DEMEANED
BUT
EMPOWERED

DEMEANED
BUT
EMPOWERED

The Social Power of the
Urban Poor in Jamaica

OBIKA GRAY

University of the West Indies Press
Jamaica ● Barbados ● Trinidad and Tobago

University of the West Indies Press
1A Aqueduct Flats   Mona
Kingston 7   Jamaica
www.uwipress.com

08 07 06 05 04   5 4 3 2 1

CATALOGUING IN PUBLICATION DATA

Gray, Obika
Demeaned but empowered: the social power of the urban poor
in Jamaica / Obika Gray

p. cm.

Includes bibliographical references.

ISBN: 976-640-153-5

1. Urban poor – Jamaica – Political activity. 2. Urban poor – Jamaica –
Social activity. 3. Patronage, Political – Jamaica. 4. Community power –
Jamaica. 5. Crime – Jamaica. I. Title.

HV4063A5G72 2004   364.2'56'21 dc-21

Cover photo by Phillip Harris

Book and cover design by Robert Harris.
Set in Bembo 11/14 x 24
Printed in Canada.

To Osonye

Contents

Acknowledgements

BUT FOR MY HAPPY ADOPTION AT a young age by an upwardly mobile aunt who snatched her nephew from the slums, and from an errant working-class sister, my own life might well have made its contribution to the vast social power of the poor discussed here.

The advantages of this escape from a troublesome destiny, the joys of loving reconnection with my still working-class mother – together with Carl Stone's inspired scholarship on the Jamaican people – made personal biography a powerful subtext for my social and intellectual preoccupations.

A nagging concern for what might have been and worry for the fate of the urban poor therefore drove me to write this political account of their lives. As the reader will discover, I do so in ways that reject both contempt and apologetics. It is possible to write passionately about this socially despised group without the fear or the uncritical favour that inform so much of the political discussion of the group today, and I have tried to do that here.

I have incurred many debts in writing this book. First of all, a heartfelt thanks to my mother, Gloria Cooke, and my sister, Suzanne Fletcher, for their love and abiding care during many research trips to Jamaica. Sharing their modest home and participating in their animated lives has been a gift and an unmatched tutorial in the travails and triumphs of the respectable poor.

I also owe a special gratitude to the faculty and staff of the Department of Government at the University of the West Indies, Mona. In the years it took to write this book, I encountered only encouragement and welcome. I owe a special thanks to Professor Brian Meeks, an engaging scholar and friend, whose steadfast encouragement and practical help facilitated the publication of this book.

Criminologist Anthony Harriott was more than an unsparing guide to the dark side of Jamaican politics. He became a friend, a wise counsellor on the politics of the poor and a patient sounding board for my ideas.

I am equally grateful to Anthony Bogues, a former member of the department and currently professor at Brown University in the United States. In the early months of this project, Bogues offered critical insights into the politics of the People's National Party, and his timely intervention years later helped this book find its Caribbean publisher. I am also grateful to Professor Trevor Munroe for making interviews with leaders of the Jamaica Labour Party possible. All this and the warm collegiality of department professors made for agreeable research visits.

This book could not have been written without extensive interviews with persons who witnessed the politics of the poor at first hand. I am especially grateful to Paul Burke for sharing his intimate knowledge of the rough-and-tumble of Jamaican street politics. Much of what I now know about the underbelly of Jamaican politics I owe to several late-night interviews with Paul in his Kingston office. Arnold Bertram offered a similar purchase on the rough politics of the People's National Party and the Jamaica Labour Party, particularly his compelling memories of ghetto notables and the party civil wars.

I am also grateful to "Churchill" and Sidoney Massop, who shared their time and unmatched perspectives on the life of Jamaica Labour Party ghetto leader Claude Massop. In their turn, Pearnel Charles and journalist John Maxwell gave riveting accounts of the "dutty politics" practised by both the Jamaica Labour Party and the People's National Party. I am most grateful to Anthony Johnson for sharing his insights into the political culture of the Jamaica Labour Party.

Janet Grant-Woodham, Frances Madden, Father Richard Albert, Professor Barry Chevannes and the late Errol Anderson also shared their perspectives on the costs of inner-city poverty, the perils of factional party politics, and the vocation of notable groups and personalities in the slums. Thanks are due as well to Mark Figueroa and Michael Witter of the Department of Economics at the University of the West Indies, Mona, for their critical yet always supportive remarks during the research for this book. A special thanks also to former front-line policeman Keith "Trinity" Gardner for an eye-opening tour of Kingston's badlands, and to Bradley Lecky for introducing me to the good citizens of Rollington Town.

Many friends and associates offered good cheer and opportunities for recreation during trips to Jamaica. D'Arcey and Dell Crooks, Clinton Hutton, Chris Charles, and Ian Boxill were unfailingly generous as they escorted me for sojourns across Kingston.

A big thanks also to Linda Speth and Shivaun Hearne of the University of the West Indies Press for recognizing the worth of this work and to their capable staff for seeing to its immediate publication. I thank David Scott, editor of the journal *Small Axe*, for his wise suggestions for making this a better book. I am indebted as well to Dr Christopher Lind and the staff of the Office of Research and Sponsored Programs at the University of Wisconsin–Eau Claire for supporting this work with a summer research grant in 1996.

Parts of this book appeared elsewhere and I thank the publishers for permission to reprint versions of them here. Chapter 1 appeared in *New Caribbean Thought: A Reader*, edited by Brian Meeks and Folke Lindahl (Kingston: University of the West Indies Press, 2001); a version of chapter 4 appeared in *Modern Political Culture in the Caribbean*, edited by Holger Henke and Fred Reno (Kingston: University of the West Indies Press, 2003); parts of chapters 5 and 10 were published in *Understanding Crime in Jamaica*, edited by Anthony Harriott (Kingston: University of the West Indies Press, 2003) and in *Issues in the Government and Politics of the West Indies*, edited by John Gaffar LaGuerre (St Augustine, Trinidad: School of Continuing Studies, 2001). Versions of this book's findings also appeared in *Social and Economic Studies* 52 (March 2003) and in *Small Axe*, no. 13 (2003).

Lastly, this book is dedicated to my wife, Tess Onwueme. Her steadfast encouragement and pedagogic love spurred completion of this work, as did the inspiring example of her own prolific career.

Abbreviations

BITU	Bustamante Industrial Trade Union
JLP	Jamaica Labour Party
NDM	National Democratic Movement
PNP	People's National Party
PNPYO	People's National Party Youth Organization
TUC	Trades Union Congress
WPJ	Workers' Party of Jamaica

1

Rethinking Power
Political Clientelism and Political Subordination in Jamaica

THE DIALECTIC OF OPPRESSIVE STATE POWER, and opposition to it, remains a compelling subject for political analysis. Studies of this phenomenon have emphasized the ability of socially marginal and disadvantaged groups to constrain power holders in ways they find hard to suppress.[1]

Although mainstream social science has traditionally paid little attention to this theme of power from below, increasing interest is being given to the subject of the social power of the urban poor and to their relations with contemporary states. It has become more apparent that the social actions of the poor are politically relevant and these actions are increasingly being examined.

Among the studies that focus on the poor and their relations with the powerful are those which call attention to their fugitive and evasive tactics. Such studies have emphasized unorthodox strategies of marginal groups, who appear to rely less on direct violence and overt rebellion in challenging political authorities than on hidden forms of opposition, ranging from dissimulation, evasion, smuggling and theft, to the ridiculing of power by gossip, character assassination and biting popular song.[2]

Still other studies have not only emphasized the critique of power by these tactics, but also shown how the rejection of a bourgeois, civic morality, in favour of the cultivation of an identity of radical otherness, has empowered stigmatized groups. These reports argue that such strategies and renegade forms of opposition secure for the poor the status, honour and respect an exploitative society has denied them.[3]

Other analysts in this tradition have also commented on outlawry and crime as forms of political defiance.[4] These analysts do not reject the importance of covert actions of the poor, but they go beyond an emphasis on fugitive acts to emphasize overt, defiant and extra-legal forms of contesting power. These forms are seen as having little to do with organized or revolutionary action. Rather, they are regarded as representing collective, autonomous acts of empowerment that strike a blow against an oppressive and unjust system by resorting to predation, criminality, banditry and other forms of social outlawry.

Commentators on these forms of social action in contexts of marginality and unequal power note their political relevance and insist that such actions be viewed as the political response of disadvantaged groups to social oppression.[5] While considerable disputes and controversies attend these formulations and query whether crime and outlawry should be regarded as political or emancipatory, it is undeniable that the states dealing with these issues have taken notice of them, recognize their political relevance, and have been attempting to crush them.[6]

The florescence of unorganized renegade behaviours, the resort to non-bourgeois identities and the formation of rebellious moral communities on the part of disadvantaged urban groups in contemporary non-Western states are increasingly matters of urgent concern for such states. Rebellious cultures of the urban poor, and their acts of defiance, pose for these states the problem of political legitimacy, the maintenance of ideological dominance and social control, and the predicament of securing obedience to law and official morality. These challenges become especially acute in contexts where the state is nominally democratic and is concerned not to be seen as contravening the rule of law.

At the same time, the expansion of these rebellious cultures in various non-Western societies opens up other interesting issues. They include the following: identifying the social bases for the cultural formation of rebellious cultures of the urban poor; locating the processes involved in the construction of their identities; assessing the contents and political resonance of their moral culture; evaluating the rules for joining the moral community of the alienated poor; and determining the effects these rebel cultures of the urban poor have on political systems and on social and cultural change.

These issues suggest the need to pay greater attention to the politics and social actions of the urban poor. Because of their growing social and political importance and demographic significance in both industrialized and underdeveloped societies, the urban poor cannot be easily dismissed as irrelevant to the politics of these societies. Despite serious problems involved in studying such groups, and notwithstanding the tremendous handicaps that confront them in their encounters with modern states, the urban poor have a political life and a moral economy whose contours require closer examination than they have received thus far.

Disadvantaged groups, while lacking political power and denied the traditional resources of their social betters, do have resources they can deploy in social conflicts. The forms such responses take, however, should not be reduced to a simple continuum ranging from mere resignation to their unequal status, to sudden violent outbursts against it. Between these two extremes, there exists a vast terrain on which myriad forms of resistance to domination are enacted. Recent studies have examined some of these and identified their significance for the persistence of domination and hegemony.[7] Despite their differing emphases, such studies share a basic conclusion that whatever power states or ruling groups might exercise, that hegemony is never total. The dominated have the capacity to resist and often find the means to elude power, constrain its effects on them, bargain with it, and adapt it to conform to some of their needs.[8] Disadvantaged groups therefore exhibit a social power that can be identified and examined for its compulsion on power and for its impact on social change.

In light of these considerations, this chapter revisits the issue of state power in postcolonial Jamaica, offers a revision of the identity of that power, examines the forms of opposition to it, and discusses the political meaning of responses to this power among rebellious, socially mobilized tributaries of the urban poor.

Jamaican Statecraft: Clientelism and the Art of Political Border Crossing

Conceptions of the identity of the Jamaican state have emphasized its paternal and authoritarian qualities. The late and influential political scientist Carl Stone, for example, has shown how clientelism, linked to a competitive electoral system, produced a faction-ridden and violent political system.[9] His emphasis on political patronage and its dynamics offers a revealing anatomy of the postcolonial Jamaican political order. His analysis shows how that order combines authoritarian, democratic, paternalist and populist features to hold together a class-divided society.

In Stone's analysis, unequal class relations in Jamaica are addressed through a combination of patronage, multi-class party alliances, and strategic uses of violence to quell popular opposition. For him, state power in Jamaica is pre-emptive, invasive, monopolistic and coercive. But he also argues that this power is flexible, adaptive, and is one that retains significant democratic content. As Stone observes, "the real strength of the Jamaican parliamentary system is clearly to be found in the resourcefulness of the party leaders that have shown over the years a remarkable capacity for adapting to the changing moods and trends of the political community". Hence, he argues, "democracy will continue to grow in strength in spite of foreboding Marxist predictions about political collapse".[10] In this view, power is not only adaptive to shifting political trends in Jamaican society, it is also exercised democratically.

Similarly, when Stone turns to the analysis of popular protest, he maintains that despite a capacity for creating disturbances and some turbulence in the social order, the protests of the rebellious urban poor, "do not amount to any real threat to political stability in Jamaica and have become incorporated into the turbulent process of often violent interparty contestations for power and popular support".[11]

This formulation of the character of state power and opposition to it is insightful. Yet it is in need of revision in two substantive ways. First, the claim that democracy is the dominant, defining feature of Jamaican politics needs to be revised to take account of contrary practices which have been ascendant and which indicate a decisive mutation in the political identity of the Jamaican state.

Second, Stone's low estimation of the significance of the rebellious urban poor's politics must be reconsidered. The defiant protests of the urban poor have not succeeded in toppling power holders and their radical claims on the society have often been integrated into the processes of the Jamaican political system. However, underestimating the significance of the urban poor on the Jamaican political scene, ignoring their growing accumulation of social power, and slighting the definite compulsion they exercise on relations of power, would be as unfortunate an error as overestimating the capacity of the poor to challenge power and to unilaterally determine the terms and conditions of their lives.

Notwithstanding these demurrals, Stone's analysis of state power in Jamaica is extremely persuasive for its emphasis on the adaptive and flexible character of power. The specificity of this form of power is its protean, mutating and flexible identity. The identity of Jamaican state power goes beyond mere clientelism; that power is not reducible to its democratic features nor is it to be identified with sheer authoritarianism and the unchecked use of force – all features exhibited by this state.

The expression of state power in Jamaica is shaped not solely by formal institutional inheritances such as electoral activity or the rule of law. Nor, again, is it purely autocratic and brutally repressive. Rather, this form of power appears to be a flexible ensemble of all these contradictory components. State power in Jamaica can simultaneously be predatory and populist; violent and paternal; as well as democratic and viciously abusive of human rights, depending on the exigencies of the political situation.

Moreover, unlike some forms of clientelism that are purely prohibitive, repressive and generative of a supine dependency among the disadvantaged, political rule in Jamaica cedes significant social space, limited political influence, and a palpable cultural agency to clients and suppliants from the lower class. Rather than being "totalitarian" and cruelly disempowering, the strategy of power in Jamaica grafts itself onto existing structures of autonomy and patterns of community culture among the poor, and permits them a modicum of independence. Despite this adaptation, power in Jamaica nonetheless feeds on, and assimilates cultural structures of the urban poor and adapts them to its protean format of rule. In this respect, the Jamaican state is parasitic rather than overtly destructive in its political relations with the poor and in its approach to existing cultural structures in poor urban communities. Unlike traditional forms of power which attempt to establish a sharp divide between the people's culture and the culture of the ruling class, parasitic rule reproduces the latter's hegemony by appropriating aspects of popular culture and blurring, even collapsing, the boundaries between antagonistic cultural forms of the poor and that of their nemesis in the class system.

Despite contrary implications which can be drawn from Stone's analysis of the Jamaican political order, his observation that the political system is essentially democratic conflicts with his other assessments which call attention to the illiberal character of state power.[12] Stone's repeated claim that stable democratic rule thrives despite widespread party-sponsored electoral fraud, massive party and state violence against the poor, and ever-expanding official corruption and resort to blatant illegality, is untenable.

It may be argued that while "electoralism" persists, albeit in a highly compromised form, and though the pluralism of the Jamaican two-party cartel
remains durable, the outstanding feature of the Jamaican political order is not
to be found in its democratic credentials. On the contrary, it is not so much
that Jamaican democracy survives and flourishes, but rather that a predatory
state, which increasingly corrupts and violates existing democratic attributes,
has flowered into maturity, particularly after 1972.

Rather than the factional, embattled, but thriving democracy depicted by
Stone, we need to revise that perspective to emphasize that political rule in
Jamaica is exercised through a mutating, opportunistic system that willy-
nilly incorporates antagonistic norms and practices, several of which are
hostile to the ones it publicly defends and selectively enforces. The implications of this mutation for the political identity of the system itself go
beyond the fact of mere turbulence-amidst-democracy. They invite a
reassessment that asks whether the democratic elements in the ensemble
have been supplanted by predatory, violent and illegal forms of rule.

Such considerations raise the question as to whether the Jamaican state
should not be more accurately identified as a violent, parasitic entity that
retains some democratic features. It can be argued that violent, parasitic rule
is now ascendant over liberal democratic rule. Evidence from the past fifty
years confirms erosion of democratic practices in Jamaica as the state has
increasingly resorted to political victimization of the poor, excessive use of
violence and misuse of public funds. More recently, public outcry against
extravagant salaries paid to public sector executives seemed only to confirm
public perception of corruption and featherbedding at the highest levels of
the state.[13]

In the past two decades, certainly, it may be argued that the balance
between official respect for democracy on the one hand, and the resort to
force and official illegalities on the other, has been tipped decidedly in favour
of the latter. This mutation into a violent parasitic state does not mean that
the democratic content of the system has been totally eliminated; it does
mean, however, that it has increasingly lost its vigour; that the forces which
have traditionally defended democratic values are retreating from the political scene; and that this "democratic" state has increasingly resorted to violence, abuse of human rights and corrupt political acts.[14] In light of these
developments, descriptions of the Jamaican political system as unambiguously democratic are woefully inadequate in describing the complex realities involving the uses of power over the past fifty years. In contrast,

therefore, to the relatively benign and optimistic interpretations of democracy in Jamaica, the mutation of the political order into the dominance of parasitic and predatory rule should be grasped.

One unmistakable feature of the Jamaican state is its shifting definition of law, morality and crime. Despite an official rhetoric of "law and order" and affirmations of allegiance to democratic values, established political parties and their agents have systematically contravened law, order and democracy in the quest for political dominance. In specific conjunctures, what is regarded by the state as "criminal", "illegal" and "morally right" gets redefined as acceptable or unacceptable depending on the exigencies faced by rival parties and their competing interests. Thus at one moment, criminal gunmen are defended by state agents as untouchable heroic protectors of their ghetto neighbourhoods, while in a subsequent period they may be regarded as social pariahs to be hunted down and summarily killed by the state. Official morality may converge with a popular morality that demands state protection for outlaws. Yet, as exigencies change, this state sympathy for popular values may be withdrawn, thereby frustrating popular expectations.[15]

Likewise, state agents may stoutly affirm, and defend as morally just, the supplicancy of the poor for material benefits and handouts. Nevertheless, as political relations change, these same supplicants may be denounced by their patrons as succumbing to an alleged "freeness mentality" that identifies them, in the eyes of the state and detractors, as indolent freeloaders and moral bankrupts.[16]

This shifting definition of propriety, morality and law extends to a variety of phenomena such as land seizures by the poor, the violent conduct of the police, the enactment of special agreements that are partial to corporate interests, and the appropriation of public funds to meet the demands of favoured political clients at the top and bottom of the class structure. A contradictory and ambiguous official stance on the lawfulness of these processes, and the stunting of independent criticism of such activities in the society, capture the ongoing mutation of the Jamaican state away from its nominal liberal-constitutional identity and toward violent parasitism.

This variable definition of law, morality and crime not only confirms the adaptability of the state to changing circumstances, but also shows the capacity of the state to escape its nominal democratic political identity and its ability to develop new repertoires of control in a disintegrating and volatile environment. As the Jamaican state moves back and forth across the border between the legal and the illegal, between the shadow economy and the formal economy, and between reliance on constitutionally mandated security forces and dependence on private, party-linked militias, it becomes something new in the process.

This new identity is its parasitism. Parasitic rule in Jamaica is the form that state power takes as dominant classes attempt to extend their political power, control a fragmented society, manage dependence in the world system, and expunge rebellious challenges from below. Yet the exercise of parasitic rule is neither essentially for the benefit of the rich nor unalterably against the poor. Parasitic rule is not based on an alien model of power and it is not so slavish to foreign interests that it ignores local political interests. Indeed, because parasitic rule explicitly draws on indigenous socio-political tendencies, those over whom it rules typically experience it as culturally familiar, and even as representative of national-popular traditions. Similarly, parasitic rule does not employ state power in favour of "order" against "disorder"; it does not valorize legal-democratic measures over illegal-mercenary tactics in political contestations, nor is it reluctant to embrace both the rule of law and the subversion of that law in making public policy.

Rather than making such distinctions as a method of establishing itself as a lawful and legitimate power, parasitic rule blurs the political boundaries between the formal-constitutional and the covert-illegal. It exploits political antinomies and employs them as repertoires to secure its own power; indeed, parasitic rule deploys and integrates antinomies to secure its control of Jamaican society. In this respect, parasitic rule is Janus-faced in its simultaneous adoption of constitutionalism and dictatorial predation.

In coping with the inevitable dissatisfaction it provokes, parasitic rule does not, however, expunge all forms of opposition to its sway. On the contrary, dissent within the rebellious cultures of the intelligentsia and the urban poor have typically encountered the solicitude of the Jamaican state. It does so by domesticating, canalizing, and feeding on elite and popular dissidence to reproduce its dominance. Thus state agents in Jamaica are solicitous of the rebellious cultures of the urban poor and the intelligentsia, and have consistently put to use in reproducing dominant class power, the outlawry of the one, and the ideological antagonism of the other.

I am sympathetic to views that assert that state agents in Jamaica are facing a crisis of political authority; that they are experiencing uncertain moral leadership and encountering a marked disequilibrium in the social relations between classes.[17] A palpable expression of this crisis has certainly been a growing deflation in the authority of the state. More than that, exit from the moral community fashioned by nationalist leaders has become the norm in recent years. Defiant tributaries of the urban poor who fashioned rival structures of social power that now seriously compete with state power are only the most notable of these defectors.[18] The widespread flouting of laws by all classes, the incapacity of the state in the face of rising crime rates, and the ability of disadvantaged groups who seem able to dictate the cultural direction of the society, all highlight a decisive shift in the social balance of power from the respectable middle class to the culturally defiant and irrepressible urban poor.

Yet despite this threat to the existing mechanisms of control, and notwithstanding the inflation in the social power of the urban poor, the Jamaican state is not at its nadir. Nor is it on the verge of collapse. On the contrary, the Jamaican state retains a significant capacity for self-renewal and reinvigoration. This recuperation, however, is not necessarily due to its law-abiding and democratic tendencies. Rather, the state owes its recuperative power in large part to its ubiquity in strategic social spaces; to its punishing violence against challengers; to its capacity for invading non-state arenas of power relations and throttling potential opposition there; and to its remarkable ability to maintain elite consensus.

That the Jamaican state may not be able to curtail all political dissidence or seems to be increasingly overwhelmed by the maturation of economic and social crises is not necessarily confirmation that it has lost complete control of the society. While parasitic rule is certainly an index of growing social crisis and degenerating social relations, the sway of parasitic rule is not an absence of political control. Burgeoning economic crises, high levels of factionalism, increasing social violence and spiralling crime rates have done little to loosen the grip of the two-party cartel in Jamaica, or to shatter elite unity. This political control has not ceased with either growing social conflicts or mounting challenges to dominant class power. On the contrary, dominant class power exerts its control in this unstable and turbulent environment. Parasitic rule may be seen, then, as a particular form of political management amidst crises in peripheral societies. Consequently, though parasitism may be a truly unflattering form of rule, and while it may be inimical to liberal-democratic sensibility, it is not a wholly unfamiliar political phenomenon. Indeed, parasitism in Jamaica should be seen as an identifiable form of managing power in contexts of underdevelopment and marginality in the international system.

The dilation of parasitic rule across moral boundaries and its straddling of political oppositions are evident, for example, in the parasitic state's approach to crime. Rather than retreat from predation in the face of growing public disillusionment and cynicism about its provocation of partisan violence, and its inability to stem violent crime, predatory rule in Jamaica assimilates public concerns about crime to its own discourse, and uses these concerns to reproduce its power. Hence, both the inability to curb violent crime and public knowledge of the state's complicit role in fomenting partisan political violence become means for pursuing even more extralegal and politically suspect measures to achieve public order.

Contrary, then, to claims which see this type of state as being in its last throes of control, parasitic rule may be regarded not so much as an expression of a collapsing state, weakened by social disintegration, but as a form of state that establishes its identity in these unstable, volatile contexts, and that tries to turn this social and economic unravelling to political advantage. In this sense, parasitic rule should properly be regarded as a political strategy that state agents employ in contexts of underdevelopment where existing structures of control are no longer able to satisfy dominant group needs.

In this respect, parasitism is a method of political management, of maintaining domination in contexts where a peripheral society is in crisis, and where neither the labouring class nor propertied groups have the capacity to exert their unchallenged dominance over the state apparatus. Parasitism thus emerges in contexts of underdevelopment and marginality in the international system where state agents are pressed to forge strategies of control in order to maintain both social cohesion and class dominance. In these contexts, both by-the-book constitutionalism and official outlawry become repertoires of power.

It should be remembered, of course, that predation is a repertoire available to both powerful and subordinate groups. However, the specificity of state predation in Jamaica is that it represents an institutionalized form of political control, whose means and resources are far greater than what most disadvantaged groups can muster. Predation by the state is also different from the predation of disadvantaged social groups because, unlike them, the predatory actions of the state often carry with them the imprimatur of legitimacy and the stamp of official authority.

Thus while predation is a strategy to which contending classes may resort, state parasitism is unique for its protean capacities. Indeed, the state not only adapts itself to a volatile political field with the intent of absorbing social tendencies there, but it moves beyond this accommodation to provoke those very tendencies, moulding and exploiting their sharp antinomies as a means of political control. By extending its political grip at the nexus of political antinomies, parasitic rule brings an inventive, generic strategy to political management in the Third World.

For example, the Jamaican state's ability to mould contradictions is evident in its harnessing of the rebel cultures of the urban lower class to the state's agenda of domesticating, disorganizing and demobilizing the rebellious poor by means of a crucifying political partisanship. In this respect, the Jamaican state has not fled from the antagonistic, rebellious customs of the urban poor, but has instead absorbed and used them to form the rival and warring "proto-nations" of the political parties.[19]

Acting much like communal groups, poor partisans of the two-party system have been slaughtering each other in political battles for over forty years. Party leaders, in their quest for political power, actively promoted this slaughter. These leaders, after all, encountered the antinomy between a dominant class antagonistic defiance among tributaries of the rebellious poor on the one hand, and the state's maintenance of unequal class relations and a discriminatory party system on the other. I argue that party leaders tried to reconcile this tension by resorting to clientelism, cultural solicitation of the poor, and the harnessing of their rebel cultures to inner-city party politics. The effect has been to transform carriers of that rebellious culture into "proto-national" tribal communities, engaged in murderous conflicts with each other. By a risky, but inventive strategy, parasitic rule has shaped a troubling political antinomy and moulded it into a form of social domination in Jamaica.

Punitive violence by security forces, instances of official corruption and party solicitation of the outlawry of the poor therefore represent more than just the seamy side of Jamaican democracy. Such troubling features of Jamaican politics are inventive forms of social domination. However, this reality should not be overstated. These extra-legal "political border crossings" co-exist in an unstable unity with some attention to the rule of law, concern for excessive corruption, and official respect for the achievements of champions of the poor such as Marcus Garvey and Bob Marley. Thus rather than failure or weakness of the Jamaican political system, these political border crossings reveal an essential feature of Jamaican statecraft: its successful stradling of conflicting political values. This parasitism, with its transgressive character, is the identity of the Jamaican state, and it has defined socio-political relations in the country for more than half a century.

Contesting Parasitism: The Social Power of the Urban Poor

Because state parasitism is the form that power takes in Jamaica, it is not surprising that the poor have developed unique responses to it. These responses show that power is not a zero-sum relationship, but rather a field of action nested in complex relationships involving dependencies, bargaining, and trade-offs between protagonists. The dynamics of this relationship give to each of the protagonists a potential leverage on the other that can produce a compulsion and constraint on actions. This constraint alters each actor's capacity to exercise unchecked influence and limits any effort to unilaterally impose outcomes.

I argue that the urban poor exercised their own leverage on parasitic state power without political mediation. Alienated intellectuals and disaffected middle-class activists did not lead this compulsion on the powerful; nor did influence from below take the form of a frontal assault on the state. Rather, the social power of the urban poor expressed itself through autonomous, small, persistent, and cumulative acts of individual and group empowerment inside and outside the state apparatuses. These small acts of empowerment, and the compulsion they exert on the society and on power holders, are referred to here as the social power of the urban poor.

As the foregoing discussion of parasitic rule has shown, this form of power is simultaneously repressive and solicitous in its relations with the poor. It is not surprising, therefore, that the poor exhibited contradictory responses to it by complicitly engaging with power holders, and defiantly rejecting their predation. Despite being ensnared in the web of parasitic rule, mobilized contingents of the urban poor have nonetheless accumulated significant social power and used it to alter relations of power.

This capacity for compulsion has allowed tributaries of the urban poor, particularly the lumpenproletariat, to influence the politics of the parasitic state. It has permitted them to jockey with the powerful for political spoils; to constrain policy choices of state agents; to bargain with them for benefits; to contest ideological efforts to fully integrate them into the moral community fashioned by nationalist leaders; and exert a pervasive influence on the cultural identity of Jamaican society. Since the late 1950s this accumulation of social power by contingents of the urban poor has not only entailed an alteration in the balance of power between classes, but also produced a reshaping of the social identity of the urban lower class, stimulating in its members a lively consciousness of social inequality and a potent sense of their capacity to challenge the state.

This insistence on the agency and political relevance of a historically disadvantaged group in Jamaica need not romanticize them. Acknowledging their leverage on power only highlights the fact that the poor are not marionettes in the hands of the powerful, or a powerless group moulded and manipulated by rulers. It is apparent that the poor are capable of fighting back in their own way, and that they at times may even capture the powerful in a shifting and complex relationship of mutual dependence and antagonism.

Recognizing this display of social power does not therefore imply that the urban poor hold advanced political views, have a coherent social project, or possess a sophisticated perspective either of the structure of domination or of the outlines of an alternative society. A few socially conscious members and contingents from the ranks of the poor may, indeed, exhibit this capacity as a function of the spontaneous consciousness of the group. But berating the poor for lacking attributes usually associated with the intellectual class is to demand that downtrodden groups exhibit an ideological coherence not seen even among more advantaged members of Jamaican society. While social disadvantage does constrain social consciousness, disadvantage is no bar to social awareness, and in no way turns all contingents of the poor into political dullards.

The political behaviour of the poor therefore shows a similar complication and heterogeneity evident among other social groups. Thus, while some contingents of the urban poor may respond enthusiastically to populist regimes and their redistributionist policies, others from their ranks rally, just as fervently, to the appeals of conservative, pro-capitalist parties that oppose confiscatory socialist policies. The claim here is not that the poor are agents with an uncomplicated outlook on power, or that they possess a capacity to represent their needs through self-organization. Instead, the concern is that these debilities and renegade forms of popular social action are politically relevant phenomena that states and power holders ignore at their peril.

Our perspective is therefore not unmindful of the deeply conflicted moral and social outlook of the urban poor. I am not unaware of the severe handicaps that limit the poor and downtrodden in urban Jamaica. Commentators on their plight rightly call our attention to their lack of traditional political resources, absence of bureaucratic know-how and exclusion from official networks of political influence. As one observer remarked of the Jamaican poor,

> The average citizen in most communities lacks the information, the organizational connection, the resources and the necessary channels of representation to solve simple problems, to pressure the bureaucracy into conceding just demands, to ensure that he or she is not taken advantage of by more privilege [sic] interests, and to provide a vehicle by which individuals with common problems can put minds and hands together to work them out rather than await the never never promises of politicians.[20]

Such handicaps are a real hindrance to the urban poor's ability to alter their circumstances, and class and social divisions within this group aggravate these obstacles. Moreover, these debilities are made worse by contradictory tendencies within an uneven popular moral culture. That moral culture reflects the often-volatile social relations in which the socially mobilized poor are enmeshed and it exhibits the contradictory customs of the diverse strata which make up the ranks of the urban poor.

The latter include myriad categories, and while it is possible to identify several strata and categories of the urban poor, as in the description of the five important strata below, it should be remembered that social reality is more complex with its overlapping social categories, protean occupational identities and dynamic moral cultures defined as much by relations of culture as by relations of production.

Within the ranks of Jamaica's unemployed urban poor are the following groups:

- Those who stoutly reject what they regard as the "slave wages" paid to the poor, and who turn to petty hustling, street trading and other self-supporting entrepreneurial pursuits as various as artisanry, street vending and popular singing.
- Those who fall into the ranks of the militant lumpenproletariat and who turn to crime and predation, drug-dealing and social banditry.
- Those who attach themselves to the political apparatus to become its fanatical supporters, militia members, "political badmen", constituency enforcers and nibbling supplicants of the state's largesse.

- The broad strata of the striving, working poor who see themselves as representing the law-abiding "respectable poor", with aspirations of upward mobility and ambitions for self-and-community recovery.
- The contingent within the lowest rungs of the working poor who retain a tenuous attachment to the wage nexus. Within this contingent are the barmaids, menial workers in the service sector, those hiring themselves out as domestics, gardeners, casual labourers and others working in myriad jobs for which it was necessary to pass a law establishing a national minimum wage.

Given this heterogeneous social composition, complex location within the production process and contradictory relationship to political power, the moral culture of the urban poor is necessarily complicated. It is well known, for example, that defiant anti-system sensibilities compete with the urban poor's complicit involvement with predatory power. The group also exhibits norms, both law-abiding and outlaw in character, that link them to a wider set of social values in Jamaican society. Communal sentiments and norms of mutuality are articulated with powerful countervailing tendencies. These latter include social cannibalism and beggar-thy-neighbour strategies, particularly in times of extreme need and partisan conflict. Though the poor may be badly victimized by parasitic rule, many within their ranks have nonetheless preyed on their kith and kin in the urban ghetto.

Alternatively, socially militant strata of the poor, using renegade and outlaw tactics, have directed their hostility against predatory power. Such acts of defiance have won sympathy from other contingents of the poor who morally underwrite these acts of uncivil anti-dominant class outlawry. Alienation, anger and deep frustration with the conditions of their lives cause many among the poor to lend tacit and active moral support to the defiant ones among them.

Still, it should be remembered that when this anti-system alienation collapses into violent crime, murder and theft from the hard-working poor, it does also elicit harsh retaliation and biting moral disapproval. Many among the poor, especially the respectable and hard-working strata, are outraged by this behaviour. They typically are embarrassed by its occurrence within their community, and unqualifiedly reject the abandonment of what is seen as a violation of an older moral standard among the community.

These scandalized contingents of the urban poor find such outlaw structures of defiance "disgraceful", and regard them as a transgression of an older community standard of dignity, marked by hard work, uplift and sacrifice. These contingents of the poor reject the criminal extremism of their marauding peers; they are threatened by it, and inveigh, as militantly as their social betters, against a descent into rapacious and anomic behaviours that target hapless members of the society, whether poor or well-to-do.

These contrasting dispositions highlight the protean nature of popular moral culture with its simultaneous possession of defiant, oppositional practices, and restraining moral sensibilities borrowed from a wider system of shared values in Jamaican society. These dispositions indicate not only that the poor are capable of resorting to crimes against each other and their social betters, but also that they are not immune to the wider network of norms and values in Jamaica. This network of values has become increasingly complex since the 1970s, and has been characterized by an erosion of the disciplinary moral leadership of nationalist leaders and their civic allies. The expansion of predation, aggressive violence and rejection of public authority among all groups confirm this loss of dominant class authority.

It is therefore not surprising that the moral culture of the urban poor reflects tendencies within a shared Jamaican moral and political culture. That culture includes aggressive personal dispositions and resort to violence as a means of resolving disputes and securing advantages. It contains intense individualism as well as a self-seeking and status-consciousness preoccupation with consumer materialism as measures of achievement and social recognition. This protean moral orientation adopts a pragmatic outlook on politics based on necessity and short-run advantage, rather than on any sustained commitment to radical politics or utopian ideologies. Finally, this moral culture among the urban poor includes a deeply ambiguous disposition toward blackness and related Africanisms as the basis for the civilization-identity of Jamaicans.

Thus, contrary to the widely held view that the social actions and moral sensibility of the rebellious poor are outside the pale of Jamaican culture, these shared traditions, in which the poor participate, show that what the rebellious poor do politically ought not be regarded as moral aberrations inflicted upon a civilized society by a criminal and barbaric class. Rather, much of what the rebellious poor do, and the moral sentiments they exhibit, should be regarded, in part, as expressions of the banal, everyday attributes of a widely shared social sensibility in late twentieth-century Jamaica.

Notwithstanding these shared traditions, the customs of the urban poor, and the politics of this group are not all identical to those of other social classes. Distinctive group experiences, peculiar to the urban poor, do separate them from other classes and give their customs a specificity of their own. The dispossessed group's role in production, and its material circumstances and social experiences, informs their political dispositions and moral sensibilities, setting the urban poor apart from other classes and strata within the Jamaican social structure.

Part of the distinctive social identity of the urban poor is closely related to the group's tenuous relationship to the system of production and its inability to provide employment for job-seekers from the poorer classes. A historic and persisting feature of the Jamaican economy has been the chronic unemployment and underemployment of urban unskilled labour, and the casualization of these castaways from the ranks of the employed labour force. Joblessness, economic insecurity and poverty have been the lot of generations of the urban poor, and few other classes in the urban milieu share this condition of chronic economic deprivation and marginality.

Few groups in Jamaica know the misery and frustration of the socially conscious but impoverished sector of the urban poor. Moreover, not many Jamaicans know what it means to be homeless in the inner city. While many among the urban poor do find shelter in modern facilities and enjoy public amenities, the vast majority of the poor live with inadequate shelter or homelessness and a lack of privacy.

Where better-off social classes can speak meaningfully of living in modern homes, the most deprived of the urban poor have long been housed in decrepit, substandard dwellings: in crowded tenement yards and in baleful shanty towns. The absence of public amenities such as piped water, electricity, modern sewage and drainage systems in the poorest slums not only makes these areas a hazard to the health of residents, but also identifies such slums as breeding grounds of resentment and sites of social desperation.

The deprived material conditions in which the poor live, and the social relations which flow from being poor, unemployed and black in a race- and class-conscious society, have inevitably spawned rebellious social dispositions and antagonistic moral responses far more bitter among the most disadvantaged urban poor than among other deprived groups. Unequal and discriminatory social relations in Jamaica helped provoke these acute responses. The list below summarizes key impediments the poor face:

- Loss of political freedom, personal liberty and citizenship rights in select inner-city communities where party-linked militias treat residents as captive populations.

- Political victimization on the basis of political affiliation.
- Imposition of humiliating stigmas based on class membership, residence and cultural attributes of class.
- Harsh state violence, cultural inferiorization and discriminatory application of the penal code.

Alienated Cultures of the Urban Poor and the Predicament of the Parasitic State

In the four decades since political independence, these unequal relations provoked hostility among the poor, producing in them a rebellious sensibility. Commentators have remarked, for example, on the dissident role and socio-political importance of the Rastafarians in Jamaica.[21] Less attention has been given, however, to other contingents of the poor, to their contribution to the social power of the group, or to the social linkages and networks of influence within the heterogeneous "society of the poor" in urban Jamaica.

This society has spawned unique customs and practices, networks of influence, distinct repertoires of resistance, and a pantheon of heroic figures. The society of the urban poor has thrown up identifiable, alienated and socially mobilized contingents who share, in different degrees, relations of conflict and cooperation with the parasitic state and with a culturally inferiorizing society. Among these alienated and socially mobilized contingents there are certain groups that are most notable:

- Legendary political sentries in poor communities who are often shielded by their political patrons.
- Heroic "Robin Hood" figures with primitive political agendas for subverting the state through hit-and-run tactics.
- A self-helping entrepreneurial stratum, defiantly assertive of its right to dignity, and protective of its niche in urban petty trading and street vending.
- A picaresque lumpenproletariat subsisting on petty crime and predation and given to political forays on the streets during heightened social conflict.
- Bandit gangs and their flamboyant leaders, thriving on the expansion of the gun, drug and contraband trade, using their criminal largesse as patronage and influence in poor communities.

- Contingents of jobless youth and allied politicized strata in ghetto communities, who resort to spontaneous political demonstrations and riotous acts. These groups also resort to recurrent bids for social respect, personal dignity and autonomy from both parasitic state power and a culturally dismissive society.
- Outriders of cultural defiance and moral tribunes of the popular classes. Their ideological appeals through popular song, music and oral-kinetic dramaturgy critique power and rally the poor to loosen respectable society's moral grip. These tribunes invariably urge the poor to demand the right to equal identity, social justice and freedom to enjoy the aesthetic pleasures of a non-bourgeois identity.

As the foregoing distinctions imply, the social identity of these important contingents of the mobilized poor is powerfully influenced by the group's insertion in complex political, economic and cultural relations. Such ties typically involve unequal relations of power that impel the poor to sometimes adopt defensive postures of self-protection and self-help.

But the urban poor are also involved in a process of cultural self-construction. The seven contingents identified above have been decisive in the cultural self-formation of the alienated and socially mobilized urban poor. These contingents have been not only a defiant vanguard, often opposed to the authority of the parasitic state, but also pacesetters in establishing the political and moral foundations for an oppositional political culture. Indeed, they have been the leading agents of an oppositional morality that has spread to other groups in the society. These militant tributaries helped fashion rival structures of power; developed models of community rallying based on natal community loyalty; carried out seizures of strategic social spaces; and established the dramaturgic and aesthetic bases of a dissident cultural consciousness.

These leading forces within urban rebel cultures in Jamaica have, over the years, provided the poor with a compelling politico-cultural tutelage. This pedagogy by the poor on behalf of those who were "politically poor" disclosed repertoires for acquiring a dissident consciousness; it offered apprenticeships in social outlawry and gave lessons in how to win social respect and constrain politicians. These tribunes issued summonses for recruits to join the oppositional moral community; they called on the poor to share in solidarities and commitments, and encouraged allegiance to a martial, combative social identity.

In the aftermath of the enervation of the Rastafarian movement in the 1970s, and in the wake of the decline of elite radicalism in the 1980s, these alienated groups, among the urban poor, became leading opponents of state predation. Their rejection of the civilized identity proffered by creole nationalists; recurrent demands for work and social respect; bold bids for social justice and peace in their communities; as well as complicit involvement with predatory power, all highlight the agony and dilemmas of the urban poor.

These dilemmas arise from the fact that urban dispossessed groups are politically poor and lack the traditional resources of organized lobbies. Given these circumstances, the socially mobilized poor have adopted alternative means of exerting political influence. Socially marginalized and deficient in the resources held by better-off groups, the urban poor have developed compensatory repertoires of defiance that over time increased their social power.

As the foregoing has maintained, and as later chapters will show, that power is evident in the florescence of independent initiatives; in the checkmating of state strategies; in seizures of strategic social spaces; and in the near-monopoly of a small vanguard over definitions of urban lower-class identities. This social power is now increasingly, if reluctantly, being recognized.[22]

The predicament of the poor, however, is that the group's status as social outcasts acts as a constraint on their capacity to overcome stigmas assigned to them. This status of the mobilized poor as social pariah has been both the source of a remarkable inventiveness, as well as a condition for an equally stunning group suppression and collective immolation.

Moreover, because of a political imagination among the poor that seemingly linked middle- and upper-class social power with unredeemable corruption, political venality and chronic victimization, defiance within these mobilized tributaries of the poor has come to assume a problematic form: rebellious outlawry, deep suspicion of middle-class politics and an abiding rejection of bourgeois norms of respectability.

In this context, it is apparent that the social power of the poor is contradictory and ambiguous. In Jamaica's predatory, violent and levy-imposing social environment, forms of subordinate-class social power have become bases of group autonomy, honour and identity. At the same time, however, the context of predation, and the conflictual relations spawned by it, has also provoked responses that hobbled the poor, made them into complicit challengers to power, and induced in them self-destructive cultural reflexes.

Put differently, the predicament of the mobilized urban poor is that the very forms of its social power that act as powerful constraints on dominant groups are themselves bases of subordinate group cannibalism and self-suppression. Their social power has altered the dynamics of power relations, but not always in ways that permit the urban poor to unilaterally dictate outcomes to the power holders. Paradoxically, then, the urban lower class – the most rebellious and feared social stratum in postcolonial Jamaica and nemesis of the powerful – finds itself in a checkmated situation anchored in the very marginality that gave them a purchase on power. Such debilities are matched, however, by predicaments of the predatory state. As this state absorbs social contradictions and becomes a leading agent in the unravelling of social relations as well as an agent of cohesion, it too is beset by contradictions.

The predicament of the predatory Jamaican state is that the measures that secure its dominance and sustain the cohesion of the society – clientelist party rule, punitive violence and elite unity – become the very sources that threaten the erosion of its power. As the parasitic state and its agents move into the shadow economy, violate democratic practices with impunity, protect fearsome gunmen, and foment a crucifying political violence in which the poor become cannon-fodder and the well-to-do fear for their physical safety, a legitimation crisis ensues and the hold on power by state agents becomes increasingly tenuous.

Recurrent attempts to surmount this dilemma, however, seem only to compound the problem. Repeat announcements of harsh crime eradication programmes appear ineffective as they provoke party factionalism, distress civil libertarians and alienate the poor, whose neighbourhoods are targeted in the fight against crime and political violence.

Similarly, official denials of state involvement in political violence, political leaders' ties to gunmen, and the parties' repeated signing of peace accords, merely earn politicians the cynicism of the poor and the unease of middle-class and corporate backers of the state. In both instances, the generic strategy of combining both "order" and "disorder" entangle the state in myriad predicaments. It is hardly worth mentioning that this loss of authority requires measures to arrest it. However, efforts to stem the state's weakening hold over economic processes and social relations are themselves sources of hegemonic decline.

The perception of growing disorder and unravelling of social relations have thus far provoked the state into devising even bolder strategies involving risky and controversial policing. But as these measures founder and become what observers cynically call "nine-day wonders", they seem only to invite scorn for the political leadership and to further the erosion of public backing for this model of the state. Still, public disgust with a foundering state that cannot maintain order, achieve legitimacy or solve economic problems has not provoked a ruptural break with predatory rule. Disillusionment has led neither to calls for military intervention nor to any support for a popular uprising and seizure of the state.

This impotence of civil society and the state's inability to unravel the tangle of social contradictions is a fitting expression of the social crisis and of the identity of power in Jamaica. On the one hand, the crisis – manifesting itself in the double handicap above – clearly shows the checkmated relations between state and society. On the other hand, however, the crisis fittingly attests to the consequences of the distinctive play of power in Jamaica. That is, the Jamaican ordeal seems to confirm what I have argued here – namely the durability of state predation and its capacity to nullify and disarm its many detractors.

2

A Fateful Alliance

THE PREVIOUS CHAPTER ARGUED THAT PARASITISM in Jamaica should be seen neither as an aberration nor as an index of the failure of political power. Instead, it is best viewed as both a repertoire of power and a mechanism to manage and contain the social contradictions and challenges unleashed by relations of power in an economically dependent society such as Jamaica.

By the early 1940s those relations of power changed significantly, as the British Colonial Office acknowledged the necessity to transfer power to local political leaders. These leaders, and their associated political organizations, emerged on the political scene in the context of the 1938 labour revolt.[1] This revolt had brought to the fore two important nationalist leaders – Alexander Bustamante and Norman Washington Manley. Both men were united in their commitment to improving the lives of the labouring classes.

Race to Power

By the close of 1938, each leader had founded an independent political base, and both cooperated in advancing the cause of the working people. Shortly after the revolt, Bustamante created several trade unions that would subsequently become part of the Bustamante Industrial Trade Union (BITU). Later, in September of that year, Norman Manley and his political associates founded a nationalist political organization, the People's National Party (PNP).[2]

Despite this quickening development for the cause of labour and for nationalism, these two organizations, with the potential for unity under joint leadership, diverged when the PNP – provoked by Bustamante's accusations concerning an alleged PNP plot to take control of the BITU in 1942 – broke off relations with the labour leader and his union in that year. In the aftermath of this split, Bustamante, anticipating national elections in 1944, formed the Jamaica Labour Party (JLP) in 1943.

Although this development was a setback for the nationalist movement, the break-up did not seem a harbinger of the violence that would ensue in Jamaican politics. Even though Bustamante's personal insecurities, authoritarianism and inability to tolerate principled opposition to his views spurred the rift, there was much that both leaders shared.[3] Besides being cousins, each possessed a residual cultural loyalty to the British Empire. In addition, during the 1938 revolt, both had strenuously avoided inflammatory political appeals to their supporters. Neither leader whipped up ethnic sentiments nor encouraged working-class attacks on the owners of capital.[4] In fact, despite the parting of ways, and notwithstanding the political ripples caused by the PNP's declaration of a moderate socialist agenda in 1940, both Manley and Bustamante were united in their commitment to improving the lot of the working people, and both men pursued this agenda within the legal and moral framework of the time. Indeed, the shared commitment of both leaders in the late 1930s to improving the circumstances of poor Jamaicans was carried into the next decade as their parties competed for voter support in the first election held under universal adult suffrage in December 1944.

That election was won in a landslide by the JLP, who secured 41 per cent of the popular vote, and twenty-three of the twenty-nine contested seats.[5] While this JLP victory was a stunning setback to the political hopes of the PNP, the small group of unions the PNP created to compete with the JLP–BITU after 1942 – the Trades Union Congress (TUC) – retained a significant role as labour representative for workers across several industries in Kingston. The December 1944 election was also notable for Bustamante's decision to campaign in the capital city as the representative of the West Kingston constituency. Despite his enormous popularity in the countryside, Bustamante had evidently recognized the political importance of trying a run for office from the capital city. Two motives might have prompted this decision.

First, the PNP and TUC were potent political forces in Kingston, and this power threatened the JLP's influence over important sections of the

Kingston working class and the unemployed. The PNP not only had support among the urban middle class, but also drew significant backing from sections of the Kingston working class and the unemployed, many of whom were organized and ideologically mobilized by trade unionists in the PNP-affiliated union, the TUC. By running in Kingston, Bustamante evidently hoped to extend his considerable popularity and national prestige among the Jamaican working class, thereby blunting the PNP–TUC's strength among workers and the unemployed there.

Second, it should be noted that the capital city was the hub of commercial and political life in the island. Major government offices, the Legislative Council, as well as leading commercial enterprises were located there. The capital city was therefore a major business centre and locale of elite politics. On this small island, therefore, events in Kingston often took on national importance. Not surprisingly, both Bustamante and his political rival, Norman Manley, contested the 1944 election from constituencies in the parishes of Kingston and St Andrew, which together formed the greater Corporate Area.

In addition to being the business and cultural centre of the island, Kingston and its environs had, by the late 1930s, also begun to undergo significant urbanization, population growth and the construction of new suburban communities. These newer middle-class enclaves were set apart from the poorer neighbourhoods in Kingston, several of which were teeming with rural migrants, unemployed workers and destitute itinerants. By the early 1940s, this residential segregation was an unmistakable aspect of urban life in Kingston, as the modern dwellings of middle- and upper-class residents to the north and east contrasted sharply with the squalor and degraded condition of the working class and poor districts mostly concentrated in the western sections of the city.[6] It was from this West Kingston constituency – perhaps the most downtrodden and benighted neighbourhood in Kingston – that Bustamante, who saw himself as a champion of the poor, first ran for political office in 1944.

With its electoral victory in that year, the JLP therefore seemed poised to consolidate its considerable support in an important part of urban Jamaica that would complement its sway in the countryside. In fact, Bustamante wasted little time doing just that, as he began using the levers of state power to reward JLP and BITU supporters with jobs, political favours, and other benefits. As his biographer George Eaton would later observe, as minister of communications, and later as mayor of the municipal body, the Kingston and

St Andrew Corporation, Bustamante put in place the discriminatory practice of allocating work primarily on the basis of party and trade union affiliation.[7]

Patronage and Political Violence

In his multiple roles as head of the government, as the Kingston and
St Andrew Corporation mayor, and as party and trade union leader,
Bustamante, with the assistance of his associates in government, controlled
the levers of both local and national government and used them to reward
only political supporters. Specifically, JLP political control of the Kingston
and St Andrew Corporation – the organization that supervised municipal
government and allocated its work – strengthened the JLP's hand in distributing partisan benefits, and cut the PNP out of the flow of patronage at the
local level.[8] As Eaton observed in his biography of Bustamante, JLP control
of local government and Bustamante's role as minister of communications
enabled him "to determine the levels and allocation of public funds for public works and in the process to control the distribution of work and employment opportunities".[9]

This discriminatory use of state largesse obviously victimized PNP supporters and those workers affiliated with the TUC. But the onset of this
politics under Bustamante went beyond merely rewarding loyalists with
jobs. It also introduced the practice of "political unionism" which linked
recruitment for government jobs to union membership. The immediate
impact of this Bustamante practice, as Eaton noted, "was that political and
trade union affiliation became the main criterion governing the employment of labour on governmental work projects as well as the recruitment
of employees at the subordinate levels in the public services. This held true
for both levels of government, central and municipal or parochial."[10]

Faced with the prospects of continued discrimination by the government, the PNP and TUC fought back. Between 1945 and 1947, the TUC
put up a stiff fight against this JLP–BITU effort to block TUC recruitment
efforts, deny its members' demands and bar fair access to government jobs.
Leading TUC organizers such as Ken Hill and Richard Hart joined hands
with top PNP leaders such as Wills O. Isaacs, in an attempt to beat back the
JLP onslaught in Kingston. This response spawned more violence in
an apparent unending cycle.[11] Therefore, within a few years of the 1944

election, the practice of political discrimination had unleashed an orgy of political violence and industrial strikes as the PNP–TUC resisted Bustamante's bid to monopolize power, dominate trade union and political activity in Kingston, and distribute jobs on a purely partisan basis.

This PNP–TUC resistance, and the JLP effort to subdue it, found partisans of the parties and rival unions battling in the streets of Kingston, and clashing outside government buildings there. In these battles, they fought over the allocation of work and the right of TUC members to challenge, through strike action, a government both engaged in discriminatory hiring and prepared to use violence and intimidation to enforce their actions. In these early years of fledgling electoral competition, Bustamante's political unionism triggered a cycle of violence in which labourers, thuggish recruits and other sympathizers fought bloody battles in the name of their respective parties with a passion and zeal resembling commitment to a messianic cause.

The intensity of this partisan fervour was apparent in a major crisis in mid-February 1946. As workers sympathetic to the TUC went out on strike on the fifteenth at the local mental hospital, a fracas ensued in which Bustamante was struck by a rock, allegedly thrown by an inmate.[12] Impatient with the strikers and smarting from the injury, the next day Bustamante rallied an angry gang of Kingston dockworkers who marched on the hospital in a bid to rout the strikers. In the ensuing riot, several persons were injured and three were killed.[13] Among them was a bystander and PNP sympathizer who, having shot dead one of the dockers in self-defence, was promptly beaten to death by the marauding mob.[14] On the eighteenth, the JLP's declaration of a state of emergency eased the tense situation in Kingston somewhat. This was the first of several states of emergency that Jamaican politicians would employ to quell violent partisan disputes.

But this unprecedented resort to the use of a state of emergency by politicians against each other did little to end the political war. By late 1947, the warring between the parties and their unions reached its zenith, as political violence engulfed the capital city. The TUC that had been fighting for its political life since the election responded to JLP–BITU violence and victimization by recruiting committed defenders from its ranks to do battle.

Between 1945 and 1947, the TUC increasingly drew workers, politically mobilized sections of the urban poor and gangs of toughs from the Kingston lumpenproletariat into confronting JLP violence with counter-violence in the Kingston streets. Violence flared between the combatants at political rallies, during protest marches and at demonstrations in front of government buildings. Each side brought into the fray not only rank-and-file activists, but mercenary figures and criminal gangs from the Kingston underworld.

The war over political spoils had begun, therefore, to introduce new political players in the dispute between middle-class politicians battling for power. These were the "hired hands" from the unemployed poor and social outlaws from among the militant Kingston poor, who had attached themselves to the parties. With politically mobilized sectors of the urban working class, the militant poor and a mercenary lumpenproletariat as their shock troops, both parties headed into a decisive battle in October 1947.

Dubbed by commentators as the "battle for the streets of Kingston", this encounter challenged Bustamante's use of street violence as the means of settling political disputes and fending off legitimate challenges to his power.[15] The battle also intensified the tendency that would become more pernicious with time: the resort to political violence to break up rival party meetings, and the onset of party-sanctioned efforts to hamper and frustrate rival party meetings in some constituencies in Kingston.

Although the PNP–TUC could not at this time be effectively barred from competing for votes, nor could its ties to labour be destroyed in Kingston, the JLP–BITU resort to force throughout the city had introduced an unprecedented violent outlawry into national and urban party politics. Moreover, in these early days the unmistakable political nature of the violence and its association with JLP patronage, as well as the JLP's bid for control of working-class constituencies like West Kingston, created an ineluctable link between the competition for power and party support of political violence.

Though not yet a fully mature process nor an institutionalized practice, there was, by 1947, the advent of a definite political tendency that saw each side attempting to undercut, by unorthodox means, the ability of rivals to hold rallies and meetings in contested political territory. Such means included not only disruptive violence, menacing of political adversaries and denying to the opposition unhampered politicking in disputed territory, but the enmity between the rivals also included expulsion of opponents from contested areas through thuggery, street violence and other forms of partisan intimidation.

At this early date, then, there was some basis for the real fears of the PNP–TUC: that they could lose not only the hard-won support among

Kingston's workers and voters, but also possibly be denied access to political territory and not find enough "political living space" in the capital city. PNP–TUC concern regarding Bustamante's determination to rout them in Kingston provoked them to retaliate violently, and to mount a successful fight against this prospect.

As part of its effort to resist JLP violence, the PNP drew militant recruits from workplaces in Kingston. The party also mobilized its own gang of political activists, including a contingent at 69 Matthews Lane, a street with diehard PNP adherents in Bustamante's West Kingston constituency.[16] There socialist PNP organizers had formed one of several political study groups that combined analysis of socialist texts and assessments of Jamaican history with PNP activism that had helped move that party to adopt a socialist platform in 1940.

Consequently, not all combatants from Matthews Lane were merely thugs and political badmen drawn from the Kingston underworld. Many partisans who were involved in the street battles were exposed to radical PNP ideas and the socialist politics of the Matthews Lane political study group. At the same time, however, several PNP street fighters were recruited from the socially desperate unemployed. They knew or cared little for the niceties of socialist theory, and were not likely to be familiar with the intricacies of the politics of nation-building that energized their more sophisticated peers. As a result, the contingents from "Group 69" at Matthews Lane who went into battle were an ideologically uneven lot, with the majority not schooled in the doctrinal disputes that preoccupied Jamaican leftists of the day.

For their part, JLP combatants were neither mobilized for battle by party and union activists who stood out as ideologues of a free enterprise system, nor were they trying by doctrinal education to inculcate their supporters in the virtues of the capitalist economic system. While fear of a confiscatory and communist PNP was an important source of anti-PNP hostility among poor JLP partisans, they were not primarily impelled by an ideologically motivated, doctrinal defence of capitalism as a superior economic system.

Rather, important JLP street fighters – such as the Kingston dockworkers, other unionized labourers and partisan JLP thugs – acted mainly out of an intense loyalty to Bustamante, because of what he stood for. Charismatic authority counted for much among the Jamaican people, and Bustamante instinctively understood this. With great success against the PNP, Bustamante employed histrionics and the symbolic power of his personality. Loyalty to Bustamante, combined with the anticipatory fears of PNP communism, fuelled anti-PNP enmities among the JLP poor. The prospects of winning the not inconsequential spoils of political war in the emergent winner-take-all political culture only intensified these communal antipathies. At this early date, then, JLP fighters and PNP activists, like those from Group 69, exhibited the sensibility which would come to define the politics of the most fanatically committed of adherents: a fierce allegiance to a party or leadership believed to be more committed to the needs of its segment of the urban poor; a compulsion to demonize opposition party supporters; and a propensity to unleash a thuggish violence against them in politically charged disputes.

The street violence, which occurred in October and November of 1947, took a heavy toll on the JLP–BITU, as several of its supporters were killed and wounded. Many fell under the withering hail of bullets, as pistols increasingly became a weapon of choice in the ongoing war. Neither JLP bans on street demonstrations nor its laws prohibiting the growing use of firearms in political battles could stem this spiralling violence linked to the struggle for power in Kingston.[17]

West Kingston: The Bustamante Retreat

When the smoke from these street brawls had cleared, it was the JLP forces that were in disarray and on the defensive. Raw PNP counter-violence had forced them to retreat. Bustamante's three-year effort to achieve political hegemony in West Kingston through outlawry, street violence, intimidation and political allocation of government work had stalled in the face of recip-rocal violence by the PNP–TUC. Indeed, this counterattack was effective enough to prompt the pugnacious Bustamante to flee his West Kingston constituency in favour of a politically safer area in the countryside.

In remarking on this unlikely exit of the labour leader from West Kingston, commentators have identified 1947 as a decisive year and stressed how counter-violence carried the day for the PNP–TUC in West Kingston.[18] On the basis of the extant research, this conclusion is certainly compelling. However, this interpretation of the JLP's reversal of fortune in West Kingston should be qualified by other considerations. First, the 1947 battle was only one skirmish in a wider and continuing political war that the JLP would eventually win in West Kingston, and in the country at large, in the years between 1944 and 1972.

Second, and just as significant, is the fact that the successful PNP assault was probably not the only determinant that provoked Bustamante's decision to take flight from West Kingston. Bustamante and the JLP also faced equally serious social, demographic and ecological obstacles in that constituency besides PNP violence, and these other factors probably influenced Bustamante's decision to leave for a more hospitable district.

The problem for the JLP was that the constituency in which Bustamante ran for office in 1944 was perhaps the most destitute and miserable place on the island. The constituency in those days contained woeful pockets of extreme poverty. These areas were marked by the absolute lack of basic amenities, including piped water, electricity and modern sanitary facilities. Residents, many of whom were recent immigrants from the countryside, lived in pitiful shacks pieced together from scavenged wood, zinc and material foraged from the nearby city dump. There were no modern roads in the worst areas such as Back-o-Wall; residents had to pick their way through narrow lanes covered by sharp, thorny brush that punctured the bare feet of South Asian goatherds and their poorer Negro customers who bought meat, fish and vegetables from the South Asian merchants, while other blacks rented bamboo shacks from petty Asian landlords.[19]

Although dockworkers and other labourers lived in West Kingston, and gave hope to some residents, these employed groups were a minority in the area. In fact, despite their membership in the BITU, the dockers were scarcely better off than their more destitute neighbours.[20] West Kingston port workers in the 1940s lived the same meagre existence as their unemployed peers, and these poorer residents vastly outnumbered them. Residency in West Kingston was also highly unstable, and whole areas were marked by itinerancy, disease and by the lawless, predatory strikes of notorious outlaws with names such as "Money Makerel" and "Absolam".[21]

In this period, to make matters worse, the cultural fundamentalism of Rastafarian groups inspired by the black nationalist ideas of Marcus Garvey had become a significant political force throughout Kingston, and particularly in West Kingston. By the late 1940s, many among the West Kingston poor were drawn to the culturally separatist ideas of the early Rastafarian movement in Kingston. Although its influence had not yet become pervasive, this social movement for racial uplift that encouraged blacks to reject a Jamaican nationality and to look to Africa had made major inroads among the urban poor in the 1940s.

While partisan and trade union appeals to remedy this condition through ties to political and labour organizations were certainly the more dominant influence among the Kingston poor, the deliberate avoidance of racial appeals by both parties was being vigorously contested by an emergent group whose demand for racial justice must have complicated Bustamante's effort to master the cultural and political dynamics in the constituency. It also did not help that Bustamante, with his light skin colour and reputed rejection of his own ancestral ties to Africa, was perceived by Rastafarian adherents as unsympathetic to their cultural and political yearnings.[22] Given these disparate impediments, political recruitment, voter registration, and union- and party-building efforts must have been nearly impossible for the JLP. Indeed, despite Bustamante's effort at slum clearance in 1945 and the passage of laws to control firearms, it is arguable that poverty, itinerancy and the fragile ecology of West Kingston were as daunting a challenge to the JLP's hold on the constituency as the tough PNP response. In these early years, then, the West Kingston constituency became altogether too inhospitable an environment in which to establish a politically safe seat for the combative labour leader.

The Hardening of Communal Identities

This early relationship among party competition for power, the political uses of violence and its deployment in urban poor communities introduced several new developments into national politics, and into the politics of the capital city. It was first apparent that by the early 1950s the anti-colonial politics of the nationalist movement had long been derailed. That unity against colonialism was replaced by a war for power and the political spoils it afforded. "Benefits politics", which linked the distribution of employment and largesse to political and trade union affiliation, were now entrenched, and enveloped the urban poor in a violent partisanship inimical to the cause of national unity against colonial rule. In an apt characterization of this destructive turn, Eaton would write the following: "[poor] Jamaicans died therefore, not in struggle against a colonial administration for political independence and freedom, but at each other's hands in the forging of the two-party system".[23]

Second, this partisanship in which the combatants were not arrayed against each other either by class, ethnic or religious differences, nonetheless found the Jamaican protagonists acting much like contending cultural communities fighting to defend an inviolable and sacred principle. In this struggle for material benefits and political advantage, PNP and JLP partisans and their union associates exhibited a sensibility not unlike that of rival national communities fighting for their very existence. In this war between the parties in Jamaica, and for the majority of the urban poor, what was at stake, however, was not the defence of religious rights, racial or ethnic identities, or even opposing class interests. Rather, the black poor and working people hurled epithets at one another, killed and maimed each other over party-and-union prerogatives, and fought over the perceived benefits that the poor associated with winning these exclusive rights. In the ferocity of their emotional attachment to the cause of the parties and unions, rival detachments of the Kingston poor became, in effect, the "proto-nations" of the political parties. Indeed, they began, in these days of early partisanship, to associate the political stakes with their very social existence, and each side joined the contestation for power as warring communities fighting as if for their cultural and political survival.

In these volatile circumstances, antagonistic political symbolism and offensive epithets were joined to hardening images of political opponents. Political deprivation, or advantage on the basis of party and union affiliation, had emerged as bases for the assumption of social identity. To be a JLP–BITU or a PNP–TUC partisan in these early years had taken on powerful social connotations and cultural meaning, and the communities being formed by such identifications began to cling to these identities, and to grasp their political consequences. In a society in which profound and destructive ethnic or religious divisions were therefore absent, highly partisan political communities had nonetheless emerged; by the early 1950s these groups had begun to exhibit the enmities and hardened dispositions more typical of social groups divided by irreconcilable cultural, ethnic or religious differences.

In urban Jamaica of the 1940s and 1950s, political identity and cultural identity were being fused, and party politics had become the cement that bonded both. To the combatants ensnared in this politico-cultural development, individual social worth and prospects for group social honour or disrepute now depended on political affiliation. Depending on which side of the social divide the combatants stood, the assumption of a partisan identity became either a badge of honour or a stigma of devilry. Party and union affiliation had therefore become not unlike an ethnic identity in these early years of contestation, and the embrace of this proto-national sensibility had launched the black poor into an internecine, destructive war for political advantage. Thus, while the urban Jamaican poor lacked the provocative and formal ascriptive characteristics and ethno-national factional heritage that could have caused them to be mobilized as competing cultural communities, by the late 1940s and early 1950s they were nonetheless harnessed to rival party projects and were provoked to begin acting like fanatical cultural groupings. The intensity of this early antagonism therefore found sections of the urban poor arrayed against each other like two hostile "national" communities. Each became a "proto-nation", determined to hold onto its sacred exclusivist rights, ready to demonize its opponent, and poised to back up this antipathy with naked violence.

Third, the struggle for power in the 1940s not only produced a violent fanaticism among partisans, but also saw the direct sponsorship of violence by the political parties and their complicit leaders. In these years of political transition, the earlier genteel politics of native elite leadership was cast aside in favour of a tough, unforgiving, bare-knuckled approach to political contestation. In this political holy war, not only were unemployed thugs unleashed against contending organizations, but also leading party officials were not reluctant to enter the fray where they contributed to the mayhem.

Violence and Cultural Affection: Two Faces of Predation

A top JLP figure such as Bustamante, for example, unabashedly identified himself with the use of force. Full of bravado and seasoned by his experiences in shepherding his fledgling union through numerous political brawls during the late 1930s, Bustamante was accustomed to these violent skirmishes and was a practitioner of the disruptive uses of violence to turn back political challenges. It is not surprising, then, that he had taken it upon himself to mobilize and lead the angry mob that had set upon the striking workers at the mental institution in Kingston. Bustamante's propensity for violence in these circumstances was well known during these turbulent years. Indeed, at one time during this period he was even charged with manslaughter for a killing at a political rally.[24] Consistent with the swashbuckling image he liked to cultivate, and alert to the stone-throwing and gunplay to which he was often subjected at political rallies, Bustamante typically came to political street meetings armed with a loaded revolver, which he occasionally discharged with a flourish into volatile crowds.[25]

A similar readiness to identify with and use violence for political purposes was also apparent among PNP leaders of the time. Ken Hill and Will O. Isaacs, for example, backed the PNP–TUC violence against the JLP–BITU challenge. Moreover, in the 1940s, Isaacs, a third vice-president of the PNP and TUC firebrand, was among the top party leaders to assume the role of street fighter in these brawls.

Undaunted by the real physical dangers in such street battles, Isaacs, like Bustamante, flung himself with gusto into the partisan fray. In time, he too became embroiled in a serious clash, as in a 1949 street meeting in which there were injuries and the loss of life. When he was indicted for incitement to riot and accused by the presiding judge of provoking a "saturnalia of hatred, intimidation, insult and abuse, violence and even death", Isaacs was unrepentant. In defending himself against the charge, he is reported to have "uttered the remark for which he will long be remembered: 'What are a few broken skulls in the making of a nation?' "[26]

But this unapologetic rationale for the political use of violence is both revealing and utterly deceptive. On the one hand, Isaacs's admission was a rare official acknowledgement of the provocation of political violence by party leaders. On the other, Isaacs's remark spoke to a reality that by 1949 had become undeniable: the urban poor had become the cannon fodder in the battle for power between the two parties. Contrary to Isaacs's high-minded rationale about "nation-building", the conflict was not about the marshalling of a people in a costly war to expel colonial rulers nor was the dispute about competing class agendas in which the urban poor died for a larger cause. Rather, in this battle for the accumulation of political power by middle-class politicians, the black poor were the major victims.

But as accurate as this judgement is, it too must be tempered with the truism that "benefits politics" did benefit the poor. From its very inception in the 1940s, the partisan distribution of benefits involved an extensive parcelling out of the largesse of the state. Benefits to the working class and the poor included the following: union and non-union jobs in the fledgling industrial economy, in the service sector and in the large agricultural segment of the national economy. Party-linked spoils included work on state-sponsored construction projects such as housing and prisons (called workhouses by the poor). Other advantages to the loyalist poor included tickets for overseas farm work and employment on myriad public-works projects ranging from the construction and repair of roads, to the building of gullies that routed flood waters from heavy rain and hurricane. In this period of the early patronage system, not even overseas emergency aid was immune from partisan distribution and contention, as the JLP government reportedly parcelled out to its supporters used clothing and aid sent by US donors in the wake of the devastation wrought by the 1951 hurricane that struck the island.[27]

Thus, despite the impediments suffered by the loyalist poor in opposition, this condition of subordination and abuse was not without its benefits, as well as contradictions and ironies. They included the fact that although both parties were not unmindful of the interests of property owners and the well-to-do, politicians did direct their populist appeals overwhelmingly to the peasantry, the working class and the urban poor. As well, such politicians did fight over the distribution of largesse to disadvantaged groups, albeit on a highly abusive and partisan basis.

The battles in Kingston were primarily for political advantage, but they were also about the disposition of political patronage to a people whose material needs were badly neglected by the still-existing colonial system. The party rivalries were therefore also about the distribution of material benefits to the downtrodden, and this competition genuinely sought the extension of economic opportunity to the peasantry, the working class and the urban poor against the background of colonial exploitation.

The fact that the working class and the unemployed poor were divided into rival organizations and were pitted against each other in a destructive war should not obscure this dimension of the conflict in which the parties had significantly identified themselves as popular, people-oriented parties, rather than as exclusive class organizations that spoke only for propertied groups. This commitment to the concerns of the poorer classes demonstrates that the parties and the trade union leaders were not going to be the mere captives of propertied groups. By the late 1940s, therefore, the struggle for power combined two contradictory impulses: political victimization and violence against sections of the poorer classes, and active solicitation of the social and labour rights of the poor and the extension of a problematic patronage to them.

The Urban Ghetto: Paths to Power

These two faces of parasitism produced another paradox in urban Jamaican politics. This was the subtle but gradual purchase on power that sections of the urban poor began to win for themselves. As middle-class politicians fought for power, clashed over the distribution of patronage and used violence to realize political aims, the dynamic in this process gave a small but perceptible leverage on power to groups historically marginalized in Jamaica's two-party system. This was so because even as the evolving political process faithfully reproduced the multi-class coalition model of Western democratic systems, the model was being transformed in the early decades of its post-1944 implantation in Jamaica.

A theoretical account of this transformation – state parasitism as a strategy of exercising power – was given in the previous chapter. But three associated historic processes can be linked to this transformation in this early period of party competition. The first is the peculiar and fateful alliance between the parties, their top functionaries, and the mobilized partisans of the Kingston poor. The second is the subtle but discernable decentralization of state violence manifest in the transfer of violent authority to thuggish partisans; and the third is the official acknowledgement and buttressing of the moral culture and social power of individuals and groups representing communities of the poor.

As the foregoing has shown, not only had party-backed violent outlawry and political unionism been introduced into national politics in the 1940s, but sections of a historically marginal and despised social force – the downtrodden urban poor of Kingston – had begun to assume a slight but growing importance in national politics. Indeed, despite the fact that the vast majority of the population in this island lived outside the capital city, it was clear that politics in Kingston, and particularly the political involvement of the small working class, and the mobilized unemployed there, was fast defining the temper of national politics.

I have already called attention to the importance of these groups to the fortunes of both the parties and unions in Kingston. But what seems particularly compelling about the relationship between aspiring politicians and the urban poor at this early date is the degree to which seasoned politicians of national reputation relied on social outcasts to win political power. These unorthodox politicians unabashedly inserted themselves in the social and cultural milieu of the ghetto, and sought the votes and loyalties of residents there as the path to national power. In urban Jamaica in this early period, top politicians from both parties unambiguously allied themselves with the working people, the desperately unemployed and even a few individuals who sprang from the predatory and opportunistic lumpenproletariat.

While notions such as "populism" and "multi-class politics" offer insight into the reasons for this association, these concepts do not fully capture politics on the hustings in small island societies where face-to-face interactions and intimacy of communication are the norm for political and personal success. Uncritically applying the generic idea of multi-class politics to the realities of small island politics runs the risk of leaving out the intimate communications politics that are so vital to political effectiveness in small island states. Moreover, a wholly strategic understanding of populism in peripheral societies might easily reproduce the patronizing role of the politician who invariably relates to his supporters from a distance and from on high. Such a traditional account of political interaction does not capture the readiness on the part of island politicians to deepen this elite–mass alliance by self-sacrificing means. Breaking down the traditional distance between the leaders and the led, these Kingston politicians went into battle, cheek-by-jowl, alongside the working class and side-by-side with the feared lumpenproletariat, the traditional target of middle-class cultural contempt.

A complementary explanation of this alliance that goes beyond populism and multi-class politics may be that emergent ties of Jamaican politicians to militant sectors of the downtrodden urban poor reveal these politicians' capacity for an inventive politics. This association with the desperate, but socially mobilized poor, shows Jamaican politicians' appreciation of the political uses of contained interpersonal violence and their grasp of the role of intimacy in political relations. This alliance forged from above suggests a boldness and acumen that gave birth to a novel tactic: the managed recruitment of violent actors to do political battle on behalf of intimately known political bosses. At the very least, such an alliance between slum-dwellers and middle-class politicians indicates a bold readiness to redefine the etiquette of power and the social space from which power could be both accumulated and deployed. In sum, the basis for the origins and coexistence of violence and politics in Jamaica in these years may be found in the intimacy and strategic sense that some politicians brought to their engagements in the urban cauldron that was Kingston.

By actively soliciting the urban working class, the unemployed and even the predatory lumpenproletariat, power was now displaying its ubiquity and ingenuity. Such a ubiquity created a basis for both a potential re-siting of power and the possible suppression of challenges to it. In this way, political power could be relocated outside official state apparatuses. It could be devolved onto alternative cultural structures; it could inhabit new social spaces beyond the formal etiquette demanded by the civic realm; and it could even recruit for its myriad purposes the most unlikely personnel – in this case the urban poor. The inventive stroke of party politics in this period, therefore, seems to have been its capacity to move boldly into the turbulent political, cultural and strategic space that was the society of the Kingston poor, and employ this space as a route to national power.

Political intervention in the urban cauldron and the enhancing of the strategic role of the militant poor in national politics in these early years were therefore clearly linked to the bid for political power on behalf of middle-class politicians. But that quest, it must be insisted, did not rule out the location of a domain of state power within the ghettos nor did it bar official incorporation of the moral culture of residents who lived in those communities. It is not surprising, therefore, that in the pitched battles for political dominance in the capital city, its several working-class districts and slum areas took on a corresponding political importance which began to give the residents there an enhanced role in national politics.

Political Interdependence in the Slums

The influence of the urban poor could be seen in the indispensable nature of their engagement in the rough-and-tumble feature of city politics. It was evident in the passion of their involvement in party politics and in the polit-ical apprenticeship won by notables among them. Indeed, because of their heightened mobilization and integration into the parties, minority contin-gents of the urban poor became more influential in shaping the temper of national politics than their demographically larger kin such as the peasantry and the urban working class. Contingents of the urban poor, particularly the Kingston unemployed and lumpenproletariat, had definitely outstripped both the working class and the rural peasantry in the degree of their com-bative, street-level partisan activism, and in the intensity of the social ideolo-gies that they espoused. Consequently, the struggle for power in the capital city had opened the way for certain mobilized strata of the poor to play an important political role, albeit an unpredictable and tenuous one, in the unfolding dynamics of power in the country.

The politicians' quest for power, therefore, could not mean a one-way exercise of influence, as a simplistic version of patron-clientelism or populism would suggest. On the contrary, the politicians' penetration of the social space of the urban poor inclined these politicians to cede some of their dominance to already powerful cultural impulses among the poor, even as the politicians sought recruits for their political wars. As the parties and unions became involved in the social and cultural milieu of working-class and poor neighbourhoods, both residents and politicians accommodated each other's needs and dispositions. Poor residents sought benefits and invariably attached themselves to the parties for these reasons. At the same time, aspiring politicians looked to poor neighbourhoods for recruits, organizers and combatants to help secure political gains in the ongoing political and trade union struggles.

It therefore seems reasonable to assume that middle-class politicians had to respond to the material wants of urban poor people, as well as adapt to their politico-cultural sensibilities. In the 1940s and 1950s, this accommodation saw the parties' concession to pressing demands from below for the distribution of patronage. In other instances, this adaptation by established power implied an ambiguous accommodation to growing social assertiveness in the slums.

This complication was evident, for example, in the uncertain response to the growing presence of religious revivalists on the streets of Kingston, and to official uncertainties concerning the expansion of the Rastafarian movement among the Kingston poor.[28] Finally, even as the state promoted predatory violence among the most non-conformist elements of the Kingston poor, state power could not always contain expressions of popular violence. Antipathies among the poor often broke through official boundaries as interpersonal clashes, partisan violence by over-loyal adherents and banditry challenged the state's ability to manage the expression of social violence from below.[29]

This nexus between the urban poor and the state highlights the complex, unequal, yet mutually dependent relationship between the downtrodden and their political representatives. This ambiguous relationship permitted sections of the urban working class, the unemployed poor and parts of the lumpenproletariat to gain limited access to the political process and to exercise a constrained but important leverage over political dynamics. Politics in these early years was therefore monopolized not by propertied groups, middle-class actors or by professional politicians. On the contrary, while the urban poor were locked out of the corridors of the state house, denied a place in the top echelons of the parties and used as cannon fodder in party political wars, at the level of the street and the constituency, and in the politics of the neighbourhood, the official power of the "big man" had to accommodate itself to the limited social power and violent political compulsion of the "small man". An informal interdependence was being forged out of this nexus and desperately poor and working-class actors were fashioning social spaces for the downtrodden both inside and outside the party structures. In the post-war years, this subtle accretion of influence from below had its effects on the dynamics of power. For a view of the uneven dialectic between power holders and the urban poor, our account turns to the early career of the JLP politician Edward Seaga, and to the deepening ties between state agents and the mobilized urban poor.

Race and Politics in the Slums: A Victory for Edward Seaga

The foregoing account has shown that by 1947 both the inhospitable conditions and violent PNP retaliation had forced Bustamante to withdraw as the JLP candidate in the West Kingston constituency. Despite this hasty retreat, Bustamante, from his new constituency in the rural parish of South Clarendon, once again led his party to a narrow victory in the 1949 national elections. For its part, the PNP, despite consecutive defeats in both the 1944 and 1949 elections, followed up its hard-won victory in the street battles of Kingston with an electoral triumph there, as Ken Hill, a left-wing labour activist, won the coveted West Kingston constituency in 1949.

Despite this breakthrough, however, the PNP's hold on the constituency was short lived. In 1952 a debilitating ideological rift inside the party led to the expulsion of Hill, along with three of his left-wing associates. This parting of ways between leading PNP party moderates and four left-wing labour activists, who had done much to bring the working class into the party, was a mixed blessing for those in the country who identified with a progressive political agenda.

On the one hand, the expulsion of the Marxists inside the PNP defused Bustamante's effective anti-communist attacks on the PNP and reassured the Jamaican public that the PNP had no intention of taking the country in a communist direction. This purging of the leftists probably contributed to the eventual PNP triumph in the 1955 national elections and gave the PNP its first victory at the polls since elections were first held under universal adult suffrage in 1944.

On the other hand, however, Ken Hill's ouster from the party hurt the PNP in West Kingston in 1955. Running as an independent candidate in the elections of that year, Hill was forced to split the pro-PNP vote with Iris King, the campaigner for the PNP. The result of this division of PNP support was the election of Hugh Shearer, the JLP candidate, and the return of the West Kingston constituency to that party in 1955.

As this political seesaw unfolded in West Kingston in the early 1950s, a curious development was simultaneously taking place in the constituency. In 1953 Edward Seaga, a Jamaican of Lebanese origin and a student of anthropology at Harvard University, was collecting ethnographic data in West Kingston and rural Jamaica for a study of indigenous religions and folk culture on the island.[30] From his research base at Salt Lane and other vantage points in the slums of West Kingston, Seaga witnessed and began recording the religious and social practices of the Kingston and rural poor. In what must have been a rare display of anthropological initiative and commitment in the slums of West Kingston at the time, the white-skinned Seaga decamped among the black settlers during his three-and-a-half years of fieldwork to share their simple dwellings and consort with them in their daily activities while studying their religious and cultural practices at first hand.

West Kingston certainly offered the young Seaga fecund territory for the study of Jamaican religious life. Between 1935 and 1955, the entire area had become a major urban outpost for the practice of indigenous religious forms, especially the variants of revivalism in Rastafarianism and the Kumina cult. Informants recall an enthusiastic Seaga participating in sacred rites, taking photographs of religious activities from ghetto rooftops and in other ways associating with the daily life of the urban poor. In recalling his participant-observation, Seaga saw his experience as that of immersion.

> I had lived in these areas experiencing life not as a visitor . . . but waking and going to bed in the households of village and ghetto, and experiencing the widest form of participation possible of everyday life. I heard and collected

folk tales, folk music, lived experiences of nine-nights, and digging sports, played ring games, attended more than 100 revival spiritual functions, and in short, was immersed and baptized in the folk culture of Jamaica.[31]

Seaga's readiness to commingle with urban revivalists, and his enthusiasm for learning about the religious cultures of the folk, brought him into a world unknown to most Jamaicans of urban middle-class origins. This was a world in which peasant beliefs, rooted in revival religious traditions, held sway. Here folk healing, divination, charismatic prophecy and the manipulation of the natural world coexisted with belief in direct communication with the Divine through ecstatic spirit possession.[32] This was a world in which protean revival practices deeply influenced popular religions as various as Myalism, Rastafarianism and Pentacostalism. Religious adepts of these faiths had begun to secure popularity and an abiding loyalty from the ranks of the Kingston poor to whom they ministered. Typically informed by a profound redefinition of the relationship between the faithful and the Divine, these religious forms and their rituals clearly set their adherents apart from the religions and practices of the respectable classes.

It was Seaga's circumspect, non-patronizing orientation to the folk and their religions which brought him to the revivalists' respectful attention. His many forays into urban communities such as Trench Town and Jones Town allowed Seaga to meet the revered kings and queens of the Kumina cult, and permitted him to become acquainted with the leading practitioners of Zion Revivalism in West Kingston. Of course, in these overwhelmingly black-skinned and impoverished communities, Seaga's skin colour and social status did not go unnoticed, and it caused some residents to be wary of him initially. However, with time and the negotiation of this potential pitfall by a seriousness of purpose, this "white man" quickly earned the goodwill and reciprocal regard of the religiously minded black poor in the area.[33]

Beyond this association with religious groups, Seaga's sojourn into the Kingston slums also gave him a privileged vantage point on working-class community life. He no doubt witnessed the flow of community life beyond religion in activities as various as domino and dice games, illegal betting, cricket and soccer matches, and self-help banking by the poor in the so-called partner system. Seaga would also have been familiar with the predation of notorious criminals and bandits in the area, some of whom won a heroic status for both their brazen acts and their evasion of the authorities.

In the early to mid-1950s, this student of cultural anthropology would not have been unmindful of heroic criminality as a form of status honour in the Kingston ghetto. Nor would he have missed the sharp rise in the cohort of unemployed youths of the area who converted an enforced idleness into rival gangs that jealously defended their turf in working-class communities. The duelling in the 1950s among West Kingston youth gangs, such as the Vikings, Skulls, Phoenix City, Phantom and Spanglers, would have caused Seaga – like many residents of the time – to become alert to this nascent but extra-legal form of gang power, and he would have been aware of some of the gang leaders and the emergent community loyalties they displayed.

In addition to a familiarity with these social relations, Seaga also frequented venues where the poor took their leisure. In addition to having an acquaintance with illegal gambling sites, the lively rum shops and the popular open-air Kingston cinemas, Seaga also visited the dance halls of the day. By the late 1950s they were among the most popular places for working-class recreation. Venues such as Chocomo Lawn in Denham Town and Forrester's Hall on North Street were packed on weekends with working-class revellers. Residents, and particularly the youth, came to these "blues dances" to hear and dance to the latest "sounds" in music, both local and foreign.[34]

Paced by the creative use of the sound system as a means of direct transmission of popular music to the working people, a vibrant, indigenous music culture and music industry sprang up, with West Kingston as its artistic epicentre. Local musicians, aspiring vocal groups and ambitious lone performers vied for the attention of working-class audiences in live performances and on records put out by a fledgling local recording industry. In these years, singers and vocal groups copied both the songs and idioms of black American music and the soulful mannerisms of its popular exponents. At the same time, the Jamaican artists went beyond simple imitation to fuse these imported styles to original, winning songs about the joys and travails of working-class life. Record producers, fast-talking disc jockeys in the dance halls and canny talent scouts scrambled to showcase the raw talent and exploding energy of this new cultural development.[35]

This florescence of popular music culture was sufficiently compelling for Seaga to enter the ranks of these sponsors and converts to the new musical forms. In 1959 Seaga had already established his own recording label and had several performers under contract, among them Byron Lee and the popular duo of Joe Higgs and Roy Wilson.[36] Seaga's budding career as an entrepreneur in the local music industry was cut short, however, by the lure of politics. As this period of cultural creativity was unfolding, Kingston had become a cauldron of the racial and class contradictions racking Jamaican society.[37]

In May 1959 political riots had erupted there and throughout the year a militant Rastafarian movement openly challenged the multi-racial ideology of the parties and adherents of the movement clashed with the police in the streets of Kingston. These tensions intensified in 1960 and were capped in June by an uprising that was quickly extinguished. Violent social unrest, spawned by social inequality, had now brought the frustrations of the urban poor to the attention of a complacent society.

While the unrest would prove damaging to the PNP and to its hopes of appealing to its record of social improvements, the disturbance and sense of national crisis did raise the political fortunes of the JLP. The JLP had lost the 1959 national elections, and with it the coveted West Kingston constituency. But the PNP's 1959 triumph was dimmed by growing social unrest in Kingston, and the rising chorus of critics who bemoaned the PNP's inability to address the social inequalities in the country.[38] The PNP also had its hands full with other pressing political concerns, including the pace of the imminent transfer of political power to native hands, and the question of Jamaica's continued membership in the West Indies Federation.[39]

In what proved a remarkable political stroke, Bustamante intervened in these uncertain circumstances, and in 1959 recruited the anthropologist-cum-entrepreneur Seaga to do battle as a member of the JLP opposition in the Legislative Council. The canny Bustamante also intensified his campaign against the PNP's defence of Jamaica's membership in the Federation. Leading this attack in early 1961 was none other than the political neophyte, Edward Seaga. In his famous "haves and have-nots" speech in the Legislative Council, Seaga marshalled statistics to show the growing inequalities between the poorer classes and the other groups that benefited from the island's post-war economic growth. He implied that the PNP had lost its way as a champion of the downtrodden, and accused the government of pursuing the retention of the country's membership in the Federation at the expense of poor Jamaicans.[40]

Stung by these criticisms, and driven by his democratic commitments, Norman Manley, head of the government and PNP leader, unexpectedly called a referendum on the Federation issue. In a stunning reversal of fortune, the PNP in September 1961 faced a humiliating defeat in that poll as voters affirmed Jamaica's withdrawal from the regional body. Observers of this debacle would credit not only an alleged PNP misstep in putting the issue to a vote, but also the effectiveness of both Bustamante and his protégé, Seaga, in exploiting insular, nationalist and class sentiments of a largely unsophisticated electorate.[41]

With this resounding victory, the JLP pressed its political advantage. It demanded and got a role in the final negotiations for independence and tried to identify itself in the public mind as a party that would uphold the interest of the poor against a PNP that seemed out of touch with popular sentiments. The date for political independence was finally set for 6 August 1962, and the PNP announced new elections for April of that year. These elections found Seaga as the JLP contestant for the West Kingston seat, and the run-up to the poll saw the JLP trading on Bustamante's heroic status as fighter for the downtrodden and a founding father of the nation. This strategy paid off, for in a major setback, the PNP was handed yet another defeat, as the electorate returned the JLP to power as the first government of the independent nation.

As JLP partisans revelled in this triumph, they no doubt took particular satisfaction in Seaga's stunning upset of Dudley Thompson, the distinguished PNP candidate who had introduced pan-African and anti-colonial sentiments into the contest. Thompson, a short, stockily built and black-skinned lawyer, had returned to Jamaica in 1955 after an illustrious career abroad.[42] He had travelled to Britain to serve in the Royal Air Force in the mid-1940s, was subsequently a Rhodes scholar at Oxford University and had practised law in East Africa. There he earned his credentials as a pan-Africanist and anti-colonial champion. This in large part because of his successful defence of Jomo Kenyatta – the jailed Kenyan nationalist – who was put on trial for leading the Mau Mau movement in that country. On the political hustings in West Kingston, Thompson tried to parlay this racial commitment and African experience into a political victory in the slums. In a remarkable aesthetic makeover for this lawyer who belonged to the upper crust of Jamaican society, Thompson began appearing at his political rallies wearing flowing African robes and carrying a tall spear.[43]

Evidently appealing to the Rastafarians and others holding black nationalist sentiments in West Kingston, Thompson complemented his new attire by assuming the provocative honorific "Burning Spear". As the honorific given to Kenyatta during the Mau Mau struggle, the meaning of this title was not lost on the Rastafarians and allied groups, including many pan-Africanists of the day, who followed the latest news from Africa. While this unabashed appeal to black racial and cultural nationalist sentiment was unprecedented for the hitherto racially circumspect PNP, and although it produced that party's most direct cultural identification with the black poor in West Kingston, this symbolism proved insufficient to win their unqualified support.

Several developments conspired to deny Thompson a victory in West Kingston. First, Seaga had beaten him to the punch on the important religious issue. As the foregoing has shown, Seaga had been active in the constituency for nearly a decade and had established his credibility with the religiously minded residents long before Thompson appeared on the scene. By his own account, Seaga had close ties with all the major religious adepts of the area. For example, he had the confidence and friendship of Malachi "Kapo" Reynolds, a "guru of Zion revivalism".[44] Seaga had encouraged the latter in his artistic effort as an exponent of African art, and in time the politician would even dare to rescue the artist's works from the police who had impounded them as evidence of the revivalist's illegal involvement in the practice of obeah.[45] Unlike many of his peers in both parties and in the wider society, Seaga was not repelled by this folk belief in the powers of obeah, nor did he shrink from acts of spirit possession and the esoteric rituals invoked by the faithful.

By 1962 the cultural sympathies of the anthropologist began paying dividends for the aspiring politician, as his genuine interest in the circumstances of the poor caused these people to support his candidacy. Seaga's close ties to the revivalists were such that their presence and spiritual invocations at his political rallies gave these gatherings a coveted cultural authenticity and popular appeal lacking in the campaign of his Oxford-trained PNP rival.[46] Indeed, the role of popular religious symbolism was so significant in the Seaga campaign that it was said that the temper of his public meetings in West Kingston was more akin to religious revival meetings than to the modern political rally.

Another advantage Seaga enjoyed was the effective martial protection that enforcers mobilized by the JLP–BITU gave to his campaign. Hoping to defend their hard-won political victories in the constituency, PNP organizers and their thuggish enforcers sought to disrupt Seaga's campaign and hoped to eventually drive him out of the constituency altogether. After all, they had earlier succeeded in routing the indomitable Bustamante, and imagined Seaga to be a political interloper who could easily be intimidated into fleeing in the face of threats, beatings, knife-wielding, gunplay and other disruptive acts. These acts of violence were carried out not only by rank-and-file activists, but also by criminal gangs whose youthful members were being drawn into the political fray. Though he was subjected to brutish assaults, nasty epithets about his alleged lack of ambition in campaigning in so benighted a district, and was even disabled by a serious stabbing that hospitalized him, Seaga survived these violent attacks because JLP counter-violence held the PNP thugs at bay.

Notable among those sending enforcers to Seaga's aid was the legendary JLP politician D.C. Tavares, who represented the working-class constituency of South West St Andrew. By the early 1960s Tavares, a tall, brown-skinned politician, had earned notoriety for being a tough politician who brooked no challenge to his power. In fact, even as West Kingston and other Kingston constituencies swung from one party to the next in national elections, Tavares had held onto his district in these early years by the application of two tactics which would be copied by other urban politicians: patronage to lock in politically faithful constituents, as well as gunplay and threats by politicized gangs to prevent incursion by rival parties.[47] While both parties would only later institutionalize this JLP tactic, in the 1962 electoral contest, Seaga's victory was in part secured through the deployment of violent JLP gangsters from the lumpenproletariat who beat back a similar PNP effort to intimidate voters in the area.

In this epic contest between the parties for West Kingston, one impoverished enclave known as "Dungle" (probably from the contraction of the words [garbage] "dump" and "jungle") assumed a controversial role in the outcome. An overcrowded, benighted area of huts and pitiful shacks, this area had been made by Dungle's impoverished but socially conscious lumpenproletariat into PNP outpost in the West Kingston constituency. This enclave had proven impervious to the interventions and entreaties of JLP contestants, including the indomitable Alexander Bustamante who had routed its settlers by razing their shacks in 1945.

In the wake of the continuing trek of poor migrants to the area, and in the context of the 1959 PNP victory in the constituency and that party's mobilization of voters in the enclave, Dungle's settlers seemed ready to vote again for the PNP in April 1962. But in what would remain a controversial and disputed event, on the day ballots were being cast, a skirmish between the police and voters erupted at the polling site. In the ensuing fracas involving the use of tear gas by the police, potential voters from Dungle were scattered from the polls and did not cast their ballots. Seaga's subsequent victory by a narrow margin of several hundred votes confirmed for PNP partisans their belief that the event was contrived to deny the PNP another victory in West Kingston by preventing Dungle's voters from going to the polls.[48]

Finally, despite the salience of this dispute, it may be argued that Seaga really outlasted Thompson by dint of effort and organization. Seaga's unflagging "house-to-house canvassing", the fact that he had lived in the community and had "close links with local constituency organizations", gave him the political edge in a contest where, despite the efforts of the PNP and others, appeals to race and skin colour did not produce the racialization of this contest or the political outcome PNP supporters had hoped for. Thus when the votes were tallied in the West Kingston constituency, it was the white-skinned Seaga who got 51 per cent of the vote and the black-skinned Thompson who received 45 per cent.[49]

The volatile constituency of West Kingston thus changed hands once again. By voting JLP for the third time in the five elections held there since 1944, constituents refused to allow consecutive electoral victories to either party. In this remarkable political contest in a district where race and class concerns were assuming dramatic proportions, neither the race nor the skin colour of the candidates proved decisive to the outcome. Instead, the materially desperate voters of West Kingston handed a pragmatic political victory to the "white man" who had lived among them; who had spoken for the "have-nots" in Parliament; and whom they believed might – unlike the four other representatives before him – make a difference in their deprived circumstances. Before turning to the startling political changes West Kingston residents would experience during Seaga's early tenure, a few summary remarks are in order.

Conclusion

The foregoing account has confirmed the extant research which shows that the use of violence as a political tactic to win elections, defend political territory against rivals, and secure representation of workers in the trade union movement, actually began in the 1940s and not in the 1960s as some observers have been wont to believe. Thus from the moment Jamaicans won the right to vote, and native politicians got the opportunity to become incumbents of state power, political violence in the ways described became an organizing feature of Jamaican politics.

This violent outlawry, driven by a war over political spoils, was actively abetted and often spearheaded by top politicians of the day and their political organizations. Competition for power led to party sponsorship of this kind of political violence. But as has been pointed out, that violence was decentralized and highly personalized. It was not the repressive apparatus of the state, the army or the police that were used in these fracases. Rather, political activists and organizers, workers and the unemployed, gangsters and other thuggish recruits became the vanguard of this dispersed violence.

This use of force in the 1940s and 1950s was episodic and primarily intimidatory in nature. It was not employed as a species of political cleansing that purged residents from communities that voted for opposition parties. It certainly did not entail genocidal acts meant to physically wipe out residents or their political representatives by murderous force. Moreover, while this violence for political purposes did countenance murder and the use of guns, their employment was secondary to the typical adoption of threats and beatings. Political street violence in the 1940s therefore involved a variety of disruptive acts as various as stone and bottle throwing, physical beatings, knifings, and selective gunfire to hamper opponents. It was carried out by hastily convened recruits from party headquarters, job sites, union halls and the slums, and occasionally with a known and feared "badman" in the lead. The police and the military were therefore not the agents of this repression, but rather were typically bystanders as this violence unfolded. Violence linked to politics in these years was therefore dispersed and decentralized, and the state's repressive authority was shared with these partisan irregulars who were recruited for battle.

This fractious form of early political contestation seemed also to strengthen a style of political leadership that emphasized the following as its trademark qualities: histrionics, charisma-as-power, personal loyalty as a basis of political reward, and the calculated, officially sanctioned use of punitive violence against opponents. Under these circumstances, urban politics in the 1940s and 1950s was not the genteel affair of a closeted consensual elite, but rather a rambunctious free-for-all in which a tough, bare-knuckled approach to rivals often carried the day.

Such a tactic required for its success an alliance with segments of the mobilized urban poor. As has been shown above, some Jamaican politicians consorted with, lived among, recruited and went into street battles shoulder-to-shoulder with many strata of the urban poor. These politicians were seemingly at ease with groups as disparate as older unionized labourers, the unemployed young, revival shepherds and Rastafarians, as well as personalities from the ranks of the predatory lumpenproletariat.

This association was remarkable for its inventive quality. It found Kingston politicians adapting and relating to the cultural conventions of these disparate groups. In this period, politicians not only spoke at rallies of party- and nation-building, but also invoked Marcus Garvey's memory; they called for the singing of hymns and the invocation of folk blessings for their agendas, and when circumstances warranted, they riled up their supporters by hurling partisan epithets and promising menace to their political opponents. By bowing to the social and cultural concerns in working-class communities and articulating them to the parties' political projects, Jamaican politicians were rather exceptional. Within a constitutionally democratic system, they had not only established a cultural consonance with the materially deprived militant and compliant poor, but also forged an intimate and complicated political alliance that would shape the destiny of the parties and the country.

The establishment of this alliance was equally exceptional because it demonstrated a remarkable strategic sense among Kingston politicians that the urban cauldron and the society of the socially conscious urban poor were sites for the assimilation of antagonistic cultural structures and arenas for the location of state power. This bold intervention in these turbulent social, cultural and political spaces disclosed a recognition by Jamaican politicians that national power and glory may not lie primarily in the bureaucratic routines of official state institutions nor exclusively with a politically relevant, but complacent middle-class and entrepreneurial elite. Rather, the vigour of the intervention in the Kingston ghettos and working-class communities, as well as the cheek-by-jowl association of national politicians with the socially conscious and martially oriented urban poor highlight the politicians' instinctive grasp of a risky, but possible route to both national power and effective political control of this fractious segment of the national population.

By the late 1950s, aspects of this political control had been achieved through the creation of the proto-nations that were attached to the parties. Moreover, the antagonistic cultural communities, and the political tribalism with which they were associated, gained even more energy. Their invigoration was spurred by the distribution of limited patronage, the winner-take-all competition for political power and the depiction of the opposition as an adversarial, proto-national community that should be fought in the name of political and cultural survival. Benefits politics in these years thus divided the working people, set them to murderous assaults against each other and inaugurated a culture of political warfare that persists to the present day.

Finally, the foregoing has shown that despite these disabling circumstances, tributaries of the militant poor retained a modicum of influence over important developments in this period. Their violent partisanship, albeit in a self-destructive cause, placed them at the epicentre of national political disputes and at the nexus of the contradiction between the people and those who held power and privilege. In this destructive apprenticeship to the power holders, the socially mobilized lumpenproletariat and allied groups were not merely cannon fodder; surprisingly they were also agents that contributed to a decisive shaping of political outcomes in this period.

Politicians relied on the politically compliant poor, as well as the alienated and violent poor, in their reach for national power. As a consequence, the protean moral culture of the materially desperate poor had begun to influence the internal cultural life of the political parties; and as violent political enforcement began to take root alongside the nefarious activities of a few heroic criminals, the violence of over-loyal partisans was already pressuring native politicians to be extensively concerned with making sure the violence welling up from the slums did not overflow the boundaries these politicians had established for it. We turn in the next chapter to an examination of the maturation of this process over the next decade.

3

Fulcrums of Power in the Ghetto

FOR ALL ITS SEEMINGLY CHAOTIC AND TURBULENT character, the violent, state-sponsored outlawry of the 1940s and 1950s had an undeniable logic. This was the effort of party leaders to achieve total supremacy in Kingston over rival politicians and their fanatical supporters. At the same time, however, while this competition for power undoubtedly provoked serious clashes between the political parties and their allied unions, this very warring created a paradoxical bond among the joisting leaders. It is arguable that even as the power struggle tore at partisans on each side, this contention did join the political bosses from both parties in a common enterprise – the domestication of the West Kingston slums and control of the fractious urban poor there. Hence, no matter their political differences, the party leaders' unleashing of the war for votes and spoils also revealed a bid to exert political control of the slums.

As Jamaica's political independence neared, however, neither the urban ghetto nor the rebellious poor were under the effective suzerainty of the parties, the trade unions or their leaders. This lack of political hegemony was apparent from a number of outbursts in the Kingston slums. They included race-conscious protest against the island's nationalist leaders; armed insurrection by a Rastafarian sect in 1960; the denunciation of Chinese shopkeepers by ghetto dwellers in October of that year; and street protests by unemployed residents.[1] This defiance by unruly inner-city dwellers not only highlighted a wider alienation and discontent among the urban poor; it also indicated that contingents among them had eluded the enveloping reach of the dominant political organizations established after the 1938 labour rebellion.

It will be recalled that this momentous rebellion led to the founding of national trade unions and their affiliated political parties.[2] Yet even as this outcome empowered these organizations' leaders and gave the labouring classes significant political and union representation, it did little for many among the urban poor, particularly those who lived in Kingston's slums.[3] Many from their ranks lay outside the mobilizing reach of party and union activists.[4] Indeed, anti-system sensibilities, high unemployment and the relative social isolation of the ghetto poor shielded them from political and civic leaders' moral and political leadership.[5]

Ideological Deficit and Cultural Challenge

This absence of elite cultural and political dominance in the slums and beyond should also be linked to an ideological deficit brought over from the colonial period into the early years of political independence. Ken Post, for example, has shown how middle-class nationalists in the 1930s and after had adopted a peculiar social outlook that expressed the demands for political self-rule without also envisaging a repudiation of their Anglophile sympathies, or abandonment of filial loyalty to the British Empire.[6]

This contradiction, which found nationalists combining claims for political self-rule with residual sentiments of European cultural belonging, exposed a major vulnerability of this elite group. For as its members went about the construction of a social identity for the fledgling Jamaican people-nation, these nationalist leaders muted appeals to both black nationalism and the widely shared Africanist sensibility among the Jamaican people. This discomfort with race, nationality and popular culture was typical of the Jamaican middle class and of most members of the political elite.[7] For example, in response to the colonial authorities' July 1941 crackdown on Leonard Howell and his leadership of the Rastafarian settlement at Pinnacle in the parish of St Catherine, observations were printed in *Public Opinion*, a publication that spoke for the middle class:

The Ras Tafari movement is an excellent example of the kind of thing which develops when popular movements become entirely divorced from the educated classes. The merit of Garveyism was that it expected the educated man of African descent to come in, that it rallied all sections. It did not renounce civilization and deify an African king because it did not renounce education.

It is striking that the Ras Tafari movement could not exist with trade unionism. During the 1938 disturbances, it entirely failed to serve as a rallying-point. It was winded out [sic]. It has now become the hobby horse movement of a few obscure fanatics who have collected themselves in a dark corner of the countryside. It is not a true symptom of present day tendencies.[8]

This negative assessment by the politically moderate middle class suggests something of the polite contempt with which they viewed Howell's politics and other militant expressions of black nationalism among the Jamaican poor.

For their part, Jamaica's communists of middle-class origins were not much better in their opinion of race consciousness among the black poor, though these leftists took a slightly different tack. While not dismissing the Rastafarian movement as a form of race consciousness gone bad, the Left, however, did share their moderate compeers' concern with the Rastafarians' isolation from the civilizing impact of the educated elite and their politics. As I shall show below, elite paternalism – the belief that progress for the black poor lay exclusively in the political leadership and organizations created by the educated classes – united middle-class nationalists of divergent ideological persuasions. For example, where politically moderate nationalists saw party and trade union politics and the influence of the educated middle class as bases of cultural uplift for the black poor, Jamaican communists assigned a similar benefit to joining the class struggle.

Thus in protesting the colonial authorities' banning of a Howell mass meeting in February 1940, the *Worker* newspaper published the following from a leading left-wing letter writer:

We do not know Mr Leonard Howell and we hold no brief for the Ras Tafari Society, but we know that they represent a *united Negro Movement* with a membership drawn exclusively from the working class; so naturally we sympathise with them and regard them as comrades. Their methods are different from ours but we feel that ultimately they will join us in the *class struggle* to achieve the emancipation of the *entire working class* of the world.

The more we unite the stronger we become; and by the strength of our unity we are confident that in spite of any curtailment of our civil liberties we will secure the liberation of the Ethiopians and all other oppressed peoples from the unmerciful exploitation of the capitalists.[9]

While this defence of the Rastafarian movement hinted at recognition of a racially based social movement and improved on the dismissive sneering of middle-class PNP activists, this communist acknowledgement of racial politics from below was itself clouded by left-wing class conceit and social-ist political prejudice on the "race question".[10] Hedged about with qualifi-cations, the foregoing communist acknowledgement of a racial politics under colonialism left much to be desired. It seemed to grant race con-sciousness and black struggle among the poor neither independent status nor importance as possible tutor to left-wing politics. Instead, it was hoped that the Rastafarians would add their protest to the working-class struggle led by the Left. As was the case in socialist and communist circles at the time, the Jamaican Left viewed "Negro politics" as an adjunct of the class struggle, soon to come under the tutelage of the "comrades" fighting against a cap-italist system.[11]

Where middle-class nationalists remained uncertain, if not dismissive in their attitude to race, such an orientation tended to cede cultural ground to more racially conscious groups.[12] The mobilized black poor in the country-side and the towns were certainly among these actors. The Rastafarians saw themselves as possessing an African identity. And unlike most, the group affirmed this honourable racial identity, in contrast to what they saw as the dishonoured status of many Jamaican blacks from the lower class.

Indeed, by the early 1960s an epic struggle over the cultural content of the island's national identity broke into the open, and set middle-class nationalists against their nemesis – the urban poor and their Garveyite sym-pathizers such as the People's Political Party.[13] These champions for an Africanist content in the country's social identity sharply criticized the nationalist elite for demoting this important cultural heritage. Both groups criticized discrimination against blacks and called for a cultural decoloniza-tion of the country.[14]

This cultural-nationalist backlash was most apparent in an expression of racial assertiveness by the Kingston poor between May 1959 and June 1960. This upsurge in black racial consciousness capped several decades of Rastafarian recruitment, agitation, and proselytizing among the militant Kingston poor and made clear their continuing dissatisfaction with the political settlement of 1938.

In criticizing that settlement, the Rastafarian activist Claudius Henry berated the national leaders as moral and political bankrupts for choosing "self-government under British Colonial rule" as the route to political independence.[15] Rastafarian leaders claimed, among other things, that political independence would be a chimera that would perpetuate racial discrimination against the black poor and continue their poverty. Henry, the leading Rastafarian activist of the day, sharply criticized nationalist politicians as misguided, and denounced them as "wicked, unrighteous and oppressive rulers of Jamaica" who would return the poor to slave-like conditions.[16] The way forward for the black poor, Henry claimed, was to reject Jamaican independence in favour of repatriation to the African continent. There blacks would be free from white colonial rule and from the policies of the native agents who, Henry felt, would perpetuate the continued subordination of blacks in Jamaica. This much was evident from a July 1959 pamphlet that Henry distributed:

> Dear Readers, should we at this time sacrifice such a righteous Government, for Jamaica [*sic*] Self-Government, or any other Self-Government, in the world? . . . shall we sacrifice the continent of Africa for the island of Jamaica? Shall we refuse God's offer for repatriation back home to Africa and a life of everlasting peace and freedom, with Him under our own vine and fig tree, and go back into slavery, under these wicked, unrighteous and oppressive rulers of Jamaica? God forbid.[17]

Henry's growing support among the West Kingston poor, his inflammatory language and his unvarnished threats against the prime minister brought him to the attention of the authorities.[18] They were alarmed by this turn of events that threatened to undo a carefully nurtured alliance that native political leaders had forged between black labour and their representative organizations, the parties and trade unions. To quell this racial outburst and protect this relationship, the Jamaican government launched several raids in Kingston in April 1960 against Henry's organization, the African Reformed Church.

In their forays against the Rastafarians, the police discovered an arms cache and not only charged Henry with unlawful possession of weapons but accused him of treason as well.[19] On the heels of these events, the police in June also pre-empted an armed attack on the government by Henry's son, Ronald, and several Afro-American associates. Therefore, in the waning years of colonial rule, champions of black racial consciousness from the slums were repudiating native political leaders' appeals to join their ranks and these rebels had even begun to amass arms in a bid to overthrow the Jamaican state.

Jamaican political leaders were not unmindful of this opposition that now verged on insurrection and, as the foregoing has shown, they moved forcefully to crush this uprising. But force was not their only response. Because of the ideological nature of the conflict, nationalist leaders developed, in the thick of this battle, a legitimating counter-ideology to the black nationalism emanating from the slums. These nationalist leaders therefore depicted the expression of black nationalism among the lower class as an unfortunate and dangerous detour that would only lead the country into a cultural abyss. According to party leaders Alexander Bustamante and Norman Manley, the real threat to Jamaican society was not the Anglophile cultural dependency of its elites, but rather the spectre of black consciousness which threatened to scare off foreign investors, set cultural groups against each other, and ruin the social harmony that elites claimed for the society.

To fight this upsurge in black consciousness, political leaders therefore turned to the ideology of Jamaican Exceptionalism. As a counter-ideology, Exceptionalism sought to blunt the racial appeal of black nationalism and promote the idea of the Jamaican people as primordially disposed to a harmonious and tolerant resolution of social conflicts. Middle-class nationalists of a certain ilk maintained that where racial strife and conflicts had torn apart other societies in the Third World, Jamaican social relations were exemplary for the social harmony that existed between racial groups there. Prime Minister Norman Manley's lament expressed this concern for heightened race consciousness among the poor and among other blacks that felt racially aggrieved:

> Ugly forces are rising in our country. All over the land people have begun to preach race hatred – colour against colour, race against race. Movements are being formed dedicated to the destruction of the very idea of inter-racial harmony. I could understand that sort of thing 20 years ago, but today I say bluntly that it is a dangerous throwback into the past that threatens to undermine and destroy one of the greatest and finest things we have ever tried to achieve.[20]

The invoking of Jamaica's purported reputation for ethnic cooperation was also used in regard to the island's development prospects. For Jamaica's nationalist leaders, ethnic harmony was itself a guarantor of foreign capital investment. As Bustamante observed during the crisis,

People in the world have come to point at Jamaica as a leading example – as a small country where reason, law and order are fundamental to the country and our people, and where races work and live in harmony with ever increasing respect for each other, and capital therefore has regarded us as a safe place to come while local capital gained faith to join in doing their part in our development.[21]

But as a political invention forged in the heat of battle, the ideology of Exceptionalism encountered problems in rallying popular support. First, the ideology glossed over the emergent racial and class contradictions in Jamaica that were causing social unrest at the time. As a legitimating ideology, Exceptionalism therefore won few adherents among the militant urban poor, and many in the ranks of black labour who were also protesting the impact of racial discrimination on them. In the late 1950s and early 1960s, these antagonisms had caused the urban unemployed to assertively protest their marginal class and cultural status in the society, and in the early 1960s they were joined by better-off groups who criticized racial discrimination against blacks.[22]

Second, the counter-ideology of Jamaican Exceptionalism, with its emphasis on the Jamaican people's primordial disposition for social harmony and tolerance, appeared unconvincing to a volatile urban population already inured to state political violence against the militant poor, and accustomed to state sponsorship of communal inter-party wars over political spoils. Consequently, the unfolding battle over the role of race in the country's cultural identity, the ongoing conflict over political spoils and disputes over the economic status of blacks *vis-à-vis* other groups in the society disclosed not the social harmony claimed by the politicians, but rather a deeply felt sense of racial discrimination and political victimization.

Indeed, the black poor's expanding agitation for social justice had already inspired an attempt, in 1960, to violently overthrow the state, and this attempted putsch clearly revealed the persisting dilemma for the state and its political agents. They faced the challenge of domesticating alienated, but socially mobilized segments of the urban poor – the majority of whose members remained largely outside integrative political organizations and dominant cultural institutions of the time, yet whose numerical weight, cultural influence and political importance in the capital city were increasing.

As the previous chapter has suggested, the parasitic state and its agents were aware of this development and had sought to address it by extending the reach of state power into the Kingston slums. In this effort to exercise dominance in Kingston, and over the national society more generally, state agents had resorted to the three powerful initiatives discussed earlier: the deployment of benefits politics, the decentralized use of political violence in the Kingston slums and the fashioning of the proto-nations of the political parties.

By the early 1960s it was also apparent that state parasitism, as a structure of power, had begun to show its dual face. On the one hand, politicians, civic leaders and members of the ethnic minority bourgeoisie, had adopted a hostile posture toward lower-class expressions of cultural and political dissent.[23] On the other hand, state agents – in particular the jockeying politicians competing for power in working-class neighbourhoods – had forged close personal and political bonds with the very lower class who were now the object of condemnation.

Moreover, as I have argued in the previous chapter, in their quest for power, these urban politicians had harnessed the lumpenproletariat and other rank-and-file loyalists to party agendas and distributed benefits to them, while deferring to these groups' vital cultural claims. The political price exacted for this concession was, of course, enforced filiation with the parties, and the obligation to display raw and violent partisanship against other contingents of the urban poor in the continuing party civil wars. At this early stage, then, state parasitism was already evincing an antinomy that captured the unity of its domination: the combination and interdependence between legal-constitutional gestures pertaining to law and civility within the formal civic realm, and the extra-legal tactics, violent mayhem and warlordism at the informal level of constituency politics in Kingston.

But while such a deployment of political power in the slums certainly functioned as a commanding pole of attraction and operated as a remarkable source of political containment of the urban poor, the compulsion of this form of state power over the more rebellious, minority segments of the urban unemployed still remained a tenuous and shaky matter. In addition to the ideological deficit described above, other systemic factors intensified the vulnerability of the emergent political rulers.

First, the harsh material deprivation of the urban poor antagonized this group, and this discontent provoked the more militant among them to resist the blandishments of the parties. The poverty, abominable living conditions and chronic joblessness of the urban poor identified them as the national group whose desperate circumstances were sharply at odds with the material improvements that segments of the manual working class and the middle class enjoyed as a result of the island's post-war economic growth. This acute impoverished condition which denied the urban poor the material benefits that came with the island's economic and social modernization marked the urban lower class as the group with the least benefits and the least stake in the prevailing social arrangements. This condition put the urban poor at odds with the wider society and with the dominant political organizations of the day.

Second, despite its attractions, benefits politics also alienated the very partisans who stood to gain from this arrangement. Because benefits politics could only deliver a scarce largesse to a limited number of loyal labourers, voters and other partisans, it forced loyalist slums-dwellers into a desperate jockeying for limited spoils. This competition in a context of scarcity tended to undermine confidence of slum-dwellers in the spoils system because of the acute uncertainty it entailed, even for the loyalist poor. Thus even as the spoils system acted as a magnet for the poor, it also caused political partisans among them to be wary and to hedge their support for the parties. In fact, as the volatile voting behaviour of the West Kingston poor in the 1940s and 1950s attests, desperate voters in search of meagre benefits switched parties repeatedly.[24] This uncertain and volatile political disposition confirmed these voters' uncertain faith in the parties and in the evolving spoils system. By denying either party political dominance in West Kingston in the nearly two decades between 1944 and 1962, skittish voters therefore issued an equivocal verdict on the spoils system. This electoral oscillation and political tacking by the poor signalled their reservations about benefits politics, and this hampered the parties' efforts to affect a thoroughgoing political enclosure of the turbulent West Kingston constituency.

Third, the spoils system also antagonized the vast majority in the slum who did *not* benefit from it. A far more serious lack of confidence in the parties was apparent among members of this contingent who were obliged to look beyond the spoils system for a livelihood. Hampered by class, racial and residential discrimination in their quest for a livelihood, this group turned to forms of self-help ranging from criminal employment, to petty entrepreneurial pursuits. This enforced form of economic self-reliance helped consolidate an antagonistic sensibility within this group. Their outlook disclosed a consciousness that reflected both their rural origins and the effects of the new social relations spawned by this group's insertion in the post-war urban milieu.

For the Kingston poor of the 1950s and early 1960s, this sensibility was marked by the combination of peasant religious beliefs, exilic impulses, antagonism to dominant class morality and cultivation of in-group solidarities based on shared lower-class experiences. This ensemble of values which contained revivalist religious currents, Garveyite race consciousness, spontaneous nihilism, and desires for economic and political inclusion, marked the urban lower class with a social consciousness that was particularly resistant to easy elite political summons.

Last, left-wing movements that attempted to win their allegiance also strengthened an anti-system sensibility among rural workers and the urban poor. The ideologies of several Marxist-oriented movements in Kingston in the 1950s and after fell on receptive ears in the slums, and many from the ranks of the unemployed rallied to the banner of these left-wing labourite formations.[25] Thus, the Marxist Unemployed Workers Council, under Ben Monroe's leadership, demanded employment for the poor and sharply criticized the main political parties for their political victimization of this group. Likewise, ex-PNP leftists and others rallied the working class and the unemployed not just to independent union activity, but also to a third party formation founded in 1954, the People's Freedom Movement.[26]

Consequently, not only did activism by the Left blunt the appeal of the established parties among the alienated poor, but the coincidence of the latter's hostility based on lower-class values, and antipathy provoked by left-wing political mobilization, made for a potent anti–status quo combination that was potentially explosive. Thus even where many among the striving and partisan poor did come under the political tutelage of the parties and succumbed to the moral appeals of their leaders, this was not the case for those members of the urban poor who were left out of the spoils system and were mobilized by radical anti-system movements.

This lack of resonance of party promises and appeals was particularly noticeable among alienated and highly mobilized segments of the urban poor such as the Rastafarians. Defined by their unremitting opposition to native rule under British sponsorship, this minority among the poor stubbornly remained outside the sway of party inducements and moral appeals. The Rastafarian movement was a dominant and combative tributary of the urban poor. By the late 1950s, this segment of the mobilized poor had created a relatively independent moral-political culture for itself, and was generally free from the constraints of the political inducements of both the departing colonial rulers and the aspirant native classes who were replacing them.

Other socially mobilized, militant tributaries of the poor such as the non-Rastafarian Kingston lumpenproletariat also lived largely outside the ken of official morality and party inducements. This group's desperate circumstances and acute awareness of class and racial discrimination tended to immunize it against the appeals of parties and politicians. This moral alienation was combined with a strong sense of class and racial belonging that inclined this segment powerfully toward black consciousness. Out of this potent fusion of class and race consciousness sprang not a coherent social consciousness, but instead a malevolent, antisocial sensibility that often erupted into violent, nihilistic outbursts.[27]

Thus, like their Rastafarian peers, tributaries of the alienated lumpenproletariat represented a distinct pole of opposition to the social and political status quo. Neither group wanted any truck with a society it deemed callous in its treatment of the black poor. However, unlike the Rastafarians who developed a coherent anti-system ideology that rallied the faithful to the political obligations of racial loyalty and called adherents to the austere disciplines and political duties of an exilic movement for racial uplift, this segment of the lumpenproletariat lacked both a coherent counter-ideology and a political project of its own. Furthermore, unlike the Rastafarians, for whom such a thing was anathema, contingents from the lumpenproletariat had no reservations in signing on as political enforcers for the dominant parties and unions.

This cooperation with power reveals an often-misunderstood disposition among subordinate groups in general and among contingents of the lumpenproletariat in particular. This is their apparent readiness to become allies of the powerful and willingness to sometimes do the violent bidding of the state. Marxists in particular have historically adopted a dismissive, even hostile view of the lumpenproletariat. In summing up the Marxist viewpoint, for example, Hal Draper has observed the following:

> Experience demonstrated to Marx and Engels that, on the whole, the elements of the lumpen-class tend to be inhospitable to social ideals socially implemented — for what is society to them, or they to society? — and that they are typically moved by cynical self-interest on the most vulgar level, however rationalized; hence they tend to be venal, available to the highest bidder; attracted to the bandwagon of the winner, or distracted by circuses with or without bread; unlikely to become serious about any social cause or motivated

by any political vision; untrustworthy even when bought up, and dangerous even as tools: "the worst of all possible allies".[28]

Contrary to this harsh view that dismisses the lumpenproletariat as a mere criminal class, wholly inferior to the working class in social consciousness and only the "bribed tool of reactionary intrigue", the group's filiation with power is far more complicated than this orthodox perspective allows.

Such a dismissive view, for example, leaves no room for the common reality that finds subordinate groups of whatever class often cooperating with the powerful because of a sheer disparity in power and resources. Arguing, as a traditional Marxist perspective does, that the lumpenproletariat is so easily seduced and so primed for political opportunism, is to ignore the myriad inducements the powerful successfully employ to compel compliance, not just from the desperate unemployed, but from all subordinated groups.

Moreover, a perspective that assigns a purely venal and criminal identity to the lumpenproletariat, as the Marxists do, is apt to miss this group's use of small acts of resistance such as dissembling, masking and feigning performance in the face of unequal power. As James C. Scott has so admirably demonstrated, the relations between subordinates and the powerful are more complex and more problematic for power holders because of this tremendous capacity for dissimulation.[29]

But if the Marxist perspective on the lumpenproletariat is unhelpful in capturing the disguised and shadowy forms of subordinate group politics, Frantz Fanon's opposite standpoint that sees the lumpenproletariat as a bold, revolutionary social force is just as problematic.[30] This is the case because Fanon exaggerated the group's political capacities in the European-dominated African colonies by assigning the lumpenproletariat a radical role in upheavals against colonialism. In his view,

> The men whom the growing population of the country districts and colonial expropriation have brought to desert their family holdings circle tirelessly around the different towns, hoping that one day or another they will be allowed inside. It is within this mass of humanity, this people of the shanty towns, at the core of the lumpen-proletariat that the rebellion will find its urban spearhead. For the lumpen-proletariat, that horde of starving men, uprooted from their tribe and from their clan, constitutes one of the most spontaneous and the most radically revolutionary forces of a colonized people.[31]

Such a perspective seems overly optimistic, given Fanon's own recognition of the group's desperate circumstances and susceptibility to blandishments from the colonial state.[32]

Contrary to Marx and Fanon's perspectives that reduce the ideological orientation and political behaviour of social classes to core essences, it is worth remembering James C. Scott's cautionary note. This is the reminder that "most of the political life of subordinate groups is to be found neither in overt collective defiance of power holders nor in complete hegemonic compliance, but in that vast territory between these two polar opposites".[33] This alternative view, to my mind, avoids the Marxist Scylla of the lumpenproletariat as a thoroughly bribed contingent, and the Fanonian Charybdis of the group as a violent, revolutionary force.

As this study will show at some length, the social orientation and sensibility of the lumpenproletariat in Jamaica's postcolonial context do not fit the rigid classical portraits described above. Rather than forming only the two contrasting social types described above, harsh postcolonial politics and deeply conflictual social relations in Jamaica instead encouraged the formation of a lumpenproletariat that was more variable in consciousness, more deeply politicized and self-owning, and possessed of more social power than the classical appraisals would allow. While the Jamaican group undoubtedly betrayed destructive dispositions, the group's political evolution in Jamaica's racialized class society – one in which the form of state power was simultaneously devouring and solicitous of the mobilized poor – yielded an assortment of social types that went beyond the conventional depictions.[34]

What this reappraisal implies is an ambiguous group portrait rather than fixed essences. It is important to recognize, therefore, that the poor may be stubbornly opposed to exploitative power, yet may contingently filiate with it to gain advantages in the short-to-medium run. While such alliances do not always redound to the benefit of the poor, the existence of such alliances does not undo the resistance of the poor to political victimization and political domination.

On the contrary, the hierarchical bond between alienated slum-dwellers and urban politicians is always freighted with conflict and is not a condition of permanent supplication to which the poor have resigned themselves. Indeed, their engagement with power ought to be seen not as a zero-sum game in which autonomy is sacrificed to subservience, but rather as a shifting dialectic of compulsion and resistance to which both parties are subject, despite their sharply unequal status and resources. In the Jamaican case, while

a minority from the ranks of the lumpenproletariat signed on with the parties as goons and supplicants, in all probability they did so fully cognizant of
the predation which it entailed.[35] Of course, they were always on the look-
out for the opportunity to plunder state resources, and they were alert as well
to the possibilities of expulsion or enforced defection because of disagreements arising from this conflictual relationship with the political parties.

While such complications may have deterred the supplicant but quiescent branch of the unemployed poor in the early 1960s, several of their
mobilized lumpen kin maintained a trademark anti-system disposition
informed by predation, banditry and social outlawry. Members of the
Kingston lumpenproletariat that committed these acts included youth gangs
fighting for turf, petty criminals who preyed on both the well-to-do and the
poor, as well as bandits who robbed the powerful, struck at symbols of
authority and gained notoriety for their lawless acts.[36] Economically desperate and condemned to a hustling existence, this alienated predatory minority was feared equally by both the downtrodden and the well-to-do. In the
turbulent, changing Jamaican society of the early 1960s, this anomic group
became the real nemesis of a society that had begun to demand the use of
"law and order" to quell the growing outbursts of urban discontent.

In summarizing power relations between state agents and their nemesis
among the militant poor, it is apparent that in the early postcolonial period
neither law nor politics had secured the effective compulsion and domestication of the dissidents, and certainly not the lumpenproletariat. Indeed, the
contingent loyalty of poor-but-hopeful voters in West Kingston, the hard-
bitten opposition of militant tributaries such as the Rastafarians and the
turn to gangsterism and outlawry in the slums confirmed a less-than-satis-
factory situation for party leaders eager to extend their influence in the
urban milieu. This riposte of uncertain allegiance and unbending opposition
from the ghetto made clear the parties' shaky grip on Kingston slum-
dwellers and highlighted the incompleteness of the attempted political
enclosure of the troublesome West Kingston constituency.

Popular Culture as an Arena of State Power

As the parties continued their struggle for ascendancy over the politically
untamed poor, Edward Seaga, in the wake of his election in 1962, boldly
intervened into this thicket of conflicted allegiances, disputed party loyalties,

and simmering PNP disappointment at its electoral defeat. Upon assuming political office, Seaga launched two decisive initiatives that would underscore the protean nature of state parasitism and highlight the importance of his recent political victory in the slums. First, in stark opposition to the "cultural commonsense" held by many in the country, Seaga championed the revitalization of the country's indigenous culture and continued his advocacy of an improvement in the circumstances of the urban poor, including social outcasts such as the Rastafarians.

Second, as minister of community development and welfare, he consolidated in his constituency the many elements that made up the partisan distribution of benefits and he did so in a manner that signalled a new departure in the uses of political power.[37] Both initiatives were important developments in the evolution of a flexible, culturally resonant, but violently intrusive parasitic state power oriented to the enclosure and domination of the urban poor. I shall address, in turn, the national significance of Seaga's cultural initiative and the political impact of his consolidation of the components of benefits politics in the West Kingston constituency.

Against the background of his earlier sojourn in both rural Jamaica and the urban slums as an ethnographer and cultural enthusiast – then later as a producer of popular music and as a politician who spoke up for the "have-nots" – it is not surprising that when Seaga assumed political office as a JLP cabinet member in 1962, he turned to the urgent question of cultural policy.

In this period, it was evident that the struggle for the identity of the Jamaican people had become particularly urgent. The ongoing clash between the middle-class nationalist ideology of Jamaican Exceptionalism and the unapologetic black nationalism of the unemployed made this clear.

For example, this conflict over race and colour as well as disputes over the civilization identity of the Jamaican people confounded the political elite and opinion makers.[38] In fact, in one notable instance, the black poor's insistence that race and colour mattered in Jamaica provoked Prime Minister Norman Manley to exasperation as he addressed a 1960 party conference:

> And then comrades, there is this matter that I so hate to have to talk about. I see people on platforms all over the place preaching colour, trying to build up a spirit of skin against skin and race against race. It is the work of the devil ... in our country, where all our political institutions are in the hands of our own people and where we are rapidly reaching the day when merit alone

counts, . . . who the hell cares that some men are black? Who cares that I am a
brown man? Who cares that comrade Arnett is nearly white? Who cares? Any
of you care?[39]

The ongoing turmoil surrounding this issue continued unabated, and
the dispute persisted, despite the fact that the island had achieved its political independence under native rule. The major issue facing the new government, then, was how to rally the black majority population to the
identity of Jamaicanness in ways that would recognize the importance of
blacks in the cultural history of the country, yet blunt the polarizing racial
appeal of groups such as the Rastafarians.

The political elite and allied groups had developed the ideology of
Jamaican Exceptionalism that was enshrined at independence in the national
motto: "Out of Many, One People". But in their effort to limit the appeal
of radical black nationalism, dominant groups had fashioned an official
counter-ideology that was troubled and burdened by a problematic narrative. Developed during the struggle against the non-compliant urban poor,
this narrative seemed uncomfortable with hailing the black nationality of the
majority population. Indeed, in summoning the national population to a
Jamaican identity in the late 1950s and early 1960s, the main exponents of
Jamaican Exceptionalism – Anglophile politicians, the culturally colonized
middle class and the defensive ethnic minority business class with influential ties to the state – seemed to depict the Jamaican people as exemplary
racial neuters, while expressing revulsion for the race-consciousness of the
politically uncooperative poor.

Wary of the Afrocentric folk culture of the displaced peasantry in
Kingston, appalled by the violence in the slums and scandalized by the urban
poor's racialized outlook, fearful politicians drew back from the rebellious
poor and rallied to Jamaican Exceptionalism with its cultural ambiguities and
racial discomfitures. Thus, in response to the upsurge in race consciousness
among the urban poor, Ivan Lloyd, a PNP member of Parliament in the
countryside, warned against black nationalism's ideological contagion of his
constituents.

> I am glad indeed, that our rural population, that the country people have not
> at all been infected by this virus. They are still living in their own original con-
> cepts of right and wrong. They have no conception and any sensitiveness as
> regards race and colour and things of that sort . . . I am sure Members of both
> sides of the House would like to see it remain so. In that respect, I hope that

our politicians, especially those from the Corporate Area, when they come to our country parts, I am hoping that they [leave] our country people alone.[40]

Against the background of the island's slave past, the now-insistent demand from the slums for racial redress and rising complaints of discrimination against black-skinned persons seeking opportunities in the new society, the ideology of Exceptionalism – and the national motto linked to it – seemed hollow, evasive and unconvincing to many from the deprived black majority group.

Yet whatever appeal this ideology might have had for others in the wider society, Jamaican Exceptionalism seems to have had limited appeal for personalities such as Edward Seaga and other contenders for power in the working-class districts of Kingston. These politicians appeared to relish the near-martial form that early political campaigning had assumed in these places. Unlike their uptown peers or rural counterparts, these urban politicians adapted quickly to the social and political turbulence in their districts. Although they were primarily responsible for provoking the political violence in the slums, these politicians were equally aware of the underlying material deprivation that informed the lives of the urban poor. Consequently, while they incited the population to violence and could be neglectful of their poor constituents in the interim between political campaigns, these politicians were not unmindful of the hardships of the poor and often tried to respond positively to their needs. Both self-interest and real sympathy for the poor were therefore commingled in the ghetto as politicians fought bitterly for their constituents' support in bruising, often bloody political campaigns between 1944 and 1962.

On and off the campaign trail, then, these fearless politicians ranged easily through the impoverished and harsh urban spaces where the working class and slum-dwellers lived. In the competition for votes, in the rivalries over the distribution of favours, in the delegation of responsibilities to constituents and in the recruitment of "security" personnel from the slums, these Kingston politicians adjusted to the pressures of the urban cauldron as they came face-to-face with forms of suffering that escaped the attention of the wider society. As these redoubtable politicians encountered the many social types in the ghetto, they struck up personal friendships, established clientelistic ties and built organizational bonds with the black residents.[41] Such encounters not only allowed the political manipulation of desperate residents, but also permitted these politicians to see and to respond variously to the debasement and the social promise of their downtrodden constituents in the early postcolonial years.

This blend of active familiarity and sympathy for the socially mobilized black poor, as well as concern for partisan advantage, gave these politicians in the ghetto an exceptional status. They had the distinction of rubbing shoulders with volatile and outcast groups in the slums – people whom most persons in the society avoided or held in fear and contempt. Moreover, in their willingness to recruit and abet political thugs for agendas of partisan political violence, these new urban politicians introduced a tinge of outlawry into national political affairs and gave a measure of political clout to contingents of the poor who were hitherto not regarded as politically relevant. Thus the close ties these politicians had to the downtrodden and militant poor and their endorsement of threats and violence by loyalist gangs against political rivals set these urban vote-getters apart from the political moderation and benign paternalism their peers typically exercised outside the urban cauldron.

As populists in the seething urban milieu that was Kingston, Kingston politicians often trafficked in a cheap knowledge of black popular culture as they invoked concern for the plight of the poor. These politicians endorsed racially informed cultural expressions from below and they gave voice to nationalist political sentiments widely held by black constituents in the slums and elsewhere. Dudley Thompson, for example, had earlier found eager adherents among the black poor for his racial and pan-Africanist appeals.

Likewise, during his successful 1962 political campaign, Edward Seaga had a ready audience for his fusion of religious revivalist sympathies and secular political appeals. Seaga, in particular, traded on his ties to the poor not only to promote the religious culture and new music in the ghetto, but to establish a cultural resonance with constituents, which helped him to secure his electoral victory. This level of comfort with the cultural outlook and sentiments of the lowly black-skinned population therefore distanced these urban politicians from their conventional peers, from the nostrums in the ideology of Exceptionalism, and from the sneering contempt with which the better-off classes viewed the black poor.

As a member of this group of urban populists and as a specialist in the island's folk culture, Edward Seaga therefore tried to steer the newly sovereign state away from its anachronistic and demeaning attitude toward black popular culture. For example, the early 1960s found him at the forefront of a state-led effort to promote the island's indigenous culture by intervening in the cultural space of popular traditions. In his capacity as minister of community development and welfare, he contributed to official plans to identify national heroes with whom both the middle class and ordinary citizens could identify; he promoted the idea of a unique Jamaican culture by organizing a National Heritage Week; and he directed the collection of oral histories from peasants and other groups that would be placed in a national archive.[42]

Beyond these innovations, Seaga also founded *Jamaica Journal,* a literary and historical periodical devoted to high-brow discussions of Jamaican culture, and his reach also extended to the founding of the influential Jamaica Festival in 1963. The latter was devised as a showcase for the talents of ordinary Jamaicans who dramatized neglected aspects of the island's popular culture in competitive performances in areas as diverse as religion, leisure activities, community life, and the cycle of life and death. Initiated during a period of racial anxieties and cultural uncertainties, this state-led effort at cultural indigenization, with Seaga at the helm, put on public display long-suppressed cultural practices from a durable folk tradition.

Yet despite its critical importance in contesting the historical marginalization of black culture in Jamaica, this state-led promotion of popular culture had its limitations. It was neither a full-blown assault on the lingering anti-black racialism of the old cultural order nor was it an installation of the cultural and political agendas favoured by partisans of radical political reform and black nationalism. On the contrary, despite the efforts of personalities like Seaga who backed these cultural reforms, the old order lived on in the country's bitter cultural disputes and in the political attacks on the black poor from official circles within and beyond the political parties.

Still, in what now appear as original and formative initiatives by politicians as diverse as D.C. Tavares, Dudley Thompson and Edward Seaga, state agents began intervening in urban-popular cultural spaces to secure a political legitimacy for the state, and to harness and appropriate elements from these inroads for more local political agendas. Indeed, by attempting to put the state's imprimatur on aspects of the people's culture, a few state agents had begun to make explicit their acknowledgement that popular culture was critical to political outcomes and their recognition that culture was itself a vital political battleground.[43]

In the early 1960s, the acknowledgement by state agents of the legitimacy of the people's culture therefore had three important consequences. It began a subtle but discernible subversion of outworn notions of an inferior indigenous culture that was allegedly no match for a superior European colonial culture. It also ceded a limited but important space within party politics – the space of urban, street- and constituency-level participation linked to political-electoral agendas – to non-middle-class participants from the slums and working-class districts. Moreover, it permitted the state and its agents to insert themselves into the irreverent domain of popular urban everyday life and moral culture – a site they now sought to encapsulate and reconfigure as an arena of state power. Having remarked on the inroads made by the state and its agents into the domain of urban popular culture, I turn now to Edward Seaga's second major intervention: the consolidation of the components of benefits politics with the creation of the West Kingston Tivoli Gardens housing scheme.

A Political Enclosure: The Creation of Tivoli Gardens

Of the many deprivations experienced by the Kingston poor in the post-war period, perhaps none was as serious as the lack of adequate shelter. As we have observed, for the most destitute poor in Kingston since the 1930s, this shelter typically consisted either of huts or of materials scavenged from garbage dumps. In Dungle, famous for its squalor and human misery, slum-dwellers subsisted in overcrowded and dump-like conditions as rival politicians, offering unlikely promises of significant relief, scoured the district for votes and supporters. Here itinerant and displaced persons from the countryside subsisted in squalor. For their part, the more fortunate poor and working-class residents in Kingston found shelter in crowded tenements, often without basic amenities. Residents in these places, living in yards without the benefit of privacy, invariably shared public baths and toilets and occupied overcrowded quarters, typically several people to a single room.

In an effort to improve this situation, the PNP administration that took office after the 1955 elections began an extensive housing construction programme in the Kingston and St Andrew Corporate Area. Between 1955 and 1962, two PNP administrations built the Mona Heights and Harbour View middle-class housing schemes in the north and east. There housing was made available to the upwardly mobile middle-class, irrespective of their political affiliation. In the same period, the PNP also developed plans for the construction of modern, low-income housing in the western, working-class districts where this housing was most needed. The Tivoli Gardens housing scheme in West Kingston was part of this project of upgrading shelter for the poor.

As the site was being prepared for construction in 1963, however, the PNP was no longer in power. It was therefore unable to establish the criteria for the distribution of the coveted dwellings. Unlike the earlier allocation of middle-class housing which seemed not to have incurred a vicious partisanship, distribution of urban working-class dwellings was already ensnared in benefits politics. For example, in the aftermath of the 1951 hurricane that struck the island and destroyed meagre working-class dwellings in Kingston, disputes had already ensued over the PNP allegation that the JLP was distributing the rebuilt shelters on a partisan basis.[44]

In the overheated and intensely partisan atmosphere of the early 1960s, criteria for the distribution of new housing in West Kingston were subject to politicization and intense scrutiny by the PNP, the party in opposition at that time. Benefits politics was by this time a pervasive feature of Jamaican politics, and partisanship had permeated the awarding of government contracts, union representation in labour markets and the allocation of work on government projects.[45] In the context of the intense partisanship unleashed in West Kingston after 1944, and on the heels of Seaga's bitterly fought 1962 electoral victory, a non-partisan distribution of new housing, under the PNP or the JLP, became a near impossibility in the political hothouse that was West Kingston.

In the context of this intensification of partisanship over housing the poor, Seaga and the JLP began, in October 1963, a forcible evacuation of residents from the Back-o-Wall area who refused to quit the site on which the Tivoli apartment complex was to be built. Among these residents were militant Rastafarians, youth gangs and hard-core PNP supporters who remained unalterably opposed to Seaga and to the JLP's control of the constituency. Supported by PNP political organizers, non-PNP left-wing activists and PNP-organized gangsters, these residents demanded assurances that they would be housed in the new apartments planned for the area.[46]

The JLP's response was to unleash the riot police on the settlers and to send in the bulldozers to begin the demolition. But the defiant settlers grimly fought back by hurling stones and marching to block the bulldozers. In the face of a public outcry at the callousness of its actions, the JLP relented by offering a brief moratorium on the evictions and extended the settlers' notice to quit until January 1964.[47]

But notwithstanding PNP and civic leaders' efforts to secure an agreement that would give apartments to the routed settlers, only persons deemed loyal to the JLP were ultimately allowed to take up residence in the apartments that were completed in the initial phase of the project.[48] By defending their tough actions in the name of urban renewal, Seaga and the JLP thus rid themselves of a troublesome political nemesis – anti-government squatters and pro-PNP settlers – and established a housing scheme that was then filled with JLP loyalists.

This foray against the rebellious poor in 1963 was extended in 1966. Between February and September of that year, in a protracted and bitter struggle involving an even bolder and controversial strike against hostile settlers in the constituency, Edward Seaga and the JLP expanded the slum-clearance policy to make way for an extension of the Tivoli Gardens apartments and the construction of other facilities near the Kingston waterfront. Here again, when notice-to-quit edicts were ignored by some five hundred settlers at the Payne Avenue and Majesty Pen sites, and by another fifteen hundred squatters in the Industrial Terrace and Foreshore Road areas, the police, accompanied by bulldozers, made short work of dispersing these settlers and razing their shacks. Although the Jamaica Council of Churches secured a £10,000 contribution from the government to assist in the relocation of these settlers, neither Edward Seaga nor the JLP was deterred in the effort to uproot hostile, anti-JLP partisans from these areas.[49] Indeed, by the summer of 1966, Edward Seaga and the JLP had successfully routed the hapless squatters and tightened their grip on another section of West Kingston.

Juvenile Gangs and Politics: The Early Nexus

As the JLP and PNP battled for political dominance in the constituency, both parties actively employed juvenile gangs as their political enforcers. These youth gangs had initially conducted their turf battles relatively free of political partisanship, but were drawn increasingly into the intensifying West Kingston political rivalry. These gangs bore such names as the Vikings, Salt City, Phoenix City and Spanglers.[50] Prior to the mid-1950s, these gangs had largely confined their activities to petty theft, violent turf rivalries and sporting competition in soccer matches. As political competition heated up in the late 1950s and early 1960s, youth gangs were actively courted by the parties and were gradually inducted into political service.

Attracted by the prospect of receiving material rewards in exchange for securing political territory for the parties, the juvenile gangs and their allies among the lumpenproletariat threw themselves into the political fray and played a direct role in the mayhem which attended the 1962 electoral contest in West Kingston. By the mid-1960s their role in street- and constituency-level political violence in West Kingston was unmistakable. The Phoenix City gang, for example, had sided openly with Edward Seaga and the cause of the JLP. In their turn, the Rastafarian- and socialist-leaning Vikings gang defended the right to their own turf and the PNP's control of precincts in West Kingston.[51]

The politicization of the youth gangs was therefore a direct outcome of the intensifying party civil wars. These wars were abetted by the conjunction of two factors that facilitated the initial incorporation of urban gangs into Jamaican politics: a gang's location in the constituency and the parties' extension of a seductive political patronage to them. Hence, if a juvenile gang was historically located in a particular neighbourhood in West Kingston, and one of the parties was politically dominant in this locale, then the gang would invariably be subject to party-generated pressures to become partisan and encouraged to provide a martial defence of the neighbourhood in exchange for political patronage. This political tactic was not unknown in Kingston before the 1960s, but between 1962 and 1967, the parties were perfecting the political colonization of youth gangs. Edward Seaga's harnessing of these gangs for political purposes is instructive of the early nexus between gangs and politics in urban Jamaica.

As the minister responsible for youth and community development, Seaga probably used this leverage to draw area youths to the party, and juvenile gang members into the JLP as enforcers. As an observer of this process noted, the JLP drew the youth into politics in areas it controlled by means of a patronage funnelled through the Youth Development Agency, a state agency supervised by Seaga.[52] Where juveniles in Seaga's constituency had long been engaged in independent, self-organizing activities including the formation of gangs, youth clubs and soccer teams, this self-organization in the constituency and autonomy among the young was undercut by the state's encapsulation of these activities under the umbrella of the Youth Development Agency. Thus government support for youth activities in the form of YDA services, facilities, sporting supplies, equipment and the like came with a political price – obligatory loyalty to Seaga and the JLP. Barry Chevannes observed this link between youth activities, gang membership and party politics: "YDA affiliation was soon regarded as tantamount to JLP affiliation."[53] Inevitably, this party-led encapsulation and subversion of youths and the juvenile gangs intensified the political violence, and deepened the party civil wars in West Kingston.

Like its counterparts in the PNP who employed similar means, the JLP unabashedly gave a hitherto pariah group – the juvenile gangs in JLP-controlled areas – an important role in the violent competition between the parties. Thus, even as the JLP relied on the police to help evict the rebellious pro-PNP settlers in West Kingston, the party also dispatched members of the Phoenix City gang to do battle with the Vikings gang who had been recruited by the PNP to defend its imperilled political territory. These politicized gangs fought each other and roamed the constituency intimidating and beating up citizens whom they believed to be politically disloyal. Party-directed incorporation of gangsters as enforcers and political gang warfare thus became pervasive features of political contestation in West Kingston by 1966. Indeed, the deployment of political gunmen, the militarized nature of the political evictions and the large numbers of settlers who were affected announced the advent of a new type of politician on the West Kingston scene: one prepared to undertake the systematic, violent resettlement of hostile urban populations and deny them housing in order to secure effective political control of strategic areas within his constituency.

A Consolidated Vision: Edward Seaga and Realpolitik in the Ghetto

The significance of this 1960s departure in Jamaican politics cannot be diminished by the claim that it was merely the continuation of a pattern of violence associated with a long-entrenched system of benefits politics. It certainly is the case that slum-clearance and the use of thugs as a means of ridding an area of hostile populations were techniques not inaugurated by Edward Seaga. It has already been shown that that distinction belongs to Alexander Bustamante. Similarly, the partisan distribution of housing was not Seaga's invention either. The practice of giving exclusive preference to loyalists had already seeped into the distribution of shelter for the poor when it tainted post-hurricane housing benefits to them in the early 1950s. Nor was Seaga a pioneer in the use of political violence to rout his opponents. Politicians from both parties in urban working-class areas had been directly associated with the use of violence and other autocratic practices against the urban poor.

Rather, what was unique about Seaga's use of political power between 1961 and 1966 was his *consolidation and extension* of the ensemble of tactics that defined or were related to benefits politics in the post-war years. Where those tactics had been applied by others in an ad hoc and even desultory fashion, Seaga, now in his fourth year in office in 1966, appeared to have brought coherence to the deployment of such tactics, while employing a steely determination in dealing with his opponents in West Kingston.

Where earlier JLP politicians seemed unable to master the political turbulence in the constituency and seemed bereft of a long-range vision for lasting control, Seaga, backed by then prime minister Bustamante, brought a warlordist, pre-emptive and strategic sense to the use of political power there. The JLP's recruitment of political gunmen in Seaga's constituency, sustained attack on the defiant anti-government settlers and willingness to defy a public outcry on their behalf, combined with Seaga's readiness to turn a housing programme for the poor into a housing programme for JLP supporters, unmistakably confirmed his autocratic inclinations and his consolidation of the array of tactics associated with benefits politics and the predatory state.

But more than that, Seaga's interventionist approach in dealing with political uncertainty and politically volatile issues placed him in the vanguard of the authoritarian and nimble politicians who campaigned in the slums and working-class areas of Kingston. Indeed, by delivering the new housing in West Kingston only to JLP loyalists in the politically explosive atmosphere of the time, Seaga not only showed contempt for his detractors, but also displayed a martial, commandist orientation in the conduct of party politics in the chaotic constituency. By enforcing benefits politics in the Tivoli Gardens scheme through such tough measures, Seaga showed that he had grasped the important emergent link between a government-built housing project for the poor and the politics of constituency control. The partisan distribution of the Tivoli housing to JLP loyalists therefore gave new vigour and a martial tinge to an incipient process that had seeped into the mix of politics under native politicians. This was the turn to politically segregated housing as a means of stabilizing party control of a constituency, and employing this tactic to deter effective political competition in the turbulent, but still politically competitive constituency.[54]

By the mid-1960s, Seaga's strategic acumen and confrontational stance, coupled with his remarkable ability for forging cultural and political ties with the poor, made him both a feared figure and a wily politician to be reckoned with. In the disruptive, chaotic West Kingston political scene, Seaga had emerged as a martial tactician who had skilfully kept his opponents off balance with repeated pre-emptive and aggressive measures that they seemed powerless to prevent. By that time, Seaga had fashioned an integrative and combative approach to power. In a hotly contested constituency, where the PNP was a constant thorn in his side and whose activists also resorted to their own realpolitik deployment of gang violence, Seaga's rule in the constituency not surprisingly assumed a sentry-like political vigilance that reflected a bunker mentality.

As Seaga secured his hold on West Kingston between 1962 and 1966, all pre-existing tactics associated with benefits politics and the predatory state – rallying the black working class and loyalist poor with promises of material rewards and official deference to the validity of their cultural life; employing political enforcers from the slums; harnessing the resources of public agencies and using them for partisan purposes; employing violence against the disloyal poor; and forcibly evicting uncooperative populations – were now cumulatively directed to holding onto power at all costs in this hotly disputed political territory.

As the JLP's third term of office wound down late in 1966, and as new national elections approached early in the following year, it was clear that Seaga – the so-called white man in an overwhelmingly black constituency – had prevailed in circumstances where his black partisan detractors had given him little chance of survival. By enacting a consolidated vision of power, he had defeated the opposition party at the polls in West Kingston, beaten back a coordinated challenge from hostile settlers and their allies, weathered a public outcry against his methods, and established a patronage-driven bulwark against his foes in the form of a housing and community development project in Tivoli Gardens on which he had lavished funds and resources during his incumbency as minister of community development and welfare.

This political victory in late 1966 by a martial figure in West Kingston represented more than a personal victory for Seaga or the triumph of one party over another in their continuing battle for power. Rather, Seaga's victory confirmed the tightening hold both political parties now exercised over working-class communities in Kingston. There, as in the rest of the country, both parties had established their political and electoral dominance.

While this dominance was certainly being tested by rebellious elements in West Kingston, there is little doubt that by the beginning of 1967 both parties had made significant gains in encapsulating urban lower-class communities into the predatory structure and political orbit of the two-party system. Thus by the time the JLP won the February 1967 national elections and had once again deployed the violence of its political gunmen against an equally violent PNP challenge, that victory completed an important stage in the consolidation of the predatory Jamaican political system. By means of a turbulent incorporation both parties had awarded an anomic and unruly social force – the youth gangs – a decisive role as street- and constituency-level fighters in Jamaican politics.

Gangs and Politics: Unsettling Consequences

This violent integration of the street gangs in the 1962–67 period accelerated two ongoing processes. First, it brought guns into national politics on an unprecedented scale, while elevating the party-recruited gunman to a heroic status among the sympathetic poor and to a feared status in the society at large. We have already seen how urban political competition had become increasingly violent in the 1940s and the 1950s. In those years, street-level violence linked to politics had grown from threats, beatings, stone- and bottle-throwing, as well as knifings, into an increasing but limited use of guns in political fracas. These weapons – primarily revolvers – had found their way into politics usually after being stolen by bandits in hold-ups, seized in house- and shop-breaking, and robbed in the hijacking of trucks whose armed drivers delivered goods in Kingston.[55] While urban gangs possessed some of these guns in the 1950s, the number of weapons was limited and gang members did not put them fully into the service of politics until the mid-1960s. In fact, the real nexus between guns and politics in Jamaica was not definitively forged until the run-up to the 1967 elections.[56] By this date, the primitive weapons of knives and stones had given way to guns, now fully deployed in street-level political violence.

Indeed, these pistols had become the weapons of choice for the warring political gangs as barking guns dominated the political fray during these years in West Kingston. Traffic in guns was extensive in this period, and the growing deployment of weapons on both sides suggested the existence of other sources for these weapons besides robberies and the hijacking of weapons by individual bandits and gangs. Other sources for the increased flow of guns into West Kingston in the period of 1966–67 certainly included the political parties who were engaged in battle in West Kingston. A search of the candidates' constituency offices by the police just prior to the 1967 elections suggested as much, as the surprise raids turned up an embarrassing cache of arms in both places.

A second effect of the incorporation of the gangs was the important status it gave to young notables among the party-recruited enforcers. Consistent with the prevailing pattern of political recruitment in the slums, constituency-based party officials – typically members of Parliament themselves – identified from among the unemployed youths those young men who displayed leadership abilities or had won the respect of their peers in other ways. For the young males in the ghetto, these qualities of initiative and leadership were usually on display in community sport clubs, on the football and cricket fields, or in leisure and other community-based activities.

Whether they were organizing a community dance, captaining a football team or heading up a juvenile gang, promising youths in the ghetto inadvertently put on display neglected talents which predatory politicians found politically useful. Thus as the party civil wars heated up in Kingston, a few influential individuals among the youth were drawn into the conflict with promises of material benefits in exchange for helping the party to defend its turf. These rewards could be as simple as outfitting the young person's football team with new athletic gear or pouring state funds into community development projects.[57] By the late 1960s, the rewards of benefits politics would become increasingly lucrative for the partisan poor, as political enforcers were awarded government contracts for work in which the enforcer would hire political recruits, and from which the recruits would make a living.

One young JLP enforcer of note at the time was Rudolph "Zackie" Lewis. Lewis began his short career as an enforcer after he was identified, probably by Seaga, as an influential in the Salt Lane community of West Kingston.[58] Lewis was both the captain of one of the many football teams organized by unemployed youths in the area and a notable in the community. In the early 1960s, he had been drawn into the JLP political apparatus as one of its top street-level gunmen and enforcers. Along with his counterpart from the PNP – Douglas "Little Keith" Campbell – Lewis fought for the JLP in the party civil wars. Both youths quickly gained notoriety for their bravado and fearless deployment of mayhem and brutality, before they were cut down in the political violence of 1966.[59]

A third effect of the incorporation of the gangs into politics was the quickened transformation of working-class neighbourhoods into martial political enclaves. The practice of benefits politics over two decades had already inclined such neighbourhoods into acting as "proto-national" communities. As political affiliation and geographic location became linked in fact and in the imagination of adherents, both parties and their loyalists behaved as if constituencies and neighbourhoods were imperilled cultural zones whose "nationals" had to be defended by violence and other non-democratic acts. Under the intensifying pressure of party politics, such neighbourhoods became thoroughly identified with one or another of the two dominant parties, and by the mid-1960s, the temptation to use political violence and other extra-legal means to keep it that way had become overwhelming.

Indeed, by this time, whole constituencies in Kingston, enclaves within them and even particular streets had in fact taken on the character of embattled politico-cultural zones. Their residents were intensely loyal to one or another of the political parties and toughs within these areas were prepared to violently defend their parties' political turf. Thus even as the West Kingston constituency remained open to electoral competition in 1967, locales within it such as Salt Lane, Pink Lane and Wellington Street had been transformed into unmistakable proto-national communities of the JLP and were off-limits to the PNP.

A similar politico-cultural identification prevailed in PNP-dominated areas. The settlers of Ackee Walk and Back-o-Wall, for instance, were intense partisans of the PNP and had jealously guarded their turf before being routed in the slum clearance of 1963.[60] Likewise, a single street in West Kingston – Matthews Lane – and its environs, had become a bastion of PNP diehard loyalists. As a result, much of the factionalism and violence in these areas of West Kingston originated not only from competition at the polls, but from the efforts of rival parties to seize or to hold onto coveted political territory.

It was precisely this contestation that had intensified the political violence of the 1960s. Hence, when Seaga expelled residents from the areas of Back-o-Wall, Ackee Walk and elsewhere, the evictions were viewed by the opposition not merely as callous, but as political expulsions and barefaced grabs for territory. In the eyes of the PNP and the evicted settlers, the forced

removal represented the eradication of a PNP political bastion. This political cleansing of the area earned Seaga and the JLP the unyielding enmity of
the PNP and its partisans.

Still, as successful as these JLP political evictions were, they did little to
diminish the level of political warfare. On the contrary, politically sanitizing
West Kingston of PNP adherents merely intensified violent communalism
in working-class neighbourhoods around Kingston. Many of the evicted
and antagonized refugees simply regrouped elsewhere, to form new impoverished settlements now filled with inflamed anti-JLP partisans. Other political refugees who had been subjected to the forced evacuation created new,
highly partisan political enclaves near the very communities from which
these refugees were expelled.[61] Thus, whether they fled to far-flung precincts
in and around Kingston, or decamped to adjoining neighbourhoods, these
settlers, and their allies in pro-PNP West Kingston enclaves such as Hannah
Town, could only be encouraged by the evictions to harden their negative
cultural images and bald caricatures of the JLP. For the PNP and its adherents, the political evictions confirmed their image of the JLP as the embodiment of political evil.

Pathways to Power: The Emergent Politics of the Lumpenproletariat

Despite the awful toll on the urban poor and on the lumpenproletariat that
came with their role as proxies in the party civil wars, influential contingents
among them fought to both evade this destiny and exploit this unfavourable
inheritance. Whereas some of their kin were seduced by the grasping reach
of the state and were battered by its incursions and victimized by the prosecution of the party civil wars, others chose a path of resistance. At the epicentre of this struggle, and participating in both the leveraging and the
evading of parasitic power, was the ubiquitous, socially mobilized lumpenproletariat. Rather than treat this group as an undifferentiated mass, I shall
offer a classification of the variety of social agents who fell into this category
in the mid-1960s.

Five major segments of the lumpenproletariat existed at the time: (1) a
vast, unskilled, chronically unemployed segment in which the jobless young
predominated; (2) a minority segment which formed part of a criminal
underworld of thieves, gangsters and others engaged in criminal employ-

ment; (3) an unskilled but wage-earning stratum which subsisted on uncertain employment and the meagre wages earned by the lowest ranks of the working poor;[62] (4) a massive, self-helping contingent engaged in a variety of petty entrepreneurial activities, including street vending and artisanal self-employment; and (5) a minority, politically aligned segment drawn from various strata of the urban poor. This latter group formed part of what might be called a political underworld, albeit in its sprouting, embryonic stage.

Nourished by the parties and alert to the advantages of a filiation with power, members of this formation assumed their place as street-level, diehard loyalists, political henchmen, constituency thugs and enforcers. Together with their equally partisan peers in the constituency who were mobilized for party duty as scrutineers, enumerators and even ballot-box stuffers during election cycles, the lumpenproletariat was gradually assuming a strategic place in Jamaican politics and society in the years from 1944 to 1970. As a downtrodden and despised group in the society in the mid-1960s, then, the lumpenproletariat was beginning to accumulate important, if unflattering forms of social power.

Several factors led to the accretion of this power including the impact of Jamaica's modernization on post-war social relations on the island. Urbanization and post-war modernization alienated the migrant lumpenproletariat and prepared them for an oppositional role in postcolonial Jamaica. It will be recalled that the country's rapid economic growth in the post-war years was urban-centred, and this bias of town over country was reflected in the significant upgrading of the infrastructure of its main towns, and especially the capital city, Kingston. The post-war modernization of Kingston saw the building of new roads, the construction of government offices and the development of modern, middle-class housing projects. The growth of commercial life, the expansion of national and municipal government, and Kingston's role as the island's political, commercial and communication nerve-centre attracted upwardly mobile groups and increased Kingston's appeal to rural migrants in search of a better life.

The ambitions of the migrant poor were, for the most part, frustrated. The trek of rural migrants to the capital city swelled the ranks of the urban poor and many of them became part of the lumpenproletariat. The hardships of these trekkers became a source of political disaffection. Their experience of grinding poverty in the city, the harsh milieu of working-class communities, as well as the class and the racial discrimination they encountered, made the Kingston lumpenproletariat not just a materially deprived group, but the most politically disaffected and socially mobilized force in the country.

This was in sharp contrast to the experience of the numerically larger peasantry and rural poor. For while they also experienced economic hardships, their circumstances were attenuated by other factors. It is arguable that the existence of a stable rural ecology, the possibility of small-scale farming, and the muffling of unequal relations in the countryside between large landowners and small peasants conspired to render these relations non-combustible, while inclining the peasants to political quiescence.[63]

A similar demobilization of the rural and urban working classes was accomplished through these groups' more stable link to the wage nexus, their trade union membership, and integration into the clientelist political parties. In sum, unlike their kin in the countryside, the lumpenproletariat's experience with urbanization and class discrimination resulted in an aggravated situation for them, and this condition gave the group a strategic role in the society as an aggrieved formation that could not be ignored by politicians.

Targeted as rival voters and loyalists in the party civil wars, sections of the lumpenproletariat struggled to transform their social alienation and conflictual relations with the state into a usable politics. In time, these antagonistic relations caused the urban poor to take initiatives that created resources for the exercise of a social power. In the post-war decades, that power was expressed in myriad ways.

For example, from the 1940s to the mid-1960s, the urban poor took advantage of the parties' attempt to incorporate them into the predatory structure of power. The urban poor gave their votes to campaigning politicians, loaned their bodies and menace to the political wars, and exacted the price for this loyalty in the form of jobs, housing, contracts, union membership and other benefits. While predation and the civil war had a destructive impact on the poor between 1944 and 1970, it is worth remembering that the lumpenproletariat and their notables never lost sight of the material advantages provided by this connection with power.

Indeed, since 1944 state predation in Jamaica had not only institutionalized the political victimization of the poor, but also solidified a moral claim among the downtrodden that the state owed them now-customary rights in the form of handouts and other welfare benefits. The parties' recurrent promises to distribute these benefits upon taking office and the urban poor's fanatical insistence on them resulted in the tight overlapping of these two inexorable claims that defined the Jamaican political order. By taking advantage of the populism of the parties, and demonstrating their indispensability to those jockeying for power, the urban poor – and particularly the lumpenproletariat – eked out a modicum of power from a nexus largely unfavourable to them.

A subtly accumulating effect of this counter-penetration of the parties from below was the gradual assimilation of popular political values by the political parties and their affiliated trade unions. We have already called attention to the appropriation of popular values by figures such as Edward Seaga and Dudley Thompson in West Kingston. And while the integration of popular sentiments by Jamaica's modern mass parties certainly began much earlier when nationalist leaders Norman Manley and Alexander Bustamante created these organizations, the process of value-counter-penetration from below intensified in the 1950s and 1960s. As the parties sought votes in the urban areas, and as the urban poor rallied to the populism of the parties, this group gained an important leverage that moderated the middle-class cultural impact on these institutions.

In these years, the parties certainly accommodated the noisy boisterousness so typical of popular discourse and everyday social interaction among Caribbean peoples. Socially advantaged political leaders in Jamaica embraced the verbal and kinetic histrionics associated with the people's everyday expression of competitive argumentation, and the parties pandered both to the people's religious sentiments and the readiness among the poor to do violence to rivals who threatened their access to power and material benefits.

Benefits politics and the spoils it afforded therefore thrived not merely on the machination of leaders, but also by way of a lively individualism and authoritarian partisanship long prevalent among the Jamaican people in causes and social activities as various as entertainment, team sports, politics and religion. These activities created outlets for creativity and avenues of individual expression in circumstances where other opportunities were denied to them.[64] Enthusiasm for these other creative opportunities was typically expressed in a jousting, often fraternal, competitiveness in which exponents became adepts and demonstrated their mastery of a unique creative domain.

Among the materially deprived but socially mobilized urban poor, this competitive individualism could assume a viciously partisan form, as scarce benefits were distributed in Jamaica's winner-take-all politics. The provocation this caused led to an inexorable turbulence in party politics, and its overlap with a popular individualism and penchant for varieties of authoritarian partisanship transmitted a popular identity to the party that now commingled grassroots concern with middle-class political influence. Thus, while middle-class and propertied groups exercised considerable, even dominant, moral–political influence inside the parties in the first two decades after 1944, their suzerainty did not go unchallenged as a nexus between politicians and subordinate partisan voters was established in working-class districts. There party activists and urban politicians jockeying for power sponsored and encouraged the contained introduction of popular needs and moral concerns into the agenda of both parties. While never going so far as to champion Rastafarianism as the cultural basis for the Jamaican identity or to promote subordinate-class challenge to the structure of unequal power, politicians on the ground in working-class districts sponsored the entry of the lumpenproletariat into party politics and facilitated their political and cultural penetration of party life.

It is worth repeating that this lumpen membership and cultural influence was confined to the exigencies of street- and constituency-politics, and did not define official party policy; nor did notables from the slums ascend to the elected positions in either party. Still, despite their exclusion from these organizational and bureaucratic domains, the urban poor and lumpenproletariat were beginning to define the political culture of the parties and society in ways which suggested that the parallel influence of the traditional middle class and their values were being eroded.

This much was clear, for example, from the cultural sea change taking place in the country after 1960. The ideological content and tempo of this change reflected the struggle for equal identity and social justice by the black urban poor. This moral leadership in which subordinate-class racial concerns were brought forcefully to public consciousness was defined almost exclusively by socially mobilized slum-dwellers. Besides increasing political pressures on the parties, the urban poor's demand for social recognition earned sympathy from influential groups whose changing views about class, colour and power in Jamaica challenged middle-class shibboleths about the poor.[65]

This erosion in the dominance of middle-class views about the status of the poor was evident in a number of developments pertaining to the battle over black nationalism in the 1960s. These events included the 1960 middle-class grumbling – and even outrage – that greeted sympathetic recommendations of a government-sponsored academic report on the grievances of the Rastafarians;[66] the irony of the 1966 official state visit by Haile Selassie of Ethiopia to the island that seemed to honour Rastafarian ideas about his divine relation to the black poor in the country; and the bold endorsement of black cultural nationalism in 1968 by hitherto politically reticent students at the University of the West Indies.[67] As defections from the ideology of Jamaican Exceptionalism occurred among politicians, academics and other professionals, and as the tempo of discontent increased in these years among the poor, it was apparent that a boundary in Jamaican politics and culture had been breached; this was the slight diminution of hostility to black nationalism, the dictation of new social values from the slums, and the discernible growth in the social power of the lumpenproletariat.[68]

Between 1967 and 1970, the rebellious urban poor increased their not-inconsiderable social power beyond their presence and cultural influence in the political parties. First, leading members of the group invented a pedagogic dissidence that carried powerful appeal for the disaffected. The Rastafarians, for example, exerted a massive moral-political influence over the lower ranks of the working-class and allied members of the unemployed. By offering the black population an alternative cultural identity based on an unapologetic racial belonging, the Rastafarians exerted a massive compulsion over disaffected populations smarting from class and racial discrimination in the early postcolonial years.

More importantly, the Rastafarians led the way in offering the disaffected urban poor a subversive structure of defiance and an identitarian clothing with which to challenge inequality in Jamaica. The invocation of this structure of defiance was nicely captured in the Rastafarians' hailing of the black population to "lick down Babylon" and stand firm for "roots and culture" in a time of social discrimination against poor blacks.[69] In the context of Jamaica's turbulent social relations, these invocations carried an explicit moral message that affirmed the urban poor's demand for social justice, equal rights and equal identity.

Second, Rastafarian dissidence was matched by outlawry and cultural defiance among young unemployed males trapped in the Kingston slums. Identifying themselves as "rude boys", these young men formed neighbourhood gangs and rebellious confraternities that challenged the cultural and political status quo. Unlike the Rastafarians, who called for a pietistic militancy linked to a black nationalist identity, the rudies combined black consciousness with social outlawry. The social consequence of this fusion was a sustained outburst of street crime, hooliganism in public places, and inversions of norms of personal and civic morality among the young. In the eyes of the alienated young, the cause of the downtrodden had to be affirmed by a racially informed indiscipline against a discriminatory society and its values. Wedded to a muscular black consciousness, this social indiscipline among the young – who began calling themselves "sufferers" – became a form of social protest through which the lumpenproletariat sought to influence developments in the country.[70]

Last, the lumpenproletariat in the 1960s exerted a social power on Jamaican politics and society by resorting to other stratagems. Contingents from their ranks fashioned formal and informal ties to left-wing and black nationalist organizations.[71] These formations defended the claims of the urban poor and mobilized them for a variety of left-wing and black nationalist projects. Although the claims of these projects were often quite similar, their ideological and organizational demands on the unemployed were often at odds with the cultural formation of this outcast group.

For example, in the black nationalist movement Abeng that they joined, the semi-literate lumpenproletariat was unable to read the movement's newspaper, *Abeng*, because writers for this press typically lapsed into academic jargon to describe social relations in Jamaica. Indeed, these alliances between middle-class radicals and the semi-literate unemployed often proved mutually frustrating to the participants. The pressing material needs of the lumpen constituency, its reflexive distrust of radical middle-class leaders and the urban poor's isolation from the wage nexus – which denied them the "norming" moralities of discipline and stable group membership valued by activists – became insurmountable barriers to the political organization of this downtrodden constituency.[72]

It is worth remembering, however, that the urban poor did not look only to better-off groups to assist them. Despite the dangers of a punitive, authoritarian state that was prepared to expunge overt protest with armed force, the urban poor occasionally engaged in demonstrative political actions to protect their own interests. As we have noted, the Rastafarians had taken up arms against the Jamaican government in 1960. Likewise, in a 1965 riot, the aggrieved poor struck back at Chinese shopkeepers in Kingston, accusing them of cheating their black patrons and allegedly assaulting a female worker. In still another riot in October 1968, the anti-JLP lumpenproletariat attempted to settle scores with its punitive nemesis, after the government

barred Walter Rodney, a popular Guyanese lecturer and critic, from returning to the island.

Similarly, the renaissance in artistic creativity among the working class and
unemployed that began in the 1950s continued unabated and expanded its
influence beyond the slums. Having pioneered reggae as a new musical
genre, musicians, singers and producers from the lumpenproletariat refined
it in the 1960s by combining religious themes, biting political commentary
and witty observations on the joys and pains of the downtrodden. These
themes, which insisted on the class and cultural concerns of the poor, resonated with the urban poor and made reggae the music of choice among
workers and the unemployed.

By the late 1960s, this vogue for discovering the roots of a national culture, rejecting political victimization and affirming cultural authenticity won
acceptance from other groups. What began as a vehicle for expressing the
travails of the lumpenproletariat was rapidly adopted in this period by dissatisfied middle-class youths, discontented labourers, dissenting intellectuals
and opportunistic entrepreneurs in the music and entertainment industry.
In this domain where old cultural beliefs were being challenged, and where
state predation was eliciting serious public outcry, the lumpenproletariat
held unrivalled sway as tribunes and exponents of a dissenting, anti-system
ideology and moral culture.

Conclusion

By the mid-1960s the socially mobilized lumpenproletariat had become a
major social and political force in Jamaica. By the end of the decade, this
rebellious contingent was of central concern to Jamaican society, particularly
to its political agents and civic leaders. Members of the clergy and other civic
leaders bemoaned the misery of the urban poor and decried their outlawry.
Radical intellectuals and political activists sought their support for social
change, disaffected groups felt the compulsion of their moral claims and rallied to their cultural critique of society, a repressive state fought to check
their riotous protests, and the political parties embraced them as strategic
allies in the party civil wars.

As the politically dominant segment among the urban poor, the lumpenproletariat had emerged as an unambiguous advocate of social change in the
society. Despite a condition of social marginality and political disadvantage,

the group had put its imprimatur on the cultural and political identity of the country. Whether through its exacting pressures on the parties to deliver benefits in exchange for votes and threats or in its capacity to affirm a cultural and political autonomy from the state, the mobilized urban poor unambiguously demonstrated a remarkable capacity to exert a social power over a resistant society.

In accumulating this power, the urban poor showed the political acumen that earned it notoriety in the post-war years. This was its remarkable capacity to turn dependence on state power into a political resource, and the group's ability to exert a social power in domains beyond the state's direct control. These skills, fashioned over several decades, would be sorely tested after 1970, with the revival of the PNP's political fortunes. We turn in the next chapters to the curious inflation of the social power of the urban poor by way of direct PNP sponsorship and to an assessment of the throttling of this power as the party civil war reached its apogee.

4

Exilic Space, Moral Culture and Social Identity in the Ghetto

IN THE RELATIONS BETWEEN THE URBAN POOR and state agents, both groups had fashioned forms of power that made each a force to be reckoned with. We have seen how the urban poor, despite its marginal status, had gained a modicum of social power by way of its political engagements. Notwithstanding the importance of these developments in which politics and partisanship loomed large, the poor's relations with the parties and the state were not the only sources that defined their identity. The social identity of the poor was shaped, as well, by sentiments of self-ownership and cultural pride based on group achievement beyond the game of politics. These activities and achievements represented a cultural unfolding from below that offered a relative protection from the encapsulating reach of state predation.

This experience of a relatively autonomous cultural life was as important to the identity of the poor as the influence of invasive political forces. In fact, although it was enmeshed within a grasping political dynamic, this parallel process of cultural formation in the ghetto evolved fairly independently of the crude factionalism and unyielding compulsion associated with the cut and thrust of violent political competition.[1] Hence, despite the invasive thrust of politics, whole areas of shared customs among the poor existed beyond the reach of state predation.

Of course, not all aspects of this cultural life in the ghetto could escape factional politics. Enterprising politicians including Alexander Bustamante, Edward Seaga and Dudley Thompson felt no compunction about making popular religion, black nationalist symbols and the vernacular language of the street a part of their political campaigns. Nonetheless, for the most part, that cultural life operated independently of politics and in the 1960s it enabled a new consciousness, social power and moral authority among the urban poor.

This social vitality did not appear as a coherent political ideology or express itself as a formal political movement. Rather, community life in the slums conveyed these facets of autonomy, and it did so in circumstances and in places beyond the exigencies and force field of political relations. As we shall see, the circumstances of community life yielded social types whose actions expressed a distinctive moral outlook. It was marked by a quest for cultural autonomy and efforts to protect the cultural life of the poor from an invasive partisan politics.

It should be emphasized that the poor's relationship with national politics was not the sole provocation for this outlook, although politics was a major determinant in their lives. Rather, everyday, broadly shared experiences that were very much related to their sense of identity formed the bases of their emergent social consciousness. These experiences included a syncretic religious life in forms as various as Rastafarianism, revivalism and pukkumina;[2] an ethno-national consciousness that affirmed non-negotiable loyalties and beliefs about the primacy of Africa and concern for the fate of Africans in Jamaica and in the wider world;[3] a vernacular language that communicated ideas and beliefs through orality and kinetic expression;[4] participation in forms of leisure and sport in which concern for mastery and group uplift were manifest;[5] and mutual awareness of a self-owning freedom that resisted the moral authority of their social betters and the compulsion of governing institutions.[6] While these resonant values and related practices were always ideologically laden and available for partisan political activation, because of their historical character they tended to be autonomous from the confining partisanships and political doctrines of the day.

The black poor lived much of their existence under conditions of social dishonour and economic marginality in post-war Jamaica.[7] This was the condition to which Jamaica's historically unequal social relations had assigned the black majority. However, the black poor did not surrender to this deprivation but developed a repertoire of defensive responses. These included complicity with power, active defiance of it, and pursuit of a relatively autonomous existence within the social space they occupied. This space helped determine the urban poor's impact on Jamaican society. In fact, whatever influence the materially deprived and socially marginal urban lower class exercised in the society at this time, it came largely from the group's historical occupancy and creative use of what may be termed exilic social space.

This space – both physical and psychological – has always been a refuge for imperilled and marginalized populations in Jamaica.[8] But other social actors, including state agents and middle-class allies of the poor, were also participants there. In Jamaica's racially charged and discriminatory society, such actors as the security forces and radical political activists invariably intervened in this exilic space to either quell or sustain dissent.

In the case of middle-class activists, for instance, their presence in this exilic space was largely episodic and tactical, rather than sustained or compelled by class membership. In fact, pragmatic reasons including the conduct of political campaigns, party protection of constituencies against encroachment and the search by radical reformers for new forms of mass support brought small contingents of middle-class political actors to this exilic site. Urban exilic space was therefore a multi-class site of social contestation in which the black poor held numerical predominance over intrusive middle-class players typically engaged in a struggle for power.

In belonging to exilic social space in Jamaica, slum-dwelling Afro-Jamaicans were neither isolated from social and political developments on the island nor wholly transformed by these processes into an upwardly mobile and socially advantaged group. Despite measurable post-war improvements in the social condition of the labouring classes, the inner-city poor and the urban unemployed saw few of these benefits.[9] Yet this materially deprived group was both racially self-conscious and subject to partisan politicking and its associated violence. In these circumstances, the social mobilization of the poor without significant improvement in their social condition fed alienation from the conventions of Jamaican society.

It is not surprising, therefore, that Afro-Jamaican residents of Kingston's slums shared a common condition. They were denied full moral membership in Jamaican society partly because of customs like their vernacular language and religious life, and also because of a stubborn, even militant commitment to an African civilization-identity. Besides poverty and the insecurity caused by lack of full moral citizenship, the militant poor also lacked the protection of the law, as it fell heavily on dissenters from their ranks.[10] Police raids of mass meetings in the slums, imprisonment of community leaders such as Claudius Henry and harsh prison sentences for lawbreakers confirmed the discriminatory uses of the law and the courts to discipline and punish the rebellious poor.[11]

Given these circumstances the poor typically retreated to their exilic space as both a social site for dissidence and venue for the repair of cultural injuries. There they developed structures of defiance and modes of existence that emphasized the quest for competence and the search for social honour. Juvenile political gangs, own-account entrepreneurship, street- and community-based messianic religious leadership, criminal subcultures and a Garveyite ethno-national awareness were among the components of this space.

In the cauldron that was the ghetto, then, these structures activated social consciousness, encouraged new forms of social power and facilitated the formation of new social identities. Thus, political gangsters not only willingly served their political bosses, but these political hirelings could also carve out "notable" identities for themselves as heroic political fighters, and as patrons to the underclass.[12] Similarly, the prophetic "work" of religious adepts in pocomania and Zion revivalism complemented that of heroic criminals – bent on earning a reputation for themselves in the slums – in the quest for a self-owning identity that was relatively autonomous from outside interference.

In these ways, the socially mobilized poor were engaged in a distinctive form of cultural labour within exilic space – the labour of self-making and self-recovery. In this cultural labour, they were placing their imprimatur on the competitive individualism that defined Jamaican cultural sensibility even as they tried to immunize lower-class cultural forms from the enveloping embrace of politics.[13] In trying to reclaim themselves, therefore, the poor fought to recover their dignity as persons and affirmed the right to an equal identity.

A major consequence of this cultural work was the steady production of anti-system identities and moralities. They included affirmations of Black Power and black nationalist cultural belonging, a heroic gangsterism in the criminal and political underworlds, and a nihilistic youth movement – the so-called rude boys – that challenged all conventional norms.[14] By the late 1960s, these identities and moral outlooks had become sufficiently generalized to constitute a new and politically significant cultural departure.[15]

Thus even though exilic social space was often confining for the poor, by the late 1960s there was little doubt about its capacity to attract new, dissenting consumers of the new morality. They included university and high school students, intellectuals and academics, as well as workers, political activists and professionals. These middle-class social groups entered exilic subcultural space to identify with the new cultural vogue. Others, however, hoped to harness the conflicting impulses in exilic space for their own designs.

Inside Exilic Space

Urban exilic social space had other relevant features. First, it was a relatively sequestered site. Although this space was subject to surveillance and penetration by the state, it remained primarily a place of refuge. Exilic space offered those who "lived" there a place to recover from cultural injuries, such as the lack of effective citizenship and the denial of law. Exilic space also permitted the fashioning of repertoires of survival and it gave the poor means to exert a social power.

Such means were always under challenge. The urban ghetto was patrolled by the police and invaded by competing politicians. At times, partisan factionalism, political violence and emergency curfews threatened to destroy an already limited autonomy in the slums.[16] Still, the level of state penetration was not so pervasive or draconian that it disabled those who had nothing to do with politics or others wishing to evade the state. Political violence and partisanship certainly roiled the waters in the slums, but daily life continued apace.

Indeed, even when factionalism and political intervention were significant, they were limited to discrete episodes and particular locales. It should be remembered that disruptive political violence occurred primarily during electoral cycles and in contexts of episodic partisan competition. For example, electoral violence that began in the 1940s grew more intense and destructive by the mid-1960s as the war for votes and scare benefits heated up. Nonetheless, while this form of state penetration in the ghetto was disruptive, and though it conditioned the sensibility of the urban poor, the electoral reach of the state was not so overwhelming that it obliterated everyday forms of autonomous cultural life. Nor did it wholly determine social consciousness in the urban ghetto.

A second important feature of exilic space was its function as a refuge for the morally excluded. In the early postcolonial period during which nationalist leaders sought to gain legitimacy by showing their empire loyalties, they largely ignored the protean cultural life of poor Afro-Jamaicans. As one commentator observed of the governing elite, "The central focus was on the claim . . . that it had mastered British culture and could therefore be entrusted with taking over from the colonial overlords the running of the institutions of state. Second, the masses they insisted were 'civilized enough' to participate more fully in the political process."[17] This neglect of popular cultural values in establishing the political legitimacy of the state quickly became a political handicap, because it had in effect denied Afro-Jamaicans of a certain class and cultural formation effective cultural membership in the new society. As Carl Stone, the Jamaican political scientist, recognized, patron-clientelism and native incumbency were poor substitutes "for the imperial legitimacy of the colonial state".[18] That was the case because "the withdrawal of imperial legitimacy left the state with only party legitimacy and the personal legitimacy of the charismatic figures and political patrons and bosses as a protective umbrella but also with the tradition of remoteness and alienation from the people".[19]

This deficit that denied cultural citizenship in the new society to Afro-Jamaicans was therefore morally exclusionary. Indeed, by assigning Afro-Jamaicans this frangible status, the political elite not only denied this group membership in the people-nation, but made them cultural nonpersons as well. Moral and cultural divorce, not moral infrangiblity, now defined the status of Afro-Jamaicans in independent Jamaica.[20] Thus even though the Rastafarians and other champions of black self-respect strove mightily to remind ghetto residents of an honourable cultural past and their role as a historic "chosen people", a palpable sense of displacement, psychic dislocation and cultural homelessness informed sensibilities in the slums. Like marginal populations everywhere, the urban poor experienced cultural disenfranchisement and it deepened their alienation.

Third, physical segregation aggravated this homelessness. As a dominated group in a class-divided and racially discriminatory society, the black poor became tenants of segregated, inferior places. Such places included gullies, street corners, slums, tenement yards and ghetto neighbourhoods. The ecology of these places, with their inferior amenities, lack of infrastructure, as well as their cramped and overcrowded conditions, aggravated the black poor's historical social confinement.

Last, exilic space was characterized by the urban poor's participation in multiple time-spaces with their contradictory impact on social consciousness. In the 1960s, three confluent forms of consciousness reflected the different "time-spaces" inhabited by the urban poor.[21] One form of consciousness was expressed in the persistence of residual Africanisms in the society, especially among rural dwellers that had trekked to the major towns and to the city of Kingston. This sensibility and its amplification in the Kingston slums confirmed a widespread assertion of a civilization consciousness powerfully oriented toward the continent of Africa.[22]

This social outlook was apparent, for example, in the unyielding insistence among the more militant sectors of the urban poor during the 1960s that Ethiopia was the font of Black civilization, and that its role in African affairs and in global culture could not be diminished. Africanisms were also apparent in the myriad cultural forms among the black poor. Such expressions were apparent in religious practices, patterns of entrepreneurship, and forms of leisure and family life.[23] This inclination to an Africanist identity found dramatic expression in the publicly and militantly expounded Rastafarian demand for repatriation to Africa. Africanist civilization-consciousness was equally on public display in the 1960s, when massive crowds of poor people came out to greet the Ethiopian emperor, Haile Selassie, during his visit to the island in 1966.

A receding but still influential culture of British imperialism defined the second form of consciousness at large among the urban poor. In the 1960s, the centuries-long impact of imperialism on Jamaican society remained a powerful force. The cultural residue of Empire influenced the entire field of consciousness in Jamaica, shaping political ideology, religious beliefs, social attitudes, marriage customs, personal etiquette, as well as tastes in food, clothing and fashion. This imperial influence on customs, taste, etiquette and fashion conditioned lifestyles, shaped social identities and inclined the poor to habits of imperial provenance.

There remained among poor and working-class women, for example, a desire for formal marriage and a hankering for the respectability of a "church wedding". For these women, this legitimate form was preferable to the myriad unsanctioned and socially disrespectable conjugal patterns that existed on the island.[24] Similarly, for broad sections of the population, a fair skin colour was preferred to a dark complexion. The black poor were not immune to these sentiments. With notable exceptions, many among them accepted norms that identified European hair as "good hair" while associating "bad hair" with a "nappy" African texture.

Similarly, the urban poor, like those above them in the class structure, retained a fondness for British royals and nostalgia for the pageantry of Empire. The homes of poor urban dwellers carried framed pictures of the reigning royals, Queen Elizabeth and her husband, the Duke of Edinburgh. All Jamaicans keenly followed broadcast accounts of the travels of these royals throughout the British Empire. Their visits to the island invariably brought the largest turnouts from poor and working-class neighbourhoods, as residents gathered en masse on sidewalks and strained behind barriers to catch a satisfying glimpse of the white-skinned visitors in their official car. A similar summoning of imperial culture was evident in the widespread preference among the urban poor for various styles of British imported goods, including shoes, hats, and choice fabrics for trousers and dresses. This inclination was typically against preferences for locally produced products. Last, popular island sports and games such as cricket and soccer, and the rituals that informed them, were also defined by their European origins.[25]

The penetration of American power and the authority of its moral culture on the island shaped the third sensibility among the urban poor. The ascent of the United States to global dominance in the post-war world was felt keenly in Jamaica. The impact of American economic power was evident in its investments in tourism, mining and banking. By the 1960s, the United States had replaced Britain as the island's major trading partner, and some of the prodigious output of the post-war US economy found an open, welcoming space in Jamaica, as economic policy threw open the door to foreign imports.[26] Indeed, American manufactured goods, its cars, food and luxury items, were the vogue on the island, and Jamaicans of all classes increasingly consumed these US exports.

The dominance of America's exports to the island matched the growing authority of its worldview. In addition to having a powerful impact on Jamaican migrants returning from the United States, American cultural and political ascendancy was felt on the island in other ways. One vector for the transmission of this cultural authority was the growing tourist traffic from the United States. The post-war period had seen an expanded tourist trade on the island, and North America – particularly the United States – had become the major source of visitors to the island.[27] Confident in their relative prosperity, visitors from the United States brought with them a seemingly boundless optimism about their own fortunes and America's place in the world. As beneficiaries of the post-war economic boom and witnesses to the authority of America's commercial, military and political power in the world, American visitors confidently confirmed for islanders – including poor and low-wage workers – the moral virtues and material rewards of the American way of life. Whether ensconced in hotel properties devoted to their leisure, living in the homes of welcoming Jamaicans or meeting poor islanders on their sojourn, American tourists and the tourist trade itself exercised a not-inconsiderable impact on the social consciousness of Jamaicans. As agents of this cultural transmission, American visitors communicated to their island hosts North American optimism, its easy affluence and its members' confident satisfaction with the virtues of the consumer society.

If North American visitors' national pride, displays of affluence and consumerist optimism failed to morally compel low-wage workers and their unemployed kin, then the latter groups were even more powerfully influenced by another key vector of American power. This was the dissemination of American popular culture by way of print, film, radio and other media of communication. The penetration of American popular culture on the island was felt through the extensive distribution of B-grade Hollywood films and in the importation of American popular magazines, comic books and pulp fiction. Hollywood films, particularly "Westerns" were extremely popular in working-class neighbourhoods across Kingston. Theatres such as the Ambassador in West Kingston, and both the Rialto and Gaiety in East Kingston carried a wide-ranging fare of B-grade films whose images of savage violence, animated gunplay and romantic melodrama proved compelling for the cinema-going poor. In all these films, white actors presented an unmistakable melodramatic narrative in which the lawful and the good triumphed over the illegal and the bad.

The cinema in working-class neighbourhoods therefore became more than just a vehicle for conveying social drama. It was also a medium for the communication of ideology and values, in this instance primarily American political ideology and social values. In addition to the social values in these films, the political newsreels of the day that were shown in the theatres also affirmed the virtues of American society and the moral struggle of the United States against communism and other evils. The "news ideology" contained in these propagandistic newsreels of world events marked out a Manichaean line for poor theatre-goers in Kingston.

For these viewers, then, there was hardly any difference between the moral dictums in the apocalyptic newsreels on the politics of the Cold War, and the normative lessons transmitted by the on-screen melodramas. If the insistent sermons of American evangelists such as the Reverend Billy Graham (whose apocalyptic *Hour of Decision* programme was transmitted by audio tape to Jamaicans on the radio on Sunday mornings) are included in this Americanizing cultural ensemble, then the enveloping reach and authority of US ideological power on the island is apparent.

Besides being exposed to news ideology, evangelical summoning and on-screen Hollywood fare, the urban poor were exposed to American lifestyles and social attitudes from other media available to them. They perused imported American glossy magazines ranging from the tabloid *Photoplay* – which focused on the lives of Hollywood stars – to the sober *Time* magazine, which served up extensive pro-American coverage of world events. The urban poor also pored over Disney fare in print; they experienced the passions of schoolgirl romantic fiction and they amused themselves in the torrent of American comic books about Popeye and the heroic Superman.

Similarly, like other Jamaicans, the urban poor consumed American culture through its popular music. They listened to it on the local radio stations, heard it in city theatres from the mouths of its leading exponents and brought it back from sojourns to the United States.[28] This vogue was particularly true for the idioms of rock-and-roll, black American soul music, the blues, as well as country-and-western music. Local artists, arrangers and singers from the urban poor embraced these American forms, adapted and imitated them, and filled them with local political and social content.

Despite such episodes of adaptive creativity, however, few local artists and other Jamaicans who imbibed American popular music could escape the simulacrum of American experience that the music and other media had introduced to the island. Indeed, locals with limited or no direct contact with American society and culture experienced nostalgia for the culture and ambience of that nearby industrial society as if it were their own. One consequence of this de-territorializing effect of America's cultural reach was that many among the urban poor experienced a palpable cultural disruption.[29] For many Jamaicans, there was a disjuncture between the misery and hardships of their lived experience on the island and the imagined experience of participating in the material well-being, consumer tastes and popular culture imported from a highly industrialized society. This contact with distant American others through travel, film, music, radio broadcasts and pulp fiction therefore transported Jamaicans – including large contingents of the urban poor – into an American-dominated and worldwide political, economic and cultural space. The urban poor, as did other Jamaicans, embraced American codes and social tastes inside this space, and many among them experienced these values as familiar and culturally their own.

Like many imperial systems, American civilization in the post-war years asserted itself as a universal civilization. Jamaicans experienced the global reach and ubiquity of American political, economic and cultural power as a universal world culture appropriate for them. Hence, even as one European civilization with claims to universality went into recession in the region, the newer authority of American power at its apogee now inclined the urban poor and others on the island to experience American ideologies and social values as their own.

This confluence of multiple time-spaces, and the cultural disjuncture between a global awareness and a lived Jamaican experience that was miserable and confining, defined the existential life of the urban poor. Such an overlapping of time-spaces gave the poor opportunities for shared customs other than the narrow partisanship offered by the political parties. Still, these alternative culture-forming experiences were not unproblematic, since they produced contradictory summonings. On the one side, a pattern of moral hailings drew the poor to Africanist obligations. On the other, a different set of appeals pulled them to the simulacrum of American experience. A third pattern linked them to the residues of British imperial culture; and still a fourth hailed the poor as either members of the proto-nations of the parties, or as obedient subjects of the ideology of Jamaican Exceptionalism.

Inside urban exilic space, therefore, unemployed male youth in the ghetto lived a hybrid cultural existence by juggling lived experiences and their simulacrum from elsewhere. Some urban youths adhered to an Africanist sensibility by choosing to "defend" Rastafarian beliefs against anti-black sentiments in the society.[30] Some tried to make their world intelligible by invoking Jamaican folk wisdom. Others adapted a media-informed and imperially transmitted male *savoir-faire*. It was expressed in the "cool pose" of the local "sweet boy" and in the flirtations of the "face-man" in the urban ghetto.[31]

By the late 1960s, many ghetto youths found the simulacrum of the Hollywood cowboy genre usable as they adapted it to the violent "screw-face" and avenging Gorgonian identities of local origin.[32] But even as the rude boys' ranging outlawry alarmed the wider society and caused acute concern in the slums, their adoption of Rastafarian beliefs concerning black pride and redemption at least immunized them against a cultural handicap that afflicted many Afro-Jamaicans. This was Jamaicans' continuing belief in the racist shibboleths of European slavery and empire that condemned non-white subjects – and particularly peoples of African descent – as the embodiment of all that was worthless, sinister and uncivilized.[33]

The rude boys' sense of racial pride protected them from these beliefs. Still, the fusion of Rastafarian cultural nationalism with Hollywood-influenced gangsterism in the slums was a mixed blessing. On the one hand, it enabled the youths to escape the cultural dependency and sense of inferiority that afflicted their black countrymen. On the other hand, this wedding of proud race consciousness and bold criminality of local and Hollywood provenance, produced hybrid social types – neither wholly Jamaican nor fully North American in sensibility.[34]

In the most extreme cases, cultural hybridity and deterritorialized experience among the young meant the juggling and combination of all these identities into an inchoate ensemble that revealed a pastiche of time-spaces, with their clashing lifestyles and moralities. Which identity or morality came to the fore in such cases necessarily depended on the wider social context and exigencies of the situation.

However, regardless of the kinds of moral apparel worn by the poor in these circumstances, what is not in doubt is that competing allegiances and moral dispositions blunted the hope of politicians for an unchecked exercise of a party-driven hegemony over the poor. These rival compulsions drew them away from the moral sway of law, divorced them from official society, and isolated them from the pressures of state politics. Indeed, competing allegiances inclined the urban poor to search for and build social and cultural empowerment zones in which they exercised alternative forms of black mastery. The construction of these zones of empowerment inside urban exilic space, the exercise of forms of black mastery within it, and the proliferation of contrary social identities and moral cultures, all acted as powerful constraints against any state-driven attempt to monopolize or dominate the lives of the poor.

Poor Neighbourhoods as Moral Incubators

The foregoing has shown that urban exilic space possessed a dual identity. It was both a site of repression and also a place where forms of social autonomy could be generated. Ghetto neighbourhoods around Kingston reflected this double feature. Poor and working-class neighbourhoods were therefore simultaneously empowerment zones and places of marginality and confinement. As with all such exilic spaces, a poor neighbourhood – by reason of its segregation and relative isolation – permitted the flourishing of relatively autonomous subcultures. Such tendencies were much in evidence, for example, in poor and working-class precincts across Kingston.

On the one hand, such low-income neighbourhoods were often tense and conflict-ridden. With narrow lanes, exposed dwellings, overcrowded tenement yards and cheek-by-jowl living, the ecology of these neighbourhoods invited conflicts and hostilities among residents. Family quarrels, backbiting and petty interpersonal strife complemented the clash of partisan difference.

On the other hand, these same communities generated forms of mutuality and self-help. Neighbours watched each other's children, passed around bounties they had acquired, and tipped each other off to scarce jobs and welfare benefits. Neighbourhood life in urban Kingston in the late 1960s was therefore defined by normal incidents of hostilities and acts of communal obligation. While these circumstances are not remarkable in poor neighbourhoods, it is arguable that the ecology of ghetto life in Kingston mostly aggravated feelings of alienation and increased levels of discontent. In the context of Jamaica's highly charged socio-political relations, with its mobilization of the poor by means of racial, class and social justice ideologies, the physical circumstances of life in Kingston's ghettos intensified residents' latent moral sentiments.

One such sentiment was the concern for dignity and social respect. Mostly poor individuals affirmed this need and they often sought to achieve it in the one place where a sense of personhood was at stake and needed to be protected most – in the neighbourhood, on the streets, and in the tenements and communal yards where they lived. In these contexts, individual concern for social regard was heightened in the 1960s, and neighbours insistently made claims on each other for social respect.

This insistence assumed dramaturgic form in a public and highly stylized manner that drew attention to the individual's concern that his imperilled, honourable self be publicly and vigorously protected. The ecology of the ghetto made public affirmation and defence of this endangered self all the more urgent.

Living in poor neighbourhoods imposed not just material deprivations on residents. The deficit of living space induced its own moral responses.

Lack of living space could provoke anger and violence among herded residents. Cramped quarters also meant a loss of individual privacy. This deprivation was particularly worrisome for a lower class that, like the rest of the society, highly valued the norm of privacy.

The crowded and close-quartered environment of the slums also had an effect on the evolution of moral culture there. Living in these circumstances in urban Kingston condemned the poor to a peculiar condition of ghetto residency: the subjection of their person to constant exposure, unyielding spectacle and public display. This intensely public nature of daily life in the ghetto caused slum-dwellers to adopt protective poses. These poses allowed the poor to assume militant identities they hoped would ward off shame and protect their dignity.

For example, ridicule and public shame were constant threats to social respect in the ghetto. Jealousy, spite, traffic in rumour and the flow of personal gossip ensnared residents and caused them to be wary of neighbours. Caution against "bad-minded" people in the ghetto arrested conviviality and led to pre-emptive moral judgements. Neighbourhood scorn for individuals, often on the basis of rumour, could scar and ruin reputations. As well, persons deemed untrustworthy or found to be "licky-licky" in their gluttony, or those regarded as "tight-handed" in refusing to share all became community pariahs. Community gossip, with its moral injunctions, put residents on their guard and stimulated in them protective poses to maintain personal respect. In such cases, targets of anonymous gossip dealt with threats to their reputation by pre-emptive and strenuous assertions of their righteousness, while promising menace to the gossips. This vigilance in the interest of personal respect encouraged aggressiveness among the poor, independent of provocation or manipulation by political parties.

But threats to personhood in the slums came not just from destructive talk. The outdoors existence typical of the slums created moral values, as residents battled for space and assumed protective identities. Life in lower-class neighbourhoods typically meant living in makeshift dwellings or tenement yards. Such yards normally consisted of simple one-room dwellings abutting a common outdoor space. Living in the tenement yard meant cooking, bathing, eating and washing clothes outdoors in this common space. Ghetto life also meant the public sharing of private facilities and the inconvenience of waiting one's turn to use scarce amenities. Individual conduct, the intimacies of family life and social interactions in the yard took place mostly in full public view and within earshot of neighbours. Thus, such activities were subject to constant scrutiny and moral judgement. While offering opportunities for mutuality and sharing, tenement yard life was cramped, and the constant surveillance of personal lives tended to undermine sociability and trust. Open disputes, fights and public quarrels punctured occasions of neighbourliness in the yards.

Tenement yard space and its relations extended into the streets. This nexus also intensified alienation. Though narrow streets and lanes in the slums were physically separated from dwellings by fences, gates and other crude delimiters, there was much physical overlap between the street and the yards. Despite tenacious efforts to maintain privacy by erecting simple fences, dwellings in the slums often abutted the streets without any protective, intervening barriers. The overlap between street and yard meant that each contributed to the public spectacle in which all residents participated. Indeed, what transpired in the open yards and dwellings of the tenements was generally visible and audible from the street. Conversely, a vibrant street life intruded into the yards.

The characteristically outdoor and public spectacle of ghetto life sharply reduced personal privacy and with it any individual effort to maintain a life or identity that kept the residents' public and private "faces" separate. To many residents this separation was important to their sense of enjoying a civilized existence. Constant exposure "at home" in the yards, and "in public" out in the street, forced residents into a struggle for personal space and denied them the social and physical context for the norms of civility they coveted. Achieving social respect under these circumstances therefore depended on the ability to manage appearances in neighbourhood spaces and to compel others to accept these protective poses. The street and the yard thus became platforms for the construction of identities and together they helped foster a moral culture often at odds with the civic culture to which many residents aspired.

In the streets and tenement yards, individual identity was closely linked to oral-kinetic repertoires. Somatic poses, variable facial utterances and verbal tonality enabled slum dwellers to compel respect from neighbours by using the body as a vehicle of moral communication. To know someone and to be someone in the ghetto was, in part, a function of the use of bodies in public space. To acquire a "self" entailed its public construction in the form of physical gestures before one's neighbours. For young men in the streets and yards, this meant the deploying of a heterosexual, manly etiquette in which voice, gesture and orality confirmed an unassailable masculine aura.

This assertive body was generally effective in addressing the everyday encounters that threatened each resident's search for a potent self.

Depending on the circumstances, threats to an honourable identity could be warded off by means as various as aggressive stances or cool poses by males. For women, protective measures might include the wearing of modest clothing or the public affirmation of a devout commitment to a religious faith. In deeply influential ways, community social relations and the ecology of the ghetto created the basis for a theatre of identity revolving around corporeal acts and the political uses of bodies.

Social relations in the slums and the ecology of the yard and the street therefore induced in the urban poor a kinetic morality that offered a somatic complement to their ideas of personal autonomy and black freedom. Public gestures often implied ideological needs. Moreover, for many in the ghetto, its streets, yards and public squares were not just places to claim public respect for one's identity as human. Social and physical spaces in the slums were also domains for the practice of forms of neo-African moral intelligence and neo-African aesthetics because racial consciousness saturated corporeal acts.

Both moral intelligence and aesthetic form were thus bearers of civilizational values and carriers of popular-democratic impulses. They affirmed the value of black personhood and the righteousness of the poor's claim to social honour.

This role of the street and the yard as powerful identity-creating platforms was strengthened in a country in which both law and society offered few protections and meagre affirmations of the black poor's right to respect. The spectacle of yard and street life therefore encouraged somatic norms and a performance culture in which residents publicly claimed protective identities against possible threats.

In these circumstances, both the aggressive "rude boy" and the menacing "screw face" identities adopted by juveniles and grown men during the 1960s become intelligible. These identities of Hollywood origin, but adapted to local circumstances, were deployed for strategic purposes: to avoid public shame and to deter threats to an imperilled self. Though the adoption of these identities may be regarded as instances of nihilistic rage against injustice and state abuse, it is worth remembering that they were also deployed to influence neighbours and to hold at bay their invasive habits. State politics induced anger in the slums and provoked these wary identities. But a life of spectacle, the threat of humiliation before one's neighbours, and the battle for space in the neighbourhood all induced in the urban poor moralities that were formed well outside the ambit and play of predatory politics.

The spectacular quality of daily life in the slums, with its risk of shame and public ridicule, therefore made already anxious individuals feel even more threatened and concerned for their dignity. A heightened sense of vulnerability to spectacle and public humiliation encouraged in residents a powerful need to dramatically affirm their dignity and claim their self-respect from neighbours. The battle for space and the avoidance of public shame in yards and tenements therefore became the goad to the well-known, stylized aggressiveness among the Kingston poor. Quite independent of the pressure of political parties upon their lives, the poor were inclined to adopt aggressive and vigilantly defensive postures partly due to the ecology of the slums. Thus the constancy of this battle for space and the search for an honourable identity in both society and the ghetto inclined poor residents to wariness and martial postures of self-defence.

Autonomous Lifestyles: Sources of Social Power and Cultural Capital

Two conclusions can be drawn from the preceding discussion. First, it is apparent that despite the tremendous power of the parties and of predatory politics in the lives of the poor, the reach of American power, the residual culture of European imperialism, and pervasive Africanisms among the poor all blunted the colonizing effect of politics. All three sources of alternative cultural existence conspired to hold invasive state politics at bay and to give the urban poor cultural living space. In the 1960s, contingents of the urban poor drew on the triple heritage of African, European and American cultural influence to invent new customs. This variable heritage helped them construct hybrid, emancipated selves that eluded the monopolistic reach of politics and the domesticating influence of local institutions and moral agents.

Second, the insecurity of outdoors existence and vulnerability to spectacle that threatened black esteem in the slums could also be employed to secure its recovery both in the ghetto and elsewhere in the society. Among such sites were public theatres where popular performers contributed to group moral culture by providing entertainment in song, music and dance. Dramaturgy and role-playing in the slums, as a response to the spectacular quality of everyday life there, could be transferred to this other theatre of identity where slum-dwellers, in their role as public entertainers, affirmed the cause for social autonomy and black esteem.

Myriad cultural practices in the 1960s seemed to confirm this assessment. The phenomenal popularity of ska and reggae music in these years offered a dramatic illustration of the point.[35] The rise to national prominence of popular singers and performing artists from working-class and poor neighbourhoods was achieved partly on the basis of the triple heritage, and partly by drawing on the availability of dramaturgic opportunity and experience. Popular musicians, DJs and singers embodied cultural styles within the triple heritage. Crooners, shouters, balladeers and religious chanters of popular song displayed in public performance the mimetic, distant inspiration for the lyrical content of their songs and musical styles.[36]

Musical and stylistic forms from Africa, Europe and the United States therefore coexisted in contrapuntal unity with local innovations. This simulacrum of worldwide experience captured in song styles and lyrical content was evident, for example, in the stage attire of performers. Formal suits, top-hats and imperial regalia of British origins were mixed with African-inspired dreadlocks and fashions of local derivation. Both on and off stage, male performers' gold-capped front teeth of local invention complemented the wearing of impenetrable, black sunglasses whose aesthetics reflected the influence of the hipster in Black American popular culture. Similarly, stage gestures echoed a medley of expressive styles and affective-libidinal norms drawn from elsewhere. The majestic struts and martial stances seen in the concert halls complemented stagy, soul-group choreography borrowed from North American rock-and-roll culture.

If public exposure and invasive scrutiny in the ghetto induced belligerent poses and self-regarding "performances" among slum-dwellers, then entertainment on the public stage was not very different in its mobilizing cultural impact. There too, public spectacle, within the context of social inequality and the triple heritage, became a vehicle for heroic performance and the communication of a dissident moral culture. The popularity of the Wailers singing group, and later of Bob Marley himself, epitomized the dynamics among spectacle, performance and moral culture. Like other reggae bands, the Wailers' public performances mirrored for poor audiences the corporeal intensities and dramaturgy of ghetto life. In Wailers' concerts, for example, performing the mimetics of libidinous joy in the slums and mirroring the cultural injury of the downtrodden won the group a huge following.

Occurring in exilic spaces beyond the reach of official scrutiny and censorship, the spectacle in concerts and dance halls in working-class neighbourhoods became an occasion of celebratory, collective racial joy. In these places, poor audiences revelled in their particularity as black "sufferers" and in their anonymity as opponents of social injustice. The sensational content of these musical performances allowed the black poor to indulge libidinous norms. Concerts found them shouting affirmations to the band and indulging in exuberant racial pride in the aesthetic content of the music. Likewise, revellers in the dance halls were capable of falling into near-hypnotic trances as they navigated the extended, instrumental "dub" interlude with its insistent, deafening bass-line. For these people, the pulsating sound of reggae music seemed as important to the formation of their social and moral identity as the race-enhancing message in the music's lyrical content.

Like its counterpart in the neighbourhood, then, the spectacle of the public concert and the dance hall created opportunities for identity-making, black mastery and heroic performance. Musical skill and creativity in oral-kinetic dramaturgy enabled performers from the slums to achieve public honour and heroic reputations. Because of his mastery of these repertoires, Bob Marley became the iconic reggae artist of the 1960s and 1970s. He was simultaneously a creative exponent, heroic performer and cultural tribune. Musicians and singers in the Wailers as well as producers and sound system engineers won similar notoriety for their creative expertise in synthesizing voice, drums, pianos and guitars to fit the demands of the new music. The public appreciated this musical creativity of singers and sound system engineers so much that enthusiastic audiences attended concerts and went to the dance halls as much to experience the aesthetic, public affirmation of their values as to witness virtuoso performances by individual artists and sound engineers.

Thus spectacle and performance in the dance halls and concert venues were nothing without the moral culture for which they were the vehicles. Public performance in concert permitted the collective assumption of poses and social identities infused with racial and class content. As a component of exilic space, the dance hall allowed the ecstatic indulgence of cultural dissidence and collective black joy. There, contingents of the black poor affirmed their equal claim to an honourable identity. Sound system engineers bearing honorific titles such as "Duke" or "King" vied with each other, and with popular singers, to bring ecstatic audiences the latest and greatest in popular music. In the specular domain of these spaces, well beyond the immediate scrutiny of an intrusive state and a racially discriminatory society, the aesthetic experience of the urban poor achieved authentic representation.

In this regard, kinetic prowess, verbal play and instrumental virtuosity by performers on stage could carry little force without related norms of cultural autonomy, personal excellence and black mastery. In the eyes of both artists and audiences, performance was never divorced from this black excellence and search for cultural autonomy. For artists as well as audiences, artistic techniques and their mastery were usually linked to racial group awareness; hence, concern for aesthetic values and technical expertise was never far from sentiments of collective cultural redemption. Consequently, even as the lyrical content of reggae music advanced an explicit moral and political agenda of black redemption and racial pride, the orienting norms of that agenda – black mastery and black freedom – were tacitly reinforced by these ethnic artists' self-conscious concern for mastering the craft. Group moral culture and its larger social concerns informed the quest for superior technique.

This overlapping of public performance, heroic individualism and moral culture can now be generalized to other cultural practices in urban space. Positive examples of the twinning of these three values were evident in popular culture in the 1960s and after. Sports and games as well as entertainment are two well-known domains in which performance values, individual mastery and socio-political values have historically overlapped for the poorer classes. Sports and entertainment verified the ubiquity of shared customs among members of this group; both confirmed the fact of cultural construction beyond the realm of partisanship, and both attested to the striving for black esteem and liberty.

If we turn briefly to sports and games, it is a commonplace to observe that in Jamaica the working and poorer classes found in them outlets for their politically constrained abilities. Talented youth across the island, but especially from poor urban communities, gravitated to track-and-field athletics and to the games of cricket and soccer as outlets for their ambitions. Stirred by their own efforts and encouraged by school, church and community organizations as well as politicians, youth in Kingston communities enthusiastically embraced popular sports as a platform for their talents.

Every community had its assemblies of sports-playing youths and teams. These collectives ranged from the scrappy, informal "pickup" teams to the organized clubs and local "Elevens" that proudly represented working-class constituencies in regional and national competition. Every community had its adult youth mentors and its natural leaders who stepped forward to organize a team and to stir community pride through sporting excellence. Sporting competition and adult supervision of the young encouraged community pride, leadership, discipline and *esprit de corps*. In these ways, poor and working-class youths found in sports a vehicle for their ambitions, a means of acquiring social respect and a sense of community identity. All across working-class Kingston, residents' outstanding achievement in sports and entertainment helped forge powerful community bonds.

The massive outpouring of working-class talent in cricket, soccer and athletics during the 1950s and 1960s is too well known to be rehearsed here.[37] These years produced legendary athletes and famous teams that won a huge following for their national and international achievements. Such sporting achievements, with their summoning of skill, courage and endurance, provided the occasion for historically stunted talents to find creative expression in dramatic public performance. The spectacle of black athletes excelling nationally and internationally mirrored the latent talent in poor communities, and confirmed for the urban poor the possibilities of black mastery in contexts of racial denigration.

In this spectacle of public performance in which heroic individualism and audience yearning for public recognition were wedded, the soccer field, the cricket pitch and the stadium track became scenes of dramatic spectacle in which athletes from lowly origins honed their talents. In the 1950s and after, new black talent was successfully apprenticed to the skills, disciplines and aesthetic values of sports. These premium values were established by legendary sport figures, particularly those that played the game of cricket. Promising teens on rival cricket teams across Kingston, for example, rehearsed the elegant stroke-play visually acquired from watching accomplished batsmen of "test match" fame.[38] Other young practitioners with an aptitude for bowling practised at home and abroad the idiosyncratic arm-and-wrist movements learned from legendary West Indian bowlers they admired. This same devotion to craft was evident in other sports such as boxing and horseracing. In both, black talent also came to the fore, as representatives from the poorer classes established spectacular careers as prize-fighters and jockeys before an appreciative national audience.

As with the game of cricket, normative concerns also infused performance in the boxing ring and at the racetrack; in each sport a moral culture, inspired by a concern for racial competence, saturated each athlete's technical performance. Every sport became an incubator of moral values as black excellence in style and technique won public acclaim. Independent striving through sporting games therefore established the basis of a unique form of cultural unfolding. It was marked by the building of a tradition of excellence and the inclination to positive leadership.

Accomplishment in sports and popular entertainment created new forms of cultural capital for the poor, and helped establish a positive basis for their widening social power in Jamaican society. In the post-war years, acclaimed sports figures and entertainers from humble origins came to exercise an unparalleled moral authority in the society, largely based on their roles as icons of black excellence.[39] Leadership, technical competence and outstanding achievement in these areas of popular culture did much, therefore, to enhance racial pride, alleviate feelings of inferiority and build community spirit. Indeed, natal community identity became a source of personal pride among poor and working-class youth, as flourishing talent and outstanding achievements earned their communities public recognition.

For residents in these urban neighbourhoods, community identity and pride came therefore not so much from the claims of partisan politics as from the satisfaction of contributing to the transformation of the nation's cultural identity by fielding talent in the areas of sports and entertainment. Social power from below came therefore from sources other than partisan political engagements. The urban poor found in these other non-political domains cultural space in which they tried to fashion a relatively autonomous existence, free from the debasing effects of factional politics.

This freedom should not be exaggerated, however. Autonomy was strictly limited, as urban politicians were determined to harness this cultural flowering to their partisan agendas. Nevertheless, even when political partisanship encroached on that existence by state funding of community sports and the fashioning of community development projects to suit partisan ambitions, politics could not control the meaning of this cultural flourishing for the poor. Indeed, the poor did not see individual excellence in sports and entertainment as an achievement won by politics, or for the glory of politics. On the contrary, in their eyes a hardy black people had excelled despite the odds and had won laurels in both domains. In this view, the poor celebrated personal striving and success for their triumph over poverty and politics.

Thus performing artists, sportsmen and community folk saw their achievements as their very own. These forms of black mastery from below were therefore something that belonged to the ordinary people and were won by them, despite political encroachment. Thus, even as these agents of cultural empowerment would find it necessary to accommodate the intrusion of politics on what they had accomplished, they tried also to keep politics in its place by recognizing its contingent, episodic role in their lives. In sum, though personal and group ambition might at times require accommodation to predatory politics, such ambitions did not countenance the suppression of black cultural autonomy.[40] Indeed, for the vast majority of the poor, cultural autonomy was sought for its own sake. As a result, involvement in political partisanship was regarded as an encumbrance and a necessary evil that was typically subordinated to the quest for group cultural respect.[41]

Here again, the quest for cultural space should not be overstated, as it was informed by a covert desire for inclusion in the cultural mainstream. For while cultural affirmation greatly increased the social power of the poor in opposition to a dismissive society, it is worth remembering that conventional morality and shared values also undergirded popular claims for respect. Thus even as icons of black excellence challenged the cultural inequities of the society by highlighting cultural empowerment and advancing alternative modes of existence, they were demanding inclusion and did so by tacitly invoking common Jamaican values and widely shared norms.

Those values were rooted in notions of personal ambition, competitive individualism, and norms of merit and reward that recognized achievement. By embodying precisely these values, the search for black excellence among the poor echoed shared but neglected values in Jamaican society. In their quest for social acceptance, then, many icons of black mastery from below sought to win respect and acquire respectability in ways that were thoroughly consistent with the values of the wider Jamaican society. In displays of ambition and in the harnessing of discipline to positive goals, icons from the poorer classes established a delicate relation between two contrary impulses within lower-class groups. One was the fashioning of a culturally grounded aesthetic that was conscious of differences in social identity between the black poor and their social betters; the other was tutoring a dismissive society in it neglected norms, particularly those that linked social worth to individual and group achievement.

Still, by the late 1960s this quest for social empowerment was not merely supportive of prevailing values. It was, as well, infiltrated by sentiments that were increasingly hostile to those values. This much was clear from the actions of a rebellious lumpenproletariat that openly rejected the dominant morality and societal norms of civility and upward mobility through lawful achievement and competitive individualism. Paradoxically, the quest for social respect and regard in the slums was expressed in two competing tendencies: the imitation and negation of official norms. Together they solidified divergent yet affiliated social identities in the slums.

The ghetto therefore had its exemplars of positive black achievement as well as its iconic rebels who were intent on challenging conventional achievement norms. Sports heroes and popular entertainers won public acclaim for succeeding despite the odds. But such exemplars had also to share notoriety and community recognition with the likes of heroic gunmen, youth gangs, political enforcers and agents belonging to the criminal underground. Poor communities held model figures from sports and popular entertainment in awe. But these communities also endowed celebrated outlaws in their midst with heroic qualities. These outlaws included urban bandits (several of whom held Rastafarian and socialist views), gun-wielding juvenile gangs and lumpen collectivities inclined to predation and street crime. In contrast to the exemplars in sports and entertainment, this latter group had also carved out alternative paths to survival and recognition in the slums by means of outlawry and a convention-disrupting indiscipline.

In the post-war years, the storied reputations of some of these outlaw actors became not just the stuff of legend; they also offered models of emulation for the unemployed young. These contrary yet kindred forms of heroic individualism illustrate the dialectics of the struggle for cultural space unfolding in the slums against the background of the island's unequal social relations and multiple historical inheritances. The following section reviews an aspect of this dialectic – the intensification of non-compliance, and the turn to self-help indiscipline among the lumpenproletariat – and comments on its social significance.

Escape from Civility: Outlawry and Indiscipline as Cultural Self-Help

In making the point that part of the urban poor's social identity was formed outside the envelope of political partisanship, this chapter has stressed positive attributes that shaped the group's self-initiated and protean cultural construction. But as the previous chapters have already shown, marginality and deprivation also generated criminality, outlawry and rebellion in the slums. Like their positive counterparts, these uncivil expressions evolved independently of party political agendas. Outlawry was not inspired solely by political manipulation. Objective, material hardship in the slums yielded its own responses and created contexts for cultural adaptation and innovation. For example, material deprivation encouraged the desperate among the lumpenproletariat to resort to predation and to self-interested acts of survival regardless of ongoing political contestations.

In the slums of post-war Kingston, pickpockets, hustlers, drug peddlers and hold-up men jockeyed with petty thieves and murderous outlaws in a common vocation of preying on the poor and the well-to-do alike. These social predators were the bane of both their neighbours and the police. They formed part of a criminal underground largely devoid of coherent convictions, but still deeply affected by the summoning of social justice ideologies that were widely disseminated at the time. Thus, though it is unlikely that these criminals held coherent political convictions, they were nonetheless aware of belonging to a class-divided and racially discriminatory society.

This awareness of inequality suggests that the island's class and race relations had inevitably influenced even this anomic group's self-image. Their offences, however, cannot be regarded as unambiguous cases where petty crimes and assaults were committed with the intention of retaliating against the rich and the powerful. Urban street crime by the criminal class took its toll not only on the middle and upper classes, but on the defenceless poor and the working class as well. Just the same, it is worth remembering that though this predation did not target the rich and was not driven by coherent political concerns, criminality still had subversive political effects. This was so because as common crime increasingly became a cause of official concern, efforts to arrest it invariably took on political overtones.

Unlike the hard-core criminal contingent, other strata of the lumpenproletariat were less ambiguous in the kinds of political association and motivations that stirred them. Contingents not part of the criminal underground seemed especially sensitive to social justice ideologies and appeared more susceptible to political direction. Five groupings seemed amenable to political mobilization and were the ones most involved in forms of rule breaking that suggested more focused ideological commitments. These were the following: (1) juvenile gangs fighting for turf in politically divided neighbourhoods; (2) the unskilled unemployed seeking work but unable to find it often because of political victimization; (3) street vendors who had defected from the wage economy and had self-consciously repudiated what they regarded as its "slave wages"; (4) a minimum-wage lumpenproletariat that was part of the low-wage, working poor subject to short-term, uncertain employment in the urban economy; and (5) jobless school dropouts not yet lost to the society and living with their kin in poor neighbourhoods. In the politically charged post-war years, these groupings rallied to Rastafarian, socialist and Black Power activists in addition to the politicians who saturated the slums with their populist appeals and political agendas. By the end of the 1960s this motley convention was probably the most highly mobilized and ideologically provoked grouping among the Kingston poor. From the ranks of these mobilized layers came the social rebels whose anti-system ideologies defined subcultural values in the slums. Within this grouping, widespread moral inversions, rule breaking and self-help indiscipline became affirmative norms informing new, subversive social identities.[42]

Rule breaking by such groups was varied. As we have seen, open political rebellion and riotous, collective actions challenged class and racial inequalities and affirmed popular perceptions of injustice. Defiant acts included aggressive assertions of black self-regard that alarmed the government and the ethnic minorities.[43] Other forms of rule breaking threw dominant values into doubt even as they revealed something of the infra-politics of the urban poor.

The rude boys flouted conventional norms and turned social etiquette on its head. Likewise, the content of popular songs, the costumes of the rebellious young and the inclination to heroic criminality became means of acquiring reputation and social honour. In Kingston and other main towns, menacing bravado, belligerent poses and raw aggression became vehicles for the assertion of popular alienation.

Vocal opposition to power, biting critiques of inequality and the ridiculing of political figures defined the political content of this alienated culture.[44] For example, linguistic innovations reflected antagonistic class relations. New words, epithets and locutions became part of the language of the slums. Mocking speech raked the party bosses as well as the privileged and the powerful. For instance, politicians were chided for engaging in "politricks", and social relations in Jamaica's capitalist society were denounced for causing the human race to become part of the "rat race". As this linguistic defiance spread, it dominated popular music and crept into the speech of other discontented classes.[45] As a result, lower-class discontent and values became generalized and this diffusion also signalled the growing social power of the urban poor.

Yet even as this insurgent social power depended on the inversion of *values*, power from below also relied on the dramaturgy of oral-kinetic opposition. In addition to their subversive *discourses*, the values of the outlaw poor were transmitted through newly empowered bodies. Voice and gestures of opposition carried moral-political overtones. Popular speech and song were resonant with political concerns. Talk behind the back of power carried ominous warnings, issued hopes of redemption, expressed libidinous joy and uttered biting invective.[46] Moreover, raw sounds connected to political discourse in the slums carried moral freight. Sneers at the powerful and curses, shouts or a plaintive cry against injustice gave sound to contested relations of identity, power and inequality. Such sounds in their cadence and rhythm lent vigour to dissidence and reinforced the elaborated, valued-laden lyrics of popular speech and song. By such powerful means did oral gestures inform moral culture.[47]

The infra-politics of the urban poor therefore depended on a dissident black body that was employed as a cultural weapon. Its target was the power exercised by the historical conditioning and aesthetics of colonial "body-politics" in Jamaica. The labour of self-construction among the poor was, in part, a challenge to the colonial idea of how the civilized, disciplined body of the black poor should behave. State- and society-inspired rituals of deference, compliance and obedience had made inroads in governing the physical body of the urban poor. Centuries of moral indoctrination, religious teachings and dominant ideologies of uplift had sought the reproduction of acquiescent, subordinated blacks.

Discipline, propriety, decorum and suppression of impulses injurious to good order were therefore the *sine qua non* of Jamaican nationalism. These values helped define the politics and aesthetics of the postcolonial order. In postcolonial Jamaica, therefore, a disciplined black body was not merely good for the stability of the new society; it had in effect become coterminous with the social identity of the people-nation. As the Rastafarians, rude boys and other rebels discovered, to lack a disciplined body was to fall outside the national moral community. Not surprisingly, therefore, denunciations of "lawlessness" and of "hooliganism" were widespread in the 1960s and exponents of public manners emphasized to the poor the need for civility, respect and obedience to law.[48]

This emphasis on etiquette produced cultural dissonance in the first decade of independence. For rather than being resonant with narratives of social empowerment, the summons of nationalist state agents and their moral allies sought the suppression of potentially unruly black bodies. Law-and-order narratives therefore dominated official discourses and complemented the state's increasing resort to violence in the 1960s.[49]

When words failed, challengers to the social order were policed and punished. This was especially so in the prisons where the poor faced whippings, hangings and hard labour for their offences. The exercise of power acted punitively and ascriptively against social rebels as civility's authority took its toll on black bodies from the slums.

Because of such injuries, the urban poor developed exilic responses and inverted norms of civility described above. Inclinations to self-governance and autonomy moved therefore from restraint to indiscipline, and a retreat from civility's authority. Insubordination and cultural sedition characterized the new moral sensibility among the alienated urban poor.

Led by the exemplary "natty dread" culture of the Rastafarians, the urban poor had fashioned a new and rival moral community in which heroic, dissident and uncivil social identities were celebrated. Truculent rudies, self-appointed Gorgons, neighbourhood "top-rankings" leaders and other anomic figures now held sway among the urban poor. In sum, sustained non-compliance and insubordination now defined the cultural politics of the urban poor.

Sharp moral censure had little effect in reversing these acts of empowerment. The alienated poor, it may be argued, regarded their indiscipline not as a source of shame, but as a mark of distinction and a matter of pride. For these downtrodden contingents, autonomy and freedom lay in demonstrations of cultural prowess, displays of hardiness against the odds, courage in the face of intimidation, and martial aggressiveness against threats from neighbours and the state. In circumstances of sharp social inequality and punitive political rule, these assertions invariably butted against norms that reinforced structures of inequality. For the alienated poor, the attainment of a potent self therefore meant retreat from official conceptions of order and civility.

In this normative exit from state and society in Jamaica, it is notable that it was not the labour-capital antinomy that produced mounting tensions. Rather, conflict over inequalities had congealed around disputed identities, questions of cultural empowerment and rival conceptions of values.

At the close of this turbulent decade, then, cultural struggle had yielded a contrary conception of self-regard among the alienated poor. It was expressed as pride in a rude otherness and conviction that indiscipline and defiance could hold better-off, politically dominant groups at bay. As the next chapters show, the destabilizing power of this group confidence and the authority of dissident identities in the slums would be lost neither on the powerful nor on their supplicants.

5

Badness-Honour and the Invigorated Authority of the Urban Poor

THE PREVIOUS CHAPTERS IDENTIFIED TWO LEADING trends in the evolution of politics and society in Jamaica between 1944 and 1971. The first was the emergence of a national state defined by predation and violence against the urban poor. State power was defined by the distribution of scarce benefits to duelling contingents of the supplicant poor and by a marked solicitousness toward popular cultural practices that set the urban poor apart from dominant social norms.

This form of rule helped the political parties to achieve an unstable social cohesion amidst deepening social divisions. Control of the restive urban poor therefore relied on spurring competition among them for political spoils, while authorizing erstwhile agents from their ranks to employ violence to maintain or disrupt the partisan flow of benefits and the control of hard-won political territory in the slums.

That violence and distribution of benefits pitted rival contingents of the supplicant poor against each other, thus shaping them into warring political communities. Violence against the poor was tempered, however, by the parties' populist ideologies that carried their own seductions. Thus, despite important differences in their agendas, and in the ideological orientations of their respective leaders, from 1944 to 1971 both the PNP and the JLP were engaged in a common agenda. This project was the disorganization of the supplicant and rebellious urban poor by means of a destructive political violence amidst rival party claims of popular uplift. Violence and populism had therefore become the *sine qua non* for the exercise of political domination in Jamaica.

The second dominant trend in post-war Jamaica was the steady expansion in the social power of the mobilized poor. Their power was especially evident in the expanding socio-political leverage of the lumpenproletariat. This compulsion on Jamaican society came through the dissident norms of the Rastafarians and the cultural rebellion of alienated youth in the slums. As well, contingents from the criminal underground exerted their own social influence. However, the greatest share of the violence in this period and after came from politically aligned street gangs who wreaked havoc on the society.[1] Their violence, banditry and outlawry overlapped with a widening cultural rebellion to influence both social norms and party culture.

We have already observed that much of the social power of the poor lay outside the machinations of party politics. Subaltern power was spurred by complex social dynamics well beyond political compulsion. They included the alienating, disruptive effect of urban life on the migrant poor that, ironically, fed their growing social authority.

Similarly, for all its ambiguity, the cultural impact of the country's triple heritage invigorated the challenge from the slums as exponents of all sorts fused clashing cultural orientations to their different social engagements. Last, frustrated social ambition in the ghetto intensified the agonism that poor residents shared with other Jamaican nationals.[2] This spur to competitive individualism in the slums marked residents there as a restless, disruptive force whose rivalry for spoils, claims for racial honour and demands for social justice could not be ignored.

Agonism and Gamesmanship in the Slums

In the post-war years, this agonism had an ambiguous effect. On the one hand, internecine rivalry blunted the poor's efforts to improve their circumstances even as it spurred slum-dwellers to take up anti-system, noncompliant orientations to power. On the other hand, a defiant gamesmanship and competitive individualism encouraged group pride based on norms of excellence in a variety of non-partisan domains. These variable circumstances, outside the scope of partisan control, abetted the growing social significance of the mobilized poor.

By the early 1970s it was evident to political observers and state agents alike that the mobilized urban poor had established multiple claims to group power and had created manifold sources of identity. Outlawry-as-identity, particularly among the alienated young, had established its hegemony over all other identity claims. Its supremacy marked rebels in the slums as a volatile, non-compliant constituency that was ill disposed to easy moral governance and cheap political blandishments.

Despite its vogue in the slums, however, hardened defiance was typical of only the most alienated elements. It should be remembered that the rebelliousness that led to crime, banditry and general mayhem among the poor was the work of only a tiny minority. Not all slum-dwellers and residents of working-class districts were driven to outlawry. A majority of these residents still remained law-abiding, even as more and more of the unemployed young in working-class communities were fast becoming morally uncaptured rebels.

Motivated variously by devout religious faith, commitment to civic morality and ambition for upward mobility, the lawful majority still adhered to racially inflected achievement norms as means to group uplift. As community exemplars whose inclinations ran neither to partisan violence nor to antisocial rebellion, this majority contingent offered to the restive young and other marginals a racially informed culture of uplift tied to traditional values.[3]

Yet despite the fortitude of these role models, contrary trends weakened the force of their example. As the dynamic alliance between the parties and militant slum-dwellers unfolded, and as social inequalities widened during the early 1970s, the restraining influence of this majority group was steadily eclipsed. That authority was supplanted by the heightened moral sway of a lumpenproletariat inured to violence and crime. As this group became immersed in the cut and thrust of constituency- and street-level politics, its desperate supplicancy and pioneering demand for racial justice imposed tremendous moral pressures on the political parties.

As we have seen, party leaders and activists responded positively to these demands. Indeed, by 1971, as the parties sought to manipulate this supplicancy, the struggle for benefits encouraged further antisocial defiance among the rebellious poor. That defiance was represented by the popularity of what I shall call the norm of "badness-honour". Badness-honour is the oral-kinetic practice in Jamaica that enables claimants, usually from disadvantaged groups, to secure a modicum of power and respect by intimidation.

By 1971 badness-honour as a cultural practice had won moral dominance within the society of the Kingston poor. There a stylized outlawry ("badness" or "badmanism" in Jamaican parlance) provoked fear in the larger society but earned raves in the slums for challenging the norm of civility and for affirming a racially charged defiance as a new basis for social identity and honour.[4] Defiance of conventional norms by juvenile gangs and political enforcers gave such rebels in the slums a martial, violence-ridden identity totally at odds with widely held norms of respectability and obedience to law. By the end of the 1960s, acts of badness-honour and the sensibility that informed them were commonplace in Kingston's ghettos; by the early 1970s that outlaw sensibility had tightened its hold on both the society and the political culture of the parties.[5]

Of course, outlawry and violence as signature features of politics in urban Kingston were neither new nor solely the acts of desperate supplicants. In the decades-long association between parties and urban masses, the moral concerns of the alienated poor had preoccupied the parties and dominated the calculations of their leaders and activists. Material want among the urban poor and their boisterous outlawry in the service of partisan politics and self-help had long compelled the parties and their strategists to acknowledge this alienated constituency.

One effect of this association was that urban politicians and activists were compelled to exhibit their own forms of braggadocio, outlawry and aggression if they were to survive in Kingston's violent political culture. There is little doubt, then, that mass pressure from below and the suzerainty of hardy politicians in Kingston had long made violent outlawry a feature of Jamaican politics that was not confined to the ranks of the militant poor.

What was new in the early 1970s, however, was the increased authority that badness-honour assumed as a cultural force in political life. To the satisfaction of the lumpenproletariat and their allies in the parties, political contestation drew increasingly on the contentious symbolism, combative dramaturgy and pugnacious etiquette of urban street life and culture.

The harsh imperatives of this street life in Kingston were in many ways no different from those facing the poor in overcrowded cities everywhere. They included survival at all costs, application of a self-helping resourcefulness and capacity for a hearty gamesmanship encouraged by the outdoor, spectatorial quality of street life. As with many overcrowded and impoverished urban centres worldwide, the streets of Kingston had become a major social space for the social relations of the poor and their public rituals. In these streets, black residents enacted a durable gamesmanship, found conviviality and affirmed an aggressive ethnic pride. This show of ethnic confidence was mixed with moments of racial self-contempt and ethnic chauvinism.[6] Displays of acute race- and class-consciousness – both confident and insecure – saturated interpersonal relations on the streets of Kingston in these years.

Those relations were defined by a never-ending ordeal of gamesmanship and individual improvisation that allowed the poor to become respected persons in their own eyes. Whether negotiating commercial exchanges in the vibrant street trade or resisting injuries to their racial pride from insensitive protagonists, ghetto locals usually made sure no slight or abuse went unchallenged.

These circumstances yielded their own dramaturgies. Slum-dwellers, for instance, were impelled to establish, protect and even bid up the value of their personae by resorting to aggressive histrionics invested with concerns for race and identity. Epithets, verbal aggression and contentious physical encounters vied with their benign counterparts such as honorific hailings, warm conviviality and a conscious, even docile mutuality that was affirmed in the name of racial solidarity.[7]

In large part, however, the culling of status honour and self-regard on the street relied less on maintaining a neutered, stoic quiescence than on exhibiting a brash dramaturgy in which oral-kinetic "boasting" – verbal skill, oral aggression and argumentation, and a muscular exhibitionism hinting of violence – signalled the onset of testy gamesmanship for social respect.

On loan to partisan politics throughout the post-war years, this agonism among the poor thus found an outlet worthy of their unchecked, jousting talents. It precipitated a factional politics that complemented the boisterous non-partisan rivalry that the militant poor employed to secure social respect on the streets. That is, socially conscious and self-seeking supplicants applied to their political engagements a trademark, tormented cultural orientation – badness-honour – to get the parties to do their bidding.

Transformation of Party Culture

This intensified compulsion from the streets induced a mutation in the cultural life of the parties. Beginning in the early 1970s, their ideologies, electoral mobilization and political symbolism drew more and more on popular street culture. This was especially the case with the PNP in the 1972 electoral campaign, but this tactic was also evident in the JLP's feverish pro-capitalist populism.[8]

While the parties were never merely the mouthpieces for popular demands, there is little doubt that by the early 1970s the militant poor had come to exercise their own powerful reciprocal influence on both organizations. This powerful impact of the militant poor on democratic political parties in Jamaica is exceptional, because it is sharply at variance with traditional patterns of class representation in democratic societies. Remarking on this phenomenon of militant lower-class influence on Jamaican political parties, one commentator has observed that

> this hard core party support is characterized by great intensity of feeling, emotional loyalties, and aggressive and combative sentiments of support. It is sustained by a number of factors that mirror the role of democratic organs in the Jamaican society. It has to be understood as a response to the need for power on the part of the majority classes (workers, peasants, unemployed, and petty traders and artisans). Unlike other political cultures in the Western industrial countries where middle class and middle income persons are overrepresented in activist party membership compared to less educated, lower socioeconomic groups, the reverse is the case in Jamaica. Hard core party membership . . . underrepresents the middle class and overrepresents the poorer classes (both urban and rural).[9]

This access to power by the poorer classes was achieved by demanding the satisfaction of their needs in return for "their votes, their loyalty, their commitment, and their enthusiasm".[10] Some of this fervour in the service of politics took the form of badness-honour; it was used to both threaten and beckon political sponsors who needed the votes and political support of the urban poor. It should be remembered that threat to political patrons lay in the urban poor's largely unchecked militancy and tendency to insubordination. At the same time, of course, politicians were drawn to the poor precisely because these very traits were politically useful. Hence, as the politics of the 1970s became more extreme and ideologically polarized, lower-class badness-honour was both nemesis and friend to party bosses and power-seeking politicians.

In the early years of the decade, then, the hustling, catch-as-catch-can culture of the streets was being felt more and more inside both political parties. The greedy, opportunist, and even mercenary culture that had come to define the life of the desperate poor saturated the political parties at the street and constituency levels. As ghetto figures and other notables became street-level political activists and enforcers, the desperate survivalism and inclination to predation, so evident among the lumpenproletariat, found expansive room for political expression.

Still, "badmanism" and a pirate's sensibility were not peculiar to the militant poor. The violent disposition of the hardened lumpenproletariat and other hard-core supporters was matched by the histrionics and outlaw populism of party leaders and political organizers. Indeed, as the lumpenproletariat grew in social and political importance, and as the leadership of the parties resorted to a combative populism to win votes, predation and factionalism became routine in the political culture of the JLP and the PNP. In both parties, the violent culture of the street gang, the bandit's eye for easy booty and the supplicants' fawning loyalty to patrons who "fed" them with benefits intensified the raw, mercenary quality in the island's winner-take-all politics.

In the early 1970s, the histrionics of a predatory lumpenproletariat in search of political booty and the showmanship and braggadocio of political sponsors in search of votes grew more intense. Older distinctions between the parties that were based on a blend of messianic personalities, contrasting policies and ideological differences now counted for less, as the mercenary, cutthroat norms of street life saturated the parties in these years. Here loyalty to the party leader as patron fed political passion. As a consequence,

> This intensity of loyalty ties often spills over into combative, aggressive and violent defense of the party and its leaders against real or imagined threats from the opposition or alternative party. The party leaders and the party are defended with violence against criticism and ridicule. Critics and detractors of the party and its leaders are defined as despicable devils deserving of violent aggression in defence of the party and the leader's political honour.[11]

By the early 1970s, such displays of badness-honour had become *de rigueur* in urban politics and party culture. Indeed, political activists and leaders bid up their dramaturgic claims to respect in these years. The histrionics of partisan competition with its outlaw tinge confirmed, for friend and foe alike, that politics in urban Jamaica were increasingly being regulated by a stunning cultural imperative: the adoption, on all sides, of martial identities.[12]

They became the carriers of new social claims and formed the basis for the allocation of status honour.

Politics and access to power on the hustings therefore paid increasing homage to an aggressive corporeal etiquette. An important claim to personal authority now relied on a capacity to deploy militant social identities that would cause others to take pause and possibly concede respect. The lumpen-proletariat led the way in proclaiming this new right to honour among the poor. State agents backed this normative turn in the slums and comple-mented this endorsement with their own forms of badness-honour. This legitimation of outlawry by state agents had two effects: it won the politi-cal support of violent supplicants and awed them with the political patrons' equally militant claims to respect.[13]

In the society of the mobilized poor, we have seen how it had become customary to break laws and to flout social customs as ways of decrying racial and social injustice. Outlawry, social indiscipline and violation of norms of respectability were justified in the name of rolling back imbalances in social power and affirming the poor's right to honour. Badness-honour among the poor had therefore become a retort to unequal power, class dis-crimination and ethnic injustice in Jamaica.[14] Now rival politicians seeking office and trying to establish their credentials with the militant poor matched this outlawry in the slums.

This showmanship by politicians helped win political office; it also worked to regulate the delicate relations of power between boisterous sup-plicants on the one hand, and their party sponsors on the other. That is, militant supplicants' irrepressible displays of aggression in the quest for polit-ical booty sometimes provoked disciplinary responses from their patrons. In Jamaica's hierarchical clientelist politics, in which authority relations mat-tered, too-feisty loyalists who overstepped their bounds and encroached on the prerogatives of the party boss were punished.

Political power holders brooked no threat even from their own backers. Consequently, "increasingly coercive methods are used to control even rank and file supporters within the respective political parties' power domain. The enforcers of these coercive means of political control . . . acquired increasing power in the political system, that at times threatens the control and personal hegemony of the political bosses."[15] Braggadocio, threats of violence and ritual aggressive displays by middle-class politicians set the oral-kinetic terms under which equally martial supplicants were compelled to grant due deference and social respect to political sponsors. The aggressive histrionics of politicians tempered violent displays from below while affirming the patrons' own right to deference. In this way, displays of badness-honour among party notables and middle-class organizers gradually established, in the eyes of the poor, the terms of submission to power, the basis for the cultural authenticity of political patrons and the legitimacy of their right to rule in the violent urban cauldron.

Those relations were driven by mutual need: politicians needed votes and the muscle of their backers, while supplicants needed the benefits and the political protection of their sponsors. However, as these relations unfolded over the post-war years it became clear that it was the urban poor who were dictating the terms for evolving claims to cultural authenticity and personal respect. After all, advocates of radical black nationalism and champions of social justice for the poor were typically from the slums of Kingston, and it was their cultural defiance that forced state agents and the wider society to take note of this important cultural turn.

State agents adapted themselves to that lead while boldly harnessing the violent gamesmanship among the poor. Racial agonism in the slums and a violent street culture dictated the etiquette by which votes were sought; they defined how constituencies could be secured against challengers; and they set the terms for claiming an heroic individualism within and beyond partisan engagements. In light of this development, it is clear that a boisterous gamesmanship and violent political etiquette had migrated from the slums to compel the wider society. This culture of violence forced the society to take contentious notice, and its entry into the political fray was both welcomed and condemned.

Despite a seeming dictation from the streets, the moral influence of the poor on the political parties was nothing without political sponsorship from above. For as the PNP and JLP intervened in the ghetto to integrate the social forces there, mass pressures for material assistance and stubborn cultural assertions by the poor drove both parties to respond, often with positive measures. The parties employed both violence and predation against the disloyal poor while disbursing benefits and showing solicitude for the cultural complaints and moral culture of the loyalist poor.

This double compulsion for material benefits and cultural recognition facilitated the parties' contained incorporation of popular demands. It also gave the Jamaican state its well-known populist appearance. Not only did top leaders and cadres articulate the moral and political claims of the poor, they also mirrored the libidinal dramaturgies that were the stock-in-trade of supplicants in the slums. From the 1940s right up through the early 1970s this meant not only the articulation of mass needs by means of an overheated language, but the adoption by parties of an etiquette that mimicked the norm of badness-honour in urban Jamaica.

The Theory and Practice of Badness-Honour

In Jamaica, badness-honour refers to a distinct dramaturgy in which claimants to respect and social honour employ intimidation and norm-disrupting histrionics to affirm their right to an honour contested or denied. Although currently high rates of homicide and lawlessness have encouraged pundits on the island to associate these developments with a peculiarly aggressive Jamaicanness, acts of badness-honour are not uniquely Jamaican.[16] On the contrary, such practices should be seen as a mundane but ubiquitous weapon of the weak. At this juncture, it may be useful to elaborate on the specificity of what I have been calling "badness-honour".

Acts of badness-honour occur among the poor across all societies. It is the assertive form that moral alienation takes in contexts of inequality and social domination. It is the social behaviour that can result from sharp deficits in power, group respect and material well-being. In post-war urban Jamaica, public aggressive displays of personal violence and defensive postures to secure an imperilled self in the ghetto qualify as forms of badness-honour. Thus the racial indignation of the Rastafarians and the nihilistic outlawry of the rude boys were quintessential expressions of badness-honour in the 1960s. Their dramaturgy and that of allied groups confirm badness-honour as a social norm and a publicly displayed repertoire employed by alienated, but highly mobilized social forces who want to change their disadvantaged circumstances.

Badness-honour is evident therefore in the public, kinetic expression and corporeal gestures employed by social agents in contexts of domination and social inequality. Badness-honour is a repertoire that employs language, facial gesture, bodily poses and an assertive mien to compel rivals or allies to grant power, concede respect, accord deference or satisfy material want. It is therefore a cultural style that may be used to intimidate others through menacing or histrionic gestures. It may also be employed to bargain and negotiate the terms by which power, social respect, deference or resources are granted or denied to claimants. Acts of badness-honour constitute a gestural-symbolic system and a carrier of moral communication. Through badness-honour, inter-subjective understanding about the basis of identity and the terms of power are conveyed by intensive corporeal acts of speech and gesture. Such acts exercise moral compulsion on social subordinates, group allies and social superiors.

While the norm of badness-honour may employ violence, it does not rely solely on the use of violence to be effective. Ominous threat rather than actual violence is the stock-in-trade of those exhibiting badness-honour. Threats and histrionics to overawe and compel are often enough to secure the claims of practitioners. Of course, when these compulsions are inadequate, they are indeed buttressed by resort to violence.

As a repertoire in the arsenal of disparate groups, violent forms of badness-honour may well be amplified where harsh social domination and sharp inequalities exist. Provoked by conflicts and social tensions in these societies, exponents of badness-honour may employ histrionic gestures to rally allies or to intimidate and overawe adversaries. These exponents, who can come from diverse social backgrounds, typically apply these compulsions not through the violent machinery of the state, but through the aggressive display of unpredictable and *ominous corporeal power.*

Gestures of badness-honour may form the basis for a heroic individualism in contexts of deprivation. And while badness-honour is a form of personal charisma, it is surely the dark side of that magnetism. Indeed, where an optimistic populist charisma had once been the primary stock-in-trade of politicians and notables in Jamaica, that heroism was rapidly eclipsed in the post-war period by a snarling, violence-provoking disposition among both urban politicians and their ghetto supplicants. The former used violence-ridden histrionics to overawe and compel respect from boisterous, reckless supplicants; the latter embraced a similar aggression both as a mark of social distinction and as leverage on discriminatory political processes.

Badness-honour is therefore a variable repertoire available to disparate groups engaged in struggles to protect or claim imperilled values, such as personal and group respect, status rights, or material want. Badness-honour is a major weapon of the powerless for whom corporeal aggression is a real form of social power. As commentators remind us, the powerless, in contexts of domination, may not tolerate abuses indefinitely. If degraded and abused they have often resorted to volcanic oral-kinetic expressions as compensatory forms of leverage over both status allies and power holders.[17]

Yet badness-honour, for all its usefulness to the poor, is not a resource available only to the disadvantaged. Indeed, power holders have also found this repertoire useful for their purposes. Slave-masters, colonial authorities, rural patrons and party bosses in postcolonial societies have also employed it for their own designs. Hence, both rulers and the ruled resort to badness-honour and they may do so in contexts where traditional values and the societies that uphold them are subject to challenge. These societies with massive and unyielding inequalities in power, honour and wealth are the ones most likely to provoke dramatic and hard-core expressions of badness-honour among both rulers and the ruled.

Despite this association between badness-honour and traditional settings, badness-honour as a repertoire of *subaltern* power may also appear in modern and highly industrialized societies. As the activities of street gangs in Los Angeles and the violent lyrics of "gangsta rap" in the Unites States make clear, affirmation of a violent, stylized outlawry *in the name of rescuing a racially impugned self* is not limited to small, economically underdeveloped countries. Moreover, as the American example also makes clear, acts of badness-honour appear in democratic as well as authoritarian political systems. Badness-honour is therefore a distinct repertoire of power and a tool of politics available to disparate groups enmeshed in power relations in many societies.

Despite these generic qualities, and the ubiquity that identifies badness-honour as a worldwide cultural phenomenon, mere domination and inequality need not lead to the adoption of this dissident norm by the poorer classes. Poverty and economic hardship are not sufficient conditions for the display of badness-honour. That may depend on other determinants. Depending on the history of the country in question, disadvantaged groups can respond to domination without resorting to our description of badness-honour.

Popular responses to domination have included revolutionary activity, political self-organization or covert non-compliance. Poverty has also led to resignation, disengagement or even flight by the poor. Deprivation need not lead to rebellion, and it need not provoke the kind of outlawry discussed here. Badness-honour seems to be only one of many political options exercised by the disadvantaged, as they respond to different kinds of social domination. Political indeterminacy, not political regularities, seems to shape the options the poor employ. It may be that only when a combination of factors exists in poor countries that norms of badness-honour are chosen over other political options.

It is arguable, for instance, that badness-honour in poor countries tends to occur in contexts where the exercise of power is harsh, pre-emptive and ubiquitous, yet not so totally monopolistic that popular defiance becomes impossible. Badness-honour may occur in contexts where certain cultural traditions are absent, while other relevant ones are decisively present. Thus, badness-honour that is reflected in widespread outlawry may be heightened in settings where a sustained martial and revolutionary tradition among the people is *lacking,* even as intense social and political mobilization of the poor is acutely present.

Similarly, badness-honour in the form that I have described may also unfold in peripheral societies where individualism and personal ambition for upward mobility are intensely shared and are among the premium values of that society. Badness-honour is likewise facilitated in contexts where the status-honour of the mobilized poor is actively impugned and degraded, and their material wants stubbornly denied. Indeed, acts of badness-honour may become the typical defiant response from below where state and non-state actors mobilize the poor for political agendas, even as these state actors simultaneously throttle – by violence and co-optation – the poor's ambitions for democracy, cultural self-regard and material betterment.

Badness-honour as outlawry and challenge to traditional norms of civility may similarly thrive in contexts where cultural self-regard and social cooperation among the deprived population are contradictory and ambiguously felt in contexts of high competitive individualism. In such societies, acts of badness-honour may take on idiosyncratic guises. In these contexts, personalist defiance and group agonism may displace other options in the challenge to political power.

Indeed, highly personalized forms of badness-honour and group agonism may occur and assume particular force in contexts where face-to-face encounters, ethnicity and other intimate interpersonal relations are the dominant bases for social interaction, the distribution of power and the granting of social respect. In such contexts, affective ties and deeply felt ethnic sentiments, rather than impersonal norms, usually govern the formation of identities and the access to power. In sum, badness-honour of the kind discussed here may thrive where significant social power and respect derive from networks of interpersonal ties and forms of intimate power relations, rather than from the play of distant, impersonal ties or bureaucratic-organizational routines.

As a consequence, norms of badness-honour leading to social outlawry may well be invigorated in those traditional societies where oral cultures remain strong, where patron-client relations persist, and where demands for personal loyalty and the securing and protection of reputations are intense and achieved through small social networks and face-to-face interactions. Such societies, with their struggles over wealth, personal power, and individual and group honour, can provoke intense and sustained displays of badness-honour among the poor as they seek to rectify social disadvantages and alter relations which injure their reputation and social standing and bar their access to power.

Where ethnic discrimination and resistance to it are decisively part of this contestation, such societies may provoke not just conflicts over wealth and political power, but also acute disputes over personal reputation, public honour and social worth. Hence, where the urban poor are alienated and highly mobilized around issues of ethnic discrimination, they may turn to norms of badness-honour as means to redress grievances, particularly those pertaining to disparities in power and obstacles to individual or group achievement.

In such circumstances, the play of power may operate at such a level of intimacy in the lives of the downtrodden that a concerted and focused group opposition to systemic power is blocked. In these contexts, the intimate play of power can elicit atomized, throttled responses that are informed by either blind anger toward patrons or by cunning efforts to align with or evade them in order to minimize hardships.

In Jamaica, this throttling has produced a distinct oppositional form in the postcolonial period: episodic protests, desperate supplicancy, exaggerated loyalty to patrons, and deep personal enmity for party bosses and their supporters. The overall effect of this disposition is that instead of provoking concerted action from the united poor, this patronizing power elicits throttled and atomized responses from them.

Equally significant is that where authoritarian power refuses to redress the personal agony of social agents, this power runs the risk that sympathetic elites may well view the norm of badness-honour as a politically justified moral response. In some instances, these elites may even mimic the histrionics of badness-honour in the ongoing conflict over power, wealth and honour.

It should come as no surprise, therefore, that in societies such as Jamaica, acts of badness-honour did spread to groups beyond the slums. Indeed, as conventional norms weaken in the face of challenges to them by influential subcultures, sections of the wider population may begin to adopt the norms of the dissident and influential subculture.

As peripheral states and societies are shaped more and more by the social determinants discussed above, they may find it increasingly difficult to repel mass pressures for cultural recognition and social equality. Moreover, as state agents and sympathetic elites in these places increasingly accommodate the moral values of alienated subcultures, allegiance to traditional civic norms may be eroded even more. Badness-honour is likely, therefore, to be invigorated when sympathetic elites and parties lend their legitimacy to this repertoire of power. Such elite groups do so by championing popular grievances and mimicking the norms of aggrieved and stigmatized groups. In these contexts, cultural counter-penetration from below by influential subcultures may in time subvert civic norms and values.

Finally, it is worth observing that as intensifying social conflicts and the accumulation of social power by the poor unfold, such developments may induce panic and political retaliation by property-holding groups and the normatively threatened middle class. Where such groups recoil from politics because of fear, or where they act to defend their class interests, these defensive responses – ranging from capital flight to cultural sneering at the poor – may in turn spur further acts of outlawry among the impugned but socially mobilized poor.

In summary, badness-honour may be encouraged in peripheral societies like Jamaica where social mobility and racial honour are denied the black majority, even as premium norms of individualism, ambition for upward mobility and the political mobilization of the disadvantaged are *simultaneously* affirmed. Consequently, where face-to-face communication is significant; where patron-client relations are salient; where propertied classes retreat or strike back against threats to property and modal values; and where state elites increasingly accommodate alienated subcultures or ethnic groups that are claimants to power and respect, it is likely that the norm of badness-honour will be invigorated.

Outlawry and Democratic Socialism

Given these complex determinants, there is no doubt that badness-honour in Jamaican political culture was given a powerful boost in the PNP's 1972 political campaign and by the aftermath of its electoral victory. That party's campaign for office invigorated the culture of badness-honour and with it the social power of the alienated poor. With Michael Manley as its new political leader, the PNP rallied with particular intensity to the cause of the poor.[18]

It is important to note that even though the PNP retained its strategy of appealing to a broad range of social classes, this multi-class strategy did not blunt the PNP's intensified identification with the rebellious urban poor. Indeed, between 1969 and 1972 the urban youth and the lumpenproletariat won special attention from party organizers and activists. During its public rallies, constituency-level organizing, annual conventions and stump speeches, the party's symbolism and rhetoric were attuned to the culture of badness-honour and were closely identified with moral sentiments in the slums. The long-neglected sufferers' cause in Jamaica thus found public symbolic validation in the recuperated martial politics of the PNP.

This development was apparent in the run-up to the 1972 election. A populist campaign marked by the playing of reggae music saw command performances by popular recording artists and the appropriation of the iconography of the Rastafarians. The PNP rode to power on the campaign slogan of "Better Must Come" to the disadvantaged poor.[19] That party's stunning political victory, in which the urban poor and its hardened lumpenproletariat assumed an ascendant role, left little doubt about the poor's importance to national politics.[20]

In that political campaign – more than in any prior instance – the party intensified its ideological and political association with the urban poor and especially with sections of the pro-PNP lumpenproletariat. In the politically polarized moment that defined the 1972 election, political gunmen commingled with militant activists and with well-heeled middle-class politicians from both parties. Opportunistic supplicants and the ne'er-do-wells from the slums jostled for power and advantage alongside workers, small farmers and unemployed youths seeking a better life. In this pivotal moment and its immediate aftermath, it was the lumpen elements supporting both parties that became the predominant cultural-political force in the capital city and in the country. Their cultural impact was unmistakable in the histrionics of the rival party leaders and in the jousting, aggressive behaviour of street-level supporters at public rallies and in community deference to loyalist gunmen's violent defence of garrisoned political communities.[21]

At this moment, then, both parties bowed to the newly affirmed social and cultural emancipation of the urban poor. But it was the PNP with its message of uplift and its championing of the cause of the "sufferers" that carried the day and increased the value of social outlawry as a form of political protest and social power. Social dissidence in the slums and the etiquette of badness-honour there had won the near-unqualified endorsement of a major party in its challenge to the status quo.[22] Under PNP sponsorship, the alienated antagonistic norms of its partisan slum-dwellers were celebrated as a vital force for changing the balance of social power in the society. In these circumstances, the so-called roots culture of the people in all its variations – and especially in its guise of badness-honour – therefore won free rein. Again, although JLP activists and party leaders abetted this cultural invigoration in the slums, only with the PNP's ascension to power in 1972 did the norm of badness-honour secure the kind of legitimacy hitherto unseen in Jamaican politics.[23]

Still, for all its popularity in the slums and working-class areas, this partisan legitimation of cultural rebellion among the poor did not go unchallenged. For while the parties had long ago folded forms of badness-honour into their political repertoire, other political actors and moral agents expressed revulsion for what they regarded as unchecked outlawry in the slums. For example, previous governments headed by the PNP's Norman Manley in the 1950s and the JLP's Hugh Shearer in the 1960s had bitterly denounced expressions of badness-honour in the slums, particularly when they were beyond the reach of partisan politics.[24] After 1972, however, badness-honour as a political etiquette and repertoire of power had been publicly embraced and given validation by the new government.

One consequence of this explicit public embrace was that assertions of uncivil outlawry – which had largely been confined to the slums and working-class precincts – moved out from their spatial and moral quarantine. Having achieved cultural leadership over workers, middle-class youths, students and sections of the intelligentsia in the late 1960s, ghetto exponents of badness-honour received official and public legitimation in the heat of political battle. Thus the PNP's cultural orientation, political message and policy positions seemed to bless the norm of badness-honour in the slums as a politically appropriate response to social oppression.

Like no political campaign before or since, the PNP's successful bid for power openly identified the party with the lumpenproletariat, then the leading exponent of badness-honour in the society.[25] This contingent was the most alienated group in the country, and the PNP, in its bid for power, identified with this group's cause and mimicked its political style. In the aftermath of that watershed election, Michael Manley and PNP cadres immersed the party more deeply into the urban ghetto and into the alienated subcultures of the urban poor. Cadres, organizers and top party figures articulated the slogans, wore the garb, uttered the epithets and bore the grievances of disenfranchised and impoverished groups.[26]

As the foregoing has shown, by 1974 the PNP had moved to the left by proclaiming a policy of democratic socialism. Yet in a compelling irony, this declaration that championed social justice and increased political participation for the Jamaican poor, did not bring democracy, social justice or socialism. Rather, after 1974, the violent etiquette that informed the struggle for spoils and political power seeped into the clash between pro-PNP socialists and pro-JLP supporters of the free enterprise model. The country therefore witnessed the novel occurrence in which the moral culture of badness-honour was wedded to the contest between socialist and capitalist ideas.

One consequence of this fusion was the deepening of piratic instincts among PNP loyalists as they sought handouts and political booty, this time in the name of democratic socialism. Thus even as the PNP's socialism brought benefits to small farmers, workers and small entrepreneurs, the lumpenproletariat also secured their share of benefits.[27] In time, they would put their own imprimatur on the local, community-level meaning of democratic socialism, as its ideals ran up against the violent, factional party competition and the predatory moral culture of the street.

But PNP policies and ideology did more than just recognize the material needs of the poor. The party also signalled its public approval of a trait that had long been a mainstay of ghetto life and politics: braggadocio and the thuggish use of violence. The growth of the latter in Jamaican political life seemed to confirm that the PNP was prepared to put both threats and violence in the service of its reformist political ideals.[28] As such, an unflattering but usable socio-political inheritance such as badness-honour could be made to serve the lofty reformist political goals that were being spelled out by Michael Manley, the articulate and charismatic PNP leader. A consequence of this expediency was the strange fusion of the culture of badness-honour with the party's long-standing progressivist orientation.[29]

At first blush this bond between the politics of outlawry and the politics of radical political reform along socialist lines might appear unseemly to the casual observer. How is it possible, one might ask, for a party with a durable tradition of seeking the moral and material uplifting of the poor through rational socialist pedagogy, to combine that radical and modernist tradition with the etiquette of nihilism and violent outlawry? The foregoing text has offered an answer to this unseemly pairing. The pattern of predation politics in Jamaica's political rule embraced the moral culture of the militant poor, set them against each other and made the delivery of scarce benefits – not the refinement of a democratic order on the basis of an enlightened and informed mass public – the supreme political value.

This destructive politics arose in the context of an underdeveloped society and a backward economy. As we have seen, Jamaica's former slave economy and society triggered conflicts in the late 1930s that set militant workers and alienated lower classes against their colonial overlords in a successful struggle for political independence. The result, however, was a political sovereignty in which two-party political representation took the form of predation, internecine violence and the managed solicitation of mass needs.

By 1974 both parties and their supporters had become inured to this tradition. Moreover, the PNP's politics of socialist reform after 1974, while always a basis for distinctions between itself and the JLP, were necessarily influenced by the island's infrastructural and socio-political inheritances. Not the least among these was the tendency to personalist political leadership and the inclination to messianic forms of loyalty among political supporters. This inheritance of a backward economic infrastructure that could foster no meaningful economic development and a culture of political messianism helped induce a violent winner-take-all political culture. Against this background, therefore, it is apparent that the PNP's socialist declaration occurred in a political party whose political culture was very much antithetical to socialist ideals.

Despite this shortcoming, however, it is worth remembering that historically inherited structures were not the only factors influencing PNP politics in the early 1970s. Indeed, PNP reformism, with its pedagogic content that sought the enlightenment and liberation of the labouring classes, was no passive victim of these inheritances. Such inheritances could be reshaped and moulded to suit the challenge of political management in contexts of underdevelopment. Power holders, for example, could harness seemingly contrary and inimical (to high ideals) socio-political tendencies in the society. Thus PNP rational progressivism in the years 1944–72 could and did find common cause with seemingly antithetical practices, including accommodation to nihilism in the streets, embrace of anti-democratic values, and resort to mayhem and the outlawry of badness-honour in politics. More than that, in the violent winner-take-all culture of the urban cauldron, both outlawry and rational PNP reformism might exhibit affinities. That is, exponents of socialism might regard outlawry among loyalists in the slums as a resource for enhancing and strengthening the party's rational and radical reformist agenda. In this sense, PNP supplicants might come to view their outlawry as means to a larger, worthy cause.

Similarly, strategizing party socialists might countenance menace, violence and badness-honour, if only to secure the party's elusive socialist ideal in a politically charged and unforgiving urban environment that rewarded only the armed and the martially prepared. Moreover, the internationalization of Jamaican politics in this period abetted the violence, deepened the ideological rift between JLP and PNP partisans, and invited opposition from the American government, from financial institutions such as the US Agency for International Development and the American Export-Import Bank, and from the US media.[30]

As the PNP intensified its socialist orientation at home, backed African liberation movements abroad and forged closer political ties with Cuba, opponents of the government at home and abroad accused it of trying to impose communism on the island.[31] These anti-communist attacks on the PNP fed partisan enmities in the 1970s as each side denounced the other for being the surrogate of a hostile foreign power and the conduit of its presumably alien values. Hence, the PNP depicted the JLP as an agent of US imperialism and apologist for a rapacious capitalism bent on undermining the PNP's policy of democratic socialism.[32] This sensibility was aptly reflected in a notable and highly partisan speech in the run-up to the fall 1976 general elections, when PNP leader Manley warned his detractors at home and abroad that no matter the opposition to his radical policies, "We are not for sale!"[33] The JLP was as fierce in its defence of free enterprise and liberal democracy in its denunciation of the PNP as an unmistakably communist party.[34]

The result of this ideological fervour was not only political recrimination, but also resort to violence to deter opponents of a sacred cause. The JLP and its supporters saw themselves as defenders of capitalism and freedom and this ardour encouraged attacks on PNP supporters. Likewise, for the PNP, the struggle for socialism meant warfare in the streets against a sworn enemy of its cause. Consequently, rather than being incompatible, for the PNP, gangsterism and socialism were joined in a complementary unity in the ghetto.

This fusion of mayhem and progressivism was not unique to the 1970s. As the foregoing chapters have shown, between 1944 and 1972, both PNP strategists and loyalists on the ground married outlawry to the party's left-leaning and reformist, rational ideals. One consequence of this coupling in the 1970s is that it may not have been too difficult for over-loyal PNP partisans to regard violence and acts of badness-honour as unfortunate but necessary means for achieving socialism and progressive reform.

For PNP partisans of the day, this was especially the case both because of the broad support that the JLP enjoyed and because of the equally fierce commitment to violence and outlawry among JLP activists. From the standpoint of PNP loyalists and leaders, there was no contradiction in pursuing socialist goals and engaging in violent outlawry. After all, in the PNP's view, a venal, violent and politically reactionary JLP that would stop at nothing to achieve its questionable capitalist goals had to be met with equal force if a progressive programme of reform was to have any chance of implementation.

As a result, decades-long PNP socialist ideals had necessarily to draw on acts of badness-honour in urban Jamaica if only to secure political ideals as well as protect coveted and imperilled political territory and personnel from the depredations of a demonic JLP. To be successful under these circumstances, a radical reform agenda required not just appropriate policies and ideologies, but also shock troops to secure political territory and create a wider social space for the pursuit of radical reform. In these circumstances, badness-honour, social outlawry and sheer thuggery found affinities with PNP socialism.

This consonance of political gangsterism and grand political ideology was not peculiar to the PNP, however. Unleashing political mayhem in the name of a world-historical ideology – in this case belief in capitalist democracy – was equally true of JLP politics in the 1970s. It is arguable that JLP partisans sought out PNP loyalists for punishment not only as persons who stood in the way of benefits, but also as political aliens infected by a dangerous ideology. The JLP's longstanding anti-communist outlook habituated its loyalists to think of the PNP as confiscatory and heedless of personal freedoms, and this outlook invigorated the struggle for benefits. Cold War ideology therefore added its taint to the war over spoils. In retrospect, this influence of the Cold War on Jamaican politics and on politics in the slums seemed wholly negative, as it gave each side a further pretext for engaging in political murder and the erosion of civil liberties in the slums.

Despite affinity between outlawry and left-wing PNP politics, however, it did little to ease inner party factionalism, especially between the political bosses and their supporters in the ghetto. Consistent with the evolving party culture, PNP loyalists in the slums had embraced outlawry as both the precondition for and the embodiment of progressive politics in the 1970s. But this fealty to party norms that allowed the faithful to make quick and violent work of their opponents on the political hustings – while remaining committed to their party's socialist agenda – also had unintended consequences. Political fanaticism provoked loyalists on both sides to extremes of unchecked violence, and this fervour emboldened outlaw types who escaped the suzerainty of partisan politics to enter the fray to satisfy their own mercenary appetites. Of course, state agents used sharp measures to quench this violent enthusiasm in the slums. In the first instance, states of emergency and curfews quelled the inter-party violence provoked by over-loyal partisans.[35] In the second, the army and police were loosed on the non-partisan criminals engaging in street crime in Kingston.[36]

Real differences in the parties' political culture abetted this violent agonism in Kingston's slums. Despite broad similarities between the JLP and the PNP in terms of shared culture of predation, clientelism and badness-honour, the PNP had more difficulty than the JLP in quelling the mobilized rank and file, as well as street-level contingents that had signed on to its agenda. Unlike the JLP's internal political culture, which emphasized the sole and unquestioned authority of top leaders such as Alexander Bustamante and his successors, internal PNP culture did not permit top party officials to ride roughshod over the concerns of supporters, including those from the slums. Indeed, the party's decades-long progressivism and socialist mobilization of the poor had given socialist-inspired contingents among them and their agents in the party far more ideological leverage over the PNP and its leaders than could be exercised by their counterparts in the JLP. This relative equilibrium in the relationship between the PNP and its supporters in the slums made for factionalism and conflicts with its rank and file. And while such disagreements could produce sharp reversals and alteration of party policy inimical to the poor, the PNP generally encouraged and tolerated a greater degree of open challenge to leaders and policies by its lower-income supporters than was possible in the opposition party.[37]

The PNP's turn toward the alienated urban slum-dwellers and the party's sharper identification with non-conformist urban groups in the 1970s was consistent with the PNP's decades-long ties to these groups and its championing of radical reforms to benefit them. PNP legitimation of badness-honour in the early 1970s thus merely continued, at a higher level of intensity, unique socio-political relations with its urban rank and file that had been established since the 1940s.[38]

Those relations not only included the disposition of benefits and the appropriation of popular ideas, but also saw both parties' recruitment of anomic figures and rebellious groups in the slums. Thus the PNP's etiquette of badness-honour and the party's unabashed championing of the moral and political concerns of the ghetto after 1972 was quite consistent with the party's protracted engagement with the urban poor. That relationship entailed negotiation, bargaining, mobilization, expulsion, punishment and integration of alienated forces in the turbulent social spaces in Kingston's ghettos. In this context, the PNP's intensified identification with the lumpenproletariat, and with badness-honour after 1972, was no mere opportunist association by a party that was unfamiliar with the urban poor and the ways of ghetto politics.

That long-standing association induced in party leaders not just the populist stance associated with heroic leaders fighting the evil of social inequality; it also inspired these leaders to deploy acts of badness-honour freighted with potent claims to due respect and deference from violent supplicants. The character of contestation in urban Jamaica caused these politicians to assume martial, combative attitudes. However, such expressions were not merely political theatre; they were also forms of cultural currency that regulated relations between powerful patrons and loyal but inordinately assertive supplicants.

Populism and Badness-Honour

In this regard, it is necessary to make an important distinction between the uses of populism and the uses of badness-honour by party leaders. For while the etiquette of populism and the norms of badness-honour do interact in Jamaican politics, they are not identical. Populism, on the one hand, rallies the poor to remedy social injustices through ideological and other ethico-political claims.[39] Concern for political fairness and claims of social justice have always informed populist ideology. Such claims are typically defended by appeal to reason and by reference to factual evidence of social inequality.

Populism should therefore be regarded as a generic political ideology because of its reliance on reason and because of its willingness to offer world-referencing evidence and justifications for its claims.[40] The morality of populism, then, is largely based on cognitive principles and on claims to rationality, even if its expressive form may sometimes provoke "mindless" acts of badness-honour.

The claims of populism are therefore primarily about creating social change, offering an agenda for reform and soliciting support through appeal to reason. This is still the case, even though populism signals to both the well-to-do and the poor that mass mobilization and provocation of lower-class dissatisfaction – not merely the hailing of reason – are also required to challenge and transform social inequality.

By contrast, acts of badness-honour involving the mobilization of the poor are somewhat different in their uses and effects. While they too are about making change and transforming social relations, displays of badness-honour primarily involve the unleashing of politically charged *emotions* and the exhibitionist display of *social aggression*. Unsuppressed rage, menacing threat and verbal abuse define badness-honour. These displays of violent emotion are neither spontaneous nor gratuitous. Rather, they are premeditated political acts enacted in contexts of unequal power to overawe and compel others.

As we have noted, acts of badness-honour occur in politically charged contexts where huge stakes involving individual or group honour and their power are at risk. Acts of badness-honour thus entail histrionic performances to retain or alter unequal power relations. In the eyes of perpetrators, those relations are susceptible to change by stirring fear and invoking awe through the use of a public-referencing and violent "body power". Acts of badness-honour therefore entail dramaturgic performances for explicit political ends: subverting or affirming the claims of power in contexts of social inequality. Thus while acts of badness-honour are about a strategy of politics, their coercive, intimidatory qualities confirm that they are not about appeals to reason or commitment to dialogue that entail justifying arguments or claims.

Furthermore, when political leaders resort to the etiquette of badness-honour, they are partly regulating deference and adjudicating claims of authority between patrons and clients. Expressions of badness-honour by the party elite are therefore part of the dramaturgy governing power relations among political leaders and their mobilized followers in the slums. Populism and badness-honour are thus similar in that they are repertories of power. However, badness-honour in Jamaican politics is unique for its enactment of a real battle within a wider war. Thus populist politicians fighting against social inequality in the wider society also find themselves battling for their own honorific lives with duelling supplicants from the slums who are fully prepared to test their sponsors' mettle with their own forms of badness-honour.

A clear sign of this pattern is evident in the relations between political enforcers and party bosses. Top party figures and veterans of the party civil wars such as the PNP's Michael Manley and the JLP's Edward Seaga exhibited in their personae the martial traits that linked badness-honour with its claims to personal honour and respect. Both men demanded and got respect for a brand of leadership in which martial personal qualities counted for much in the eyes of their aggressive ghetto supplicants. The resort to badness-honour for both Michael Manley and Edward Seaga was therefore a means of exercising moral leadership over alienated, rebellious and socially mobilized loyalists who respected this method of claiming power in the ghetto and were themselves inured to it.

With the PNP's ascension to power, badness-honour – an etiquette now affirmed in the name of the redemption of an unjust, errant society – became an acclaimed aesthetic and repertoire of public power. Because of this legitimation, a distinctive form of political communication that hitherto had been contained in relations of power in the island found open political recognition in public life. This fact gave badness-honour particular vigour, and also gave its exponents access to a much wider political terrain after 1972.

Because of a long-lived association between the ghetto and the political parties, slum-dwellers had therefore become agents of a decisive compulsion on Jamaican society and its political parties. After decades of involvement in the slums, years of close political and personal ties with notables in the ghetto, as well as sustained contact with lower-class subcultures, the political parties and their representatives were saturated with the cultural and political influences from the slums.

The gradual cultural transformation of the PNP was one result of this association. For although the PNP in the early 1970s was still regarded as a middle-class party with multi-class support, politics on the hustings and in the volatile urban constituencies around Kingston had moved it into a more intimate nexus with non-middle-class social forces there. By

1971–72 the social power of these forces at the street and constituency levels exerted a profound influence on the society and on the PNP's political culture.

In fact, this compelling social power outpaced the rival influence of the middle and upper classes at that time. Heightened social contradictions and direct pressures from the rebellious urban poor deepened their cultural penetration of the PNP and shifted the balance of cultural and social power away from traditionally hegemonic middle-class groups in favour of the mobilized slum-dwellers.

Outlawry and Group Honour: Rastafarians and the Criminally Employed

This change in the social weight of groups inside the party and in the country at large invigorated the social authority of the lumpenproletariat over competing groups such as the peasantry and the urban working class. In fact, the PNP's official blessing of badness-honour as a legitimate cultural expression in the struggle for power intensified the already considerable emancipation from conventional values that contingents of the urban poor had established for themselves in the post-war years. During these years the social conventions and moral codes which bound them to traditional values and the moral leadership of an earlier generation of PNP political actors were loosened considerably.

This emancipation from traditional norms was apparent in dissident innovations in music, dress styles, as well as in lifestyles, language forms and social identities. To one degree or another, these cultural forms were infused by the norm of badness-honour. These forms contained a corporeal etiquette and moral culture that sought to win social respect by means of publicly affirmed rituals in which the aggressive defence of an imperilled self was paramount. These forms of cultural expression in Jamaica typically asserted claims to a coherent, honourable and racially defined self in the face of an unjust political order.

We have already observed that the Rastafarian movement represented the iconic protest movement in post-war Jamaica. It was a leading exponent of a version of badness-honour in this period and norms of badness-honour were closely linked to the movement's emancipatory ideology. That ideology contained popular-democratic values that included the defence of "truth and rights" as well as norms of social justice and equal identity.

Because of the powerful association between their dramaturgy and their emancipatory political ideology, Rastafarians were rightly considered exemplars of the emergent norm of badness-honour in the society.

Yet it should be remembered that despite its anti-system character, the Rastafarian form of badness-honour did have a civic content. Largely because of its overwhelming concern with ending racial discrimination against the black majority and with establishing respect for democratic political values, the Rastafarian form of badness-honour contained an unnoticed but vital civic-democratic impulse.

For even as the Rastafarians made claims to racial honour and militantly rejected demands that they defer to their social betters, they also employed a discourse that invoked democratic norms. By linking respect for majority-group racial honour to the need for civic-democratic practices, the Rastafarians reminded Jamaican society of a vital nexus for the realization of democratic rule in the island. That conjunction, of course, made racial respect an integral part of democratic practice.

Thus while the Rastafarians' unconventional lifestyle, unusual religious orientation and radical otherness inclined the group to express norms of badness-honour and an exilic stance, this did not imply their complete divorce from positive social conventions and broad democratic alternatives. For all its disconnection from the conventional norms of Jamaican society and despite militant demands for repatriation to Africa, the Rastafarian movement represented a powerful democratizing thrust against a racially oppressive political order in Jamaica.

The Rastafarian movement therefore contained a positive and highly subversive agenda for change: its project for social reconstruction not only demanded the right to equal identity and respect for neglected democratic values in Jamaica, but also sought the firm coupling of law with social justice for the black majority. Again, it was this wedding of racial honour to vital democratic practices which made the Rastafarians the arch-enemy of the Jamaican system of predation.

In contrast to this positive project for reconstruction within Rastafarian forms of badness-honour, the lumpenproletariat that belonged to the criminal and political underworlds offered no clear redemptive agenda. For those engaged in criminal employment, plunder and the search for booty were unambiguous expressions of predatory self-help and survival at all costs. As victims of Jamaica's savage form of inequality this segment of the urban poor embraced gangsterism, thuggery and marauding crime.

In contrast to the Rastafarians, badness-honour among the criminally employed was predatory and uncivil. Their moral culture inclined the group not to the development of a democratic project, but to a murderous social cannibalism. Indeed, acts of badness-honour among this group in the early 1970s amounted to self-helping indiscipline and murderous crime. Still, despite this disabling circumstance, even this predation from below possessed an extremely weak, but nonetheless discernable politics of emancipation. For even as this hardened criminal class sought easy booty and committed vicious crimes, it too was preoccupied with overlapping issues of honour and respect in a class-divided and racially discriminatory society. On the one hand, as members of a criminal class, those in the underworld had to be concerned with establishing a pecking order and affirming respect for their role and status in the criminal trade. On the other, as members of a racially demeaned group and target of violent state power, the criminally employed were deeply invested in the black poor's broader quest for respect, status honour and material well-being.

These overlapping determinants of status honour caused those in the criminal underground to exhibit a curious form of badness-honour. Because their quest for status honour in the criminal underworld was intertwined with the black poor's broader search for group honour in the wider society, this overlapping, dual quest for honour made the criminally employed, whose motivation was partly criminal and partly political, a nemesis of the state. Their opposition to racial injustice and their willingness to use violence and crime to secure honour and booty in the criminal trade caused the criminally employed to resemble other ideologically motivated opponents of the regime that were engaged in protest crime.

It should be remembered that the criminally employed were a contingent of the lumpenproletariat that were doubly engaged in securing their rank in the underworld and in battling for racial respect in the wider society. Under these conditions this hardened contingent produced not only heroic outlaws, but also politically inspired criminals. The quest for rank and personal honour in the criminal underworld and its link to the broader search for racial respect for blacks in the society thus produced a stunning development: it created the potential for politicized outlawry and a turn to protest crime within the criminal underground. The activities of some hardened criminals from the slums revealed this nexus among protest, crime and power in Jamaica.

For the society as a whole, however, the 1960s and early 1970s left little doubt that crime and outlawry had become levers of social power and compulsion. As part of the community of the mobilized poor – several of whom shuttled between the criminal and political underground – this hardened criminal contingent no doubt saw in the manner of the PNP's ascension to office a powerful confirmation of the moral rightness of their lawless acts, and the ratification of their claims to material improvement. The same could be said for the sentiments of other contingents of the urban poor who were unemployed, engaged in petty entrepreneurship or working as part of the minimum-wage lumpenproletariat.

The PNP's victory and the etiquette with which it was achieved enhanced the social authority of all these groupings. The party's integration of gangsters valorized their form of badness-honour. The party's moral affiliation with the low-wage lumpenproletariat enhanced their social status; the PNP's embrace of the Rastafarians and the "culture of dread" seemed to give unqualified approval to the emancipation from social conventions and cultural norms within and beyond the slums. A variety of alienated and socially mobilized groups therefore discovered, in the PNP's victory, room for still greater emancipation from the conventions and moral compulsions of a society they deemed to be discriminatory, if not violently racist.

Lifting the Veil: Political Gunmen and Political Bosses

That the sufferers' cause and quest for emancipation found new authority in the PNP's victory should not obscure an important fact that bears repeating. Others in the party and in the wider society did, in fact, contest the moral deregulation in the slums and the elite accommodation to changing values there. Other party figures and moral leaders sharply countered the subversion of conventional values after 1972. These groups' paeans to conventional social codes sought to limit the moral deregulation among populations in the slums and elsewhere. Hence, whatever stimulus the PNP gave to the sufferers' cause was therefore rivalled by contrary though weakly supported sentiments within and beyond the parties.

Here again, such a conflicted stance among Jamaica's political and social elites was not new. In the post-war years, competing voices in the parties debated the most practical means for securing public order and obedience in the slums. Yet the flexible character of power in Jamaica was effective in large part because of this multi-vocal state ideology and because of the state's capacity to rule by straddling moral and political boundaries.

It will be remembered that this was a state that ruled by violence against the disloyal poor; that integrated criminal gangs into its ranks; and that retained solicitousness toward a dissident popular culture. This was also a state that had warlord agents who sanctioned norms of badness-honour while their respectable peers championed positive citizenship and respect for law.

It was this multi-vocal discourse which gave state predation in Jamaica its distinctive political and ideological character. After all, the parties' simultaneous articulation of opposing claims and their adoption of contrary policies effectively established the contrapuntal dynamics by which state predation operated in the country. These dynamics and the political dilation they entailed permitted both the ubiquity of the state and the extension of its political domination.

Hence, as the parties' street- and constituency-level mobilization of badness-honour clashed with lofty civic appeals for lawful behaviour, this stance – both for and against law and violence – had a curious effect. Rather than lead to a destructive incoherence in the state's legitimating ideology, dilation across moral and political boundaries facilitated ideological unity and social cohesion.

It was achieved, in part, through what I have called the state's multi-vocal ideology. In that ideology, contrary assertions of badness-honour and the use of political violence at the street level matched affirmation of democratic tenets and civic norms. This multi-vocality and its ideological oppositions became important organizing principles of predatory rule in Jamaica. Its dogma maintained that "law and order" policies and state violence were essential to holding the line against threats to civility and the rule of law. One negative result of this stance was that public outcry against spiralling violence in the society merely encouraged the Jamaican state – already complicit in the production of the violence – to employ and justify even more violence in the name of order and for the defence of a democratic society.

Despite the Jamaican state's unity through ideological oppositions, it is still the case that the parties' simultaneous encouragement and repudiation of badness-honour did send mixed moral messages to the wider society and to ghetto residents in particular. For as some state agents affirmed the importance of democracy and equal opportunity for all, other agents on the hustings undercut these claims by their pursuit of benefit politics and the violent party civil war.

In fact, neither party could escape the major moral predicament of predatory politics in Jamaica: the violent winner-take-all politics abetted and provoked a dysfunctional and generic badness-honour in the slums. In turn,
badness-honour among the poor invited violent crackdowns by the state;
that crackdown invariably encouraged more alienation and rebellion and the
expansion of the very outlawry and moral deregulation that exponents of
civility and democracy sought to curtail.

This vicious cycle had the effect of alienating contingents of the lumpenproletariat. But the cycle of violence and counter-violence also enhanced
the fortunes of thuggish recruits in the urban political underground. For
example, political gangs – already fully formed after the bitterly fought 1967
elections – assumed increased importance in party life. In the aftermath of
Michael Manley's victory, they assumed a more significant role in urban
constituency politics.

By 1972 in West Kingston, for example, this district was effectively off-
limits to the PNP and its supporters. The construction of the Tivoli Gardens
housing units, with its violent JLP gangs and partisan distribution of
dwellings only to loyalists, had closed the constituency to meaningful political competition. Gang violence and the residents' enjoyment of state
largesse barred the exercise of democracy in this now-captive constituency.
There over-voting and the stuffing of ballot boxes confirmed the *fait accom-
pli* of the party's earlier martial conquest of political territory between 1962
and 1972. By the latter year, residents in West Kingston had essentially
become a captive population corralled in what political analysts have rightly
called "garrison communities".[41]

One major consequence of this captivity was the stifling of political competition: it had a negative impact on the right to freely cast a vote in the constituency. Remarking on this development, one commentator noted that
"garrison-style voting was not apparent in West Kingston until 1972, after
the settlement of Tivoli Gardens, where 1,935 votes were returned for Eddie
Seaga compared to John Maxwell's".[42]

Credit for this unfortunate result was no doubt due to the acumen and
martial preparedness of Edward Seaga, the constituency representative. But
his victory was equally the achievement of the mobilized loyal lumpenproletariat ensconced in the Tivoli enclave. It was their martial effort on Seaga's
behalf that carried the JLP to victory in West Kingston in 1962, and in every
election thereafter. Likewise, it was the resort to violence perpetrated by
political thugs in PNP strongholds such as Central Kingston that made

effective JLP campaigning there difficult. During both the 1967 and 1972 elections, an infamous PNP gang deterred all challengers and wreaked havoc in Kingston.[43]

Known as the Garrison Gang, this group of PNP toughs carried out acts of intimidation, and perpetrated violence and mayhem on behalf of constituency representative, Michael Manley. This group from the political underground was apparently so effective in expelling JLP threats in Central Kingston in 1967 and 1972 that Manley felt compelled to thank them publicly for their services. Hence, at a public rally late in 1974 he commended the enforcers by their popular names: "I thank the Central Kingston Executive. I thank my Paseros of the Garrison – Skully, Val, Boots, Vinnie, Burry, Bernard, Spar, as a glory."[44] This spirited and public acknowledgement of the link between gangs and politics would prove embarrassing, as opponents of the PNP turned over a recorded tape of Manley's speech to JLP parliamentarians, who pounced on it to discredit the PNP leader.[45]

Notwithstanding the partisan nature of this disclosure, the airing of the connection between gangs and top party figures was significant. For although no public outcry greeted the news, its publication in the island's leading newspaper was a rare instance that confirmed the direct association between shadowy gunmen and a top party figure.[46]

The muted debate about the incident in Parliament, isolated press reports about it and the continuing realities of violent balloting after 1944 thus confirmed for a wider public what political insiders already knew. It confirmed for the politically insulated middle classes a stubborn but then little-known fact of Jamaican politics: the parties' connection to a criminal underworld that had been steadily incorporated into national politics. We turn in the next chapter to a closer examination of this underworld and its role as a constituency-level actor, and key players in national politics.

6

A Fettered Freedom
Warfare and Solidarity in the Ghetto

PREVIOUS CHAPTERS HAVE EMPHASIZED THE STEADY inflation of the social power of the urban poor across a number of social and political domains. This chapter examines in some detail the expansion of the authority of that branch of the lumpenproletariat that made up the political underworld associated with the political parties in the 1970s.

Inside this underworld were political henchmen, street-level enforcers and over-loyal fanatics. Regardless of their nefarious deeds, the duelling parties supported them all. Early in the decade this political underworld emerged as a major political actor and decisive force in the ghetto and in national politics. Encouraged in its growth by social polarization and ideological division between the political parties, this underworld, which had remained largely in the shadows and out of public view, emerged full-blown onto the political landscape with unparalleled destructive force. It thoroughly reshaped the character of urban political contestation and altered the moral temper and the trajectory of national politics. Along with other contingents of the poor, this party-based underworld left the remarkable cultural imprimatur of the urban lower class on politics and society in Jamaica.

The broadening influence of this armed party-linked lumpenproletariat could not have been accomplished without the active direction and complicity of the state and especially the political parties. After all, the political parties recruited notables from the most alienated elements of the lumpen-proletariat and encouraged the decentralized political violence for which members of this underworld had become famous. Moreover, in the 1970s, both organizations stoked new antipathies that drove rival militias and their fanatical allies into an orgy of violence and political frenzy. In that decade, the island's destructive winner-take-all politics found new strength in a renewed struggle between the JLP – then the allegedly demonic champion of free-enterprise capitalism – and the PNP, its presumed nemesis and expo-nent of democratic socialism.[1]

In this continuing battle for party dominance in Kingston, loyalists on both sides conducted a scorched-earth approach to political war in the streets, ostensibly in the defence of opposing political ideals. Yet, as we shall see in this and subsequent chapters, in this street war the contest was not pri-marily about a struggle between defenders of capitalism arrayed against those of socialism, even though a lively political rhetoric might have sug-gested otherwise. Rather, the politics of the 1970s – while riddled with ten-sions brought on by class and policy clashes – were also about something more mundane and something more destructive. This was the parties' abid-ing quest for political power and their blood-drenched struggle for the con-trol of political territory in the ghetto. The priority of these concerns gave special leverage to the political underworld and accorded it unprecedented influence inside the parties and ultimately in national politics. After decades of maturation and especially because of the close nexus with the parties, the political underworld reached the apogee of its social power in the years between 1972 and 1980.

These years, however, were not entirely about politically motivated mur-der and party communal war in the slums. They were also years in which policy and ideological differences between the parties and the social tensions they provoked reached their zenith. For example, consistent with its reformist commitment to social and economic uplift for the Afro-Jamaican majority, the PNP in 1974 adopted a democratic socialist ideology. This ide-ological shift in 1974 extended the party's populist initiatives of 1972–73.[2] The turn to socialism extended the call for social justice for the black poor and affirmed Jamaica's right to pursue an independent foreign policy free of constraints imposed by the country's traditional ties with the United States.

In the years 1974–79, for example, the PNP announced several notable domestic policies. They included a national minimum wage, formation of sugar cooperatives, a bauxite production levy on multinational corporations, worker participation and maternity leave with pay. On the international front, the PNP shifted the overall direction of Jamaica's foreign policy from accommodation to challenging the structure of the international system. This entailed, among other things, support for liberation struggles, backing for such Third World forums as the Non-Aligned Movement, and partnerships with Cuba and the socialist bloc. In sum, the PNP's democratic socialist agenda confronted local patterns of class and racial inequality while challenging the island's traditionally close economic and political ties to the United States and to the West.[3]

In extending this ideological radicalism into the international arena, party leader Michael Manley became a leading advocate for the grievances of Third World countries. He took up the cause of bauxite-producing countries against multinational corporations; he spoke out against the apartheid system in South Africa; and he backed poor countries' demand for a new and fairer international economic order. The PNP leader also established close economic and political ties with Cuba and with its leader Fidel Castro. Thus on both the domestic and international fronts, the PNP's democratic socialist agenda posed a radical challenge to the status quo at home and abroad.

The extent of this ideological radicalism is apparent from the comprehensiveness of its concerns and the combustible themes that entered Jamaica's already inflamed socio-political context. PNP radicalism was wide-ranging.

Issues such as class domination, class exploitation, the economic power of racial minorities, imperialism, dependency, pro–Third World versus pro–First World allegiances, the nature of capitalism, the role of the state in the economy, economic democracy and people ownership, land hunger and an array of controversial questions that were carefully kept off the agenda of JLP-PNP political debates were now at the center of the agenda of public discussion, political commentary and political communication.[4]

These issues that were of interest only to a minority of radical intellectuals and left-wing political activists in the early years after independence, now became the basis of rapid social mobilization and ideological polarization as the JLP opposed this turn of events.

Between 1974 and 1979, politics in Jamaica entered an extremist phase, as protagonists for socialism and advocates of private enterprise denounced each other in the most virulent terms. The PNP and its backers painted the JLP and its supporters as champions of an uncaring, devouring capitalist system and as mere pawns of Washington. In the overheated political atmosphere of the time, party leader Michael Manley, for example, denounced local businessmen as members of a reactionary "clique" determined to turn back socialism by using propaganda, guns and violence. Manley's retort to this challenge that he accommodate the concerns of local and foreign capital was pronounced in the bluntest of terms: "We are not for sale!"[5] The JLP in its turn returned the favour in equally overheated language, by depicting the PNP as confiscatory, fiscally irresponsible and hostage to communists within its ranks.

Remarking on this sharp conflict over ideas, values and policies, the political scientist Carl Stone noted that "as the PNP redefined the agenda of political debate in 1974 by projecting the political symbolism of socialism and a new image of itself as party devoted to the interests of the poor and advocating populist ideas for social and economic change, this generated a counter mobilization of anti-socialist ideas and ideology from the JLP".[6] The JLP therefore warned of the threat of a communist takeover of the island and it rallied property-owning groups, rank-and-file loyalists, and others to turn back this radical challenge to the status quo in the name of political freedom and an imperilled private enterprise system.

In throwing down this gauntlet, the JLP was helped by anti-communist and pragmatic orientations that were so much a part of Jamaican political culture. Consequently, despite extensive public support for PNP reformism on the island and for an alteration of Jamaica's international relations, polls in both the late 1970s and early 1980s nonetheless showed that a majority of Jamaicans would not abide repudiation of the United States and the positive things they believed it stood for.[7]

As conflicts over culture, social policy and ideology racked the society, both propertied and subordinate classes rallied to the democratic socialism of the PNP or to the anti-communist private enterprise claims of the JLP. These contrary policies sharpened political differences between the parties and stimulated latent class tensions in the society.[8]

The provocation of these tensions in turn had a ramifying effect on patronage politics by intensifying violent communalism in the slums. This was so because the PNP's bid to alter social and political relations unavoidably threatened not just the opposition's political standing, but also its embedded patron-client relations.[9] A reciprocal and nested relationship now existed between conflicts over policy and ideology in the wider society and conflicts over territory and political predominance in the slums. These two conflicts overlapped; they were inextricably bound and each one fed the other.

This fact of a political war in the slums that set the poor against one another, and class tensions in the wider society that set workers, small farmers and sections of the urban poor against dominant classes, was particularly noteworthy. It confirmed not so much the rebellious power of the poor, but rather the monopolistic and predatory nature of state politics in Jamaica as state agents and parties attempted to maintain control in the midst of social upheaval. Calculations of state and party power were central to the advent and provocation of the two conflicts. The clash between PNP state agents and the JLP opposition fed each conflict, and each side hoped to reap political benefit from these different kinds of contestations. State and party dominance in this period were therefore enhanced by both a war of attrition in the ghetto – in which the urban poor became cannon fodder – and a social conflict involving sharpened contestation over ideology and public policy.

Despite this party and state dominance, however, conflicts in the 1970s deepened social contradictions and raised the spectre of unintended consequences that could threaten state and party power. Yet rather than being eclipsed by mounting social tensions, state and party actors seemed ready to harvest and reorganize them, the better to maintain the predominance of party and state power. Thus when the JLP party leader famously criticized the PNP in 1975 using leaked documents, the revelation not only provoked an outcry against the PNP, but also enabled that party to rid itself of an offending cabinet member.[10] Thus in the Jamaican political system an embarrassing disclosure was both fillip for the opposition and an occasion for punishing dissenters inside the ruling party. In these ways, both state agents and the parties lived off the contrary dynamics and tensions they had provoked.

This dynamic in which power was simultaneously threatened and recuperated persisted in the 1970s. In these years, for example, PNP state policies and PNP party politics sided with the poor against certain aspects of social inequality. Simultaneously, however, PNP state politics and JLP party policies abetted a war that snuffed out lives and dimmed hope in poor urban communities.[11] Given the scale of inner-city destruction, political murder and violent mayhem that occurred in these years, it is difficult not to conclude that war on the poor and the parties' selective mobilization of their grievances defined Jamaican statecraft and the *raison d'être* for party politics.

Notwithstanding this destructive hegemony that kept the poor at bay, the parties' rival populisms did provoke fear, uncertainty and resentment among dominant groups. Despite a variety of policies that for the most part had secured their interests in the postcolonial era, it was clear to dominant groups that the parties' mobilization of the lower class had emboldened the latter in its historical quest for respect and material betterment. This fact provoked dominant class alienation from the politics of the state and encouraged revulsion against increasing lower-class political presence and social power there. This hostility to PNP radicalism was apparent in the tone of *Gleaner* coverage and editorials during the PNP's tenure.[12]

Concern for the PNP's socialist turn was also apparent from the fears expressed by Jamaican entrepreneurs.[13] The same was true for civil servants who witnessed a loss of influence before the increasing power of radical intellectuals inside the PNP. Commenting on these changes Stone observed that they "upset both senior civil servant and private sector interests. The former eventually retired from the service in significant numbers from key posts and the latter increasingly became alienated from the policy-making process and the policies it generated."[14]

By the mid-1970s, therefore, an unusual political situation had unfolded in Jamaica. On the one hand, increasing social polarization had alienated dominant groups. Some sections of the middle class and propertied groups who were revolted by PNP policies and lower-class social power retreated from social life and trimmed their involvement in public affairs. In the most extreme instances, dominant groups, fearing a communist takeover, fled the island. On the other hand, rising conflict over policy and ideology gave new life to the communal war and strengthened the power of the party militias. They now fought the communal war in a dual role: as sentries guarding garrisoned communities and as militants on opposite sides of the unfolding struggle for social change. Street fighters were therefore being compelled to declare themselves champions of competing social projects. Politics thus spawned rival and relatively autonomous militias whose presence was now being felt not just inside the ghetto, but also within the emergent conflict over political change and empowerment of the poor.

Within the context of political battle over policy and ideology, therefore, the delegation of violence to armed militias headed up by notables from the lumpenproletariat had the predictable effect. That is, the conflict unleashed by the PNP's turn to democratic socialism was experienced by the downtrodden urban poor – and ultimately by the entire society – not just as a clash of ideologies or a conflict over policies. Rather, the whole society experienced conflicts in the 1970s primarily in terms of the all-too-familiar contestation between violent and embittered party factions.

As the struggle over the society's political and ideological direction raged, the conflict mutated into a struggle that pitted allegedly "socialist" PNP gunmen and loyalists against their allegedly "capitalist" JLP counterparts. A major political effect of this evolution was that post-war structures of domination in the country – state predation and communal war – thoroughly absorbed and redefined emergent class and ideological relations into the familiar terms of violent partisanship. The logic of the communal war had therefore trumped the imperative to social and class transformation.

In these circumstances, as the war in the slums and the class tensions in the society intensified, the political underworld and its armed militias accumulated more, not less social power. For as social forces were mobilized and ideologies deployed for and against democratic socialism, party militias grew more important as they became front-line troops in the war for territory in poor communities. As policy differences and ideological clashes bid up the political stakes in the class conflict, the stakes also increased in the communal war and with it the importance of the political underworld. By 1973 this underworld had already assumed a formal role as praetorian guards in some urban constituencies, defending poor communities that were garrisoned against opposition party territorial encroachment.[15] Within a year, partisans were also guarding against any cultural-ideological incursion from the other side that would weaken their resolve.

The consolidation of cultural and political unity was therefore paramount for both sides after the PNP's declaration of democratic socialism. Armed militias and their allies in the ghetto thus fought to protect more than just imperilled political territory. They also tried to secure other values that were as equally compelling and heartfelt as barring the opposition party's territorial grab.

These other values among the ghetto poor included both loyalty to the aesthetics of their party's culture and reinforcing partisan identity norms. Political violence in the ghetto was thus the sum of both the impulse to violent territorial control and the compulsion to secure a street-level party culture against competing partisan claims. Wholly entwined with the culture of the streets and driven by ideological fervour at the top, PNP and JLP party culture invariably assigned loyalists identities based on a capacity to exhibit a stylized violence in the name of opposing social projects. This party culture encouraged political aesthetics that called forth demonic images of political adversaries and transmitted apocalyptic norms that iden-tified highly charged political differences as life-and-death threats requiring the demonization and even the elimination of opponents.[16]

The aesthetics of Jamaican party culture at this time was captured in the fusion of martial values, political ideologies and popular norms. Indeed, the temper of political rallies was not unlike war preparations. Widely shared biblical notions of redemption and deliverance from political bondage were wedded to a political discourse that was already freighted with extremist language. The party faithful demonstrated their loyalty by turning out in huge numbers at public, open-air mass meetings. There party bosses and activists, typically resorting to explicit language or a vernacular language with popular allusion – promised menace to their opponents and all-out victory to supporters. The aesthetics of street-level party culture encour-aged a tense competitive dramaturgy. In this culture, raging acts of stylized violence and a political demonology targeted opponents as the embodi-ment of deviltry for holding contrary political views.

Street rallies and annual party conventions became the primary venues for the enactment of this political aesthetic. Call and response patterns of com-munication – singing, dancing and chanting as well as the hurling of epithets and the use of raw, vulgar language – were *de rigueur* at outdoor rallies and party conventions. Such was the frenzy created at these political affairs that they were often capped by the hoisting of the party boss on the shoulders of frenzied supplicants who then enacted warmongering political rituals.

When enough frenzy was created at these rallies, it sometimes triggered an unfortunate assault on communities or persons known to belong to the other side. In brief, the aesthetics of street-level party culture therefore revolved around political thuggery. It was practised in the name of political redemption from the treasonable acts of an incumbent party, or its political opposition. Invariably, political expression in the 1970s found its true reso-nance in communal war and in the frenzied expressions of badness-honour, now put to partisan purposes.

Yet this hardening of martial faith did not exhaust the framing of polit-ical identity. As political conflicts intensified in this period, partisans on both sides of the political divide made complementary aesthetic choices. It is well-known, for example, that PNP loyalists in the 1970s began wearing knitted tams, donning African-style kareba jackets and embellishing this dress with Rastafarian colours of red, gold and green. Some PNP enthusi-asts even went so far as to distinguish themselves by the brand of beer they drank. For these loyalists, the locally brewed Red Stripe label was preferred because drinking it was deemed more consistent with patriotic values. Needless to say, JLP adherents distinguished themselves by embracing their own notions of partisan cultural identity. Hence, where PNP tribalists exhibited the raised fist, wore bright orange and threatened their opponents with "heavy manners" (violence and force), JLP tribalists rang bells, celebrated while wearing bright green and affirmed their own forms of counter-violence.

In this political war, then, the donning of party "uniforms" and the deployment of vernacular idioms stamped partisans as belonging to distinct and allegedly irreconcilable moral communities. As a result of this kind of political mobilization and ideologically driven *encadrement*, volatility of disposition and hair-trigger responses to perceived political threats and offence were typical in these years. While commentators have remarked on these traditions, what has not been fully appreciated until quite recently is that these responses were both rituals of self-making and rituals of state and party power.[17]

In these terms, violent balloting and mayhem committed at the polls and elsewhere by the underworld were not some random, mindless anarchy of the ignorant partisan poor in the slums. Rather, orgiastic violence and its associated political frenzy were critical to the reproduction of political power.

This nexus of violence and political extremism strengthened state power and the violent partisan identities that undergirded that power. Violent factionalism was therefore neither external to state politics nor alien to JLP and PNP party culture. On the contrary, violent relations were constitutive of political power in both political parties. Violence was essential to these parties' identities and to their strategies of political renewal. Power and political culture in Jamaica were therefore embedded in and defined by relations of violence.

Yet violence was not all there was to this nexus between power and culture. Power and political culture in Jamaica operated within a structure of affection and solicitation that disclosed the intimacy of patronage politics in Jamaica. Much like their betters who also received political favours from the state, poor supplicants and their families secured housing, social welfare, schooling, jobs, access to foreign travel and work abroad, because of their ties to political parties. Poor children were schooled and given uniforms, and even decent burials for relatives became possible largely because of monies distributed by patronage-based political parties. Indeed, to many among the urban poor the political party was both family and kin, providing means as well as succour and identity in a harsh environment. In this economy of partisan gift-giving, loyalties to top party officials and powerful affections of gratitude toward them were accumulated and discharged primarily in the parties' favour.

As with family loyalty, party allegiance became emotionally charged and communal with the powerful inclination to close ranks against outsiders. In this context, the violent and passionate unleashing of rival communalism in the slums merely confirmed a fact of everyday politics in Jamaica: the seduction of the poor by a victimizing party power in all its fabled violence and powerfully familiar intimacy.[18] It is not surprising, then, that a sense of solidarity and communal identity among the poor was built on violent rituals and experiences of intimate "family" bonding. These two faces of party political culture led therefore to a violent defence of political territory and aggressive loyalty to party bosses. In this political ritual, violent party culture and supplicants' desperate need for handouts fed each other.

One result was of course mounting violence. The other was the development of a consolidated partisan identity fashioned by both violence and patronage. On both sides of the political divide, loyalists could find in party membership a potent social identity far more personally meaningful than either nationality or class belonging. Hence, though class and nationality remained powerful sources of identity and solidarity in the Kingston slums, party praetorians and party supplicants found, in territory and in the intimate bonds of party culture, even more potent bases for identity and social belonging.

For actors in the political underworld and their associates, protecting personal honour and defending party honour became essentially one and the same. Responsibility for the defence of sacred political territory and protection of party cultural life and honour in the street and constituencies was as much a matter of personal honour and survival as it was a defence of political obligations. In the Kingston slums this responsibility fell primarily to armed contingents whose sense of personal identity and even manly honour were firmly connected with communal war and disposition of largesse.

It is therefore difficult to exaggerate the importance of the armed lumpenproletariat in the shaping of party culture and in the struggle over strategic political territory in the 1970s. The twinning of warlordist impulses to sharp cultural, ideological and policy differences gave the political underworld huge influence in these years. Exercised through possession of guns, as well as expressions of badness-honour and access to power, this leverage gave the underworld an unprecedented role in redefining social relations and shaping the dynamics of political conflict.

The social power of the political underworld and allied groups was so pervasive in this period that its influence in national politics eclipsed other strategic groups, such as the politically divided working class and the terrified and politically intimidated middle class. The sway of lumpen social power in national politics was thus startlingly out of all proportion to its minuscule size and its relative social and moral isolation from the main classes and the dominant social institutions in the country.

Yet as social and political tensions deepened in the 1970s, the prestige and authority of this party-linked contingent only increased. That was so because the mobilization of antagonistic social groups and the heightening of anticipatory fear by the duelling parties boosted the already important status of the political underground. In sum, as the struggle for social and cultural change unfolded after 1972, rival and armed militias became key arbiters in the inter-class politics of social transformation and in the intra-class politics of communal war.

As a result of these circumstances the political underground was involved in more than just a war for identity, a defence of street-level party culture and territory, and a quest for political predominance. It was also a force contributing directly to the momentum and character of political change. By means of badness-honour, ties to community values and access to power, the lumpenproletariat of the political underworld powerfully influenced the trajectory of party politics.

Urban politics in the 1970s became increasingly identified with street wars, political murder, warlordist ambitions and the political expulsion of populations. Members of the political underground were pivotal to these developments. They were the parties' shock troops in urban contests and indispensable to the retention of power in select communities. More than that, members of the underground received special benefits, patronage contracts and protection from the law.[19] Most important, they were deemed important players in national politics and received the accolades of both party sponsors and the communities they represented. In short, the lumpenproletariat that formed the political underground was encompassing in its cultural influence and extensive in its political reach.

From the foregoing it is apparent that the political underworld that had arisen in the 1940s to uphold rival territorial claims had become quite powerful by the mid-1970s. Its purview encompassed powerful party ties, inflection of ideological relations, violent constituency management and control, patronage distribution and identity construction. The social power of the political underworld had therefore become both pervasive and strategic. In its colonizing hegemony over a range of contentious social issues, the partisan political underground became, in part, an embodiment of the operation of power in Jamaica. That power was expressed in the ability to construct ambiguously configured social agents and to fashion practices – even among detractors – in which predatory institutional relations were inscribed.

This intersection and reciprocity between communal warfare for territory and influence on the one hand, and contention over social inequality on the other, is exceedingly familiar.[20] Where a war for political territory or booty is intertwined with conflict over social transformation, it is possible that the broader struggle over social transformation might be derailed and even subsumed by the narrower imperatives of communal war. The unfolding battle over social change in the 1970s was not lived primarily as a frontal clash of unified class antagonisms. Rather, the contention over issues of class and ideology was converted in the heat of battle into old, yet highly charged and emotionally laden structures of predatory rule. Among various classes in the inner city, this was primarily a lived experience of tribal war.

In this contestation involving overlapping imperatives to secure ideological party positions and defend territorial party gains, a violent war of attrition for political territory became a primary means by which ideological differences were settled and political advantage established. Again, in this kind of battle in the ghetto, it was not sharply defined antagonistic classes that were arrayed against each other, but rather opposing, same-class communal armies of the poor doing battle for their respective parties. Thus as the two conflicts unfolded, the PNP's attempt to alter social inequalities and usher in its version of social transformation was converted into partisan terms and was canalized into the rituals of communal war. This political subordination in which emergent challenges to the political and ideological status quo are absorbed by party communal and territory-seeking war machines is the defining feature of Jamaican politics and has been so particularly since the 1970s.

Yet, it should be said that not even the ferocity of this partisan warfare could erase the stubborn fact that no matter how fervently loyalists from the underground fought for their cause, the nexus to which they belonged was a sharply unequal one. That inequality sometimes interrupted the flow of dominant power over supplicants. After all, despite the grip of the sharp partisan divide, power holders and members of the underground were caught in an unstable, volatile and increasingly complex relationship.

On the one hand, because of the superior power and resources of the state and the parties, they invariably dictated the terms of their relationships with supplicants. Consequently, efforts from below to move beyond the suzerainty of political sponsors were repeatedly throttled.[21] The early years of this complicated relationship therefore entailed considerable lower-class subordination to party strategies and a reinforced dependence on leading party figures. Party militias and their leaders – whom the poor fancifully referred to as "top-ranking" members of the political underworld – served as direct representatives of party power at this time. They carried out political directives, distributed patronage and acted as agents of decentralized violence in the ghetto. In short, dependence, subordination and complicity initially defined this nexus between community enforcers and the political parties.

On the other hand, though dependence on sponsors could hobble the political underworld, complicity with party power was always subject to the critique of self-interested calculations amongst the needy. Covert or unabashed, supplicant predation from below at times threatened party hegemony and the authority of political bosses. In many instances, considerations of lower-class self-interest did not always conform to the needs of political sponsors or to the zero-sum logic of party contestation.

For example, autonomy gave actors within the underworld not just room to wreak violence on their political opponents. Freedom of action in the political underworld also opened a contested social space. In it, ghetto notables became not just clients of their parties, but also members of a downtrodden class. Thus the political underground was deeply conflicted. Obligations to patrons pulled it in one direction while the moral and political concerns of the disadvantaged poor, to which enforcers belonged, pulled the political underground in another.

This other relationship between the underground and the larger constituency from which it sprang created opportunities for expression of a range of solidarities and allegiances. Loyalty among the poor was not driven solely by party politics. Compulsions pertaining to feelings of black cultural pride; class concerns for eliminating the inequalities that blocked opportunities for the poor; retention of loyalties based on neighbourhood identity; and lower-class respect for iconic figures in sports, entertainment and outlawry, together comprised an alternative system of popular allegiance, motivation and self-making in the ghetto. Those among the lumpenproletariat who belonged to the party-linked political underworld were thus not immune to these powerful compulsions, and enforcers' efforts on behalf of the parties were conditioned in significant ways by these non-party considerations. Indeed, from time to time, these larger commitments did conflict with partisan allegiances.

Such contrary loyalties provoked instability and corroded relations between political sponsors and their supplicant notables from below. Thus while core party allegiance remained powerfully compelling for committed members of the political underground, it should be remembered that this highly partisan identity was always leavened by competing cultural, community and class-inspired inclinations. These rival claims reflected a wider set of class-driven motivations that overlapped with the immediately powerful obligations to party identity. Again, the combination of the historic class claims of the downtrodden urban poor, the aspiration for racial respect and dignity among the black poor, and the immediacy of sharply felt partisan obligations introduced an unstable element in the political enforcers' relations with power holders.

The import of this uncertainty is that enforcers in the underground could take things into their own hands during highly charged political episodes. Instability of ties could encourage members of the partisan underworld to race ahead of their sponsors and try to alter, by various means, longstanding impediments to lower-class advance. In short, filiation with power did not wholly satisfy the lower-class quest for power, material well-being and cultural respect. These considerations highlight the potential instability of this nexus between ostensible powerless clients and their politically powerful patrons. Such cross-cutting sentiments and contrary loyalties introduced volatility into what might superficially appear to be a one-sided and unequal relationship.

Because these counter-currents were potentially disruptive, the predatory state and its political parties were alert to them lest a once-compliant political underground become defiant in ways that could reconfigure power relations. After all, in the island's dynamic and highly charged socio-political context, with its stubborn historical class differences, once-partisan loyalists could quickly change into self-seeking and voracious predators, eating away at the same political and social system that had created and sponsored them.

Alternatively, individuals in the political underground could be transformed into class-interested actors and agents for a larger group cause: that of moving beyond the bounds of sheer complicity with power to independent action on behalf of the downtrodden. To be sure, in contexts of inequality and sharp material deprivation, this scenario of an open break with political sponsors should not be carried too far. Severe limits hampered easy defiance of any sort. Nonetheless, these considerations cannot be ruled out, and indeed Jamaican politics in the 1970s and after provides some evidence for an oppositional turn on the part of once-loyal enforcers.[22]

The varied careers of political henchmen from both sides of the political divide in the 1970s offer a good illustration of these conflicting dynamics. The political careers of Claudius Massop, a JLP enforcer and top ranking in West Kingston, and Winston "Burry Boy" Blake and the Garrison Gang that operated from the PNP's stronghold of Central Kinston confirm the underground's complicated loyalty to political sponsors. By way of contrast with the political tendencies exhibited by Massop and the Garrison Gang, I shall discuss the peculiar case of George "Feathermop" Spence, another PNP enforcer in the 1970s. His career attests to the predatory form that the yearning for self-emancipation sometimes takes in the ghetto.

Leadership from Below: Claude Massop

Claude Massop was born in West Kingston, in 1949, during the early years of the party civil wars. Like many young men from poor neighbourhoods, he became part of the network of unemployed, idle youth that occupied themselves in desultory ways. Some engaged in petty hustling and theft. Others formed juvenile gangs, but many found an outlet for their energies in neighbourhood youth and sports clubs. Young men in these groups lived for the popular weekend dances at venues such as the Chocomo Lawn, then a popular working-class dance hall and sports venue in West Kingston. There they fraternized with peers and raved at the new ska music performed by working-class musicians. These jobless young men also enjoyed the sporting life available to venturesome youths of the day. They frequented local theatres that offered a steady diet of B-grade Hollywood fare. They gambled, smoked the widely available marijuana weed and engaged in petty sales of the drug. Others competed in domino and dice games and jousted for the affections of women.

But there was more to their experience than the sporting life. The early 1960s were a time of upheaval in the slums as political turmoil and partisan rivalry converged with growing cultural ferment. Rastafarianism, black consciousness and defiance of social conventions were also the vogue. These actors became outriders in challenging social and cultural conventions and were an irrepressible social force demanding change in the society. Massop belonged to this group and he moved easily among this cohort of the unemployed young.

For a time, young Massop frequented the Ladd Lane and Tower Street areas of Kingston where he apparently engaged in a remunerative petty trade. According to those who knew him, Massop's hustling life included collecting the earnings from local women who made forays among sightseers, tourists and sailors passing through Kingston's waterfront and its environs.[23] As a street hustler, Massop developed the acumen to survive in a locale where criminal teen gangs, opportunistic predators, warring political forces and a brutal police force enacted their violent rituals.

Even as he matched wits with the prostitutes under his thrall, Massop also had to protect his fleshly trade from the law and other dangers. He also had to accommodate a rapidly encroaching political world while turning back predators and other ne'er-do-wells that might threaten his livelihood. To deter predators, caution rivals and awe admirers demanded extensive street smarts and pre-emptive displays of badness-honour. Massop had these skills and they allowed him to prevail in a turbulent context whose features were defined by the non-conformist rebellion of ghetto youths and society's vigorous efforts to suppress it.

These rude boys earned a reputation for their social defiance and destructive violence in Kingston. Yet even while the society seemed stunned by their nihilism and cowed by their violence, the mayhem took its toll on the rebels: brutal horizontal violence consumed their ranks. As one who belonged to this constituency, Massop contributed his share to the disorder. Yet he also established his notoriety through a combination of other traits. He had a tough reserve, engaged in self-supporting ventures – which he sometimes shared – and was known as a sporting "roots-man" committed to the Rastafarian ideology then in vogue among the Kingston poor.

Possession of these and other traits meant much in the ghetto. In fact, deference and leadership were typically granted only to hardy males that possessed that enigmatic combination of hard-hearted brutality toward opponents, and protective commiseration for allies and the needy in the enforcers' natal community. Notoriety as a top ranking in the slums therefore depended on fashioning a reputation in which an arch toughness was combined with warm solicitation and practical deeds that benefited one's own community.

On the one hand, then, status in the ghetto could be earned through mutuality and the norm of reciprocity. A willingness to share opportunities and one's possessions – including food and monies – ranked high among the values of the Kingston poor. Mutuality toward neighbours and a fulsome generosity with coveted goods invariably earned community respect. The needy appreciated neighbours who shared what they had. If you sprang from the poor, showed them generosity and assisted them in their travails, that was one route to community respect and reputation in the slums. Correlatively, selfishness or being "tight-handed" earned parsimonious offenders the sneers, ridicule and contempt of a watchful community.

Similarly, reputation in the slums could be won by demonstrating organizational talent and skills, especially where these enhanced community betterment and secured material gain for the downtrodden. Demonstrating talent and skill at any endeavour of community consequence invariably won notice. Talent in sports and games by a resident was especially noteworthy, since it brought sportsmen and women personal honour and their respective communities gained modest fame as a result. As we have noted above, outstanding sportsmen and -women from the ranks of the poor confirmed for the latter their sense of *racial* worth and respect. This racial commonality buttressed powerful feelings of natal community pride. For many working-class communities across Kingston, a hardy, worthwhile sense of positive cultural identity was transmitted by the worldly success of native sons.

But community notoriety could also be won by other, less respectable means. Ghetto males, juvenile gangsters and hustlers such as Massop, who exhibited a credible claim to badness-honour, were also accorded respect among the restless and the reckless young. Many of them had already formed youth gangs whose members not only engaged in petty criminality, but also participated in juvenile, male rituals of identity based on notions of manly honour.

As in the wider society, manly honour in the ghetto was based first and foremost on notions of sexual prowess, martial valour, skill in gambling and domino playing, as well as athletic prowess. A society-wide male capacity to drink and "hold" one's liquor without getting drunk was also of some importance. That and respect for an ability to smoke large quantities of marijuana with masculine ease, all pointed to alternative norms by which some male ghetto-dwellers sought respect. In sum, proud manliness, overweening heterosexuality, norms of badness-honour and yearnings for community racial uplift distinguished these contrary jobless youths in the ghetto from their conformist peers.

As a ghetto-dweller on the move, young Massop was a hardy personality with these traits and more. His personality combined broad and open generosity with a self-seeking attitude and a touch of menace. This combination put him a cut above other youths in the area. Like the few young men from Kingston's ghettos who distinguished themselves in similar fashion, Massop established his reputation as a community rude boy who was known for his street-wise acumen and badness-honour outside the realm of politics.

Partisan politics, however, intruded on this lifestyle, pulling some youths into the political fray. In Massop's case, his independent popularity would have caught the attention of the canny Edward Seaga, then member of Parliament for the West Kingston constituency. By tapping into these networks, Seaga no doubt hoped to harness for politics the independent popularity of personalities such as the young Massop.

But there was more to the political encapsulation of ghetto youths than their own notoriety. Besides being tapped for their leadership potential, ghetto youths also succumbed to the lure of party politics because of material need and because of violent opposition-party incursion into their neighbourhoods. In this broader context, residency and desperate need combined to influence political affiliation in the slums. By the mid-1960s, for example, mere residence in constituencies such as East and West Kingston, and South and South West St Andrew was beginning to determine political affiliation and membership in a partisan political community. This was the case because as parties struggled to gain political control of territories, they brought inexorable pressures to bear on residents in neighbourhoods, streets, enclaves and whole constituencies by demanding their loyalty in exchange for material favours.

It will be recalled, for instance, that in West Kingston the youth gangs and independent youth clubs were lured into politics through the distribution of sports equipment by the JLP-controlled Youth Development Agency.[24] One effect of this relationship was that the fortunes of individuals as well as prospects for community development in these working-class districts came to depend not on objective need, but rather on securing the goodwill and the largesse of the member of Parliament for the constituency.

In parts of West Kingston, jobless youths were therefore caught in the unenviable vice grip of JLP blandishment and PNP warmongering. The result of this political squeeze was not just the encapsulation of notable individuals or the juvenile gangs in the neighbourhood, but also the political colonization of the entire population in the constituency. In response to political constraints and survival needs, poor residents were therefore forced into choosing sides based in large part on where they happened to live. As a result, in some working-class areas of Kingston, residence – not political ideology – began to play a major role in determining political loyalty, establishing political identity and allocating membership in partisan communities.

This was certainly the case for Massop who lived for a time on Wellington Street in the Denham Town section of West Kingston. By the early 1960s this street and its environs had become a JLP stronghold. In fact, the JLP's national office was headquartered there and JLP political power and largesse radiated from this centre to the entire West Kingston constituency, including hard-core enclaves such as Bread and Salt Lanes. Jobless youths in these places who previously had belonged to non-partisan gangs, such as the pro-JLP Phoenix City youth gang, were thus gradually pulled into the party communal war because of the nexus between residence and party control of the area. In sum, JLP patronage to needy Salt and Pink Lane youths and PNP gang-led incursions into the area evidently drove unemployed males such as Massop into the political game. As a result this ghetto notable, not yet out of his teens, came of age politically as a member of the Phoenix City gang in West Kingston. As a rising figure in this gang, young Massop helped repel the PNP's violent bid to unseat Seaga in the 1966–67 period. His success in protecting strategic areas such as Wellington Street and Salt Lane from PNP attacks enhanced his reputation. With Seaga's second West Kingston victory in the 1967 elections, Massop's political fortunes grew and with it his fame as a ghetto fighter in the political underground. With the JLP in power for another five-year term, the party used its incumbency to extend its power. In so doing, it relied even more on members of the political underground such as Massop to secure this power in the street and in the now-garrisoned constituency of West Kingston.

The political underground and the hardened lumpenproletariat associated with it therefore became more important in this period because victory at the polls in Jamaica invariably meant the discriminatory awarding of jobs and government contracts. Yet as this odious policy ran up against the determined opposition of civic leaders, it had to be defended against critics in Parliament, in the press and in the streets. Enforcing contracts, protecting the discriminatory distribution of jobs and defending territory from political incursion worked ineluctably to increase the influence of the political underground from which both parties drew their fighters. One effect of this linkage among politics, elections and contracts in Jamaica was that violent enforcers such as Claude Massop became indispensable to the maintenance of the political power of key office holders in the country.

Still, it should be remembered that the distribution of state contracts was not always a violent affair nor was it exclusively a matter of helping only the poor. Between 1962 and 1972, for example, influential backers of both political parties – particularly in the tourism, manufacturing, commercial and construction sectors – gained extensive financial concessions and won large state contracts without much dispute. Favoured construction firms got awards to build houses in middle-class suburbs. Other locals helped develop the Kingston waterfront for modern shipping, expand the facilities at the new national stadium, and upgrade roads, bridges and infrastructure. Both public works and private market construction contracts were at the core of the contract system. This system overwhelmingly benefited favoured entrepreneurs, big political donors and the politically connected of both parties.[25] One commentator noted this connection between political donations and favouritism: "Essentially what is achieved from funding political parties is not the ability to influence government policy but preferential treatment in the award of contracts and concessions or licenses that private sector interests seek from the state."[26]

Nonetheless, consistent with the two-party practice of rewarding both the "big men" and the "small man" with government contracts and benefits, both parties gave awards to loyalists from the street. For example, the JLP gave street-level operators such as Massop a share of the state's largesse and a role in its disposition. Contracts for big projects were therefore awarded to big firms and major entrepreneurs, but these beneficiaries had to share the largesse with the "small man" and street-level loyalists by parcelling out smaller contracts to them.[27]

In Massop's case, he began earning his keep as a JLP "contractor" during the construction boom in Kingston in the early 1960s. As a "small man" from the ghetto who was also a JLP enforcer, Massop was given a strategic role in the long-established process in which government jobs were distributed on the basis of political affiliation. As a JLP loyalist, Massop was the "personnel officer" to whom the Ministry of Labour and the construction companies turned for the hiring of day labourers and others seeking employment at job sites.[28] Since many of these jobs were awarded strictly along party lines, Massop therefore wielded tremendous influence over the livelihood of workers and ghetto youths who were to be denied or given recommendations for these coveted jobs. As one who saw to the hiring of these supplicants, Massop thus became a key intermediary in the contracting process and something of a patron to the poor. Again, this intermediate status in the distribution chain enhanced his reputation in West Kingston politics and among supplicants there.

But Massop did more than distribute party largesse at job sites. The political fighter also rendered an invaluable service for which he was eminently qualified: recruiting and organizing political thugs to protect contested job sites. In the highly volatile period of the 1960s and early 1970s, these sites were often the scenes of pitched battles as PNP and TUC activists and thugs rallied against discriminatory employment in the construction sector. At some job sites, that effort by the PNP often proved futile, as the JLP often relied on both the police force and party thugs to contain challengers. At a contested job site such as the National Arena, for example, armed JLP thugs – recruited and led by Massop – successfully beat back challenges to the JLP-BITU monopoly on the recruitment of labour there.[29] Massop's role as contractor and enforcer beyond the confines of Tivoli Gardens thus enhanced his notoriety and confirmed his strategic place in the reproduction of JLP power.

But it was his role in the unfolding politics of West Kingston in the 1970s and his place as avatar for the rapidly changing cultural dynamics in the ghetto that cemented Massop's place as icon, a champion of the poor and a ghetto-based player in national politics. Three facets of his experience captured these changes: his status as the top-ranking militia leader in the garrisoned Tivoli enclave and his image as an unyielding "rootsman" culturally attuned to ghetto norms of emancipation. A third – his eventual defection from the communal war to become a peacemaker – will be examined in a later chapter. These developments sealed Massop's reputation as a gifted ghetto leader who kept the concerns of the poor among his priorities. Massop's intertwined roles as an enforcer, cultural tribune and eventual peacemaker made him a valued son of hardscrabble West Kingston and hoisted him as heroic champion of the sufferers' cause there.

Massop's crowing achievement in the 1967–78 period was his position as the "top-ranking" enforcer for the Tivoli enclave. As the successor to "Zackie the High Priest", another young JLP gunman who was eventually killed by a PNP gunslinger, Massop inherited the mantle of the fallen gunfighter and the responsibilities and aesthetic obligations that went with being a "ranking".[30]

This nomenclature concerning social status in the ghetto highlights the politics of language in the slums and calls attention to an important disposition among the urban poor. In popular parlance, a "top ranking" is a ghetto leader who wields credible power and influence in the unstable nexus that joined the downtrodden poor to power holders. The term is an honorific in the ghetto and is emblematic of an unyielding desire for social respect and autonomy among the poor. More immediately, the honorific refers to the "top gun" militia leader and political street fighter who leads armed men into battle. Though the salutation connotes the possession of skill in organizing men and using firepower to deter or launch armed assaults against political targets, it has a much broader meaning. Although it alludes to the ghetto leader's use of gun power to protect garrisons and coveted political territories, the "top ranking" salutation applies more broadly to those ghetto leaders who are party functionaries rather than mere killers. The term properly belongs to ghetto leaders who are linked to party bosses and are responsible for organizing and distributing party largesse. In addition, these notables also exercise the important function of settling community disputes and punishing infractions of community values.

Thus as political sociologist Carl Stone has noted, these gunmen "operate under the cover of community support in those areas where their role is to defend the party's territory from external attack or political infiltration. They serve further as enforcers who keep the dissidents and troublemakers in the community in line by methods varying from banishment, beatings, and threats to actual murder."[31] Top rankings are therefore ghetto community leaders who typically have armed men under their command and are both intermediaries and functionaries in a patronage distribution chain.

As the top ranking for the Tivoli Gardens enclave in West Kingston, Massop wielded considerable power in Seaga's constituency. Because of his link to this political boss during the heyday of JLP power in the 1960s, this political gunman had ample means to distribute gifts to the needy poor, to find work for job seekers, and win contracts for both himself and JLP allies. Massop was therefore an important ghetto leader who disposed of significant largesse while seeing to the armed defence of the Tivoli enclave.

Still, a cautionary note should be sounded at this point. It should be remembered that Massop had no independent political power. His leverage and influence were purely derivative. He served at the pleasure of the constituency leader; he depended on the politician's political power and beneficence and, for a time, seemed at ease with this arrangement. Indeed, for most of his tenure, Massop neither challenged the unequal nexus he occupied nor tested the suzerainty of the constituency leader.[32] Instead Massop dutifully accommodated himself to the hierarchical relationship and did so for more than a decade.

Notwithstanding this dependency, however, it remains the case that the exercise of power in Tivoli was a shared responsibility. On the one hand, influential individuals in the JLP facilitated the acquisition of guns and booty and provided overall strategic guidance. On the other hand, the political enforcer distributed patronage from above and maintained order in the constituency.

But while this relationship was based on a division of labour it remained an unequal relationship. Hence, even as Massop provided fighting men and withering firepower, the young enforcer's gunplay in the ghetto largely followed strategies set from above. One consequence of this explicit support from the top party brass was that political gunmen such as Massop were put beyond the reach of the law, yet were simultaneously subject to the personal power of party bosses who could turn them in. For most of the 1960s and 1970s, political gunmen remained thoroughly immune to the legal authorities, yet deeply subject to the personal authority of party bosses.

In this relationship, then, the power of the party boss was nearly supreme. It protected the political underworld and provided political cover for enforcers. The political influence of top party bosses, especially their access to state patronage and state power, was therefore more important than the enforcer's mere use of the gun. Indeed, political gunplay directed from on high meant little in the ghetto without the flow of patronage to clients. Thus, satisfying the bellies and pockets of JLP suppliants was critical to the maintenance of power in the ghetto, and powerful politicians who had the means to deliver coveted goods were the only ones who could provide this

patronage. It is arguable, therefore, that the JLP's spending on modern housing, schools, services and infrastructure in West Kingston made Massop's job
as enforcer in Tivoli Gardens much simpler as these bounties eased residents' discontent.

In sum, while guns and gunmen were vitally important in securing political territory and enabling the poor to enjoy party largesse, political gunmen
could not at this time act independently of their sponsors nor could their
violence compensate for the lack of patronage. We have already seen how
the compelling power of both guns and butter were applied in West
Kingston in the first decade of independence. From the harsh evictions in
1963 and 1966 through to the final completion of the housing complex in
1968, the JLP's grip on Tivoli Gardens never loosened. Violence and patronage saw to that.

Especially noteworthy against this background is that even as the PNP
stormed back to national power in 1972 on a wave of popular expectation,
Seaga's patronage and Massop's militia turned back the PNP's attempts to
make the vote in West Kingston a competitive affair. This combination of
state patronage and firepower by lumpen elements proved so intimidating
that in the decade of Massop's reign as ghetto leader (1968–78), Seaga's constituency became a fortress. This achievement was so exceptional that the
PNP would itself copy this model of the politically and militarily impregnable fiefdom that Tivoli Gardens remains to this day.

Notwithstanding the JLP's vital role in orchestrating overwhelming
power in the constituency to achieve this victory across the years, Massop's
personal power as an enforcer was not insignificant. Major credit for the
JLP's achievement in West Kingston belonged to him and to men of his ilk.
The intimidation and routing of disloyal residents, and the martial control
of strategic areas against PNP incursion – in advance of any balloting –
invariably secured a corrupt victory and sealed the political fate of this jealously guarded constituency.

It has been said without exaggeration that elections were won and lost
in such volatile Kingston environs long before the first votes were cast.
Indeed, the political parties' prized electoral triumph in places such as West
and Central Kingston after 1967 typically came only after a decisive victory
had been scored in a violent contestation between paladins fighting for control of the streets. Understandably, partisans on the ground in Kingston's
ghettos credited leaders of the armed political underground for achieving a
singular feat: discharging the punishing violence that created the conditions

for corrupt balloting and the related phenomenon of one-partyism in a few urban communities.

Despite Massop's fabled reputation and vaunted position as a JLP top ranking, dramatic changes in the 1970s affected the JLP's and Massop's political fortunes for the worse. After being out of office for a decade, the PNP swept to power in an electoral landslide in February 1972. Under the populist leadership of Michael Manley, the PNP had successfully mobilized a grand coalition of the disaffected. It included the restive urban poor, dissatisfied workers, alienated capitalists and professionals, radical students and intellectuals, and hardscrabble farmers.

Despite the importance of the members in the coalition, it was the mobilized and rebellious urban poor – particularly the militant lumpenproletariat and the socially conscious but jobless working-class youths – that were in the vanguard demanding social change. As a result, their needs moved to the forefront of the PNP's policy concerns in both the run-up to the election and in the months after the first flush of victory. Having identified itself as the reinvigorated champion of the poor prior to the election, the PNP moved sharply to the left of previous government policies, and by December 1974 the party had declared its support for a policy of democratic socialism.

Coming in the context of urgent social needs, rising anxiety among propertied groups and mounting expectations among the Jamaican poor, the PNP's victory and its surprising declaration triggered a sea change in Jamaica's social and political life. The tempo of politics quickened and new actors from downtrodden classes came to the fore. As well, policy disputes rooted in partisan ideological differences raged. Moreover, tense social relations between dominant and subordinate classes became polarized. Last, the decades-long internecine violence that racked Kingston's ghettos assumed epic proportions.

Several commentators have written insightful accounts of this watershed period in post-independence Jamaican politics.[33] Because most of these accounts focused largely on explaining the turn to democratic socialism and assessing its political and economic consequences, I shall not rehearse those assessments here. Rather, because few of these studies have looked closely at the relationship between the PNP's popular democratic appeal and its policies in the ghettos, I shall focus on this issue.

A striking anomaly was painfully evident in the politics of the PNP in the 1970s. This was the spectacle of a popular-democratic regime that, on the one hand, pursued a policy of economic redistribution and a politics of empowerment and social change. On the other hand, this same party also waged a vicious war of attrition that consumed the poor on both sides of the political divide and laid waste to poor neighbourhoods across Kingston. This paradox raises several disturbing questions about PNP politics in that period.

What, one might ask, explains the persistence of such a destructive policy during the halcyon years of PNP socialist mobilization? Why the prosecution of a violent communal war amidst social struggle over policy direction and socio-political values? What relationship was there between PNP socialist mobilization and the political war in the ghetto? Equally pertinent to the main theme of this chapter, what consequences did the politics of democratic socialism – and the startling opposition it provoked – have for ghetto leaders such as Claude Massop and other paladins in the political underground?

In attempting to address these questions, it is important to keep in mind the unflattering nature of ghetto political culture at this time. With the PNP's sweeping electoral victory, its supporters in the slums expected the inevitable swing of the benefits pendulum that attended a change of political office-holders. With the party's stunning victory, PNP supplicants therefore had every reason to expect that it was their turn to enjoy the patronage benefits of this triumph. After all, the PNP had mobilized the lumpenproletariat to its cause, and the party's electoral campaign had highlighted a commitment to the pursuit of social empowerment, economic justice and greater political participation for the poor.

The party's return to power therefore not only provoked high expectations of patronage, but also implied a consolidation and possible extension of that power into new domains. In the aftermath of the JLP's violent and pre-emptive victories in the 1960s, and its use of power to dramatically favour only JLP loyalists in West Kingston, the PNP could be expected to try to stem and even roll back the erosion of PNP influence in Kingston that had occurred since that time. Not surprisingly, after 1972 there were high expectations that the party would redress this imbalance of power and adopt policies that would benefit its supporters. Correlatively, in the context of the ongoing politics of political victimization, JLP supporters could justifiably assume that the services and benefits that had flowed to them would be diminished, if not halted all together.

These opposite sentiments, it should be emphasized, were not unique to the 1972 elections. Rather, they came as a consequence of entrenched patterns of political victimization, state predation and party-driven communal consciousness in the slums. Hence, despite its progressivist and emancipatory discourse, the PNP's incumbency after 1972 neither altered the politics of victimization nor tempered attitudes of mistrust and political hatred in the slums. On the contrary, the PNP victory emboldened its activists and gunmen to attack JLP strongholds and its supporters there. Decades-long partisan relations therefore drove these developments, despite political claims affirming a new politics of emancipation.

In addition to provoking old enmities, then, the PNP victory also unleashed a pent-up demand for handouts and patronage to its supporters in the slums. That fervour also introduced a vicious dynamic into a volatile situation as supplicants pressed the party for handouts while others of their ilk in constituencies such as South St Andrew jealously eyed an apartment complex currently occupied by JLP supporters.[34]

In response to this demand for patronage and because of the high rate of unemployment among the unskilled, the PNP launched the Special Employment Programme that benefited thousands of its poor supporters. But though the jobs programme temporarily satisfied yearnings for quick handouts, the "crash programme" for the unemployed did little to weaken attitudes of mistrust or trim partisan hostility. In fact, changing political circumstances between 1972 and 1975 had introduced such a crisis atmosphere that political reconciliation between the warring political parties seemed impossible. As well, PNP mobilization of militant slum-dwellers that wanted to settle accounts with their "Labourite" nemesis only made matters worse. In these circumstances, it is not surprising that within months of the PNP's victory, PNP enforcers began attacking JLP strongholds and pro-JLP enclaves in Kingston.

One sector that came under violent attack in the early 1970s was the Wilton Gardens housing project and its environs. Known as "Rema" by its residents, the housing complex was built by the JLP in 1963 with monies from the US Alliance for Progress programme.[35] This working-class housing complex was in sharp contrast to the pitiable shacks it replaced. New Rema housing was constructed from prefabricated concrete slabs and had piped water as well as modern lighting and sewage. In contrast with earlier ramshackle dwellings, housing for Rema residents stood two and four stories high around a modern courtyard. Such improvements in the material circumstances of poor residents solidified JLP support and made Rema a pro-JLP area in what was still a politically competitive constituency.

In the aftermath of the PNP's victory, however, the Rema enclave became a political flashpoint. This occurred for two reasons. First, after the 1972 elections, Rema was located within the now PNP-controlled constituency of South St Andrew. Rema stood north of the Tivoli housing complex in the adjoining West Kingston constituency, and immediately south of Arnett Gardens, another state-built housing project and pro-PNP neighbourhood in the South St Andrew constituency. With the build-up of PNP ideological fervour and political mobilization after 1972, Rema's location in a PNP-controlled constituency became an irritant to newly victorious hardliners determined to contain if not eliminate this JLP presence in their midst.

Second, Rema became a zone of intensified conflict after Anthony Spaulding took office as the new PNP member of Parliament for South St Andrew. As one of the new breed of tough, urban politicians in ghetto communities, Spaulding was a PNP hard-liner impatient with Seaga's predominance in West Kingston. Having won the election in South St Andrew by the narrow margin of 102 votes in 1972, Spaulding moved quickly to counter the JLP's and Seaga's political sway in western Kingston.

Much like his predecessors who held the same position in JLP administrations, Spaulding, as minister of housing, adopted the time-tested practice of using the construction of state-built housing to solidify his political power in the constituency. After 1972 Spaulding heaped such largesse on Arnett Gardens that the construction of high-rise dwellings, a school, sports facilities, a training centre and infrastructure outstripped the already considerable bounties enjoyed by residents of the Tivoli Gardens complex to the south. Fulsome PNP patronage in South St Andrew therefore fuelled this significant effort to counter JLP power in Tivoli Gardens. The political significance of this largesse was not lost on most Arnett Gardens residents, who gratefully accepted occupancy of the new apartments on condition of political loyalty.

Despite such partisanship and beneficence, however, the design of the new apartments received poor reviews from some residents. The more critical among them referred to the new complex as a "concrete jungle" because of its dense concentration of apartments and narrow passageways that limited entry and exit. Despite the negative estimation, this judgement nonetheless spoke to an important feature of the new high-rise complex: its character as a concrete fortress to halt JLP incursions. Grudgingly admired for its political monopoly, Tivoli Gardens now had a political counterweight in the newly expanded construction in Arnett Gardens.

But the build-up of PNP power in South St Andrew went beyond constructing new housing projects and stocking them with loyalists. As if to match Seaga's political acumen, South St Andrew also boasted its network of hirelings, "contractors" and enforcers from the lumpenproletariat. Consistent with established practice in West Kingston, power in South St Andrew was based on a patronage distribution chain that reached down into the ranks of the lumpenproletariat to reward loyalists with housing, favours and state contracts. Also like their JLP nemesis to the south, PNP political bosses had personal ties with the gunmen of South St Andrew who stood ready to assist in maintaining a grip on the constituency and confronting the JLP beachhead in Rema.[36] Anthony Spaulding was the immediate beneficiary of this constituency power.

Large political ambitions and increased constituency violence therefore marked Spaulding's incumbency in South St Andrew. His tenure was thus characterized by two overriding imperatives. One was to replicate in Arnett Gardens the Tivoli model of monopolistic political control. The other was to pressure, by violence and intimidation, Rema's residents into fleeing the area, thereby permitting total PNP dominance of the constituency. But even as the PNP progressively attained the first imperative through patronage, violence and housing construction, the effort to expel Rema-ites from South St Andrew, as a later chapter will show, would fail miserably.

Just the same, the inexorable logic of warlordist PNP consolidation of monopolistic power in southern St Andrew had its pernicious effects. For Rema-ites, it meant imminent danger of violent assault from Arnett Garden toughs. For the West Kingston and South St Andrew residents, the Rema–Arnett Gardens conflict continued the violent factionalism between old antagonists in rival constituencies. Consequently, enmities between West Kingston and South St Andrew worsened as Tivoli gunmen came to the aid of their political kin in Rema.

More ominous was the reciprocal relationship that was developing between political conflict in the wider society over the policy of democratic socialism on the one hand and war over spoils in the ghetto on the other. Each polarizing step in one seemed to trigger a correlative extremism in the other. Between 1974 and 1979 this resonance produced unprecedented violence, mounting crime and widening street wars across Kingston. Duelling gangs brought new, high-powered weapons to the engagement and fought with ferociousness unprecedented in the country's history. Democratic socialism and PNP mobilization of its supporters seemed therefore to have simultaneously emboldened PNP activists while provoking their JLP rivals to a matching extremism.[37]

This intensified polarization introduced a new element into ghetto politics. It now wedded struggle for patronage in the slums to societal battles over grand ideologies and rival political agendas. Political gangs and communities that had once fought over patronage and territory solely in the name of the parties and for the honour of their bosses now added new political slogans to their partisan hectoring. The struggle for patronage in the ghetto was now leavened with scripts and polarized ideological themes from the unfolding social struggle in the country. That polarization was conditioned by the internationalization of Jamaican politics after 1974 and by reinvigoration of Cold War sentiments that gripped ghetto supporters of the two main parties. Yet rather than create class unity among the struggling poor in the ghetto, the ideological clash between advocates of capitalism and defenders of democratic socialism was assimilated with the communal war and was rapidly converted into the familiar language of partisan factionalism.

In this period, terms such as "socialist", "comrade" and "capitalist" found their way into the discourse of PNP gangs, into the language of street-level fanatics and even into the mouths of ordinary community members. The mouthing of these slogans clearly showed the tutelage of party ideologues and activists who continued a long PNP tradition of left-wing political and ideological inculcation of the rank and file. Whether in study groups, constituency organizations, strategy sessions or at huge party rallies, PNP activists and leaders disseminated the terms and ideas from the party's left-leaning tradition.

By 1975–76 this progressivist outlook had become even more radical. As the PNP hurled democratic socialist epithets at the JLP opposition they were backed by left-wing and communist organizations that employed even more extreme depictions of the unfolding social struggle and of the venality of the JLP.[38] Inevitably, both the political underground and the party rank and file picked up this language and adapted it to their cause. Now words such as "imperialists" and "bourgeoisie" fell from the mouths of laypersons and activists alike, complementing already powerful sources of PNP cultural identification.

For the JLP hard-core, anti-communism and protection of freedom from left-wing tyranny reinforced belief in party boss charisma and "Labourite" culture as bonds of solidarity. Cold War ideology therefore gave a fillip to pre-existing enmities on both sides and confirmed the articulation of local and global politics on the island. Still, despite the political uses of anti-communism by the JLP, it is worth noting that neither Bustamante nor his successors had established a formal system of educating the rank and file to see capitalism as a peerless world-embracing and humanity-enhancing system. JLP support for capitalism was therefore unreflective and spontaneous, in sharp contrast to the PNP's long-standing practice of teaching socialist values and socialist history to its supporters.

The cult of personality substituted for this deficit in schooling JLP supporters in the origins and positive legacies of capitalism. It is arguable that the JLP's tendency to concentrate power in a maximum leader, to the neglect of formally stated doctrinal values, encouraged spontaneous thinking among its members who mimicked the scripted remarks of JLP leaders on the threat to freedom posed by PNP reforms at this time.[39]

This point should not be pushed too far, however. Because of economic desperation and illiteracy among the Jamaican poor, it is unlikely that the rank and file of either party grasped the theoretical fine points in the clash concerning the merits of capitalism, socialism and freedom. PNP strategists have a point when they insist that the PNP faithful have always enjoyed a historically higher level of participation in party matters. They are less persuasive when they claim that because of this, the poor people who support the PNP exhibit a higher level of cultural and political development than their JLP counterparts.

The reasons for rejecting this conceit are quite straightforward. The legendary guile of the Jamaican poor in matters pertaining to their own interests, regardless of partisan identification, is too well known to belabour here.[40] The urban poor in particular have been especially adept in seeing through the guises employed by politicians seeking their support.

Likewise, defenders of the cultural superiority of PNP supporters neglect the dark side of PNP socialist tutelage. They ignore its shallow roots among the masses and they gloss over the overwhelming power of the patron-client, dependency-inducing relationship between rank and file and top PNP leaders. Last, the image of the JLP poor as mere dullards enthralled by venal and trickster leaders ignores similar practices within the PNP, even if the political language there is more "schooled" in left-wing ideologies and in the nuances of political economy. Certainly the capacity of JLP supporters to independently define their own needs and to do so in opposition to both parties in the high-stakes game of Jamaican politics undercut this claim of cultural inferiority among JLP supporters. Based on the challenge to JLP power from its urban rank and file in the 1970s and after, there is no basis in the lived experiences of the urban JLP poor for this invidious cultural distinction.

Regardless of how well the rank and file of either party understood the technical meaning of terms handed down from party ideologues, by 1975 a new reality was apparent to slum-dwellers. Hard-core JLP "Labourites" with booming guns and an invigorated anti-communist identity were fighting a violent war of attrition against triumphant, self-styled "socialists" and PNP "comrades", also with their guns booming. The battle over the country's political and ideological direction was now identified with the politics of party factions in the ghetto communal wars. In this regard, the activities of the Garrison Gang led by Winston "Burry Boy" Blake offer a compelling instance of the indispensable role played by political gangs at this time. Equally important, their predation also shows the tight relationship between this expanding communal war and related socio-political developments.[41]

At a time of acute social crisis marked by worsening economic conditions, rapid social mobilization and sharp ideological polarization, the predation of the Garrison Gang was remarkable. The impunity with which the gang roamed across Kingston attacking JLP supporters and beating up individuals and groups deemed unsupportive of the PNP and its new values must have been particularly shocking to these victims and to the public. Yet the gang's unfettered actions were nothing new. It will be recalled, for example, that the Garrison Gang had already seen duty in the political wars of the late 1960s, particularly in the Central Kingston constituency. There, Blake and his gang members had helped secure Michael Manley's victories in the national elections of 1967 and 1972. By late 1974, the gang was operating out of Arnett Gardens and had grown more powerful and bolder in its predation. Several developments at this juncture facilitated the gang's growing influence and social power.

First, the influence of a left-wing faction inside the PNP enhanced the gang's status in the slums. This party faction, led by PNP general secretary D.K. Duncan in 1974, stressed mass mobilization; ideological education of peasants, the working class and the poor; and support for the armed underground that protected PNP supporters and communities. This radical faction's mobilization of the lumpenproletariat, workers and progressive youth across Kingston and beyond threw down a gauntlet before the JLP opposition and its supporters. Coupled with mass rallies across the country that inveighed against social inequalities and the complicit role of an allegedly traitorous labour party, these developments whipped up popular sentiments and threw enforcers like Blake and the Garrison Gang into a violent frenzy.

At the level of the street, the heated political language and inflated promises of PNP rallies encouraged party loyalists to link their prospects to the party's wider agenda of social and political transformation. After months of this summoning of the rank and file, the party's declaration of democratic socialism in December 1974 merely confirmed the widespread belief among street-level enforcers like the Garrison Gang that they were indispensable to the party's great mission in this period.

Second, the gang seemed emboldened by more than the party's radicalism and the leader's public accolades for their predation. PNP distribution of patronage after 1973 favoured this gang and signalled its importance to the party. By late 1974 and into the following year, gang members were flush with the so-called socialist money that was sent their way from now-growing state revenues in 1974 resulting from a bauxite levy on foreign mining companies.[42]

In this period, monies from the Special Employment Programme, state contracts for work on public projects and other handouts flowed to Garrison Gang members and to partisan supplicants in the ghetto. This bounty was evidently so plentiful that in January 1975 gang members – by one count some thirty of them – now rode the brand new Honda motorbikes popular among sporting males in the ghetto.[43] By mid-year, gang members' importance to the party was further confirmed when several of them enjoyed the ultimate patronage: inclusion in the prime minister's retinue on his historic state visit to Cuba. Finally, with such vital ties and explicit support at the party's highest levels, there were now few restraints on a gang that had become indispensable to PNP power in the ghetto and elsewhere. In fact, as party hard-liners moved in this period to challenge the JLP's electoral hold and political influence in South West St Andrew, the ability of the PNP's underworld to intimidate opponents with near impunity became stunningly apparent from press reports.

The social power of Blake and his gang is evident from press reports that detailed the group's unchecked mayhem in Kingston between 1974 and 1975. In November 1974, for example, the gang was accused of shooting a JLP loyalist, attacking mourners at a memorial service for a slain seventy-nine-year-old JLP supporter and mobbing opposition members of Parliament as they attempted to enter the legislature at Gordon House.[44] Likewise, in December 1974, its members disrupted an industrial dispute involving disaffected port workers belonging to the National Workers Union, the trade union arm of the PNP. As members of the rival left-wing University and Allied Workers Union sought to poll the disaffected workers, the Garrison Gang set upon them.

In the ensuing melee, the meeting was broken up, but not before the defecting workers were assaulted and Trevor Munroe, University and Allied Workers Union organizer and professor at the University of the West Indies, was chopped and nearly killed by the machete-wielding gang.[45] While this event appeared to be just another clash in a long history of violent rivalry in the industrial sector, the assault carried ominous implications. The attack on the University and Allied Workers Union and its leaders showed that PNP-related violence could be visited not only upon BITU and JLP supporters, but also on disgruntled PNP voters and disgruntled unionized workers – not to mention those such as Munroe of the University and Allied Workers Union who tried to get these workers to defect.

Given this hardening of attitude to dissent within the PNP fold, JLP supporters in Rema and in the competitive South West St Andrew constituency fared even worse. In a stunning display that unnerved seasoned warriors such as the combative Edward Seaga, the gang unleashed a reign of terror intended to expel JLP sympathizers from the enclave and seize it for the PNP.

Known to Member of Parliament Anthony Spaulding, and operating from their base in South St Andrew, gang members – riding like a posse on their shiny motorbikes – wreaked havoc in both South and South West St Andrew. In the course of a single week, they disrupted JLP gatherings in South West St Andrew; they shot at and assaulted its organizers and supporters and they pillaged the JLP's office there.[46]

In a remarkable display of unquenched ferocity, the press reported, on 20 January 1975, some sixty members of the gang riding two to a bike invaded the JLP's headquarters on Retirement Road in South West St Andrew. They smashed furniture and equipment, tore up documents, tried to burn down the building and stabbed a security guard. All this occurred with hardly any interference from police in the area.

Nor were there reported arrests or interdiction of the gang. This neglect caused William Strong of the *Daily Gleaner* to opine the following: "This doesn't speak well for the police. But the fact is there, staring them in the face ever since the unforgotten days when politician Wills O. Isaacs, then a fire-eating TUC front-liner placed on the record the cynical but historic statement that broken skulls are but the milestones on the road to nationhood."[47] A similar consternation greeted the gang's rampage of the JLP offices, as the *Daily Gleaner* marvelled the following day that "during it all, the men uttered not a word".

This outrage led to a public outcry and provoked a JLP boycott of Parliament the day after the attack. Yet neither Seaga's desperate plea that the gang be reined in nor Michael Manley's qualified criticism of the assault and intensification of anti-crime measures stopped the mounting political violence.[48] The gang's predation continued into mid-March and within days the enforcers had wounded JLP supporters at a construction site on the Kingston waterfront and boldly attacked a community centre in the very heart of JLP territory on Salt Lane.

Of course, these attacks did not go unanswered. The PNP's gunmen and its stone- and bottle-throwing fighters – many of whom were drawn from workers in the Special Employment Programme – encountered the bitter determination and firepower of Claude Massop's men. They in turn assaulted PNP supporters that had taken up residence in the newly completed four-story high-rise apartments in an adjoining neighbourhood called Lizard Town.

Like the Rema enclave that was isolated in South St Andrew, Lizard Town stood vulnerable inside West Kingston. More worrisome for Lizard Town residents, their new apartments overlooked JLP dwellings in Tivoli Gardens. This affront to JLP suzerainty made Lizard Town yet another targeted community and flashpoint in the West Kingston wars.

Before the month was out, the war had claimed its first major gang leader. The drive-by shooting of Winston "Burry Boy" Blake removed from the fray a leading member of the gang and a popular PNP top ranking.[49] Though Blake's death on 14 March earned only brief front-page mention in the *Gleaner*, the same could not be said of the outpouring of grief in PNP communities.

Blake's funeral reportedly drew an estimated twenty thousand mourners from the ghetto who came to weep and to pay their respects to the fallen PNP activist. This display of grief for the slain gunman confirmed for the wider society what was well-known in Kingston's war-torn working-class precincts: Blake and others like him were regarded not as criminal gunmen, but as community leaders, worthy patrons and even heroic figures. In losing this warrior for the party's cause, the PNP community felt it had lost an exceptional figure. For many in Central Kingston, South St Andrew and elsewhere, Blake did more than carry a gun. Rather, as a poor youth from the ghetto with few prospects, he had risen through street-level community ranks, participated in PNP constituency-level political discussions and faced down the enforcers in Tivoli Gardens. Here was a "small man" from the slums who had not only won patronage for himself and his community, but also earned the affection of PNP activists and shared the confidence of some of the most powerful political figures in the country.

In these terms, it was entirely fitting in the eyes of PNP loyalists in the ghetto that the prime minister and several cabinet members should have led the procession of mourners. This was the case despite the dismay of the public and the harsh "criticism" of bullets and rocks that greeted the cortège as it wound its way through hostile political territory in West Kingston.[50]

Biting the Hand That Feeds: The Case of George "Feathermop" Spence

The activities of George "Feathermop" Spence of the PNP offer further insight into the relationship between the parties and members of their political underground. Like Blake and Massop, Spence was an enforcer and recipient of patronage. Spence also came from the ghetto and shared the urban poor's cultural inclinations and political sentiments including holding strong Rastafarian sympathies.

However, unlike the other two, Spence was not regarded as a top ranking. He had far less political clout with top party figures than did Blake and Massop. Spence also lacked the affection and respect the other two men enjoyed in their parties and communities. More than that, even though Spence was undoubtedly a PNP loyalist and could wreak havoc on party enemies, he brought to his client status a disruptive, even disloyal disposition that the other two notables had seemingly held in check.

Unlike Massop and Blake, Spence showed a readiness to challenge his own party's customary rules for the distribution of benefits to loyalists like himself. Such party customs tacitly but unmistakably emphasized deference and respect for the party leader and his authority. Party culture also required that enforcers accept handouts through established channels and procedures without a fuss. Party political culture was therefore intolerant of behaviours that could be deemed a personal insult to the leader and his authority, or be regarded as a gross violation of rules concerning the distribution of benefits.

To be sure, these customary practices did not entail constant humiliation and personal abuse of key loyalists such as Spence. Camaraderie between party bosses and members of the underground certainly existed, and disagreements could be voiced. Consistent with this flexible relationship, PNP party enforcers had some autonomy but not so much that they were allowed to impugn the leaders' authority or engage in unsanctioned activities that could bring public embarrassment. In other words, the unequal relationship between PNP bosses and their enforcers, while allowing for some give-and-take, emphasized tight management of power by party bosses and affirmed the supplicant, subordinate status of their enforcers.

This hierarchical relationship began breaking down inside the PNP as the level of state patronage to the rank and file increased and as popular pressures for support monies and benefits intensified. By the mid-1970s the distributionist policies of democratic socialism produced two related but conflicting phenomena. The policy of handouts reinforced perceptions among the disadvantaged that the PNP was engaging in the traditional sharing out of benefits to its supporters, even though the party was describing these as socialist measures. The supplicant poor, however, recognized the disposition of political spoils for the patronage it was, and they jostled to feed hungrily on the new largesse that had come their way. In this desperate competition to get at benefits, the party's rank and file supporters sometimes overstepped boundaries, committed acts of indiscretion and exposed to public view the sharp factionalism that attended the political distribution of benefits.

By the mid-1970s, embarrassing public displays of supplicants' feeding on state largesse became a particularly worrisome problem for the PNP. Contractors and loyalists with political connections sought their handouts without regard for socialist niceties or for the PNP's grand design for social transformation. Because the party's public image in this period rested largely on its claim of introducing progressive social transformation and a change in public culture that encouraged sacrifices for the nation, any evidence of political corruption, waste or plunder of public funds would be seized by opponents and thus hurt the PNP's image.

Despite this danger, there is little doubt that jockeying for spoils as well as the waste of public funds became more intense under the PNP. Thus even as party elites and activists took the PNP's socialist embrace seriously, predation and plunder by favoured grassroots clients remained powerful inside the party. Thus while the party imagined itself to be remedying gross social inequities by "sharing out" benefits to the urban poor, the latter – desperate for scarce benefits and material improvements, and less interested in political matters of social transformation – turned to eating out the bounty of the presumed socialist state. Hunger and material desperation, not transformative political agendas, invigorated PNP loyalists in the slums. As the PNP's bounty awakened partisan appetites, the poor devoured what they understood to be the spoils of war and the scarce benefits that came with Jamaica's unpredictable politics. For them, patronage was socialism.

In sum, a redistributionist policy that was being justified largely on ideological grounds had been transformed into something familiar and something new. This was the continuation of the old benefits politics with a new twist: the onset of a desperate, aggressive feasting on the state and the triggering of sharp inner-party factionalism that would pit the party against its own jostling supporters. As this insurgency for more benefits grew, PNP control of the political situation and its leaders' authority over grasping supplicants began to unravel.

George "Feathermop" Spence became an embodiment of this disruption and unravelling of political authority. Where others among the politically connected lumpenproletariat had ritually and quietly taken their share of jobs, favours, contracts and payments, Spence, as a relative latecomer to the game of contract politics, evidently wanted to feed excessively and to "eat" his share hurriedly. His bid for unmolested feeding was accompanied by a menacing bravado and was marked by gross insensitivity to the party leader. Spence neither deferred to the superior status of the party boss nor accommodated calls for restraint on his outrageous public conduct.

For example, Spence became notorious for storming into municipal offices to demand disbursement of funds for contracts he had won from the PNP. Less interested in the growing political conflicts of the time and unmindful of the unfolding ideological debates and controversies surrounding the redistributive policies of the PNP, Spence embarrassed his socialist sponsors at every turn. He failed to complete contractual work for which he had been paid; he was accused of collecting overpayments for work; and a public outcry greeted the disclosure that he had received payments from the government while denying his workers their wages.[51]

One particularly noteworthy case came to light in 1975 when it was disclosed that Spence was being paid nearly twice the original amount of a contract to repair the Lilford Gully, which had been damaged by flood waters. The disclosure of the overpayment proved embarrassing enough to his PNP sponsors that the prime minister, under partisan pressure from his political opponents, was forced to call in the police to investigate the illegal payments.[52]

On another occasion, Spence embarrassed his Jamaican sponsors and Cuban hosts while on an official PNP trip to that country. As a member of the entourage that accompanied Prime Minister Michael Manley to the communist country, Spence became something of a loose cannon. According to press reports, Spence and his associates were accused of ripping off goods from a hotel gift shop while in Cuba.[53]

Also on this trip, to the dismay of everyone else, it was alleged that Spence and his comrades from the streets had unceremoniously overturned tables with food prepared by their Cuban hosts; this because it contained the offensive pork that these Rastafarian adherents abhorred. These and other violations of party protocol and etiquette eventually made Spence *persona non grata* in PNP circles. To the dismay of very few within PNP activist circles, Spence, in late 1975, was surprised in a tavern and killed by an assassin.

Spence's fate calls attention to differences in attitudes and political orientations among members of the lumpenproletariat that became a part of the political underworld in the 1970s. Spence's career shows he was not the top-ranking and trusted intermediary that Claude Massop was. The latter, it will be recalled, carefully managed the disposition of work at job sites, respected constituency member of Parliament Seaga, dutifully paid his workers, ritually collected his largesse from the state and organized party militias during election seasons.

Spence, on the other hand, represented that predatory element of the lumpenproletariat for which politics was merely a gateway to material opportunity and state largesse. For him, the redistributive bounty of democratic socialism was primarily a "feeding tree" for his own desires. He, like others in this layer of the lumpenproletariat, was very much part of a self-helping, predatory category. This segment saw the opportunity presented by lax supervision of state funds in this period, and individuals such as Spence took advantage of it.

Spence thus fed on the largesse of the state without apologies or bows to left-wing ideological notions of sacrifice for political ideals. Devoid of ideological commitments, Spence laid claim to the state's bounty and expressed his unbridled demand that it disgorge its wealth to him on pain of intimidation, public scrutiny and violence. Unlike other fearsome gunmen who paid ritual respect to their political sponsors, this enforcer ignored the political niceties and the delicate etiquette that defined the boundaries of respect, camaraderie and deference between political bosses and their materially deprived clients from the ghetto.

While others in the political underworld may indeed have worried themselves about the political destiny of the nation and debated the merits of this or that path to political liberation, Spence feasted in the here and now. While flouting party customs, he sated his appetite on the material goods and perks of the redistributionist state and he satisfied, for a time, the emancipation of his own needs in a context of material scarcity, social chaos and extreme personal danger.

Commentators on Jamaican politics have been inclined to sneer contemptuously at the Feathermops of the Jamaican underworld, seeing them as nothing but the "social scum", lacking in civility, devoid of political principle, bereft of liberation ideology and devoid of communal values. This is a partly valid assessment. Indeed, Spence appeared to threaten the very system that gave him sustenance by demanding and even forcing it to give him what he needed. This reciprocal and mutual predation between a parasitic state and one of its clients is not a pretty encounter to watch. However, the exercise of a wilful indiscipline and the assertion of independence by a hitherto marginal figure like Spence did create real political phenomena that threatened the unchecked hegemony of the parties and their bosses.

Spence, in being the cunning predator that fed off the state and who defied the cultural etiquette demanded by his elite political sponsors, was also guilty of executing the small acts of empowerment that threatened the powerful. Here again, predation from below may not be revolutionary, but it can lay waste to the state's resources and even threaten a corrupt system. George Spence, who was guilty of seeking the emancipation of his own needs and securing it without the approval of his sponsors, showed once again the structural tension between state agents in Jamaica and their materially poor clients.

Conclusion

The foregoing has shown how the lumpenproletariat – and key enforcers in particular – inside the political underground became decisive actors in the contentious politics of the 1970s. In a stunning progression of influential steps, this underworld assumed an authoritative position in urban and national politics in the first half of the decade. This authority was apparent from the character of urban contestation after 1967. In this period, guns, gangs and political violence had become pervasive and strategic in Jamaican political life. Political violence had also become a critical means of acquiring power, and this violence ruled out democratic competition in several urban communities.

A combination of desperate struggle for patronage among the urban poor, the mobilization of communal loyalties and the parties' quest for total victory gave an armed political underground unprecedented influence in these years. In the quest for total political victory, each party strengthened ties to its militia. To strengthen this nexus between decentralized violence and politics, both political parties placed a premium on the new values of gun power, badness-honour and violent intimidation of whole constituencies.

The immediate effects of the parties' incorporation of a violent and mercenary street culture were stunning. Political gang wars increasingly defined urban politics. Warmongering and warlordist ambitions gave rise to protracted street wars. Top-ranking notables with men under arms emerged as heroic community leaders, valued political enforcers and key associates of top politicians. In a context that saw the absorption of a predatory and violent street culture into party culture and agendas, duelling political gunmen and their gangs became icons that defined politics in the 1970s.

Nowhere was the influence of gunmen and their militias more apparent than in the nexus between the communal war for territory in the ghetto and the social struggle over democratic socialism in the wider society. As I argue above, the decades-long communal war and its paladins found new vigour as the battle over democratic socialism unfolded after 1974. Partisans on both sides of the war in the slums, with their deeply vested interests in patronage, personal honour and partisan identities, were invariably swept up in the unfolding social conflict as bitter antagonists. Armed gunmen in the political underground therefore became dominant actors in this drama, ostensibly mobilized to either protect or defeat any radical reordering of social relations. The political impact of this mobilization was unmistakable: a conflict over Jamaica's political future was transformed by and experienced as a partisan tribal war.

The penetration of street culture into political life, the constraining influence of a desperate urban lower class on the parties and politicians' warlordist bid for supremacy set the moral tone for political competition. These allied influences percolated through the political process, altering its moral temper and redirecting its trajectory. As a result, political extremism, violent settling of political scores and intimidation of populations wishing to exercise their democratic rights became accepted political norms. Whether it was the parties' unquestioned appropriation of state funds to establish political monopolies or the public accolades by party leaders for assassinated top rankings, a corrupted political culture had become an institutionalized feature of national politics.

In their search for unchecked power in ghetto communities, the nation's political parties had fashioned an unusual alliance with an alienated, socially mobilized but politically throttled constituency. Though divided into rival factions, the lumpenproletariat of the political underground gained a pivotal role in national political affairs. This political force kept party bosses in power in their constituencies and helped them establish political monopolies. Abetted by the parties' unchecked quest for power, the political enforcers' moral influence and compulsion became extensive. Thus as the war for power in the ghetto encountered the social struggle for change in the society, the moral culture of the street redefined the latter struggle, subordinating it to the deadly logic of communal war.

Yet, as the case of George "Feathermop" Spence shows, there were additional risks in the dynamics of this fateful alliance. Joining with the lumpenproletariat and making both latitude and influence in politics and society available to all tendencies among this group could lead to consequences harmful to politicians. The next chapter examines the growing social disorder that attended the continuing influence of the lumpenproletariat as a social and political force.

7

Crime, Politics and Moral Culture

IN REVIEWING THE LUMPENPROLETARIAT'S RISE TO prominence, I have emphasized the honorific status that notable enforcers enjoyed in poor communities and remarked on the gunmen's political and strategic importance to the parties. As we have seen, the political prominence of ghetto leaders and their militias had a paradoxical effect on power. Certainly the militias helped create political monopolies in urban communities that benefited politicians. But these militias provoked factionalism, urban violence and political criminality. By the latter half of the 1970s, the disorder created by rival militias was so severe that the ensuing chaos threatened not just party power but the very legitimacy of the state. Corrective action was thus urgently needed to curtail the partisan violence and reduce related street crime that threatened to engulf the society.[1]

But staunching this widening disorder would not be easy. It will be recalled that party militias and their political violence defined party and state power. Low-intensity but constant political violence was therefore a normal feature of Jamaican politics. But while steady-state political violence buttressed state and party power, an unchecked, runaway expression of that violence threatened both institutions. To make matters worse, criminal gangs and independent freelance gunmen with their own agendas and no obligation to parties or political leaders were becoming a serious political threat.

State agents and politicians therefore had to strike a balance among backing PNP paladins in the communal war, deterring criminal gangs and freelance gunmen, while forestalling the threat of anarchy. But assuring that steady-state partisan violence would not provoke lawless anarchy became increasingly difficult after 1974. In this period, PNP politics moved to the left and this turn led to an unprecedented upheaval in the society. Ideological disputes raged, factional violence increased, and criminal gunmen seized the moment to pursue their predation. In confronting these challenges, the government adopted ever-tougher measures. It asserted its authority by using the security forces to crack down on perpetrators of the unwelcome violence. It also passed anti-crime legislation and issued emergency edicts.[2]

But even as the PNP sought to dampen the spiralling violence in the run-up to the 1976 national elections, more difficulties lay ahead. They included criminal violence by perpetrators beyond the ken of party politics and political opposition by JLP tenants who challenged the PNP's bid to exercise unfettered power in the South St Andrew constituency. This chapter describes the PNP's contradictory attempts to manage the disorder by squelching violent challenges while releasing a terror of its own. The chapter concludes by considering the impact on power and politics in the ghetto of this holding and unleashing of violence.

The Unravelling: Crime, Politics and Moral Culture

As rival militias fought each other in the 1972–80 period, there can be little doubt that their mayhem contributed to the increasing level of violence in the society and to its destructive effects. Carl Stone, for example, notes that while murders had increased from about 50 per year in the early 1960s to approximately 150 per year by the end of that decade, this tripling of the annual rate paled in significance when compared to the raging murders during the 1970s. Then, according to Stone, "the level of murders linked to politics was approaching a yearly average of 400".[3] Likewise, in the twenty years between 1940 and 1960 there was no major increase in violent crimes, yet between the mid-1960s and mid-1970s, the violent crime rate doubled.[4] Between 1965 and 1966, for example, there were 228 reported homicides and 898 cases of felonious wounding. By 1979–80 those numbers had skyrocketed to 1,299 and 36,540 respectively.[5]

Furthermore, as violence from political warfare and violence associated with the drug trade converged in the 1970s and after, incidents of violent crime soared. Thus while just 10 per cent of all crimes were violent in 1974, that figure had quadrupled to 41 per cent in 1984.[6] Indeed, reported violent crimes went from 15,893 in 1977 to 22,279 in 1981 (the rate increased from 757.9 per 100,000 to 1,009.8 over that period).[7] Why did this happen?

A large part of the answer is that political opponents killed each other in unprecedented numbers in the ghettos because politics had become an overheated zero-sum game that triggered powerfully felt consummatory values held by opposing adherents. Criminologist Anthony Harriott has observed, for example, that rates of violent crimes peaked in election years and even persisted after the elections were over. Hence, "by providing guns, protective organizational networks (often extending into the police force) and a measure of legitimacy for their 'fighters', the political parties have helped to propel the rate of ordinary violent crime in the post-election years".[8]

In Jamaica's winner-take-all politics, access to political power for the poor was inextricably linked to party membership. For the rank and file of both parties, this membership established customary rights to the enjoyment or denial of scarce benefits. This membership and partisan access to power also conferred distinctive social identities on JLP and PNP loyalists in the slums. For loyalists in Jamaica's zero-sum politics, accesses to power and the enjoyment of benefits and filiation with the culture of party-driven identities were scarce resources that were constantly imperilled, hence the resort to violence.

This was so because the political game ensured that these goods would be always at risk. They therefore had to be constantly fought for and won anew, typically by violence and intimidation. Much was therefore at stake for combatants in this struggle to secure power, benefits and identities. For losers in the political game, political victimization reduced slum-dwellers' access to power and trimmed their enjoyment of material benefits. Indeed, as we shall see with housing for the poor, benefits won in an earlier period could be lost by outright eviction. Denial of power endangered or reduced benefits and reinforced grievances that invariably produced intense feelings of tribulation and distress. The result was the provocation of sentiments that found partisans adopting extremist dispositions they hoped would strike a Gorgonian fear in political opponents. In zero-sum Jamaican politics, then, the struggle for power, defence of scarce benefits and battles for identities were reinforcing and consummatory – a threat to one entailed a threat to the others. With greater access to high-powered weapons that were often superior to those in the hands of the police, it did not take much to spark violent clashes in the ghetto.[9] It was the provocation of this ensemble of combustible associations that sustained the violent frenzy across the decades.

In the incendiary political contestation that is Jamaican politics, these were the stakes for which rank-and-file and street-level activists of both parties fought and no more so than in the ideologically polarized 1970s. Scarce material goods, uncertain access to power and imperilled politico-cultural identities – fed now by polarizing ideologies and heightened economic and political crises – drove extremist political frenzy and caused street-level loyalists not merely to harass but to kill with abandon.

Hence, while a variety of violent and criminal acts had long been a staple of Jamaican politics since the 1940s, the changed circumstances of the 1970s brought a massive shift in the intensity of the violence and in the scale of its destructiveness. As economic crisis, ideological polarization and internationalization of domestic politics were telescoped in this period, political contestation became ever more vicious. Again, this extremism was driven by the high-stakes partisanship of the time and by the easy availability of guns, including high-powered weapons, in poor communities. The result was an orgy of violence that consumed residents in these communities. In them, political and moral constraint gave way to vicious assaults and wanton murder.[10]

Once regarded as unthinkable in the political culture of the early post-war years, politically motivated murder on a huge scale was *de rigueur* in the 1970s. In this period, hapless residents were consumed by the political violence not because of any specific harm they had done to the other side. On the contrary, residents were assaulted and murdered with impunity because they dared exercise a basic democratic right: choosing to favour a competing political party.

Notwithstanding the viciousness and sovereignty of political terror, what was especially noteworthy about violence and crime in the 1970s was the variety of forces responsible for the mayhem. Political violence and its associated crimes were the major sources of convulsions. But groups outside the cut and thrust of partisan conflict also contributed to the intense and sustained levels of criminal violence. For instance, lone gunmen, independent criminal gangs and opportunistic predators were perpetrators of violent crime. As guns became more readily available in the slums and as chronically unemployed males grew increasingly desperate, they became a force to be reckoned with.[11]

Several criminal gangs and bandits thrived in this period and they did so independently of the parties or, in rare instances, in association with the political gangs.[12] After all, independent criminal gangs existed long before a few among them found a political vocation in the 1960s. Autonomous gangs in the criminal trade found greater scope for their activities in the turbulent 1970s and after. These gangs also became a significant source of outlawry along with their peers in the political underground.

This widening criminal predation outside the realm of politics also contributed to public unease and to a growing sense of insecurity in the country. The unease caused by political violence and the plundering of freelance gunmen was aggravated by "domestic" horizontal violence arising from interpersonal disputes in poor communities. Violent clashes of all sorts on the street and in the yards of poor neighbourhoods testified to the grit and danger that came with living in the slums. For instance, reported cases of felonious wounding went from 898 cases in the mid-1960s to 26,976 in the early 1970s. These and other sources of violence beyond the political fray became part of the turbulence and upheaval in this period.

Criminal street-level violence in particular was perpetrated primarily for material gain. As Bernard Headley notes, violent street-based incidents in Kingston usually involved a gunman who plundered or killed with "no particular grudge against the victim, personally".[13] Hence, for Headley violent crime in Jamaica is "essentially depersonalized", and driven primarily by the quest for coveted goods. The motivation to criminal behaviour, according to this view, is to be found not in any antagonism to class relations, but rather in simple predation.

But calling attention to the predatory instincts of independent gangsters is not to say that these disruptive actors were bereft of politically conditioned motivations. To be sure, urban crime and violence in the 1970s occurred primarily in poor neighbourhoods where political ideology was the least of most residents' concerns. Where violence in the ghetto involved neither political rivalry nor domestic disputes, street crimes in the period were mainly acts of predation committed primarily by unemployed males who were part of a criminal underground.[14]

Like its counterpart in the *political* underworld, the lumpenproletariat in the *criminal* underground knew poverty and economic hardship. Lacking the restraining and normalizing influence of family, church and school, a minority of the unemployed youth in the ghetto increasingly made outlawry a way of life. They thrived on the political disorder racking the society and were largely unchecked in their predation. In light of the collapsing moral order in the 1970s, it would not be an exaggeration to say that common criminals had room to act with impunity despite efforts to deter them. This confident defiance was made possible by a politically volatile and ideologically saturated era that weakened moral sanctions against individual responsibility and growing outlawry.

But while predation was a primary motivator, criminals did hear a variety of emancipatory appeals and these summonings did not fall on a cultural and ideological *tabula rasa*. Many criminals imbibed Rastafarian doctrines of racial injustice and were aware of radical appeals from other actors. While this awareness is not the same as having a grasp of the social system, exposure to anti-system ideas did connect with lived experience. Thus, it was not sophisticated understanding that came from exposure to radical doctrines, but permission to act in the context of lived experience. In a large measure, party-driven political violence, anti-system ideologies and radical political programmes of the day did embolden lawbreakers by creating a permissive environment for their activities. Left-wing socialists, PNP–JLP populists and Rastafarian black nationalists had for more than thirty years mobilized the disaffected poor and fostered their intense dissatisfaction with the status quo. By successfully summoning the poor to their radical agendas and anti-system outlooks, these agents and their ideas had a tremendous political and cultural impact in the ghetto. Their agitation contributed significantly to ghetto residents' alienation from conventional values and to this group's confident and racially informed defiance.

As part of the ghetto population, criminal gangs and lone gunmen won permission to act from powerful appeals for dissidence. They heard radical political movements of the day hail the ghetto poor as victims of an unjust and class-ridden society that had robbed them of opportunity and denied them justice. At the same time, the tremendous popularity of anti-system songs and political ideas reinforced discontent and summoned the alienated poor to rebel.[15] Both popular music and popular culture unapologetically affirmed the right of the poor to defy the authorities and to wrest from them the social goods and material benefits denied to underprivileged groups. In sum, it is arguable that the criminally inclined among the poor could probably find in these bracing messages a rationale for their predation.

Calling attention to the resonance of dissenting ideas among the urban poor is not to argue that gunmen and criminals were being transformed into a politically sophisticated, revolutionary vanguard.[16] Nor is it the case that anti-system ideologies and reformist movements openly encouraged or justified criminality and predation. On the contrary, cautionary themes in popular music and the appeals of both radical movements and the populist parties warned against recklessness and violence as means to redress grievances.[17] As well, it is worth noting that the law-abiding majority that made up the "respectable poor" in the ghetto consistently uttered their own plaintive censures against lawless forces in their midst. Despite these restraining impulses, however, it is nonetheless the case that a handful of gunmen and criminals did commingle crime with explicit political agendas.[18] As we shall see, Dennis Barth, the notorious criminal gunman, was one such bandit with an obvious political agenda.

Such individual acts of criminal defiance that were linked to political programmes thus found a hospitable moral environment in the slums. Widespread alienation there had produced sustained challenges to dominant forms of authority and criminal gunmen generally belonged to the most alienated group. Hence, despite contrary sentiments among law-abiding ghetto-dwellers and civic leaders, opposition to all forms of restraining authority had become an increasingly appealing orientation in the slums.

Paradoxically, however, despite the power of this expanding moral defection and its limited association with overt political agendas, it is still worth emphasizing that most street crimes in the 1970s were not political acts - in the sense that the perpetrators acted in wilful concert as part of a class rising to strike a blow against injustice – nor were most criminals motivated by radical political creeds. It should be clear, then, that political motives, an explicit revolutionary ideology or doctrinal commitment, impelled only a tiny minority of gunmen in the criminal underworld. Consequently, street crimes were predominantly acts of predation committed by a seemingly unredeemable section of the lumpenproletariat that was unmindful of moral censure and bereft of ideological commitments.

An immediate effect of this purely self-seeking tendency was that such criminals targeted both the well-to-do and the less fortunate. The latter group bore the brunt of criminal forays into impoverished communities. There outlaws made the hapless poor repeat targets of mercenary opportunity and violent assault. It is therefore fair to say that politically driven and ideologically motivated criminals were rare in the ghetto, as was the phenomenon of protest crime.

Dennis "Copper" Barth: Social Bandit

Among the tiny minority of politically motivated criminals in the 1970s none won as much notoriety and anxious concern from the authorities as did Dennis "Copper" Barth. Born in Kingston in 1951, Barth's turn to crime came at an early age after he dropped out of the Rennock Lodge Elementary School at age twelve. By the time he was eighteen years old Barth had been convicted of several major offences, including murdering a policeman, for which he was sentenced to life imprisonment.[19] By the mid-1970s, Barth, who operated out of the Rennock Lodge area in East Kingston, had been declared "public enemy number one". By age twenty-six, Barth was the youngest of the "most wanted" men in the country since the violent reign of "Rhygin" – Vincent "Ivanhoe" Martin – a feared gunman who was killed in 1948.[20]

Like most of Kingston's unemployed males, Barth was drawn to the politics of the Rastafarians and he evidently shared their hatred of a police force that was perceived to be throwing its weight around in poor neighbourhoods. Other political influences on Barth included the ideological impact of entrenched gangs-turned-guerrillas that operated in East Kingston in the 1950s and 1960s. For years these gangs from the Wareika Hills region had launched forays against lawmen and a government they regarded as both unjust and illegitimate. As late as September 1978 they were still waging a war against the state. At that time a police raid turned up weapons including guns, explosives, radio and medical equipment, Leninist booklets as well as a do-it-yourself manual – *The Complete Guide to Gunsmithing*.[21] Isolated and cut off from the majority of the law-abiding poor, these guerrillas sought to topple the Jamaican government with a do-it-alone militarist strategy that relied on hit-and-run tactics.

This approach, it appears, was derived from the gangs' embrace of a revolutionary ideology that synthesized ideas from Rastafarianism, Cuban communism and other left-wing sources, including Maoism.[22] Barth studied these ideas and related guerrilla tactics, and employed them in the 1970s against the police and other targets of opportunity. Barth thus embraced a variety of doctrinal creeds and they fed his criminal engagements.

In the ideologically saturated ghettos of Kingston, a few gangsters had therefore succumbed to the appeal of Third World revolutionary thought. Politicization of crime was thus a constant possibility in the ghetto and some outlaws rummaged through revolutionary literature to find connections between their own predation and ideas about neocolonialism in the Third World. If Barth's perusal of Lenin and other radical authors is any indication, then it appears that for a tiny minority of urban bandits, anti-capitalist and anti-colonial theories of revolution did inform their violence.

In this respect, Barth appears to have been the quintessential social bandit in Rennock Lodge – a Robin Hood who commingled crime, doctrinal creeds and anti-system politics.[23] He was among the rare few in the ghetto that consciously wedded these strands in ways that won community support and the unremitting enmity of the state. For a social bandit such as Barth, alienation did lead to protest crime and the harnessing of black-nationalist and left-wing ideologies to his predation.

This much was apparent to activists of the day who reported, for example, that Barth was familiar with Philip Agee's exposé of US imperialism in the latter's book, *CIA Diary*.[24] During stints in prison, Barth read Maoist literature as well as V.I. Lenin's *State and Revolution*, a political manual that had become obligatory reading for Jamaicans of leftist convictions. It was even said that Barth was sufficiently sympathetic to the PNP's socialist cause that he offered to put his men and guns at the disposal of the party in the deepening class war of the 1970s.[25] Befitting their wish to be perceived as representatives of a lawful, democratic party, PNP leaders refused the bandit's entreaties.

Whether Barth found broad-based support in the ghetto for his revolutionary ideas remains unclear. While a few residents may have been exposed to socialist ideas through left-wing and PNP activism, it is doubtful that the majority of residents in the Rennock Lodge and Rockfort areas of East Kingston understood or even subscribed to Barth's revolutionary ideas. Just the same, the revolutionary-minded gangs' accumulation of guns, bombs and other weapons over many years marked the criminal-cum-revolutionary underground in Wareika Hills and its environs as a subversive, ideologically driven anti-government enclave.

This rebellious defiance with its taking up of arms against the state was serious enough to invite massive army and police surveillance and repeated punitive raids. The regularity with which such raids were carried out in Rennock Lodge, for instance, probably provoked enough hostility for the police that these raids more than compensated for the residents' lack of interest in or sophisticated knowledge of revolutionary ideas.

As for Barth's career, despite being given a life sentence, he escaped from his captors and continued a life of crime while on the run. He pulled off bold bank heists, baited and taunted the police, and engaged them in repeated shootouts from which he typically escaped unscathed.[26] The fear with which the official society viewed him was evident enough from pronouncement by the judicial system. When Barth was being sentenced shortly after his eighteenth birthday, the presiding judge, in passing five terms of life imprisonment on him, was quite bitter in his observations:

> You know, I am sorry for you. Something must be radically wrong with you. You were just 18 in September. What you have been convicted of already is murder, five counts of shooting with intent. You are now serving 41 years. The only thing to do is to get rid of somebody like you. You must be put away forever. You are a dangerous fellow.[27]

Despite the court's determination to be rid of him, Barth, with the help of Rennock Lodge and Rockfort gangsters, made a mockery of such claims. They twice engineered his escape from the St Catherine District Prison, once in February 1973 and again in March 1977, after which he was never recaptured. Moreover, according to the *Daily Gleaner* – whose editorialists had little patience for such ideas – urban legend had it that Barth "could not be caught because he was protected by a DeLaurence ring. Only when he did not have it on could he be harmed."[28]

Despite this criminal career, it is perhaps not surprising that Barth was regarded as something of a folk hero and Robin Hood to the residents of Rennock Lodge. According to political activists who knew him, Copper used the booty from his robberies to deliver patronage to the poor in Rennock Lodge; it was said that he bought books and shoes for school children and gave money to their mothers.[29] Patronage to the poor was therefore not the sole prerogative of the politician. Indeed, by the late 1970s, urban gangsters from both the political and criminal underworlds had become independent sources of patronage with which politicians had to compete.

Such patronage contributed to the social power of the gangs as their largesse trimmed the parties' ties with communities in which these social bandits operated. Moreover, this patronage provided the context for the protection a bandit needed in order to disappear within the stony silence of his complicit, sheltering community. In Copper's case, community collusion and active protection were indispensable to his survival, and community assistance permitted Barth to elude capture for some sixteen months.[30]

During this time, Barth not only engaged the police and robbed banks with impunity, but he reportedly went beyond crime to begin fashioning a crude political agenda. In addition to being a respected "general" who commanded armed bandits, Barth also moved easily among the rankings and enforcers of East Kingston and among their PNP allies in the Rema and Tel Aviv political enclaves.[31]

By 1977 Copper's outlook had evolved from bold banditry and avenging acts against the police to a consciousness informed by ideas for the creation of "real" socialism in Jamaica (hence the offer to PNP to permit him to form a militia in its defence). By the late 1970s, Barth had evolved into a peacemaker of sorts as he attempted to stop the political gangs from fighting each other. He achieved the nearly impossible when he helped broker the stunning but short-lived 1978 political truce between the warring political gangs. Notwithstanding this evolution in his outlook, Copper remained primarily a bandit, albeit one whose banditry came with a political tinge that reflected his own political development and the values of the community to which he belonged.

Of the several outlaws who belonged to Kingston's criminal underground, Barth comes closest to being a true social bandit. He participated in a web of defining relations that shielded him from the law for a long time. These nested ties included powerful links to the Rennock Lodge community, including the activation of a patronage role there. His associations included ties to gangs in the PNP's political underworld, alliance with left-wing sympathizers, and shared antagonistic encounters with lawmen and a predatory state.

Barth was neither a common criminal devoid of political ideology nor a revolutionary prophet from the slums. Rather, he was a combination of the avenging independent criminal gunman with a band of men who initially tried to settle scores with the security forces, and a Robin Hood securing booty for his community and seeking peace and unity among the warring poor. Barth was detached from the two-party political underworld, yet he sought to transform it into something more radical. He was both patron and feared avenger to the Rennock Lodge lumpenproletariat and a dangerous competitor who challenged the state's grip on the desperate poor.

In the eyes of his community, this avenger was not a criminal; in the moral logic of the ghetto, it was the system who pursued him and whose abuses the poor endured that was the real outlaw. While Barth was not a revolutionary figure and though he certainly belonged to the criminal underground, his career appears to defy state attempts to caricature him as a rogue figure and common criminal inured to mere plunder and outlawry.[32]

Moral Decay and Criminality

Barth's exceptionalism and the rarity of his political motives and daring within the criminal underworld does not mean, however, that its members were inoculated against the rebellious sensibilities of the urban poor. Nor were the crimes of this group without political consequences. Lawlessness and street crime did have political ramifications, since both the proliferation of crime and its extremism intensified public anxiety and threatened state legitimacy. More than that, the society's restraining civic moral culture was no match for a common political culture inured to law-breaking and to changing norms in the slums that increasingly accommodated social outlawry.

Appeals for adherence to law and calls for a return to civic morality therefore went largely unheeded as political rivalries swept aside moral restraints and as the dissenting poor turned increasingly to forms of badness-honour as a response to their marginal status. It is therefore fair to say that party-driven political violence, divided public opinion on crimes by the poor and the vogue of rebellion in the slums weakened moral restraints on the poorer classes. The coincidence of these factors did much to encourage the view that outlawry and crime in the slums were understandable, if unfortunate responses to deprivation. This was certainly the dominant opinion among left-wing activists, liberal groups calling for reform and top figures in the major parties. Ultimately, these shifts in social and cultural norms within and beyond the ghetto gave moral cover to the criminal underground and to its predation.

These circumstances involving weakened moral sanctions, intense political mobilization and growing tolerance for law-breaking empowered the criminal underworld in other ways. Freed more and more from having to morally account for its actions and provoked by anti-system ideologies and unconventional norms to break with the status quo, members of the criminal underground increasingly became a law unto themselves. They revelled in this status and reinforced this identity with pride of race. The combination of proud racial consciousness and conceit in outlawry undoubtedly drove many in this underground to rationalize their criminal acts as responses to the social oppression of blacks.

This attitude among criminals was not at all exceptional. On the contrary, badness-honour in all its variety was the dominant sensibility among rebellious contingents in the slums. Indeed, this moral provocation to crime within the underworld was the corollary to the wider moral alienation, class grievance and aggressive claims to empowerment already widespread among all sections of the urban poor. Urban criminals thus shared the confident racial self-regard of the alienated poor and some gangsters invariably saw themselves as outlaws who were victims of an oppressive and racially unjust society. Striking out at the police, for instance, or robbing the well-to-do could thus be rationalized by perpetrators of these crimes as morally justified acts against an oppressive system.[33]

Consequently, while such forms of defiance were certainly not the norm for the majority in the slums, criminals and predators were aggrieved moral agents in a society widely perceived to be woefully neglectful of the poor. Violent crime and law-breaking that was not connected to political partisanship therefore carried powerful political overtones beyond merely exposing the inability of lawmakers to deter crime. Precisely because criminals were embedded in a pervasive subculture of defiance and since predators shared the sentiments of morally alienated and rebellious communities of the poor, their criminality and its consequences cannot be divorced from the society's highly charged socio-political relations. Violent crime and law-breaking not connected to the party communal war cannot therefore be divorced from the erosion of conventional norms or from the decentralization of violence that were in full swing in the society at this time.

But this nexus among crime, politics and moral culture carried huge risks for the state, for poor communities and for the criminals themselves. First, the more street crimes were regarded as justifiable acts of badness-honour and as the militant poor's riposte to injustice, the more likely that the criminally inclined would be encouraged to adopt these attitudes. Inevitably, the proliferation of this confident criminality threatened law-abiding citizens, even as it called into question the legitimacy of state agents.

Second, the more public unease with rising street crime increased, the more likely it was that the PNP would be tempted to use harsh measures to deter predators and would-be Robin Hoods. Crime and unwelcome violence by renegades who terrorized the city and flaunted their badness-honour therefore faced swift and inevitable retaliation and interdiction. Yet because the PNP wished to be rid of all violent challengers to its authority, it was inevitable that fighting non-partisan street crime would mean not just assaults on freelance gunmen, but also attacks on defiant JLP communities and their street fighters. Hence, regardless of whether the targets were alienated, but racially confident, freelance gunmen or armed members of the partisan underground, fighting urban crime and violence meant interdicting not merely criminals but political foes as well. In sum, the more the PNP sought to stop criminal violence, the more it was likely to be perceived as targeting its political opponents, and by implication the more it would be seen as using the law to frustrate democracy.

Last, any crackdown on JLP street fighters, independent gunmen and other badmen entailed troublesome risks for the PNP. Besides inflaming JLP sensibilities and heightening political violence, harsh anti-crime measures in these volatile circumstances could backfire. This was particularly true where such measures encouraged the security forces to trample on the rights of suspects. Being tough on crime without due concern for the legal rights of the innocent ran the risk of antagonizing poor communities that invariably bore the brunt of crime control measures.

Moreover, harsh and arbitrary security measures could be unnecessarily provocative and destructive of public confidence in the security forces in the volatile environment of the 1970s. Because the security forces typically treated residents in poor communities as if they were potential criminals, it was difficult for lawmen to interdict perpetrators of street crimes without also sweeping the non-criminal but uncooperative poor into the dragnet of police-military operations and subjecting these suspects to the whimsy of repressive law. Such a broad-brush approach to prosecuting crime worsened relations with poor communities and elicited sympathy for the criminals there.

The startling increase in urban crime in the politically polarized 1970s, the prominence of a morally provoked criminal underworld in this period and the difficulties of suppressing a widening social outlawry reveal the complex circumstances governing the nexus of law and politics and their relation to crime and violence in urban Jamaica. Criminal acts and their suppression occurred in the context of radically transformed moral values and heightened social and political conflicts. Both the general dissidence of the urban poor and the growth of a criminal underworld in the 1970s should be regarded, then, as discrete yet connected effects of an unprecedented moral and political crisis. This crisis had three major attributes: the ubiquity of radical anti-system ideologies that emboldened the poor; the existence of a political alliance that assigned the lumpenproletariat a privileged place in national politics; and fear and timidity in a society that was in retreat from its demands for moral conformity from lawless groups. The convergence of these factors in the 1970s discredited power holders and marginalized the standard-bearers for civic values while encouraging lawless defiance from below.

This untimely coincidence of such disabling processes relaxed vital social restraints. In turn, these circumstances caused the militant poor to assume an exaggerated self-confidence and encouraged their rejection of all forms of authority. In the face of these assaults on authoritative values, power holders and dominant groups that had fought for those values increasingly, albeit reluctantly, acceded to the social power of the rebellious poor and retreated before the encroaching hegemony of their subcultural norms.

The moral retreat of a panicked middle class and the complicity of the state in this process created a huge moral vacuum and political opportunity for rebels in the streets. Rebel cultures of the urban poor, including hardened criminals, exploited this disarray and seized the opportunity to assert their own claims. The result was near social anarchy and the onset of a degeneracy that testified to an unhinged society that was now morally adrift.

Rising urban crime in Jamaica, then, was not simply a function of poverty and want. Rather, it was spurred by dramatic socio-political factors, not the least of which was a fundamental rejection of conventional values by strategic urban groups such as the defiant poor and ambitious politicians in search of power. Rising crime was, significantly, a consequence of expanded social power and a peculiar sense of empowerment among the mobilized lumpenproletariat. This rising crime rate was thus abetted by the moral retreat of strategic elites, crumbling conventional values and their replacement by subcultural norms from the street. As one commentator usefully observed, "It is not poverty per se but structural changes occurring in the make-up of values and attitudes in urban Jamaica in the sixties and seventies that gave birth to high levels of violent crimes."[34] It was in this unenviable context of the inflation of the social power of the urban poor and their widespread defection from conventional norms that the PNP tried to roll back crime and restore public order.

In the effort to reclaim its authority, the PNP passed the 1974 Suppression of Crime Act and the Gun Court Act. The first gave the security forces wide powers to interdict crime, and the second created a special court for crimes involving firearms and the possession of unlicensed weapons. Though no state of emergency had been declared, both measures gave the state and the security forces unchecked powers to interdict street crimes. Joint military and police patrols, for example, could detain or arrest citizens with impunity. Both laws infringed on basic liberties and they imposed harsh punishment on poor communities who were the primary targets of these laws. The Suppression of Crime Act, for instance, permitted arrests without a warrant. Citizens could be detained on the mere suspicion of a crime. Likewise, conviction in the Gun Court could mean a mandatory life sentence. Both measures therefore suspended constitutional protections for populations and neighbourhoods which were victimized by both criminal predation and party-sponsored political violence.

Despite their tremendous constitutional reach, these laws had a negligible impact on suppressing either street crimes or quelling the raging political violence in this period. On the contrary, the violence became more intense.[35] This was particularly the case as the parties and their activists jockeyed for advantage as the prospects for new national elections loomed. In a manner reminiscent of the 1966–67 contestation and warfare in West Kingston, the run-up to the December 1976 national elections displayed the well-worn tactic of using violence to establish a political monopoly in select urban communities. As with the street battles in West Kingston a decade earlier, the combatants in the mid-1970s turned to organized violence and intimidation in a bid to secure territorial control in advance of the balloting.

The Politics of Partisan Evictions

As we have seen, establishing a political monopoly or garrison meant organized, savage violence and intimidation by rival militias. Their purpose was the expulsion of residents and with it the political cleansing of the area. Typically this meant employing threats to force residents to leave their homes. Where this failed, various tactics ensured that recalcitrants fled – gunfire, stone throwing and the hurling of crude bombs that set tenements ablaze. The repopulation of the area with over-loyal supporters and the construction of

dwellings and provision of social services usually followed such harsh measures. A praetorian guard that maintained the armed defence of the captive
constituency would then shield these invaders and the strategic areas they
now occupied.[36]

This tactic of violent political cleansing – in which residents were chased
from neighbourhoods, their homes bombed and destroyed and partisan territory seized – turned ferocious and disrupted the lives of residents in the
adjoining constituencies of South and South West St Andrew in 1975–76.
In the former region, the presence of the JLP-supporting Rema enclave
and the presence of JLP voters in parts of Trench Town still rankled PNP
activists including constituency leader and housing minister Anthony
Spaulding. At the same time, JLP partisans in Trench Town and the Tivoli
Gardens area were equally determined that all of Trench Town, and in particular the Rema enclave, would not be gobbled up by the PNP in this
round of violent exchanges.

As for the latter area of South West St Andrew, a hotly contested war for
that constituency had broken out and it drew fighters from all over Kingston.
In South West St Andrew, deputy JLP leader and trade union activist Pearnel
Charles had taken up the challenge of retaining JLP control of a constituency
now violently coveted by the PNP. As the JLP candidate vying to represent
the constituency in the upcoming election, Charles showed he too was a
combative, no-nonsense fighter fully prepared to give as much as he got.
Predictably, this martial JLP effort to shore up and expand its power in both
South and South West St Andrew encountered stiff PNP resistance.

In December 1975 PNP activists attacked JLP supporters in Trench
Town. Hundreds of residents were forced to flee gunfire, bombings and
intimidation. It was clear that the street-war phase of the 1976 electoral
campaign was unfolding in earnest. As the combatants on both sides were
well aware, political dominance in Kingston's western belt of urban constituencies came not from peaceful balloting, but rather from crushing political opposition in the streets and routing terrified residents. Guns, not votes,
therefore determined political outcomes in the western belt.

This knowledge undoubtedly informed political calculations on both
sides. Yet political frenzy in the area was driven not just by the urgency of
the upcoming elections. It was also fed by tremors from the unfolding social
and economic crisis in the country, by the bracing martial identities of gun-
carrying partisans and by the huge ambitions of duelling political figures
such as Pearnel Charles, Anthony Spaulding and Edward Seaga – each insist-

ing on being lord of his political domain. In the battle between Spaulding and Charles, it was alleged that both men had bragged that with their political victory, apartment blocks occupied by the other's supporters would be razed – the better to give the victorious politician a view of his domain unobstructed by dwellings occupied by supporters of the opposition.[37] Given these imperatives it is not surprising that a ferocious battle unfolded in the communities of South and South West St Andrew as the combatants fought to hold onto or gain political territory.

Against this background of social crisis and continuing war and enmity, the new year was greeted by a new round of violence. On Monday, 5 January 1976, JLP gangs attacked PNP residents in the Rose Town area of South West St Andrew, damaging their homes and destroying both furniture and personal belongings. On the same day, PNP gunmen in Arnett Gardens and their nemeses from the Tivoli and Rema areas also fought pitched battles. They fired on each other from rooftops in daring exchanges that saw no police interference, even as residents scurried for their lives. Savage hand-to-hand combat took place in close quarters while other embittered partisans exchanged gunfire, threw firebombs and hurled bottles and stones at each other.[38]

The mayhem persisted into the following night, this time in the Rema enclave. There, gunmen from Arnett Gardens set upon JLP residents. Their doors were kicked in and homes set ablaze. But terrified PNP supporters in Trench Town also met the fury of JLP gunmen. These residents were assaulted and driven from their homes by JLP arsonists who reportedly promised death to all socialist-leaning "comrades" in the area.[39]

In the ensuring terror, some five persons were shot – one fatally – and hundreds of residents were sent fleeing from bombed-out and burning homes. By late evening when the flames were doused and the police had imposed a curfew in the area, it was apparent that terrorists from both parties had accomplished their mission. In Rema, for example, huge swaths of the population were sufficiently intimidated to flee for their lives, leaving only a brave few to return to salvage their belongings later that evening. Reporting on the debacle the *Daily Gleaner* mournfully described a motley collection of "trucks, vans, cars, and even donkeys and handcarts [that were] busy moving old and young out of the area".[40] The foregoing pattern of strike and counter strike in 1975–76 that sought the expulsion of populations deemed to be sympathetic to another party confirmed once again the destructive nexus between politics and urban violence in Jamaica. Gangs with the active complicity of both major parties were politically sanitizing neighbourhoods in which both parties held significant voter support.

In an address to the nation following the mayhem, Prime Minister Michael Manley gave a gripping account of the politics of partisan eviction.

> Gunmen had commenced a systematic campaign in the area. Working late at night, they would single out people who were known to be strong supporters of the PNP. Their technique is then to surround the home and tell the helpless victim that they have a certain number of days in which to pack up their belongings and leave the area. This was being done for the purpose of destroying the [PNP's] local political organization. It becomes more significant when you realize this is being done on the eve of a new voter registration drive.[41]

As accurate as this account was of the expulsion of PNP supporters, Manley's address scarcely touched on both parties' complicity in the terror and ignored the role of PNP gunmen in the outrage. In calling attention to paid gunmen and to "the criminal political gangs" in the area, Manley made it appear that the violence was the work of only JLP thugs. But in seeking to blame the violence wholly on that organization, Manley had evidently succumbed to a disabling condition that afflicted members of the duelling parties at the time: constant recrimination, attributing all blame to the other side and accusing it of engaging in dark conspiracies to destroy its rival. As a result, every act not to the liking of one side became an occasion for seeing a connection to a wider, sinister plot.

For the JLP, the larger danger was an alleged PNP plan to impose communism on the island. For its part, the PNP cast the JLP as a treasonous organization, allegedly conspiring with international allies and local terrorists to overthrow the government.[42] The terror in Trench Town was therefore not the shared responsibility of the parties in a long-standing war for political advantage, but rather the dastardly deed of an opposition party bent on overthrowing the government by force. In sum, despite a preponderance of evidence that pointed to the primacy of partisan competition as the cause of the terror, and notwithstanding his recognition of this fact, Manley insisted that this and other incidents across the island pointed to the JLP's role in a larger plot to remove the government from power.[43] Given this pointed attack on the opposition, one could scarcely fault Edwin Allen, a JLP member of Parliament, for reminding the prime minister of his own earlier accolades to the PNP gunmen from his Central Kingston constituency for having fought a successful war on his behalf in 1967 and 1972.

Against a background of worsening economic conditions, spiralling crime and raging violence – including the murder of several policemen, the death by arson of West Kingston residents and the killing of the Peruvian ambassador – the embattled PNP administration declared a state of emergency on 19 June 1976. This edict detained some 593 persons and lasted 351 days.[44]

With JLP activists and outlaw gunmen as the main targets, the security forces arrested numerous gunmen from both the political and criminal underworlds. Notable among the detainees was Pearnel Charles, the JLP deputy leader and candidate for the South West St Andrew seat. He was seized as a security risk and detained for allegedly possessing tape recordings of police conversations. Since Charles was a seasoned trade union organizer who did not flinch from combat with the PNP, his tough and combative campaign and readiness to confront the PNP on the hustings made him a feared nemesis in urban Kingston. Jailing Charles, then, was evidently the PNP's way of trimming the sails of a campaigner who challenged PNP ambitions in hard-fought urban constituencies such as South West St Andrew. Charles, along with other martial JLP activists, was thus detained not because he was involved in a violent bid to overthrow the state, but because he countenanced the use of political violence as a means of deterring the PNP and challenging its predominance in Kingston.

In these circumstances, however, the emergency decree did little to quell the political violence over the long term.[45] Even though the emergency permitted a relatively peaceful election, it did little to remove the suspicion among detractors that it was imposed to shield a vulnerable and embattled regime that was clinging to power in a deteriorating political and economic climate. It was not surprising, then, that the JLP decried the edict and referred to its detained members as "political prisoners".

While this language was an exaggeration, there was a modicum of truth to the JLP's protest. Although previous emergency edicts meant the imposition of strictures on political opponents, no political candidate was ever incarcerated on those occasions. Hence, in the context of the ideological polarization and political warfare of the day the jailing of the JLP officials did nothing to lessen the perception that the emergency was imposed to hamper the opposition's electoral campaign.

PNP partisans have suggested the unprecedented violence pointed to a JLP and externally based effort to destabilize the government[46] though no serious evidence was ever produced to support the view that there was a concerted and organized JLP plot or CIA attempts to overthrow the government.[47] In fact, an independent commission of inquiry into the emergency would dismiss these claims, arguing instead that the emergency was called on the basis of inconclusive evidence.[48] One implication of this finding is that political opponents were typically detained not on the basis of treasonous acts, but because of fear of these opponents' capacity to cause disruption. Hence, while the level of violence was certainly acute in 1976 and even though JLP politicians such as Pearnel Charles appeared to countenance it, most violent incidents that cost lives and destroyed property were provoked primarily by intensified factional political competition.

The continuing mayhem discredited the PNP, undercut the party's political legitimacy and made effective governance all but impossible during its second term. In order to address the real threat that violence in 1976 obviously posed to its incumbency, the PNP glossed over the systemic violence that had become a part of political contestation in the country and instead made overblown claims about the JLP's motives prior to the 1976 election. For the PNP faithful, it was JLP subversion in concert with hostile parties abroad – not heightened contestation through two-party competition – that accounted for the upsurge in violence.

Such exaggerated responses to perceived threats have long been a staple of Jamaican politics and the circumstances leading to the declaration of the 1976 state of emergency were no different. As communal wars have grown more violent and spiralled out of the parties' control, incumbent parties in Jamaica have historically resorted to the emergency laws to regulate the violence flowing from their competition. It is arguable, therefore, that violent political rivalries and factionalism, not coup plots, invariably provoked states of emergency in Jamaica. Of the several states of emergency that have been invoked by Jamaican politicians since the 1940s, every one has been linked to rising factionalism between the two major parties. It is fair to say that as far as major threats are concerned, no emergency decree has ever been issued in connection with a genuine national emergency involving a planned overthrow of the Jamaican state. As with earlier emergency declarations in the country's post-war history, it is hard not to conclude that the imposition of the 1976 edict was thoroughly tainted by partisan considerations.

The Cruelty of Power: The Rema Expulsion

If the 1976 state of emergency betrayed the contamination of law by political rivalries, then the PNP's latest bid to expel JLP supporters from the Rema enclave within weeks of the PNP's return to power confirmed that party's determination to crush all opposition to its dominance in strategic areas of urban Kingston. After 1972 that opposition had come not only from Edward Seaga's domain in West Kingston, but also from the JLP's beachhead in South St Andrew. In the four years since the 1972 PNP victory, this enclave had withstood every assault, including arson and gunfire, that PNP activists could throw at it. Yet not only had the enclave survived, but the martial determination of its gunmen and the ardour of its pro-JLP residents outweighed what limited gains the PNP had achieved from getting a few JLP residents in Rema to capitulate to the PNP's "socialist" hegemony in South St Andrew.[49] By 1977 such defiance clearly mocked the ambitions of constituency leader Anthony Spaulding and the JLP residents' effrontery provoked him into action.

After his narrow electoral victory in 1972, Spaulding had taken the measure of his opponents and had established himself as a redoubtable leader and equal to Edward Seaga. Not only had Spaulding established a powerful political base in Arnett Gardens, but his tenure had given the politically loyal poor in the constituency unprecedented access to modern housing in addition to a variety of amenities and social services. Spaulding's tenure also saw the consolidation of a fighting force of hardened political gunmen and the growth of his own popularity among grassroots supporters. The fanaticism of these loyalists and the reckless outlawry they enacted in his name had already become legendary across Kingston. This was so much the case that the Arnett Gardens gunmen's propensity for destructive violence terrified even battle-scarred veterans in the ghetto.

Spaulding's political dominance in South St Andrew was significant in other respects. It was in part his consolidation and projection of power in 1975–76 that pushed back the fighting force assembled by the JLP in South and South West St Andrew and it was this martial supremacy that prepared the ground for the PNP's Portia Simpson to score her electoral victory in the latter constituency in 1976. That Spaulding could tap the budget at the Ministry of Housing to finance the cost of his reign was perhaps another advantage he used to good effect. By dint of his formidable personality, political acumen and readiness to confront his foes in battle, Spaulding had become an inspired and respected warlord.

By early 1977 this distinction had won him a huge following among the martial-minded and socialist-leaning elements in the PNP. Now ensconced in a seemingly impregnable domain after his 1976 electoral victory in South St Andrew and enjoying a fanatical following among the grassroots rivalling that of the charismatic Manley, Spaulding seemed politically invincible. It was in this context as well as his rise to power as strategist, urban combat veteran and lord of his domain that Spaulding boldly moved to expel still-defiant JLP supporters from the Rema settlement.

The first blow was struck in late January 1977 when the Ministry of Housing approved the eviction of tenants for the non-payment of rents.[50] If it was not for the highly politicized context in which this eviction occurred it might have gone unnoticed. After all, expulsions for failure to pay rent were not unknown in working-class and poor neighbourhoods. Bailiffs and police with firearms regularly enforced landlords' eviction orders against tenants who had fallen behind in payments. Bailiffs and policemen were therefore not an uncommon sight at the gates of tenants as these lawmen made their rounds in urban neighbourhoods.

For the unfortunate tenant, however, the presence of the bailiff and the onset of eviction were shameful and humiliating occurrences. They usually testified to the tenants' straitened circumstance. Because eviction entailed the forcible removal of furniture and personal belongings to the sidewalks in full view of the neighbourhood, it became an exercise in public humiliation. For most tenants, arrival of the bailiff was therefore an experience to be avoided at all cost. All across urban Kingston, residents in poor neighbourhoods scuffled as best they could to meet the rent for the typical one-room dwellings that many called home. Yet because of their meagre incomes, many residents fell behind in payments to a variety of landlords, including the national government.

The Jamaican government had become a major landlord in the post-war years due to an extensive programme of housing construction that benefited thousands of poor residents. These tenants and apartment owners living in government-constructed housing were required to pay rents and mortgages to the national government, usually through the Ministry of Housing. On its face, this policy suggested that rents would be collected from all tenants regardless of their political sympathies and without reference to the vagaries of politics.

That was not to be the case, however. By the early 1960s, the payment and the collection of rents and mortgages to the national government had become wholly politicized. By the mid-1970s, garrisoned populations whose party was out of power typically lived rent-free under the protection of their militias. Populations deemed loyal to the party in power generally paid no rent. In both cases, where rent was due, inflamed political circumstances made the collection of rents nearly impossible. By the 1970s, payments for utilities and rents for government-owned dwellings were collected in the breach and only from populations and neighbourhoods where it was politically safe to do so.

Collecting rents from government-owned dwellings, especially in politically contentious neighbourhoods, was therefore a highly uncertain affair that permitted whole neighbourhoods to avoid paying rents entirely. This was especially the case in the Rema settlement where no rents had been paid for years. Indeed, a commission of inquiry into the eviction would find that "it is a fact without the slightest shadow of a doubt that the incidence of non-payment of Housing dues have [sic] grown to alarming proportions within recent years".[51] But for the sustained assault on JLP supporters in Rema since 1972, the eviction for the non-payment of rents by the national government might not have seemed unseemly.

The Rema evictions had less to do, however, with the non-payment of rents, as Spaulding would later claim, than with a historical partisan conflict and PNP desire to be rid of JLP supporters there.[52] Consequently, where arson and vigilantism had failed to dislodge the defiant residents, eviction for financial delinquency was now being used - presumably to give a patina of legality to a patently political act – to rid the area of JLP supporters.

Initially the pretext of a non-partisan eviction seemed to be holding as residents were expelled on 26 January, evidently without incident. But even here, all was not what it seemed. For although the eviction team had secured the apartments and barred the doors before they left, the policy still encountered the covert defiance of a hostile community. Opposition came in the form of a cat-and-mouse game that saw residents reoccupying the dwellings upon the eviction team's departure.[53] The provocation of this defiance as well as partisan agitation denouncing the evictions and encouraging residents not to pay rents now led the PNP to take more stringent measures. Paradoxically, those measures unleashed a chain of events whose fury would tear apart Spaulding's claim that the exercise had nothing to do with settling scores with a hated political enemy.

On 2 February a new round of evictions began. Armed policemen, whose presence went beyond merely upholding the law, accompanied the eviction team. Because inner-city policemen were located in contested or one-party dominant communities, members of the force were often caught in the crossfire of partisan politics. In practice, this meant that policemen were often expected to enforce partisan edicts or to stand aside while partisan mayhem was being unleashed. This politicized status had become the norm in the post-war years because the police force as an institution was increasingly buffeted by partisan pressures of the day.

This unenviable status had a divisive effect on the police force and it led to indirection and ambiguity in the ranks. On the one hand, the force as an institution took seriously its duty to enforce the law without fear or favour. On the other, as the political parties relied more and more on the police to adjudicate their wars, the force was subject to increasing political pressures that compromised its function. Hence, while the upper echelons of the force retained a professional *esprit de corps,* the impartiality of the rank and file was increasingly compromised by political clashes in urban communities.

As political conflicts worsened over the years, several police stations and many policemen around urban Kingston became increasingly identified with the cause of one or another of the political parties. Police stations in South St Andrew, for example, were cited for their pro-PNP sympathies. Communities in South St Andrew similarly regarded policemen from the Trench Town and Admiral Town stations as being sympathetic to the PNP.

This pro-PNP tendency among some police stations was evident elsewhere in Kingston. Even the Denham Town police station, which was wholly within Edward Seaga's West Kingston constituency, was regarded as a major PNP outpost. Indeed, a supervising officer from that station was on the scene during the Rema crisis, where he evidently won little respect from JLP partisans there. Derided as "Labourites" by partisan policemen from Denham Town, Admiral Town and Trench Town, Rema settlers understandably regarded representatives from these stations as incubi and parasitic agents of a hated PNP administration.[54] It is not surprising, therefore, that the hostile residents in Rema derisively referred to policemen on the scene as blood-sucking "ticks".[55]

Given these strong sentiments, the expulsion that was to take place under the watchful eyes of these policemen quickly went awry. As they readied themselves for the expulsion a vengeful, boisterous crowd of Arnett Gardens partisans including several gunmen met the lawmen. Evidently tipped off about the impending evictions and impatient to seize the apartments, this crowd gathered at the Seventh Street border dividing the Rema and Arnett Gardens communities. At the same time the presence of this hectoring mob inflamed Rema residents who, it was apparent, were not going to give in without a fight.

Recognizing the potential for a major conflict, senior police officers attempted to deter persons in the crowd by calling over megaphones for them to return to their homes. But while parts of the crowd beat a hasty retreat, others rushed past the police into the Rema sector to begin occupying the not-yet-vacant apartments. These overeager invaders were greeted by incensed residents and by a hail of bullets.[56] As the gunfight ensued, Arnett Gardens gunmen answering to fanciful *noms de plume* such as "Shine", "Mosquito", "Coir" and "Dasheen" fired back, all the while shouting party slogans and hurling epithets.

The invaders in particular seemed incensed that the Rema-ites had refused to capitulate to the PNP's socialist rule. As one eyewitness would later testify, the invaders declared that "our minister [Anthony Spaulding] send us dung ya . . . im sey we fi cum capture this. Who no want tun socialist wi have fi leave ya."[57] Witnesses also reported hearing such taunts as "Whey de Rema man dem dey – dem naw tun Socialist?" as the Arnett Gardens gunmen sought out their counterparts in Rema for violent retribution.[58]

As with earlier denunciation of PNP "comrades" by JLP activists, the PNP gunmen's threats against those who refused to embrace socialism confirmed a stubborn reality behind the political clashes in the slums. That is, the conflict over territory and power in the ghetto was redolent with the ideological issues racking the society. Epithets in the heat of the Rema battle confirmed the nexus between war over territory in the slums and conflict over policy and ideology in the wider society. For their part, JLP activists in Tivoli Gardens were equally incensed that some of their allies in the Rema enclave were breaking ranks and "getting soft and going socialist".[59] No matter how crude the expression or unsophisticated the understanding of socialism in the ghetto, sentiments in the Rema clash reflected conflicting views at the grassroots level about the significance of socialism for the poor and the meaning of radical social change for the country.

Where PNP gunmen in Rema evidently saw in democratic socialism the possibility of social justice and empowerment, JLP supporters saw just the opposite. They regarded the policy as a mechanism for PNP domination and ideological supremacy. Even though this critical view of power was increasingly being shared by dissenting voices in the press and elsewhere, such criticisms had no impact on the most rabid of PNP loyalists. For PNP "contractors", far-flung gunmen and the over-loyal rank and file, democratic socialism remained indisputably beneficial and empowering.[60]

Given these clashing perspectives it would not be an exaggeration to say that for those firing weapons from the JLP's side, the planned seizure of their apartments and the presence of unsympathetic police officers constituted a striking local case of democratic socialism in action. Rema-ites might therefore be forgiven for believing what champions of democratic socialism could not: that PNP policy in the ghetto entailed not social emancipation and improvement in the condition of the poor, but rather imposition of an unwanted authority and local subjection of the JLP and its dissenting adherents.

Subsequent developments confirmed the residents' dismay with the police and attested to the victims' understanding of the expulsion as a wanton act of political victimization. First, the police on the scene generally stood by as vengeful Arnett Gardens invaders dashed into the high-rise buildings and began hurling the furniture and belongings of JLP settlers over the balconies, smashing them on the ground below.[61] In their partisan enthusiasm, the invaders "declared that they wanted a whole building a complete high rise building for themselves and they started to throw out regular legal tenants to make accommodation for this their declared ambition and intention".[62] Despite the entreaties of frightened tenants, the protestations of an army officer on the scene and even the cry of peacemakers from the community, the destruction continued without meaningful police intervention.[63] Lawmen thus watched as the invaders who had arrived aboard trucks loaded with furniture set about seizing the not-yet-vacated apartments.

As the Small Commission would observe, it was only after

> several truckloads of furniture new and old, and families young and old arrived to take over the vacated apartments . . . that most people realized for the first time that this occupation was to take place immediately and even before the eviction exercise had been completed. The wrath and fury of the newly evicted should be better imagined than described by testimony when they discovered that not only the evictors but also the new occupiers were all junglists and PNP adherents.[64]

To be fair to the police on the scene, some did attempt at the start of the fracas to deter the invasion by various means, including beating back the PNP invaders. Moreover, as the threat of violence got worse, senior officers also tried to get housing minister Spaulding to call off the eviction.

For the most part, however, lawmen on the scene were compromised by past police accommodation to political victimization in Rema and by police deference to the PNP's reign in South St Andrew. PNP harassment of Rema residents had therefore become routine, with hardly any ability of area lawmen to stop it. Thus, even when the violence and destruction of property in Rema finally impelled senior officers to seek an end to the eviction, the lawmen proved incapable of asserting themselves against the PNP and their effort failed to override Minister Spaulding's unyielding insistence that the eviction continue.[65]

Second, JLP supporters' mistrust of the police as impartial enforcers was confirmed when soldiers on the scene intervened to forcefully halt the eviction. Where the police had dithered in the face of PNP violence, soldiers fired on the armed invaders, killing at least one gunman who had refused to stop and surrender his weapon. This shooting had a chastening effect on invaders already in the buildings and they "came running out with their hands above their heads".[66]

In this surprising turn of events, the army demonstrated its independence and affirmed its immunity to PNP insistence that the eviction be completed on its terms. Faced with the abrupt abortion of his plan, Spaulding, who was on the scene dressed in a populist bush jacket and knitted working-class tam, backed down and took a different tack. To save face the minister of housing uncharacteristically offered the improbable proposal for a committee to assist him in resolving the problem of illegal tenants.

Finally, if JLP supporters in Rema despaired of ever getting a hearing of their grievance, judicial censure of this PNP predation was scrupulous in its findings and harsh in its judgement. Remarking on the terror in South St Andrew, sole commissioner and retired justice Ronald H. Small called the eviction "a horrible stain on the pages of this nation's history".[67] His findings also put on record the ominous cooperation between gunmen and politicians and their role in this eviction. Remarking on the housing minister's close ties to gunmen the commissioner informed the public that "for a number of these Mr Spaulding claims and enjoys more than a passing acquaintance and they in turn look up to him for more than a passing salutation".[68]

To this indictment Commissioner Small added an assessment that appeared to speak the pain of all slum-dwellers who had ever experienced the sting of political victimization:

> Eviction at its best is an archaic repressive measure ill-suited to the rehabilitation of our poor and needy and oppressed. It can carry with it tremendous shock and undesirable and untold suffering and distress as was experienced on February 2nd, 1977, when violence and the threat of greater violence prevailed and had to be suppressed with violence.[69]

We turn in the next chapter to measures of empowerment to which the aggrieved among the lumpenproletariat turned in dealing with the sting of predation and the pain of marginalization.

8

The Struggle for Benefits

THE TRAVAILS OF JLP SUPPORTERS IN the Rema enclave and supplicants' indentureship to the parties point to a seeming triumph of predatory power and incapacity of the poor to escape from this captivity. However, the proliferation of myriad initiatives by the poor – within and beyond the political and criminal underworlds – achieved something of equal importance. This was the checkmating of predatory power by a severely disadvantaged group. Its response to inequality was to employ tactics that could not be easily expunged. Such measures were informed by a dynamic infra-politics whose variation exerted a compelling and subversive social power.

Compulsion from above was exercised by means of a seductive intimacy and the promotion of an appalling, internecine violence. This twin feature of power gave the Jamaican state its legendary ubiquity and loaned it a formidable penetration into the lives of the supplicant poor. This predatory power was sufficiently invasive that it is difficult to identify social spaces inhabited by the poorer classes that were not in some manner influenced, penetrated or occupied by the state and the political parties.

For example, family life, recreation and creative outlets, as well as schooling and work lives were subject to state and party interference in many urban constituencies and neighbourhoods. We have seen that this was particularly the case in those garrisoned communities where the reach of state and party politics was both extensive and intensive. But one need not live in a garrisoned community to know the influence of these two dominant political structures. Because of the reach of power in this context of predation, party–state relations pervaded any number of social spaces – some that were clearly a part of the state apparatus and others that were ostensibly independent of it. It is important to keep this in mind as we examine those arenas in which popular actions occurred.

As I have argued elsewhere, we may think of political action and social relations as occurring both within and beyond state structures in urban Jamaica.[1] While this distinction is analytically useful, there really is no social space that is so thoroughly controlled by the state that the poor can be barred from it. The urban poor's massive cultural and political penetration of the political parties makes that abundantly clear. Likewise, in contexts of predatory power there are no cocooned non-governmental spaces to which the supplicant poor can retreat in isolation. All social spaces where the state or the people attempt to exercise a predominant influence are themselves sites of great contestation. Epic struggles are enacted in them as state agents, party bosses, entrepreneurs and myriad subordinate groups fight for advantage with unpredictable results. Outcomes of contestations in these spaces are therefore decisive since they powerfully shape both the flow and character of power in Jamaica.

We should be careful, however, not to exaggerate the state's weaknesses in these circumstances. For whatever the indeterminacy of outcomes, it in no way vitiates the massive advantages of predatory power. The relationship between patrons and clients was fundamentally unequal and not just because of an imbalance in the capacity for violence. Indeed, for the urban poor state predation was not merely a banal, bureaucratic domination that was brutally exerted from the centre of power. Rather, predatory power expressed itself as intimate clientelist rule that transformed party identification into a communal, proto-national sentiment. By extending this compulsion into nearly all areas of the supplicant poor's social existence, the state and parties exerted a massive political and socio-cultural influence on poor people's lives.

This authority was felt, therefore, not just in the obvious political space where party and state politics dominated. Coercion was also exerted in ostensibly non-party, non-state spaces to which the poor increasingly retreated. Popular social spaces such as the informal economy were subject to both state and party pull and domesticating influence. State and party power reached into a variety of relatively autonomous spaces that were vital to the existence and identity of popular social life.[2]

It cannot be emphasized enough that this penetration was employed not merely to expunge or to discipline by harsh and brutal measures. Rather, in its differentiation and ubiquity across social spaces, state predation reached down to nuzzle the poorer classes, binding them to its rule by a patronizing affection. It accomplished this intimacy with seductive benefits and sympathetic concern for the cultural and material needs of the poor. In short, the predatory state incorporated the urban poor both violently and affectionately inside its variegated and dilating power. This, then, was the thralldom into which the supplicant poor fell.

For all its seductive power, however, predation had obvious limitations. It typically sought to compel by blandishment and force. On a number of occasions after 1972, these measures provoked sharp responses from subordinate groups and these challenges interrupted the flow of power and dispersed its effects. Likewise, even though predatory power won a modicum of consent by forging powerful communal, proto-national loyalties, the strategy of divide-and-rule based on provoking a frenzied partisanship fell victim to powerful, competing forms of solidarity. These were mostly class-specific allegiances that sought the poor's own empowerment beyond the state and in opposition to it.

For all its fabled capacity, state predation in Jamaica could not completely silence opposition, eliminate challenges or halt defections from its domination. Myriad challenges to dilating state power emerged willy-nilly, were sometimes dramatic in expression and were sustained in the years after 1977. Defiance occurred in a variety of social spaces and had the most unlikely consequences for state power. Remarkably, these oppositions not only disclosed the existence of a counter-system of power and values, but also highlighted the advent of unique forms of social power. By their variety, accumulation and ubiquity, these forms of social power confounded the state and blunted its power. This chapter examines the growing turbulence produced by this opposition.

Jockeying for Customary Rights

Contention in Jamaican politics is as much about intra-party factional disputes as it is about conflicts between the parties. Commentators have rightfully called attention to the importance of inter-party factional strife.[3] This focus neglects significant conflict *within* the parties. While there has also been extensive commentary on conflicts at the top between senior party figures and elite factions in both parties, there has been hardly any discussion of the issue of patron-client conflicts.[4] In particular, not much light has been shed on the relationship between party patrons who wish to restrain the poor and clients who bravely insist on trespassing on these patrons' power.

Parties and their patrons in Jamaica typically face the challenge of securing an orderly distribution of benefits in ways that respect the patrons' authority. Benefits politics encourages a vast supplicancy among the poor, yet it must also curb the enthusiasm and ambitions of boisterous dependents whose hunger for political bounty sometimes seems to know no limits. Over the years, desperate supplicants wishing to devour the spoils of political war created turbulence within the clientelist parties by leaning on them to deliver the benefits of political loyalty. Moreover, militant activists contributed to the agitation by going beyond the demand for handouts to making ambitious claims for a role in the sponsorship and disposition of benefits. Both inclinations, it is clear, conflicted with elites' desire to exercise unencumbered control over the distribution of benefits. From this vantage point clientelist politics are not just about the functional distribution of handouts by a bureaucratic organization. Rather, this politics also pertains to inner-party power relations and patron-client power struggles over contentious issues. None perhaps has been the source of more conflict than the presumed customary right of loyalists to enjoy untrammelled access to political spoils.

This presumption, as we have seen, has been the *sine qua non* of post-war Jamaican politics. A consensus that the poor are entitled to political handouts united both parties, even as disagreements over the distribution of that patronage became the major contributor to factional politics. This contention over benefits and the entitlement of political victors grew more raucous in the 1960s as supplicants at job sites, union halls and party offices clashed with their own party officers and with the political opposition to assure privileged access to spoils.

After 1972, and particularly in the aftermath of the PNP's 1974 adoption of democratic socialism, the battle over entitlements and the disposition of political benefits became more acute and especially so for PNP loyalists. This was the case in part because the 1972 populist electoral victory gave a fillip to the inevitable expectation of a sharing out of political bounty. Activists, well-connected entrepreneurs and the faithful rank and file seized the occasion of that victory to satisfy their appetites. Moreover, the successful imposition of the 1974 bauxite levy on foreign mining companies added to this enthusiasm for political handouts as the levy brought a financial windfall that was used to open up further avenues for public spending.[5] Funds from the levy, for instance, helped finance services and social programmes for the poor including the controversial Special Employment Programme.

This programme, which was wildly popular with the poor, provided some twenty thousand poor persons with menial jobs.[6] A so-called crash programme to provide employment especially for women and unskilled youth therefore became a magnet for that most desperate of urban groups – the lumpenproletariat. After 1972 this contingent increasingly came to associate the PNP's democratic socialism with handouts, public works programmes and unchecked distribution of largesse. As the predominant force among the party's urban supporters, the lumpenproletariat led the clamour for patronage, and it was from their ranks that the parties felt the greatest pressure to deliver it. The militant lumpenproletariat's growing social consciousness, sharp eye for the main chance and overweening partisanship made it an irrepressible social force at a moment of great uncertainty and mounting conflict.

How did an unruly group, which lacked education, was bereft of job skills and had no stable relationship to economy or society assume such importance in the calculations of power? Jamaica's post-war politics suggests that the lumpenproletariat achieved its pre-eminence because it was an institutionally uncaptured and politically dangerous social force that had to be contained. Neither could it be bought off by integration into the trade unions as members of a wage-earning working class, nor could its socially degraded members be domesticated as law-abiding citizens. And though the group's huge influence and entitlements in both parties confirmed an indentureship to power, that relationship remained volatile and highly contested.

Just the same, tactics of divisive and uncertain patronage as well as contained incorporation and crucifying violence were measures by which the state and parties attempted to control this dissident group. Quite simply, members of the militant lumpenproletariat were feared because they were unruly, undisciplined and were loath to accept their domination lightly. At the same time, there can be no doubt that the lumpenproletariat possessed politically relevant sentiments seemingly muted in other groups.

The lumpenproletariat's robust self-confidence and acute awareness of its marginal racial and class condition also made it a force to be reckoned with. Certainly the group's capacity for badness-honour counted for much in Kingston's political badlands. Urban politicians were particularly aware of this resource. Trafficking in badness-honour, as a political commodity, was something the political parties did routinely. As the previous chapter showed, the PNP and its urban political barons relied extensively on the mobilization of badness-honour to get their way in the communal wars.

Beyond this incorporation of the political underground, however, the PNP, more than any other force, facilitated the lumpenproletariat's expanded entry into party affairs while raising the militant group's profile in national politics. All strata of the chronically unemployed including unskilled youths, common criminals, "own account" workers in the petty trade as well as casual labourers and minimum-wage workers found in the PNP's socialist appeal something to satisfy their yearnings. In sum, the PNP's strategic incorporation of a highly disadvantaged group, redistributionist policy, aggressive self-help by the poor, and popular perception of the regime's plenitude and hospitality gave the militant unemployed strata their social pre-eminence. It was this compelling combination that encouraged the group's race for power and abetted its quest for benefits.

And there was much bounty to be distributed. Party largesse in the city included cash payments to casual labourers, monies to small contractors to undertake public works projects, tickets for farm work abroad as well as funds for beautification projects in unsightly urban areas. For decades this bounty had confirmed supporters' entitlement to handouts. Yet as with most entitlement programmes, receipt of benefits transformed these favours into a jealously guarded right. Thus, even though patronage created a loyal constituency, patrons had to be careful not to offend recipients who had grown accustomed to their rights. Paradoxically, by the mid-1970s the PNP, facing straitened economic circumstances and political challenge from below, offended the very group it had done so much to cultivate, by attempting to curb its power and appetites.

In that period, PNP socialist mobilization introduced a new twist to the entitlement process. The party's political mobilization had caused urban youth and the chronically unemployed to take a renewed interest in political affairs and to join the party. The result for both groups that entered the

PNP in the thousands was enthusiasm for democratic socialism. Once there the vast majority joined the clamour not only for jobs but also for the numerous contracts that were being given to grassroots supporters.[7]

This provocation of appetites and mobilization of consciousness had a dramatic effect on power relations. On the one hand, mobilized clients from the streets became bolder in their demands, even going so far as to wrest state resources from the party by sly theft and open plunder. On the other hand, this audacious self-seeking trimmed patrons' ability to regulate the disposition of spoils. Consequently, the ability of patrons to restrain agitation and block unauthorized access to benefits by the now "socialist" constituency of the unemployed was not only sharply reduced but, in the end, thoroughly undermined.

These relations amounted, in effect, to a nasty civil war within the PNP. That is, patrons striving to manage the process of benefits allocation faced off against emboldened clients determined to strip the party of its largesse. The conflict revealed the travails of those that would be champions of socialist values and disclosed an unflattering dimension of mass consciousness under the thralldom of political clientelism in its democratic socialist phase.

One notable instance of this tension occurred in the mid-1970s as disputes of this kind reached their apogee. In this period, PNP activists were given contracts to repair several gullies in Kingston that were damaged by floodwaters. As with the case of George "Feathermop" Spence and his diversion of funds from the Lilford Gully project in 1975, PNP contractors in 1977 "ate out" monies disbursed for repairs to the Sandy Gully. There, Arnett Gardens gunmen-cum-contractors including such notables of the political underground as Anthony "Red Tony" Welch, Dennis "Dasheen" Grant and Benroe "Venites" Bailey, devoured this largesse. This feeding from below thus left the work at Sandy Gully unfinished and an embarrassed PNP had to seek additional funds to complete it.[8]

Repairs to the McGregor Gully reportedly met a similar fate when PNP contractors and others also siphoned monies from that project. As a result, even though a contract for almost J$3 million was allocated for repairs to the gully, within months the funds were nearly depleted with very little work completed at the site.[9] Other monies disbursed to help the poor were similarly wasted in this unprecedented plunder, even as municipal budget keepers were euphemistically documenting payments to "no show" workers under the rubric of "non-productive preliminaries".

The lumpenproletariat's assault on their sponsor's power was not confined to theft. Journalists and opposition politicians who spoke out against the practice were intimidated and their lives threatened.[10] By mid-1975 the abuses and pillage of funds had become so worrisome that none other than the prime minister was driven to summon the police department's Criminal Investigation Division to investigate the disappearance of these monies.[11] This intervention by the party leader disclosed the continuing significance of the conflict: party bosses had their hands full containing this determined nibbling from below, with its direct assault on the patron's power and on the state's resources. Yet not even the involvement of party leaders could halt this frenzied feeding on state resources in 1975.

Two years later the extent of predation from below became so troubling that Paul Burke, a left-wing activist, PNP organizer and champion of the poor, was driven by frustration to alert the party leader who reportedly ordered the termination of the funds for the McGregor Gully project.[12] This bid from various levels of the party to rein in the PNP's own support-ers was too little and too late. As the lumpenproletariat's hunger for the PNP's so-called socialist money grew, members of the group became even more reckless. On 16 June 1977 someone from their ranks apparently mur-dered a key government official who was inquiring into the malfeasance.[13]

This alarming turn of events and the sustained plunder it revealed threw an unwelcome spotlight on venality within the PNP. Public disclosure also focused unwanted newspaper attention on the corruptions of democratic socialism.[14] Journalists and other observers expressed their dismay and exco-riated the PNP for supervising a giveaway of public funds.

Expressing widespread sentiments on the matter a leading critic observed that "this government in particular has tended to its role simplistically as the trade-union of the masses, striving to alleviate the distress to which their condition gives rise, and doing so at the expense of those whom they regard as privileged members of the society".[15] Another influential commentator joined the chorus by noting that both parties shared the country's predica-ment:

> The parties attracted a disproportionate number of pimps, hustlers, lumpen types, rip-off artists, the unemployed, the least productive and those most dis-connected from the main centers of productive activity in the society. The combined weight of rip-off artists and romantic utopianists and intelligentsia with little understanding of the practical culture of work and productive activ-ity and organization made the parties dysfunctional or useless as a source of

generating ideas, work discipline and collective action useful in the management of the economic system at a time when the state under both JLP and PNP . . . was assuming a larger and larger role in economic management.[16]

As valid as this criticism was, many critics neglected a hidden but equally salient issue. This was the flagrant disrespect for the patrons' authority and the near impotence of political power in the face of determined challenges from below. Hence, even as critics rightfully used the occasion to question the PNP's socialist credentials, the public discussion of giveaways and theft fell victim to the ideologically polarized climate. Proponents of democratic socialism, for example, saw only the best intentions in the PNP's agenda. As a result, they uncritically hailed its empowerment of the poor while harping on the wickedness of detractors.

On the other side, the consensus among critics that the misuse of public funds was testimony to rank PNP hypocrisy and predictable avarice by a venal lumpenproletariat was equally flawed in its understanding. PNP corruption did confirm that a few of its officers and many supplicants had used the occasion to plunder state resources. But while those incidents contravened the ideology of democratic socialism, they did not define the political character of the regime and they paled in significance with the party's real commitment to change that resulted in several programmes that benefited the poor.[17] Likewise, the sniping at the lumpenproletariat that viewed them as a morally bankrupt rogue culture that despoiled the national character merely engaged in long-standing class contempt for the poor. At the same time this attitude ignored the manifestation of similar traits within the larger population, especially the presumptively morally unblemished middle class.

In sum, blinded by differences in their ideological commitments, both camps reduced the drama in the ghetto to a contest of good versus evil that was expressed in an alleged struggle between capitalism and communism on the island. In holding this formulaic view, commentators obscured an issue of profound significance in the political process: the epic inner-party struggle between embattled patrons and emboldened clients.[18]

Socialism and Predation from Below

Rather than confirming a shared commitment to socialism and seamless consensus to plunder the public treasury, relations between PNP clients and party bosses disclosed protracted and acute conflicts between allies. While the PNP's redistributionist policy certainly encouraged what detractors have called a "freeness mentality" among the poor, political handouts were not a PNP invention nor was theft of public funds peculiar to the 1970s.[19] These were long-institutionalized benefits and entitlements enjoyed over the years by supplicants from both parties.

What was new and decisive for the PNP in the 1970s was not the misuse of public funds by disbursing it to the loyalist poor, but rather contestation over the drawing down of those funds and the uses to which they were put. The repeated attempts by party bosses and PNP investigators to staunch the flow of funds to the lumpenproletariat and the party's dismay at its own contractors' misuse of monies indicate not collusion, but a sharp divergence of motives and a shifting balance of power. The militant lumpenproletariat in the 1970s was hungry for benefits, bidding for greater influence over the disposition of funds and plainly interested in getting something for nothing. Guided by self-seeking and the national norm of conspicuous consumption, whole layers of the lumpenproletariat were interested in nothing more than getting monies to acquire the trappings of status in the ghetto such as motorbikes, fancy clothing and jewellery.[20]

These motives were often at odds with the intentions of party ideologues, their political bosses, as well as civil servants such as Edward Ogilvie, who found the plunder wholly untenable and lost his life because of it. It was not that party officers were opposed to patronage for the poor, but that they viewed unauthorized siphoning of funds without any obligatory work by their clients as an abuse of party generosity and a flagrant challenge to party authority at a time of shrinking resources and increased public scrutiny. What had occurred, therefore, was a sharp clash involving the claims of power and the terms of patronage in a highly charged and fast-changing political process. The attempted cutback on funds to the lumpenproletariat therefore had less to do with the PNP's ethical concern for the use of the public purse than with reasserting the party's authority over its supporters and rescuing its reputation from the sensational charges levelled by its critics.

PNP patronage in the mid-1970s was therefore not entirely about "freeness" – as the critics would have it – but also about demanding that recipients exercise a modicum of personal if not social responsibility in exchange for benefits.[21] Moreover, ideologues in the PNP were well aware that if the goal of democratic socialism were to have any chance of success then loyalists would have to become less self-seeking and more attuned to broader issues of social change. In short, impelled by its commitment to socialist values, pressed by the country's rapidly eroding economic situation in the mid-1970s, and facing public scrutiny as well as insurgency and insubordination from below, the PNP seemed ready to consider a change in the terms of entitlement for its supplicants in the ghetto. Patronage in the late 1970s would, after all, require a reciprocal obligation to show up for work at job sites and complete tasks; it would require honest completion of contracts reserved for the "small man" in the ghetto; and it would entail taking seriously the socialist challenge of giving up short-run benefits in the interest of the larger goal of social transformation.

It was precisely those revised terms that were being challenged by an emboldened lumpenproletariat that saw no need to respect norms of integrity in the disposition of public funds or give a fair day's work for the patronage they received. Remarkably, defence of socialist values appeared to be the least of their concerns. This unflattering use of their counter-power did more than threaten party barons' authority and the public purse. The modality of unauthorized confiscation of state largesse – feigned defence of socialism, sly theft and unabashed plunder – brought both public embarrassment and enervation of critical state functions including disabling the respected norm of fiscal prudence in public affairs. Worse still, the unquenched desire by benefits-seekers for unmolested feeding endangered the PNP's larger agenda of social change. That agenda required more than unyielding political loyalty from the poor, and it needed more than their awakened consciousness of inequality. In its most exacting form, the party's agenda called for a political awareness that valued transformative change and the capacity to sustain the quest for it over the long haul.

This is how party leader Michael Manley posed the issue years later as he considered the PNP's predicament in the 1970s and reflected on the gap between the party's larger transformative agenda and the limitations of consciousness among its supporters:

> It is my experience that one of the fundamental difficulties that we face in the political process is that the average supporter does not understand the difference between change in the sense of transformation, changes in the sense that alters his or her relationship to power, from change in the sense of more benefits. How to distinguish transformation from what we may loosely call "more" . . . we must never be confused into thinking that more of the same is change.[22]

In other words, Manley was decrying both the party's and supporters' habituation to the idea that more benefits were what politics was all about. The PNP understood this danger in the late 1970s and had begun a retreat by altering, ever so delicately, the terms of its patron-client ties. But the urban poor did not take kindly to the trimming of benefits and the modification to their entitlements. By insisting on securing these rights regardless of the party's high-flown doctrine, the urban poor derailed the plans of political bosses and ideologues, upending their high-minded calculations for decisive social change.

Paradoxically, as Manley's chagrined account attests, it appears that the successful adhesion of the culture of benefits politics had effectively destroyed the party's ambitious plans for social transformation. Thus the very entitlement values that fed the communal war on which the parties relied destroyed any hope of mobilizing the country for the hoped-for social transformation, including the alteration of the poor's relationship to power.

But should this failure be blamed primarily on habituation to handouts and an alleged lack of ideological sophistication among the poor, as Manley's comments imply? I think not. As several commentators have agreed, the foundering of the PNP's socialist agenda had more to do with other issues than with the poor's hunger for benefits.[23] As the following comment demonstrates, Manley recognized as much:

> It is the nature of traditional popular democracy, ... that it separates in the mind of the electorate, the question of benefit from the question of process, that is to say, it creates a situation in which the shouting competition of the political parties is the dominant reality. Thus the process itself obscures from the people how to accomplish and maintain beneficial change. It creates ... a fatal disjuncture between the political process on the one hand, and the economic and the social process on the other.[24]

While this points unerringly to a fundamental problem for radical change in capitalist democracies, Manley's self-criticism avoided an equally important element of the story. This was the party's wilful prosecution of the communal war of divide-and-rule at a time when the party was ostensibly pursuing a break with the past. Remarking on the negative effects of this strategy, an insightful commentator would tellingly note that " 'politics' has split the ghetto in order to rule it by throwing crumbs to the egregiously savage while they slaughter each other or are mowed down for their excesses by the forces of law and order".[25]

This factor, too, was deeply inimical to socialist values and to the inculcation of transformative norms among the poor. Indeed, state predation produced among the urban dispossessed the opposite sentiments of intraclass hostility, violence, self-seeking and enmity for the state. Manley's *mea culpa* therefore elided the fundamental incongruity in the PNP's simultaneous pursuit of democratic socialism and the political tribal war.

In light of poor people's defence of their entitlements and their relative success in interrupting the political plans of their sponsors, it is worth exploring the neglected issue in the urban poor's choice of material fulfilment in opposition to their party's high-minded commitment to a social ideal. The obstacle to social change resided not only in poor people's habituation to handouts, but also in their active distrust of a state that compromised them with handouts and crucified them with political violence.[26] Because they found the state an anathema akin to the blood-sucking "tick" they knew it to be, they were not averse to returning the favour by feigning support for socialism and positioning themselves to "eat out" its largesse.

This first choice of satisfying popular appetites derives not from a lack of political sophistication or moral failure, but from the poor's instructive experience from decades of exposure to the cunning of predatory power. It impaled the poor on its violence and destructive policies, shared out to the "big men" their portion of public contracts and exposed the "small men" to public vilification for receiving theirs. In the consciousness of the Jamaican poor, politics is about predation and how to minimize its impact on their lives. For them it is a cannibalizing experience in which they imagine themselves being eaten by a vampire.[27] Popular language has historically invoked the vivid image of the state as a predatory beast tearing at the bodies, unity and esteem of the black poor. No wonder that in popular parlance the poor see the state's relations with them as the manifestation of "politricks", defined as "the experience of being eaten up by the parties" and dismembered of their humanity by strategies of the state.[28]

If the poor then choose to devour – no matter how unflattering the resulting portrait – what they believe to be their entitlement – in this case the spoils of political war – then that act within a corrupted system might be better regarded as an understandable self-defensive manoeuvre to protect the corporeal body of the downtrodden poor from the "bites" of the invasive state. In this respect, predation is mutual, as the poor take their turn at "eating out" the state's bounty. Stolen monies, unfulfilled contracts, theft of state property, indolence and absence from the job are all evidence of this feasting on the devouring beast.

The epic that is Jamaican politics is really about this mutual predation in which a leviathan eats out with its levies and punishments the humanity of the poor, even as these same supplicants try to nourish at the body of the predator with or without its authorization. This contest of consuming wills, involving the debilitation of state power by cunning clients, was as much a nibbling-away of goods from party bosses and the state as it was a giveaway of bounty by them. Recognizing this subtlety highlights a little-understood fact of power relations in Jamaica: in the popular imagination, behind the facade of apparent unity among allies in the patron–client game, a high-stakes drama of who gets to feast on whom is being played out. That drama, in which neither protagonist is capable of declaring total victory, sometimes finds the predatory state and party barons on the receiving end, momentarily trapped in the web of their own creation. As the foregoing has shown, it is at these moments of weakness and opportunity that allegedly helpless supplicants scramble to assert their power and nourish their bodies.

The Lumpenproletariat: Pre-eminence and Ubiquity

It is clear, then, that in the 1970s a war of attrition was being fought on several fronts and all of them involved the lumpenproletariat as a major player. There were at least four major flashpoints in the ongoing battles. These were the communal war, the state campaign against crime and independent criminal gunmen, the battle over entitlements demanded by PNP supplicants, and class warfare pitting workers, peasants and the urban poor against dominant groups. It is of some consequence that by the late 1970s not only was the lumpenproletariat a party to all four conflicts, but the group's concerns and moral culture wholly defined the politics of that period.

This was so, to begin with, because in the battle against crime, the state had identified the criminal underground as a leading menace. Second, the lumpenproletariat from the political underground became the cultural standard-bearers for the parties at the street level and acted as its front-line troops. Third, members of the group were the sly protagonists in the struggle over entitlements that found them jealously guarding those rights. Finally, the whole group in all its diversity figured prominently in the ongoing war over the country's political direction. This was the case despite the fact that few from their ranks understood or cared much for the finer points of democratic socialism.

They did, however, recognize in its agenda some of the remedies for their needs. It was precisely the bold lobbying for their cause and the extremism it sometimes assumed that made them the nemesis of their social betters. It is not surprising that the latter in their public commentary depicted the rebellious poor as an alien, destructive rogue force. As political clashes involving them moved front and centre on the national stage, the lumpenproletariat became the repository of social fears, a source of moral panic and target of derision.[29] There can be no doubt, then, that the lumpenproletariat's political presence across a number of domains placed the group at the nodal point of national conflict.

This pre-eminence and disruptive ubiquity explains the concerted war against this rebellious group. Clashes on several fronts disclosed the high-stakes campaign to suppress the group in every domain where their presence was being felt. This broad assault on the group was very much the case despite the masking effect of both the communal war and the clashes over the county's political direction.

By their prominence the wider contentions of party warfare and conflict over democratic socialism made it appear that these were the only important disputes. They certainly conspired to obscure the raging battle and test of wills between patrons and clients. The former contention obscured this hidden "struggle within the struggle" by wearing the veil of seemingly irreconcilable partisan difference between thoroughly united parties. The latter clash over democratic socialism contributed to the occultation by masquerading as a battle between capitalists and communists. These two conflicts were real and consequential. Yet it was this very dominance of the clash over social transformation and the clash of partisan tribes that cast a veil over the nodal conflict underlying all other differences: the enduring clash between the ghetto-based vanguard of the people's cause – the lumpenproletariat – and predatory power. This was the case regardless of the parties' political labels and ideologies.

By the late 1970s the urban poor had fashioned discernible structures of defiance that went beyond jockeying for power and foraging for benefits inside the parties. Opposition and a quest for autonomy from the state multiplied, became cumulative and grew more intense in these years. The bid for self-ownership included the organization of criminal enterprises by free-lance gunmen and independent criminal gangs. They amassed an arsenal of weapons and used this firepower to pillage the urban economy. Warring political gangs also captured the battle for autonomy in the stunning bid for peace in 1978. The next section examines the provocations for these conflicts and their consequences.

Bandits, Gangs and the State

The PNP's move to trim the influence of supplicants within its ranks was matched by the party's attempt to crush gunmen in the criminal underground. The state found this contingent particularly worrisome because unlike the political underground, its members came under no party supervision. Although the state's approach to the early gangs had been to incorporate them into the party apparatus, by the last years of the 1970s easy integration was no longer possible. Economic decline and austerity policies, especially after 1976, trimmed the state's ability to distribute benefits to the poor. Criminals among the latter therefore had to become more resourceful to survive alongside their supplicant kin inside the political parties. Hence, where the armed political underground was largely dependent on the state for its tribute, freelance gunmen and independent gangs looked not to the parties, but to criminal employment for their booty and survival.

Several circumstances favoured the turn to crime. Unemployment, greater access to guns, the destruction of the infrastructure of urban Kingston, demoralization of the police and pervasive political violence created vast opportunities for pillage by a criminal underground that had been in formation since the 1940s. By the late 1970s this tributary of the unemployed had matured into a bold, organized and well-armed independent force that became a major source of violence in the Kingston Metropolitan Area.[30]

Unlike their counterparts of the 1950s who had few guns and had to combine the limited use of firearms with skill in wielding the ubiquitous switchblade knife, the gangs of the 1970s had an arsenal of sophisticated weapons. They acquired large guns and automatic weapons from a variety of sources. When weapons did not fall into their hands from the extensive arsenal that supplied the political wars, criminal gunmen acquired weapons primarily by exchanging both drugs and monies from the drug trade for guns. This trade primarily involved the sale and export of marijuana. By the late 1970s, however, as the island was drawn into the regional drug trade as a transshipment point to North America, that traffic also included cocaine.[31]

The criminal underground also procured guns from policemen and soldiers who sold their weapons to both the political and criminal underworlds.[32] At the same time, the island's largely unpatrolled coastal waters, heavy airline passenger traffic from the United States and importation of cheap consumer goods in barrels for the burgeoning local trade created additional opportunities for the importation of guns. These weapons provided the means for economic independence from the parties as criminal gangs engaged in drug running, bank-and-payroll heists, extortion of businesses in the ghetto as well as a variety of other rackets.[33] The massive importation of guns was thus decisive in the proliferation of criminal gangs in the 1970s and in turning an inchoate group into a formidable force. Guns, as one observer noted, "spawned a new and expanding network of criminal gangs all over the city, starting in West Kingston and expanding into other poor communities".[34]

With guns in the hands of the political and criminal underworlds, a distinct gun culture and its associated power was now starkly evident. Political enforcers were nothing without their weapons, and this arsenal combined with badness-honour conferred on the top rankings a coveted status as fearless and seasoned fighters. These praetorian guards were known and honoured for their zeal, courage and skill in wielding weapons, discharging violence, and managing men and controlling political territory. Political enforcers also derived power from the control and defence of captive populations in the garrison communities. Thus while politicians were the ultimate source of power in the ghetto, the enforcers on the ground made political control from above possible. As the manifestation of the decentralization of violence, "political guns" in the hands of the poor created formidable alternative centres of power beyond the state.

Possession of a gun in the slums was also linked to gender and sexuality. Owning a gun reinforced heterosexual notions of manliness and the image of male potency. While homosexuality was a horror and a bane in the slums, to be a gunman of any consequence did not entail avoidance of men. On the contrary, heterosexual male bonding necessitated minimizing contact with women in favour of constant bonding and expressions of martial solidarity with other men by communing around the heterosexual male ideal.[35] Guns, male friendship and participation in warfare generated new solidarities anchored in martial identities. The power of the gun was therefore both a "source of command over populations and a symbol of swaggering, male bravado".[36] Violence and a virile badness-honour – not conventional norms of respectability – were key bases of social power in the ghetto.[37]

This nexus of gun-based violence, sexual identity and social power was repeated among the criminal class. As with their kin in the political underworld, the criminal's possession of the gun went beyond its utility. Weapons conferred on these gunmen the kind of personal power and efficacy that Jamaican society denied them in other areas. Legendary criminals achieved Robin Hood status in the slums precisely because of their gun-toting defiance. A violent, dramaturgic extremism was therefore to be enjoyed for its own sake. It was a skill to be mastered and deployed with both style and verve. In the politics of the gunman, aesthetic values and self-seeking often trumped doctrinal politics. But, while crime and revolutionary protest were rarely joined in the political underground or among the criminal class, for ghetto gunmen crime and social power were inextricably yoked.

Yet there was more to the gunmen's social power than either crime or aesthetics. By the late 1970s, criminal gangs had increased their ability to disburse patronage, just like the politician. Handouts to the poor contributed to gunmen's social power and growing popularity while their open defiance of the law gave them an aura of invincibility. The gangs' social power drew on patronage and community support and the protection they provided. In the corrupted social and political system of the day, criminal gunmen and gangs were effectively insulated from the law by the active complicity of their neighbours. What has been written about the "don" – a moniker for the criminal gunman in the 1980s – is an apt description of the status of the famous "generals" who ran criminal enterprises in the ghetto in the late 1970s:

> It is this social power which allows the Don to dictate to politicians, to chuck badness in the community, to demand protection money from private sector companies, to organize . . . hard drugs networks without fear of being caught, to break the law without any fear of being dealt with and to kill people without any fear of being found guilty of murder.[38]

This proliferation of criminal gangs, their possession of a significant arsenal of weapons and the impunity of their conduct provoked another major crackdown by the state. The war on armed ghetto leaders, which had begun in earnest in January 1976, was extended through the continuing state of emergency.

The latest attempt to repress the criminal gangs came in January 1977 with the establishment of a roving SWAT team of heavily armed policemen known officially as the Mobile Brigade. Given a free hand to hunt gunmen of all stripes, the Mobile Brigade took the war on gun crimes to the ghetto. There the police conducted a merciless, no-holds-barred war of attrition against the criminal gangs. This campaign of exterminism would take a huge toll on both law officers and their targets.

Despite the severity of this state repression, notorious gunmen eluded the state's dragnet. Guarded by wary and complicit communities, the gunmen hid behind a wall of silence. It was so effective that almost a year after the declaration of the emergency, the police were desperate enough to turn to the public for help. Notices were posted in the local newspaper seeking assistance in finding several gunmen including Dennis "Copper" Barth, the elusive, light-skinned paladin. In the midst of the crackdown on gunmen, he had engineered a second escape from prison and had been on the loose since March 1997.[39]

A similar "most wanted" notice carrying a J$3,000 reward was posted in the same month for Anthony Tingle, a fearless twenty-two-year-old gang leader. Known as "General Starkie", Tingle was, for a time, the head of the Wild Bunch gang in Kingston.[40] Members of this gang plied their trade from PNP-dominated areas such as Arnett Gardens, Rose Town and Lizard Town, and Payne Avenue. Tingle himself was wanted for a variety of crimes, including murder, armed robbery and rape.[41]

That Tingle and Barth remained at large — despite the rewards on their heads and a publicized manhunt for them — was cause for consternation among the upper ranks of the state system, not to mention frustration among the security forces policing the streets. That both men continued their mayhem while nested in the protective cover of their neighbourhoods was especially galling. After all, the moral collusion that hid these perpetrators pointed to an unmistakable closing of ranks against the police, and a rejection of norms of the wider society that viewed both men as common criminals.

Dirty War: Green Bay and Its Aftermath

This impertinence and the impunity of the gangs provoked a crisis of the state that intensified hostility to it in poor communities, further eroding the state's credibility with critics and the poor alike. In an attempt to show the ghetto the wages of defiance, army officers who were evidently impatient with failures of the police hatched a plot to lure several gunmen from the JLP's Southside enclave in Central Kingston to their deaths.[42] The plan called for entrapping the men from this JLP neighbourhood with the promise of jobs and guns and then ambushing them.[43] Killing the men would presumably send a tough message to the slums while strengthening the PNP's law-and-order claims. Yet instead of killing them all in the ambush on 5 January 1978 at the army's firing range at Green Bay, the soldiers' plan went awry.

As they opened fire on the unsuspecting victims that morning, only five of ten men lured to the site were cut down and killed. The others scrambled to safety, fled the area and reported their shocking experience to the ghetto.[44] The next day the *Daily Gleaner* dutifully reported the army's false story: the gunmen had gone to the firing range with guns and were surprised by a military patrol.[45] By the time of publication, however, the real story and meaning of the incident had raced through the stunned ghetto: the state that hired gunmen to carry out its policies had sent a death squad to carry out summary executions of the ghetto poor. Raw terror and exterminism was being employed in a bid to shore up support for the regime and to reassure the public that it was, indeed, serious about curbing crime. Putting the rebellious poor in their place would reassure a fearful society that was thoroughly intimidated by them. That the gunmen were from the JLP enclave would also further the PNP's campaign to convince the public that the dead men were in fact part of a continuing plot to destabilize the government.[46]

The attempted execution proved to be a huge political blunder and it galvanized the ghetto. The immediate effect was the ripping away of the veil of partisan difference and ideological contestation that had thus far divided the poor. The veil had obscured the poor's perception of their condition and shrouded the extent to which they had become merely fodder in the communal wars. Laurie Gunst's description was apt; the shock of recognition was undeniable: "It had been one thing to war with one another over scarce scraps from the bosses' tables, and to take one another's lives in a struggle that had come to resemble some terrifying kind of blood sport. But now they saw how expendable their lives really were."[47] The urban poor's own estimation that "Is a whole heap of yout' man an' dawta dead because dem use we" (Because of political exploitation, many youths and women died) was an oft-repeated refrain in the wake of the killings.[48]

As the poor awakened to their predicament, the gunmen from both parties – in a stunning move that took their sponsors by surprise – buried their differences and within days of the massacre publicly declared their own truce.[49] Several personalities led this bid for unity. Claude Massop, the Tivoli top ranking, and the PNP's Aston "Buckie" Thompson led the way. These two respected fighters took the risk of standing in the spotlight to promote the truce, but other activists, such as the PNP's Anthony Welch and the JLP's Carl "Byia" Mitchell, worked in concert with these two.

Hard times in the ghetto and common experience facilitated this surprising concordance. After all, none of the champions of the truce were strangers to one another. Hardship and growing political awareness caused a few gunmen to breach the rigid partisan divisions even before the truce. They had begun fraternizing and were already crossing into each other's domains, and even cooperated in criminal exploits to supplement their shrinking funds.[50] They had fought across the political divide, had done jail time for various crimes and were prison mates during the state of emergency that netted several gunmen.[51] In addition, they experienced the hardship of the 1970s with its ever-greater economic pressures on the poor. The squeeze brought about by a continuing economic downturn, cuts in public spending and a looming International Monetary Fund (IMF) agreement drove supplicants including these gunmen to seek means other than patronage to support themselves. This economic squeeze together with the experience of incarceration proved to be a sobering prelude to the truce, as these gunmen realized their common predicament. Thus while the massacre created a rupture in its own right, its timing dramatically summoned latent social and political interests in the ghetto.

Several of these bubbled to the surface with the announcement of the truce. First and foremost was the demand for peace and the cessation of the decades-long war. Community leaders, and the ghetto poor who rallied to their cause, repeatedly affirmed the call for peace. In one instance, as a crowd of some seven hundred persons gathered to celebrate the truce on 10 January, a chant demanding "Peace! Peace! We want peace!" filled the air.[52] Five days later, as Arnett Gardens residents joined a march that crossed into formerly hostile areas such as Tivoli Gardens, the same appeal for peace rose from their lips. Tivolites who repeated the exercise in Arnett Gardens and other areas that were previously off-limits matched this imperative.[53]

This groundswell for peace was so strong that it prompted some in the ghetto to consider "parking" their guns. As one youth remarked to a reporter, "When peace [spreads] island-wide and we achieve equal rights and justice then the guns get rusty and throw away. Then there will be no need for even police."[54] Another remarked that "In this area youth have no father. Father dead from gunshot. We want to park gun. Mek gun get rusty and throw away."

This war-weariness was matched by the desire for unity. Activists affirmed this imperative: "We who have been observed by elements in the society as being the foundation of all badness will now demonstrate that we can live in love and unity. We will demonstrate that we can survive without the shedding of blood."[55] Yet as important and unyielding as was the desire for peace and unity, it was the demand for drastic improvements in their material condition that revealed the urgency of their claims and their possible limits. When the mobilized urban poor gathered for a public meeting at the National Heroes Circle on 11 January, Aston Thompson addressed this issue directly: "After peace now, we want to see improvement in living conditions. We want work in general and government must put more [monies] in youth programmes."[56]

Thompson's plea was echoed by others who emphasized the need for training centres, the establishment of literacy programmes, and the creation of factories and productive enterprises in the ghetto. Ras Rupert, a resident in the West, echoed the demand for meaningful programmes: "Unity wonderful but we want better housing, better living standard for all people whether JLP or PNP. We cannot allow politicians to come into West Kingston and divide youths anymore. The situation must remedy. We have to get together. We are the ones living in degrading conditions."[57] As this observation indicates, some among the poor were acutely aware of the tentacles of power and its suffocating effects. For all that, however, the poor were united in their aspiration for a better life – "one in which they could find an elusive justice, live in peace and unity, find work without discrimination, and be housed in accommodations fit for human beings".[58]

This yearning for uplift proved powerful enough to pull into its orbit areas beyond Tivoli Gardens, Matthews Lane, Hannah Town and the communities of Pink, Rose and Luke Lanes. Communities in North West St Andrew and their partisan gangs from Tower Avenue (JLP), Waterhouse (PNP) and Mall Road (PNP) joined these pioneers.

Likewise the communities of Fletchers Land (JLP) and Allman Town (PNP) signed on after being reassured by the top rankings.[59] Other Central Kingston gangs from Tel Aviv (PNP) and Southside (JLP) declared their truce on 19 January. And though the embittered Arnett Gardens and Rema communities had remained aloof from the widening peace, these important holdouts eventually came on board, thus adding their considerable political weight to the defections.[60]

Unity in common purpose thus proved more powerful than old enmities. The challenge the protesters faced, however, was how to satisfy their pressing needs when these could only be fulfilled by a state and society that had put in place the very conditions from which the poor hoped to escape. Indeed, the state's and political parties' reactions were hardly encouraging. Caught off guard by the bold initiative from below, state agents and others tacked between qualified support for the truce and outright attempts to undo it. Prime Minister Manley, for one, welcomed the truce, but insisted that all illegal guns be turned in. Bereft of positive proposals to address the poor's concern, this unilateral demand in the face of the gangs' determination not to hand over their guns seemed to be a recipe for further distrust, if not open warfare. For his part, Edward Seaga was less combative; he offered J$5,000, half his salary as a parliamentarian, toward a fund to finance new projects in the ghetto.[61]

The most ominous response, however, came from Dudley Thompson, the newly appointed minister of national security. Thompson was unambiguous in his rejection of any claims the rebellious poor might have on the society. In response to queries from the island's leading newspaper about the execution of the men from Southside and the policy toward the gunmen, Thompson made no concessions: "I don't have any time to reform them, my life is too short for that." And again, "I have no quarter to give them. They have no place in our society."[62]

This message was clear in Thompson's address to members of the Jamaica Defence Force on 7 March. There he endorsed the executions with the assertion that "No angels were killed at Green Bay", and implied there would be more Green Bays on his watch.[63] As if his endorsement of the massacre were not enough, Thompson was reported to have said, in the newspaper's words, that "the only thing that went wrong was that all of them were not killed".[64] Given this endorsement of murder and state terror, the truce-makers and other gunmen had much to worry about.[65]

Still, this danger did not deter the search for peace in the interim. In the face of the state's foot-dragging in releasing funds for needed projects, truce leaders turned elsewhere for help.[66] An appeal, backed by the *Daily Gleaner*, went out to the nation for contributions to a peace fund. The Jamaica

Council of Churches, which founded an advisory body to mediate between truce leaders and the government, also launched its own fund drive.[67] In February truce leaders sought funds and food aid from the United States[68] and in April, Bob Marley and other leading musicians gave a fundraising concert dedicated to the historic event.[69] All these efforts bore fruit, but they were never enough to support the several projects that had been envisioned. Fundraising, in particular, fell short of the amount needed to finance renewal in the ghetto. The efforts of the influential Jamaica Council of Churches yielded only J$19,000 at the end of May when its members ended their role as mediators.[70] Similarly, after several months of canvassing, the *Gleaner*'s Community Peace Fund secured donations of only J$30,807.[71] Disappointed by the meagre response, the newspaper closed the fund in April.[72]

Collapse of the Peace Movement

By that time hopes for the fledgling peace were being outpaced by a conjunction of fateful circumstances. First, there was a fundamental contradiction between the goals of the truce and the imperatives of the state system. The key to maintenance of the peace and to prospects for a hopeful future for the ghetto lay in two critical needs: the parties' commitment to change, and the immediate infusion of significant funds to create jobs, training and the upgrading of infrastructure. In other words, sustained peace required an end to political victimization and creation of a major spending programme that would create employment and enterprises to ease the pent-up demand for income and livelihood in the ghetto.

Five months into the truce, neither institutional change nor massive investment funds were forthcoming. In the former instance, the politics of the state had become more instead of less hostile to the upheaval in the ghetto. In the latter, financial investment in the slums faced the barrier of historical neglect of Kingston's poorer precincts as well as shrinking revenues brought on by economic downturn and capital flight. That the PNP was also engaged in frantic negotiations with the IMF did not augur well for the new programme of public spending. Consequently, an agenda involving a massive investment programme of this sort, while not impossible to achieve, faced enormous difficulties. But in this struggle between patrons and clients over the urgent need for infusion of funds, the evidence points overwhelmingly to foot-dragging and temporizing by the state.

Respectable advocates for that investment spoke critically of the government's do-nothing policy on this issue. The Reverend C.S. Reid, for example, accused the politicians of filibustering because of the threat to their power.[73] It is not surprising, then, that neither corporate capital nor the state responded with the significant financial package that would have been necessary to secure the peace.[74]

On balance, then, the old institutional and representational relations between state and society, and between party and masses endured. In truth, the truce needed the state's and parties' cooperation to succeed. But as their responses showed, these organizations sought, predictably, to subvert the exercise in peacemaking whose purpose was to supplant state and party control over the lives of the poor. In these circumstances, their cause was expendable and their needs were met by continued neglect and temporizing. Relations of power – not the urgent needs of the most deprived and the most rebellious of the poor – determined outcomes.

Thus, while the truce challenged key facets of domination in the country such as state violence, patronage and communal war, and though it exposed the destructive character of predatory power, truce-makers had no capacity to topple the regime or to compel it to dramatically reform the system in ways that favoured the poorer classes. In this long war of attrition, the ghetto had tipped the balance of power ever so slightly, but by itself it could not alter unequal social relations. The consequence was foot-dragging, continued repression and frustration for the poor.

This repression, both cultural and physical, was a second factor that undercut the peace. Hope for the ghetto depended, in part, on relief from the sustained, ideological and physical repression to which its residents had been subjected since the 1940s. Yet ideological repression – expressed in the rhetoric of cultural expulsion – and exterminism by police death squads continued in invigorated form. Norms of black cultural affirmation in the slums, derisively referred to as the "I-man" culture and "Trench Town ideology", were conflated with notions of ignorant criminality and moral depravity and dismissed as "a threat to the future of Jamaica".[75] For a leading exponent of this one-sided view, the poorer classes were monsters of history:

> Three hundred years of brutality, oppression, deprivation and neglect have created a Caliban, a monster without conscience, bereft of fine feelings, remorselessly vicious, coarse, grasping and improvident. A major problem with the present populist trend of politics is its tendency to bring the political and economic life of the country more and more under the influence of this Caliban.[76]

Hope of any progress for "this Caliban", it was suggested, "cannot lie in . . . imputing a spurious significance to its Rastafarian religion; but rather in joining the mainstream of human thought, and in mastering modern knowledge, ideas and techniques. To do otherwise is 'to issue to oneself a certificate of poverty'."[77]

The claims of the urban poor that were grounded in race and nationality were thus transformed into indices of ignorance, criminal depravity and moral degeneracy, deserving of eradication from the body politic. In a society fearful of the defiant black poor, this conflation of aggressive, urban lower-class cultures with racial degeneracy permitted easy cultural stereotypes and abetted the policy of exterminism. With few voices raised to contradict him, Dudley Thompson could thus indict the "I-man" culture and its alien values for abetting horrific crimes against the society.

This repression of all that seemed culturally alien in the ghetto had escalated in the 1970s to the point where state terror became the effective crime control policy.[78] The soldiers' death squad and the summary executions at Green Bay were stark expressions of the official mindset toward the defiant poor that the security minister's remarks so clearly expressed. This policy of exterminism joined to cultural contempt was maintained throughout the truce and after, despite the fact that truce leaders had secured an agreement giving them immunity from prosecution.[79]

Further confirmation that persons of their ilk were marked for murder came with the state's response to Copper's death in April. He was killed in an attempt to carry out his boldest heist yet, by robbing the payroll at the Caymanas Park racetrack.[80] Consistent with the policy of exterminism, and the moral panic triggered by the so-called Trench Town ideology, Copper was dismissed in death as no more than a common criminal. In the discourse of the day, he was nothing but a "wild animal" and a "mad dog" to be disposed of.[81]

Elimination of this spectre from society continued throughout the year as the police killed nineteen of twenty-four "wanted men" in the first eleven months of 1978.[82] This toll in dead men who faced no trial would prompt the journalist David D'Costa to remark with astonishing prescience that the use of the police as a death squad was likely to produce two casualties – justice and the truce itself. Such a policy was untenable, he warned, because though "Most Jamaicans may have a scant respect for 'law' . . . they do, surprisingly, continue to believe in 'justice'."[83]

Thus justice for the criminally culpable and the culturally alienated remained elusive in this period, as did a stable peace. Both became casualties in this period of mutually assured terror.[84] In it, the criminals' terror was met not with patient investigative work, precision strikes to interdict weapons or arrests that distinguished between gunmen and the uncooperative poor. On the contrary, state policy was marked by vengeful, indiscriminate killings by policemen whose barbarous conduct was "virtually indistinguishable from the criminals with whom they were at 'war' ".[85]

The third and final development that would undo the truce came from within the ranks of the truce-makers themselves. After bravely holding out for four months against savage state violence, cultural repression and lack of meaningful investment in their cause, unity among the peacemakers and their allies began to unravel. Unfulfilled expectations took their toll as frustrations mounted. Gang members became embittered as politicians attended fewer and fewer meetings to secure the peace. PNP gang members who "wanted independence from the politicians, though they had no intention of switching party loyalties" did little to disguise their contempt for the do-nothing politicians.[86] According to one observer, "Gang leaders were interested in money and power. If they thought you could deliver either or both they listened to you with respect. If not then their impatience was undisguised."[87]

That impatience among the unemployed bubbled to the surface in a violent outburst on 17 April. Residents marched along the Spanish Town Road demanding jobs, housing and improved sanitation while looters plundered nearby businesses. However, the no-nonsense policemen from the Harmon Barracks set upon both groups, violently dispersing them and killing three looters in the process.[88]

Disillusionment with a process that brought few rewards now eroded the remarkable discipline that gang members had imposed on their communities since the truce began. Persuasion combined with rough justice had brought peace to several communities and trimmed, for some ten months, the decades-long internecine violence. These months saw truce-makers adjudicating community conflicts and developing a parallel system of justice. In it, they determined which cases before the nation's courts that involved defendants from their communities would be permitted to hear witnesses. Equally important in this maturation of an underground judicial system, gang leaders also dealt rough justice to transgressors in their communities.[89]

By September the underground structure of power and the truce itself finally buckled under the demands and frustrations of the benefits-hungry poor, the booty-starved criminals and the partisan warmongers. The common denominator that had held these motley groups in check – hope for a livelihood and expectation of significant improvement in their condition – gave way to factionalism and social cannibalism.

Rogue elements that were obligated to no political alliance, but whose predation was curtailed by the peace, shrugged off all constraints and renewed their plunder. Warmongers returned to their old habits. As a result, a football match at the National Stadium that was to be the occasion for reinforcing bonds of trust between Arnett Gardens and Tivoli Gardens degenerated into verbal sniping in the stands. This was followed by raw violence in the parking lot between the combatants, with JLP supporters getting the worst of it.[90]

General Starkie, the independent gunman and PNP sympathizer, led this renewed assault. He still hoped to force the "capitalist" JLP and its supporters in Rema to retreat before the truth of socialism and superiority of his militia. In this left-wing, militarist vision of social change, peace was now the greatest obstacle. With guns blazing, Starkie and his men routed the "softies" protecting the truce. In so doing, they sacrificed the hard-won peace for the more invigorating and familiar *esprit de corps* that came with making war on Rema and the JLP.[91]

Finally, peace in the ghetto took perhaps the hardest blow of all when it was discovered that persons from within the movement's own managing group – the Central Peace Council – had swindled monies from the peace fund. As one report on the fraud observed, "The funds have dwindled under suspicious circumstances and it is felt that the signature of the Abba of the Ethiopian Orthodox Church was forged and over $30,000 withdrawn by fraudulent means."[92]

As the year drew to a close, these debilities sounded the death knell of the momentous search for peace. This courageous effort by proud but handicapped peacemakers was ultimately defeated by a conspiracy of circumstances in which state repression was the decisive factor. In the end, political domination yielded its predictable and dire results: hardening of partisan positions, reversion to old "tribal" boundaries, plaintive cries to save the peace and, worst of all, recurrent, mutual bloodshed in yet another violent paroxysm. The next chapter examines variations on the social power of the poor and draws a portrait of a society scarred and transmuted by the permanence of violence.

9

Uncaptured Rebels

THE FOREGOING DISCUSSION HAS AMPLY SHOWN how unique relations of power between a politically dominant class and its urban nemesis led to profound alterations in the Jamaican social order. This chapter discusses the identity and scope of this foundational change and traces its disruptive effects on power, forms of social organization and cohesion, and patterns of moral culture in the 1980s.

The mutation in the Jamaican social order had five attributes whose nested and reciprocal effects were carried over into the 1980s to define that decade. The transmutation of the social order in the 1970s may be summed up in the intensification of the following attributes: (1) the gangsterization of social and political life; (2) the rise of an uncaptured lumpenproletariat whose prominence was defined by its accumulation of countervailing forms of social power; (3) the expansion of exilic agonism from the slums to the wider society; (4) the centrality of violence as motor of change, basis of solidarity and source of disorganization; and (5) the existence of social tensions marked not by the labour-capital conflict but by clashes between a highly mobilized but socially throttled lumpenproletariat on the one hand, and a predatory state, known for its suppressive violence and "affectionate" incorporation of the loyalist poor on the other.

These dimensions of the change did not, of course, begin in the 1970s but had their roots in the first decades of the century, particularly in the wrenching transformation of the 1930s and after. In particular, during the thirty years since 1948, all five attributes had become extensive in their reach and amplified in their power. The result was a remarkable reordering of social and political relations.

To appreciate the depth of this transforming shift one need only consider the profound contrast between the social and political tone of the 1940s and that of the late 1970s. In the former period, an elite group largely determined political life. Its values oriented the society toward constitutionalism, democratic practice and the developmental values of economic growth, infrastructural expansion and social investment. Though politics in Kingston had entered its violent phase, elite consensus on the rules of the democratic game – not the claims of political gangs and gun violence – defined the temper of national politics.

Similarly, whereas social conflict in the 1940s revolved largely around competition for shares of the voting and unionized population, that competition implicitly had the labour-capital antinomy as its orienting impulse as parties and unions championed the cause of labour against employers. By the late 1970s these worker-capitalist relations and associated tensions had all but ceased in their ability to cause fundamental ruptures in social relations. Those earlier tensions were replaced by variegated clashes of which two were dominant. The first pitted politically represented tributaries of the urban poor against each other in the communal wars. The second arrayed criminal bands and other strata of the rebellious poor against the state. In neither case were workers, peasants or employers central to these conflicts. Instead the great conflicts of the society all emanated from troublesome structures of political representation.

Finally, social organization, moral culture and cohesion during the 1940s reflected the "common sense" produced by the long years of European colonial rule. Stable family life organized around the nuclear unit of husband and wife remained the social ideal, though the majority population would hardly attain it. Likewise, schooling – no matter how unequal its reach – retained its appeal as the preferred route to status and social mobility, and especially so for the subordinate classes. At the same time, moral values reflected the predominant influence of religion both in its folk and institutional forms. Correspondingly, thrift, hard work and deference to law and authoritative institutions – no matter the latter's violation of the ideals of justice – were watchwords for workers, peasants and the respectable poor. Equally important, while class and racial hierarchies sorely tested the basis of social cohesion, these stratifications remained essentially unchallenged in the 1940s, save for the activism and insurgency of politically marginal groups.

One generation later, these relations had been dramatically transformed. A variety of forces had upended and disorganized family life among the majority classes. Poverty, unemployment and migration took a heavy toll on poorer family units, leaving children and youth neglected and forced to fend for themselves in a harsh urban environment. At the same time, city life and pressing economic circumstances encouraged new forms of gender relations including the relaxation of sexual mores. Urban life and economic hardship pushed more women into the workforce and accorded them some independence. But low-wage work and fluid social relations in the urban economy had the negative effect of encouraging both men and women to participate more openly in multiple unions of unpredictable duration. Where these unions produced children, the instability of parental ties led to an uncertain future for their progeny.

Work discipline in particular declined among the hard-core unemployed. For this group who lacked a meaningful relationship to the formal economy, poverty and hardship weakened norms of group uplift, undercut the salience of spiritual values and diminished the worth of personal sacrifice. They were replaced by indiscipline and powerful materialist values reflected in a compelling orientation to consumption.

Erosion of traditional social structures and their values weakened belief in deferred gratification, spiritual suasion and the value of wage-work among the young. Indeed, joblessness, social oppression and the frustrations of throttled ambition among the hard-core unemployed and the reckless young led not to the schoolhouse, the church or the workplace, but to criminal employment and the prison house. In particular, the turn to illicit activity, whether for political largesse or for plain booty, encouraged those so engaged to rely on violence and badness-honour as routes to respect and social honour. Trafficking in badness-honour thus became a new standard of respectability in the political and criminal undergrounds, thoroughly displacing civic norms and lawful behaviour as standards of conduct in the ghetto.

Hence, within one generation, social rank and status honour were no longer defined by the values of a civilizing middle class that maintained its cultural governance of the society. Rather, countervailing norms deeply influenced by structural changes in the society and a dominant-class antagonistic street culture asserted itself in the 1970s and after.

In particular, urban street culture assigned new identities and moralities that drew on powerful inherited traditions. The emergent moral culture was now based not on the enfeebled multiracial ideals and civic norms of creole nationalists, but on martial values of a street culture that drew on competitive individualism and on the agonism of heroic outlawry.

Consequently, norms of deference and accommodation characteristic of the previous decades now gave way to aggressive assertions of individual and group claims – some of which were infused with class and racial grievances. Provoked and mobilized by politics and driven by the disruptive experience of urbanization, the restive lumpenproletariat turned not so much to political activism as to crime and outlawry.

Political sociologist Carl Stone, in reflecting on this dimension of the change, correctly observed that "their alienation expressed itself in the form of crime and violence as against collective political action which was the weapon of challenge forged by the workers and peasants in 1938".[1] The cultural impact of this unemployed contingent was no less important than its social and political influence. Rather than being marginalized and eclipsed in importance by demographically larger groups such as the peasantry and the working class, the lumpenproletariat exerted its considerable influence in the post-war and postcolonial years. That influence was contagious. It spread to adjacent groups that shared the urban poor's political and cultural sympathies. These groups ranged from middle-class youth in search of an identity to radical intellectuals and others who championed the cause of the black poor. We have already seen that journalists, state agents and civic leaders were acutely aware of the group's seeming ubiquity and its tremendous compulsion on the society. Again, in his discerning manner, Stone recognized this radiating authority and its significance:

> The lumpen influence in the society spread beyond the hard-core unemployed youth in the ghettoes. It spread to the rural youth, to middle class youth and to the younger age cohorts in the working class. The lumpen culture espouses unbridled sexuality and violence, mastery of the gun, hostility to all symbols and figures of authority, class and racial militancy . . . . unrestrained individualism, egocentric behaviour and a disdain of work, particularly manual work.[2]

There can be little doubt, then, that as a social category the lumpenproletariat played a pivotal role in the mutations described above and did so out of proportion to its size and capacity, relative to socially advantaged groups. More than that, as an uncaptured social force the lumpenproletariat provoked, benefited from and was harmed by the very changes in the social order it had helped inaugurate. Among all these mutations, the repertoire of violence left an indelible mark on both the society and on residents of poor neighbourhoods.

Violence in Jamaica is a universe in its own right. It is a complex whole that simultaneously organized and disrupted the flow of power in the society. Yet as this system generated high levels of social disorganization it also fashioned powerful solidarities. Hence, gunmen of all kinds and their ilk found common bonds in the warlike and Gorgonian identities that the culture of violence both spawned and encouraged. But while solidarity and self-construction through violence offered a passage to identity for the poor, that violence was also the cause of death and grievous injury. Consequently, violence in Jamaica was as much a source of group efficacy and social potency as it was a disruptive and scarring force.

Paradoxically, this very identity adapted well to inherited traditions of venturesome striving, risk-taking and picaresque adventures that are so much a part of the biography of the Jamaican people. Like the migratory journeys to which they were accustomed, martial risk for the ghetto poor not only held prospects of failure and disaster, but offered hope of redemption, status mobility and achievement. Thus where traditional routes to opportunity were blocked, the repertoire of violence became a means of navigating social hierarchies. In this respect, the risks of violence for the throttled poor were merely the opportunity costs of social mobility.

But while this violence had a certain symmetry with cultural traditions, and even as it operated as a systemic and unified whole, violence in urban Jamaica was remarkably heterogeneous in character and plural in its deployment. Rather than being a congealed entity dispatched from a single political source, violence was dispersed, decentralized and variable.

For example, we have already seen that the state was neither the sole purveyor nor the only agent charged with its legitimate use. Consequently, institutional violence emanated from both state security organs and from militias linked to the political parties. While having a common origin in the state apparatus, however, these twin forms of legitimate violence were often at odds with each other.

This was apparent, for instance, from the attempted PNP seizure of the Rema enclave, where segments of state security intervened against militarized groups that came under party barons' authority. Authorized agents of state violence both cooperated and clashed with each other. Moreover, though violence was the right of the state, it was equally the prerogative of criminal gangs and individual gunmen independent of the party militias.

Hence, in the fluid and changing dynamics of urban politics, alliances were forged and disrupted in violent contestations between criminal gangs, state-security agents and party militias.

Last, the universe of violence included the fury of the distressed poor and those suffering political and economic hardship. This frenzy was expressed in street demonstrations, marches and riotous acts that sought remedies for grievances of various kinds. The so-called Chinese and Rodney riots (of 1965 and 1968 respectively) typified one form of this upheaval in the 1960s. Though displaced by partisan clashes in the 1970s, this social violence in which ordinary citizens took to the street to express acute grievances remained a recurrent, even permanent feature of political life in Jamaica.

Leaving aside significant and rising levels of so-called domestic violence, these five sources listed above were the major elements in the universe of Jamaican violence. With varying levels of intensity, every component contributed its distinctive energy to the complex process of organizing and disrupting power, shaping moral culture, fashioning solidarities and influencing the character of social organization. Drawing on the analysis outlined above and on the foregoing political profile of the 1970s, we turn now to the fateful mutations of that decade and their disruptive effects on the 1980s.

We have seen thus far how state terror, the violence of party militias and the predation of criminal gunmen dominated the political stage. In succeeding years, these three segments would continue their monopoly in energizing change, generating and polarizing loyalties, and rupturing social organization. Following on the heels of the collapse of the truce, the frenzy of all three segments became fiercer.

The context for this intensification was, of course, the acute social crisis. The failed truce was part of the enormous social contention over the country's economic and political direction that began in 1974. Thus the aftermath of the 1978 truce was invariably determined by the logic of the social crisis, a major part of which was economic in character. As much as political factors, this dimension had an influential role in shaping the direction of politics after the truce.

In the economic field, mounting difficulties since 1973 – including inflation, high import costs, balance of payments shortfalls and declining production – had forced the PNP to adopt a variety of restrictive measures.[3] In particular, in 1977 a worsening economy forced the PNP to reluctantly conclude an agreement with the IMF. The collapse of this agreement in

December of that year extended the crisis and caused the government to strike yet another, even more demanding agreement with the Fund in early 1978. Agreements with the Fund restricted public spending, curtailed the flow of imports and forced job cuts. In particular, currency devaluations required by the 1978 pact added to hardships in the ghetto and aggravated the already serious reduction in the country's standard of living.

These straitened circumstances trimmed the parties' ability to distribute patronage. This reduction of largesse and the deteriorating national economy invariably increased the economic squeeze on all classes and especially on the poor who could least withstand it. Coming on the heels of the failure of the truce, reduced access to benefits at year's end could only increase frustration and desperation in the ghetto. The collapse of the truce was therefore a tremendous blow for the peacemakers and their allies. This was so because in the absence of real jobs and economic investment, a livelihood for many in the ghetto meant not a scuffling existence, but rather continued predation, both criminal and political.

In the context of narrowed economic circumstances and raging two-party contestation for national power, the demise of the truce left gunmen and the desperate poor with the old, limited options. Such pinched circumstances in which urgent material want and frustrated ambitions loomed large allowed old animosities, bitter rivalries and familiar patterns of plunder to resurface.

Yet even as the partisan war reignited the gangsterization of politics, the bottled-up concerns of other social actors burst forth in unexpected and dramatic protest. On Monday 8 January 1979, the Kingston poor took to the streets. They rose to challenge a planned announcement of a hike in fuel prices brought on by the rise of international prices. The country, it will be recalled, was rocked by tremors in the global economy that began in the early 1970s. In 1973 the OPEC countries had increased the world price of oil and the Jamaican government had over the years responded with fuel price increases of its own.[4]

The most recent hike had come in May 1978 when the price of premium gasoline moved from J$2.25 to J$3.00 per gallon.[5] But in less than a year, shortfalls in revenues, a widening budget deficit, IMF demand for deficit reduction and a coming round of OPEC price hikes pushed the government to raise prices again in 1979. Reports were that the government proposed to increase the price of premium gasoline to J$3.75 with smaller increases for regular gasoline, diesel and kerosene oil.[6] More speculative

reports had even tagged the impending hike at J$1.00. This pushed the price
of premium gasoline to J$4.00 per gallon.[7]

Developments in the world economy therefore had its disruptive effect
on Jamaica's political economy. Indeed, this latest change in global economic
relations pushed sectors of the Jamaican population to end their circumspec-
tion. Where many outside the ranks of the well-armed poor drew back from
direct confrontations with the state, this latest turn of the economic screw
pushed the otherwise conformist poor to bold protest.

The result was an unprecedented social explosion that greeted the
impending price hike. Though a formal announcement was yet to come,
the urban poor – responding to calls for a campaign of civil disobedience
by the JLP-affiliated National Patriotic Movement – rallied and huge
demonstrations shook the island. With Kingston as their epicentre, the
protests brought the Corporate Area to a standstill by Monday afternoon.

Kingston protesters employed the well-honed tactic of the roadblock.
They dragged tree trunks, piled-up rocks and cobbled debris to block both
major and secondary arteries to the capital city.[8] Unemployed women,
restive youth and other strata spearheaded this disruption, much to the chagrin of businesses, middle-class commuters and the government. When not
blocking thoroughfares in city and residential streets, demonstrators marched
with placards that ridiculed the government.[9] As was their habit in these circumstances, criminals and the hard-core lumpenproletariat joined the fray.
They threatened drivers at knifepoint, slashed automobile tires, damaged
buses, and assaulted and robbed their crews.[10] By nightfall on Monday, PNP
thugs were already on the streets in search of JLP demonstrators, as the government imposed a curfew in West Kingston.[11]

Caught off guard by the fury of the demonstration, the PNP denounced
it as "an organized act of political confrontation". Consistent with the habit
of politically tribalizing the country's difficulties, the PNP blamed the opposition for providing a cover for "acts of terrorism and the destruction of
property".[12]

But neither overblown rhetoric nor repressive law could stem the tide of
popular opposition. Demonstrations against the increased cost of living
rolled across the island. Early the following morning, protesters in Montego
Bay set up massive roadblocks around that city. By noon, traffic in this central city was forced to a halt.[13] Similarly, hundreds of demonstrators took to
the roads around Morant Bay on Tuesday, halting early morning traffic in
St Thomas, in unison with protesters in St Ann.

Protest swept other rural areas as more roadblocks and agitation interrupted normal business in Westmoreland, Hanover, St Elizabeth and St James. Though a few motorists tried to circumvent the demonstrations, their efforts came to naught as hostile protesters stoned their vehicles and made their passage difficult.[14] In Kingston and significant parts of the countryside, banks, schools and businesses were forced to close their doors as workers stayed out and demonstrators took over the streets. The contagion was so threatening that on Tuesday the government reimposed the Suppression of Crime Act in several rural parishes.[15]

As ominous as these far-flung demonstrations were, they were no match for the bold actions of workers in the bauxite as well as other industries who walked off their jobs in the countryside on Tuesday morning. In a challenge to the PNP refrain that the demonstrations were purely a JLP creation, workers belonging to the National Workers Union – the PNP-affiliated trade union – at the Reynolds, Kaiser and Alpart bauxite plants left their jobs to join the protest. These miners took to the streets and blocked roads using boulders, logs and motor vehicles.[16]

The activism of Alpart workers at Nain, in St Elizabeth, was particularly noteworthy. By walking off the job, 950 mineworkers at Alpart and their 750 peers at the Reynolds and Kaiser plants broke ranks with their union, the National Workers Union.[17] These mineworkers had, in effect, engaged in a work stoppage against the wishes of union delegates, the PNP government and its political party. These were the very units with which the mineworkers were ostensibly aligned by virtue of political tradition.[18]

The strike thus revealed a major fissure between the government and the well-paid, unionized bauxite workers. They had thrown their support to the less well-off strikers in Kingston and in the larger rural towns. This intervention had therefore established an unlikely class alliance between rural mineworkers and the urban and rural low-wage, hard-core unemployed. In forging this unlikely alliance, the mineworkers behaved not like dupes of a scheming opposition party but as aggrieved labourers protesting the new round of price hikes and the erosion in their standard of living.[19]

That the protest attracted such a widespread following gave the government pause. Indeed, its trepidation was expressed during Monday's demonstration when, late in the evening, it finally disclosed the exact amount of the hike. But rather than the rumoured increase of fifty to seventy-five cents, the government announced a much smaller increase of twenty cents.[20]

This was a significant retreat. In light of the urgent need to close the budget deficit and the government's admission that the cost of premium delivered to the pump had risen by forty-one cents since the May 1978 increase, it is clear that but for the protests, the government would likely have imposed a larger increase.[21] The protesters thus scored a major victory by causing "the Government to act as the Government could hardly have intended to act".[22]

Yet the modest hike did little to dampen the outrage and protests continued. By Wednesday the government had seen enough. It turned to bellicose language and backed it up with force. The prime minister not only condemned the protest as an instance of JLP manipulation, but denounced it as expression of "raw naked fascism" that sought the PNP's ouster.[23] In his turn, Dudley Thompson, minister of national security, assailed it as "illegal, wrong, wicked and premeditated" and hinted darkly that the security forces, which had been held in check to this point, would be let loose on the protesters.[24]

This tough response led to violent clashes in Kingston. Protesters exchanged gunfire with police there along the Old Hope Road. That led to the deaths of two civilians and the wounding of three others.[25] Tear gas was hurled at marchers at Half-Way-Tree and Olympic Gardens and as far away as St Catherine. There an overwhelming police presence complemented the massive show of force in Kingston.

But where tear gas and police batons failed to rout protesters in the Corporate Area, the marchers were forced to retreat before the surly threats of PNP gunmen who brandished their weapons.[26] JLP supporters bore the brunt of this intimidation as "cars full of PNP gunmen and trucks of PNP machete and pickaxe handle wielders" descended on them during the day and later that night.[27] The security minister's threat was therefore realized with this combination of violent party goons and gun-wielding policemen, several of whom stood by as the political thugs did their work.[28]

This stifling of the protest had the desired effect. Normality returned to the Corporate Area on Thursday as the protesters retreated and firms, schools and banks reopened for business. Surprisingly enough, as state violence curtailed the militancy of the poor in Kingston and elsewhere, resistance continued in some parts of the countryside. There defiant bauxite workers at Kaiser and Alpart refused to join their peers at Reynolds in a return to work on Thursday. Ironically, as this upheaval – characterized as "the most popular demonstration held in the Corporate Area since Independence" –

reached its denouement, the politically stranded bauxite workers in St Elizabeth stood ready to extend the protest against economic hardship.[29]

However, that was not to be. Repressive violence, partisan division, quiescence on the part of the wider public and stunning left-wing hostility to the demonstrations marginalized the militant mineworkers and their allies.[30] For all that, the protest was a chastening retort to a regime that had survived by tribalizing public issues. Mass protest in 1979 weakened the stranglehold the regime and partisan groups exerted on public affairs. The protesters' intervention allowed other social agents and aggrieved groups into the political fray to articulate their concerns. These actors, including industrial workers, spoke out – authentically and in unison – against a regime that had, indeed, worsened their economic lot.

The freeing of these independent voices was an uncomfortable turn of events for the old order, for it highlighted the growing escape of swaths of the population from the tyranny of partisanship. As with the abortive truce in the ghetto, other significant sectors of the population had begun a withdrawal from the cul-de-sac of blind political loyalty. From the ghetto to the bauxite minefields, self-interest, economic need and corporate group interests appeared to be supplanting narrow political loyalties.

One consequence of this development was that whatever satisfaction the JLP might have gained from the PNP's setback, this expression of autonomous interests among the mass public did not augur well for an opposition party equally inured to tribal politics. Defections from party-driven identities by the mass public and among small groups of party activists signalled a potential sea change in political attitudes. That is, as the public became more issue-oriented, blind allegiance to partisan positions diminished.[31] In the short term, however, traditions associated with partisan politics remained powerful, and especially so in the slums. This incompatibility between emergent autonomous group interests and the claims of a stifling partisanship were apparent from yet another detonation in 1979. This was the extra-judicial killing of Claude Massop by a police patrol, scarcely a month after the January demonstrations.

From Claude Massop's Murder to the PNP's 1980 Electoral Defeat

Despite the growing importance of issue-oriented politics in 1979, this development was too new to have much of a role in tempering polarized relations in the country. Inflamed sensibilities were the norm especially for party activists, gunmen of all stripes and members of the security forces itching to settle scores with the paladins who remained a law unto themselves. Moreover, relations between the state and fugitive gunmen remained unchanged while distrust between politicians and the truce-makers persisted. Worse still, the failure of the peace left gunmen such as Massop politically exposed if for no other reason than that these gunmen had spearheaded the opposition to political domination. In Massop's case, the gunman had set his face against all machinations from the party bosses and had stoutly defended the cause of peace even when it had grown unpopular with loyalists in West Kingston and Arnett Gardens.[32]

As the killings increased around him Massop had cautioned the youth against "destroying each other" and questioned the motives of the powerful for failing to do more for the peace. "We want to know from the dignitaries," he asserted, "how they see peace. We don't want no more youth blood to shed [sic] in uncalled for ways."[33]

But as partisan guns barked once more in the ghetto, the enforcer-turned-peacemaker seemed out of step with fast-moving events. First, the security forces kept up their pressure on independent gunmen and criminal gangs, even as the latter defiantly accepted the deadly terms of this savage war of attrition. Second, Edward Seaga had intensified his bold campaign for power. Beginning in 1977 and continuing into 1979 the JLP had assembled a campaign that employed multiple tactics that kept the PNP off balance. The JLP's quest for office included civil disobedience; whipping up public fears of communism; identifying the country's plight with PNP tyranny and economic mismanagement; campaigning in Washington against economic aid to the Jamaican government; and mobilizing street-level cadres for an electoral showdown.[34]

Third, the PNP had its back against the wall. It not only had to defend itself against a withering JLP assault, but it had to grapple with the problems of IMF budgetary constraints, spiralling violence, and rising public discontent over the state of the economy and the growing social disorder. As the regime moved to end negotiations with the IMF and construct an alternative economic plan, it also looked to its cadres on the left and its armed militia in the slums to hold the line against Seaga's unrelenting push to undermine the PNP and return the JLP to power. In short, all parties to the conflict seemed ready to settle their differences not by negotiation but by confrontation.

Massop's stubborn pursuit of an agenda of peace in these polarized circumstances of all-out political war must have seemed an annoyance to West Kingston constituency boss Seaga – not to mention the unreconstructed warmongers on both sides, arrayed anew in hostile opposition. This redeemed JLP gunman-turned-peacemaker, who enunciated an anti-system message of unity in the midst of a harsh, unforgiving political war, must have seemed to detractors a political anachronism: a target of opportunity if not a downright traitor.

Such cascading and unenviable circumstances conjoined with harsh judgements of his relevance probably cost Massop his life. The end came as he and two friends in an automobile approached the precincts of his Tivoli stronghold on 4 February. The men were stopped by a police patrol and ordered from the car. This time, in a manner reminiscent of the Green Bay massacre, the trio – with Massop's hand above his head in surrender – were all executed in a hail of gunfire.[35]

Massop's murder confirmed, yet again, an unyielding reality for the mobilized poor: any serious challenge to political power from their ranks, regardless of political persuasion, would be met by terror and unforgiving violence. Competing forms of power from below could be appropriated and even accommodated, but they would not be allowed to supplant political class power. For Massop and his ilk, trafficking in badness-honour was permitted only as long as it did not challenge political class rule. Any such attempt typically led to martyrdom.

Still, it is of some consequence that JLP politicians, PNP enforcers and tens of thousands of poor residents of the western belt attended the slain gunman's funeral. This remarkable show of respect for the ghetto notable demonstrated once again the importance of the political underground in national politics and the huge loyalty it had garnered in poor communities. The outpouring of grief for the martyred gunman showed as well how routinized the political uses of badness-honour had become, and how vital this form of trafficking was to both state predation and the social power of the urban poor.

Emphasizing this dimension of subaltern power, however, cannot gloss over a harsh and continuing reality: not only were rebel leaders martyred, but the urban poor as a whole – a group deficient in resources and capability – was still throttled socially. Thus in addition to being materially deprived and made the target of a dirty war, the mobilized urban poor remained a morally discredited, socially isolated and culturally stigmatized group.

Violence and marginality therefore left the most defiant among them with unenviable options. These included martyrdom, flight, criminal employment and indentureship to communal war. Subordination to these injurious choices only compounded the agony of these mobilized-but-throttled supplicants.

In the raging political crisis of 1979–80, these limiting options trapped the militant poor. Where state terror did not create martyrs, such as Massop, criminal employment caused more deaths by extra-judicial murder or armed clashes with the police. Indeed, the "dirty war" against ghetto outlaws had become sufficiently threatening that the PNP's Anthony "General Starkie" Tingle and Aston "Buckie" Thompson both fled the island for Canada in 1979.[36] That both men were on the country's "most wanted" list but still were able to leave the country without interdiction pointed not just to the laxity of the customs services, but to their corrupt collusion with a criminal enterprise.[37]

It is apparent from the foregoing that this gangsterization of Jamaican politics had several ramifications. On the one hand, it had given the outlaw poor a disputed leverage on national politics and political culture. On the other, this same capacity provoked the state into a violent, "dirty war" against challengers from the slums. Because communal war bound rebellious supplicants to a testy relationship with the parasitic state, that nexus ineluctably abetted the florescence of gangster politics.

Criminalization of politics in this period therefore made for a volatile nexus among patrons, clients and the state. Moments of cooperation were punctuated by horrific terror as the state targeted supplicants and outlaws for punishment. At the same time it is worth noting that state security forces were occasionally divided. From time to time, the political and security arms of the state were at odds. For example, contingents from the military and the police intervened in the communal war in ways that did not always redound to the benefit of politicians. This was apparent from the army's interruption of Anthony Spaulding's violent empire building. The army's pre-emptive role in the Green Bay killings and the partisanship of police contingents around Kingston confirmed similar disruptive tendencies. Last, tensions also increased when party barons were compelled to call in the security forces to help beat back the insurgency of overly ambitious supplicants belonging to the party's militia. In short, the patron-client nexus was rife with conflict in the late 1970s as throttled supplicants and party sponsors struggled to adjust the relationship to their advantage.

By 1980 that advantage had shifted in favour of politicians and state agents. The seesaw struggle between patrons and clients that had provoked a brief moment of unity within the ghetto was displaced by the clash of communal warriors as national elections approached. In this year, indentureship to communal war returned with a vengeance as the JLP employed all its resources to dethrone the PNP. The latter reciprocated by marshalling its cadres in a fight for political survival.

As the electoral campaign heated up, leading PNP politicians were shot at and one was even killed by the security forces in the violent paroxysm.[38] The JLP also suffered its share of attacks in 1980.[39] Stone reported, for instance, that of the 152 cases of politically motivated violence recorded by the *Daily Gleaner* during the year, 102 were reportedly against the JLP. Similarly, during the month of October when the election was held, there were seventy-five reported incidents of political violence, forty-seven of which were directed against the JLP.[40]

But it was the poor in politically contested areas that paid the highest price. Political gang warfare swept poor neighbourhoods across Kingston, destroying infrastructure and consuming lives. Armed assaults on rivals' meetings and festivities were matched by horrific arson that claimed innocent victims.[41] Indeed, gun violence reached its apogee in this campaign as protagonists on both sides deployed high-powered weapons including M16 machine guns.[42]

The death toll from this carnage was huge. In 1980 alone, gunmen killed 556 persons, while the security forces felled another 234. In the battle-scarred Rema–Newton area alone, political warfare claimed 150 lives.[43] Together some 933 Jamaicans – the overwhelming majority of whom lived in poor urban neighbourhoods – died in the political conflagration.[44]

As war raged in the 1970s, the destruction of community property was equally devastating. Politically motivated violence ripped apart lives, made thousands homeless and destroyed dwellings on a massive scale. Commenting in the early 1980s on this mayhem, geographer Alan Eyre observed for the Rema–Newton area that

> between 1976 and 1982, 1096 tenement yards or 43 per cent of the total in the study area were destroyed. These compounds housed almost 17,000 persons. An equal number and percentage of high-rise and redevelopment units – the residences of almost 5,000 persons – were destroyed or rendered uninhabitable. In total, an estimated 21,372 poor ghetto dwellers were directly deprived of shelter by fire, eviction, or gunplay.[45]

With this carnage and heightened social polarization as backdrop, 67 per cent of eligible voters braved the violence and cast their ballots in the 1980 election. In a stunning verdict, voters dealt the PNP a massive defeat and returned the JLP to office with 59 per cent of the popular vote and fifty-one of the sixty seats in Parliament.[46]

Several factors precipitated this rout, but none was more important than economic concerns. Evelyne and John Stephens cited poll data confirming the primacy of those factors:

> By far the most important reason for the PNP's dramatic loss of support was the state of the economy, followed by violence and the communism issue. In a September 1980 poll, voters were asked which was the most important issue in the election. Economic issues, predominantly unemployment, economic recovery, and shortages, were mentioned by 51 per cent of respondents in the Metropolitan Area, 66 per cent in other towns and 61 per cent in rural areas. Unemployment topped the list in all three areas. . . . Whatever the particular economic concerns, the general perception was one of an economy – and a people – in deep trouble, and of a government incapable of solving this fundamental problem.[47]

The centrality of economic issues in the PNP's defeat was a dramatic illustration of the limits of pure partisanship and the constraints on social consciousness in this country. In a society in which issue voting had increased and where political pragmatism retained strong appeal among all classes, for voters pocketbook issues were more important than party loyalty and ideological fervour. To be sure, a host of political problems undoubtedly crippled the experiment in democratic socialism. However, it could not survive the alienation caused by the sharp reduction in the standard of living of manual workers, farm labourers, the middle class and the unemployed.

Poll results revealed that significant components of all major classes switched their votes and swung heavily toward the JLP in 1980. For example, white-collar workers, 75 per cent of whom had voted for the PNP in 1972, defected with only 40 per cent casting ballots for the party in 1980.[48] Likewise, skilled and semi-skilled manual labour also voted heavily for the JLP, as did employers and big-income professionals.

But it was among its ardent supporters in the unemployed category that the PNP lost significant support. Among the urban poor, for example, the PNP suffered a massive erosion of support as more and more jobless workers and the unskilled turned to hustling and petty trading to survive. Indeed, in the months preceding the election, unemployment had increased to 35 per cent of the labour force with the urban unemployed making up a significant proportion of that increase.[49] According to Carl Stone, this run-up in the rate, was part of a dramatic structural shift that brought "a more than 50% increase in the level of unemployment between the early and later stages of the PNP's period of government".[50]

Given this blow to the economic fortunes of the poor, it is not surprising that among the unemployed and the unskilled, PNP support dropped from 60 per cent in the 1976 election to 40 per cent in 1980.[51] In summary, even as the PNP retained significant support among the electorate – the party did garner 41 per cent of the popular vote – and though support for its political objectives remained strong among blue-collar workers and the unemployed, neither partisanship nor a radical political agenda could surmount the urgency of supporters' economic needs.

The political meaning of this development was sobering. For while manual workers and the urban poor possessed an honourable tradition of insurgency against wealth, power and inequality, their rebelliousness did not go beyond trade union militancy and political supplication. Indeed, these groups' partisanship for a reordering of social relations did not embrace the kind of radicalism that could withstand the rigours of Jamaica's sharp economic downturn. Hence, the politics of pragmatism held sway among the urban poor as self-enclosure and self-help revealed both the boundaries of social consciousness and the uses of social power by this erstwhile insurgent social force.

The next sections explore the persistence of this tradition of insurgency in which self-defence and self-help – not far-reaching radical projects – informed the activism of the poor in the 1980s.

Self-Help Strategies: The Informal Economy

As gunmen and political supplicants evolved their complex strategy of filiating with, yet challenging political power in the 1970s, their compeers seeking a livelihood as traders and vendors were simultaneously engaged in their own self-help project and bid for power. Hurt by the country's worsening economic situation, and casting about for a livelihood, enterprising sectors of the urban unemployed joined the widening ranks of those who had already retreated to the informal economy. There a newly emergent group laid claim to the critical import-export niche as petty traders who now competed with big importers and merchants. As with their kin in the political and criminal undergrounds, poor persons in this sector of the urban economy sought to transform this commercial economic space into a means of livelihood and a path to power and respect. Similarly, like their counterparts in the political domain, vendors in the urban informal economy would also clash with powerful forces seeking to contain their quest for power and upward mobility.

The informal sector was a significant social space within the national economy and part of the country's economic landscape at least since the eighteenth century. First slaves, then peasants and eventually unemployed labourers had turned to forms of self-employment and petty entrepreneurship as a means of survival. As jobless persons trekked from the countryside looking for work in the first decades of the twentieth century, informal economic activity not only spread to the major cities and towns, but attracted huge swaths of the population unable to find work in the formal economy.

Ironically, despite significant growth and industrial expansion, the postwar Jamaican economy could not provide enough jobs for a steadily expanding labour force. This failure in Jamaica, as in many parts of the Third World, led to the mushrooming of petty entrepreneurial ventures outside the formal economy. Thus by the 1950s, a lagging economy, social discrimination and lack of skills among young entrants to the labour force meant high and sustained levels of unemployment. These unemployed labourers turned increasingly to the informal economy where they soon became a significant economic group and a disruptive political force.

By the 1970s, significant changes had occurred within the group. Where the 1960s saw them expressing their discontent in cultural nationalist terms, the 1970s and after found that alienation transmuted into a unique form of self-help politics. The entrepreneurial poor now acted as a corporate group, asserting its right to compete with others in the urban commercial sector for a share of the profits there. Economic nationalism had displaced cultural nationalism as a form of activism. In sum, where the crisis of the 1960s had inclined the politics of the petty trading poor toward cultural nationalism, the complex crisis of the 1970s transformed the group into an aggressive, self-representing entity and newly volatile political force in search of economic mobility.

The character of the national economy had been so dramatically transformed in that decade that the changes had their inevitable effect on the contours and functioning of the informal economy. By the late 1970s, the urban informal economy had become more complex in configuration, heterogeneous in class composition and highly politicized in its functioning.[52] Where market women who sold foodstuff alongside vendors in the artisanal and petty commodity trades dominated the urban informal economy in the post-war years, the 1970s and after saw a significant shift that was marked by the presence of new entrants. Declining economic fortunes, for example, pushed working-class women and their salaried lower-middle-class compeers into the informal economy where they supplemented their income. They did this by marking up for sale, both out of their homes and on the job, imported goods such as clothing, jewellery and other items that they had secured from abroad.

Other participants in the new informal economy included members of the political and criminal underworlds who were connected to the drug, gun and contraband trade. As gangster politics flourished and as the country's economic crisis worsened, the influence of both underworlds ballooned in the new informal economy. Entrepreneurs of all sizes also became part of this shadow economy. They operated outside the law or on its margins in order to secure their businesses in a politically uncertain and rapidly changing economic environment. Likewise, as the national economy declined and state regulations multiplied, the presence of state agents in the informal economy increased. Where opportunities for enrichment were sufficiently tempting, policemen, politicians, bureaucrats and fixers of all types – from the lowly municipal worker to the senior civil servant – nibbled at the state's largesse or leveraged their positions to earn income.[53] Typically most were paid to expedite tasks and to cut the tangle of red tape that had grown with the introduction of new economic regulations.

But what was most remarkable about the changing identity of participants in the informal economy was the great number of youthful traders and vendors who had taken to the streets to sell their wares and, most importantly, to engage in the importation of commercial goods. Citing a variety of surveys on Jamaican vendors, Witter reports, for example, that while older women selling domestic agricultural products in municipal markets remained the largest contingent among vendors, a parallel, newer group with an average age of less than twenty-nine years had taken to the sidewalks in the 1970s to sell their wares.[54] Of these curb-side vendors, 85 per cent sold their goods in the environs of the capital city and the most disruptive and politically volatile area: Kingston and St Andrew.[55]

From the foregoing it is apparent that, contrary to myths of the informal economy as the exclusive preserve of only the poor, the downtrodden and the irremediably criminal, the domain is very multi-class in composition. Over the years, the variety of forces there evolved into three identifiable group structures. These were the state, big business and people sectors. All these sectors competed with each other, with the business and the people sector vying to wrest advantages from the state.

The state, in its turn, has strategies and interests of its own which it often pursues inside the informal economy. Thus, far from being a threat to the state, the informal economy may be instead one of its resources. Indeed, in normal periods, as well as in times of economic crisis, the state and its agents are often powerfully present in the underground economy.[56]

As the foregoing has suggested, the informal sector is not uncoupled from the formal economy, but rather is coextensive with it. This characteristic explains the otherwise odd but firmly institutionalized practice in "democratic" Jamaica of distributing monies, benefits and favours strictly on the basis of political ties. When George Spence, Claude Massop and others collected and distributed their largesse, those handouts were premised on the devolution of some state functions to the informal sector. State predation in Jamaica therefore necessitated strategic resort to the shadow economy to pay and maintain political activists and supporters in ways that were free from public scrutiny. These hidden transactions were necessary, because they could not be defended within a constitutionally democratic political system. Consequently, besides being a domain inhabited by the poor and far from being a threat to the state, informal economies are vital arenas for state agents and their strategies.

Lest this point concerning the dilation of the Jamaican state into the informal economy be pushed too far, it is worth remembering that

> where democratic control of capitalist economic activity retains some usefulness for the state and entrepreneurs – as it does in the Jamaican context – then neither the bulk of economic activities nor the scope of economic regulation will be developed predominantly on the basis of hidden transactions. In such circumstances, economic regulation is premised on the principles of the formal economy and on the transparency of transactions that take place there.[57]

In short, it is the case that as states cope with a variety of challenges, their resort to the informal economy may become episodic or institutionalized.

However, in democratic systems these economic transactions are *prima facie* illegitimate and thus must be withheld from public view. In these systems, disclosure of malfeasance and the scandal that accompanies it typically bring sanctions for perpetrators and often lead to meaningful reforms. It is the viability of this principle of accountability in Jamaica's predatory state that distinguishes states of its type from the more corrupt patrimonial forms of power elsewhere in the Third World.[58]

From what has been said, it will be clear that retreating to the informal economy gave no security to vendors attempting to hide their transactions and income from the state. Worse still, vendors who turned to the petty import trade in the 1970s found themselves subject to growing state scrutiny and criticism. As their numbers multiplied and as their boisterous presence at the airports, customs offices and on the sidewalks drew public attention, these vendors' activities became politicized.

The problem for the thousands of new vendors who had turned to the importation of consumer goods was twofold. They were competing with big commercial importers already ensconced in the lucrative wholesale-retail trade and they were accumulating capital not yet subject to taxation. Furthermore they blocked the sidewalks with their goods, disrupted the operations at the docks and airports with their not-yet-taxed barrels of goods, and were vulgarly aggressive in defending their business. This did not endear them to their detractors.

As these informal importers brought in consumer goods and sold them on sidewalks next to the big merchant stores, the large commercial importers were provoked into action. They decried the presence of these competitors who were literally on their doorsteps, and grumbled to the state about new vendors "who stole their customers, paid no income taxes, and avoided duties on their imports".[59]

Because PNP policies sought to empower the poor and since much of its political support in poor neighbourhoods across urban Kingston came from the unskilled and the unemployed, the PNP was understandably dis-inclined to rein in the vendors. Taking on the unruly and politically volatile traders was apparently not a top priority of a populist government fighting major battles on other fronts. Still, increasing public concern and growing tensions in the commercial sector did force vendors to organize and prompted the state to review policies toward them. Facing creeping state regulation and police harassment the traders in 1977 formed the United Vendors' Association to protect their interests.

In the aftermath of the JLP's political victory, however, the war of attrition in the urban retail sector became intense. Policemen made brutal forays against sidewalk vending, the state stepped up its bid to regulate the errant trade and merchants pressed their claim to be treated fairly. In this triangular war between vendors staking a claim to the retail import sector, antagonized big commercial importers seeking to expel them and an embattled state attempting to adjudicate all claims, the tide shifted against the vendors.

Change came in the form of carrot and stick inducement: vendor operations would be recognized as legitimate businesses, the state would build modern arcades near business districts, but vendors would give the state its due in import licences, taxes and other fees. Should these measures be contravened then vendors' goods would be impounded and any return to prohibited sidewalk sales would invite eviction by the police.[60]

In 1982 increased regulation saw the Revenue Board assigning vendors the apt nomenclature as informal commercial importers.[61] The next year import licences were required of all small importers and the JLP made good on its promises by opening an arcade named for Pearnel Charles, the minister of public utilities and transport.

Vendors remained wary and undeterred by attempts to regulate them as the battle for space in the commercial retail sector continued. Indeed, hundreds of vendors across Kingston were hardly impressed by efforts to keep them off the sidewalks. As soon as the latest campaign to evict them had run its course, they promptly took up their positions anew on the sidewalks. As late as 1988, Kingston's municipal body, now called Metropolitan Parks and Markets, was still dispatching heavily armed policemen to demolish hundreds of illegal stalls and evict their occupants.[62]

Notwithstanding the seemingly endless warfare between vendors and the state, by the late 1980s the latter had succeeded in imposing its will. Weary of the travails of sidewalk vending, many informal commercial importers saw the government-built arcades as a superior alternative to the uncertainties of the street. Others resigned themselves to the main inconvenience of the arcades: the relative isolation from crowds and the hustle and bustle of Kingston's main thoroughfares with the likelihood of a fall-off in customers. Whatever their opinion about the state's involvement in their affairs, all petty vendors swept into the net of state regulation – whether they participated in the import trade or not – now paid rents for their stalls, while the importers among them paid for import licences and handed over duties levied on their goods. Consequently, even though the state had yet to corral the vast majority of vendors in the informal economy, its regulation of the *importers* among them was a major breakthrough permitting the capture of part of the economic surplus created by this ever-expanding contingent of traders.

As with political clashes of this type, successful regulation of the vendors was not a one-sided victory for the state. The redoubtable vendors also secured some of their needs. First and foremost, they won recognition as legitimate entrepreneurs and registered businesses. This gave them access to scarce foreign exchange and benefits enjoyed by long-time importers. The vendors had also wrested an equally significant and crucial concession from both the state and large merchants – the right to compete as importers in the lucrative commercial retail sector, an economic space that hitherto had been monopolized by large ethnic-minority merchant houses. Here again using their trademark insubordination and insurgency, the mobilized urban poor had secured another triumph, this time in the burgeoning commercial sector against adversaries with far superior resources.

A Parting of Ways: From Supplication to Criminal Self-Organization

Having fought his way back to political power in a campaign that emphasized freeing the economy from the strictures of democratic socialism, Edward Seaga and the JLP predictably reversed political course and undid many PNP policies. The regime adopted untrammelled free-market measures, ended the country's diplomatic relations with Cuba and looked to its political ties with the United States at the highest levels to put the island onto a different political and economic path.[63]

But even as the JLP's hard-won political victory raised hopes that its policies would bring the economic deliverance it promised, a major transformation was already underway within both the criminal and political underworlds. Violent crime remained a major problem and threat to both the economy and public safety. The long years of political confrontation had left an arsenal of weapons in the hands of not only political enforcers but also a growing number of criminal gangs. Their capacity for violence remained undimmed and the impunity with which these gangs acted threatened the JLP's hold on power and challenged larger structures of political domination. It was not surprising, then, that despite sharp political differences with the PNP, the JLP directed the security forces to continue the assault on the gunmen and criminal gangs. In this regard, the JLP was at one with the PNP in maintaining the policy of exterminism of criminal gunmen. Yet, as with the PNP's earlier crackdown, the JLP's hunt for violent outlaws left untouched the party's own militias. Politically loyal gunmen in the JLP's main garrisons such as Tivoli Gardens, for example, received continuing political protection and were not molested by the security forces.

That was not the case, however, for the left-wing PNP-affiliated gangs and individual gunmen who had fought in the war of 1979–80. The JLP's return to power and its "take no prisoners" approach to crime-fighting left little doubt that a settling of scores was in the offing. As a result, politically "hot" gang members from the Hotsteppers and the Christopher Henry organizations fled to Cuba and to Canada. Top paladins such as Anthony Brown and George Flash of the Hotsteppers, for example, left clandestinely for Cuba. Others followed, usually by boat, as the security forces trained their firepower on the left-wing gangs.

By the early 1980s these gangs had matured into sophisticated criminal enterprises with leaders who had clear left-wing political convictions. The Hotsteppers gang, based in the Wareika Hills, espoused socialist values even as its members committed robberies and other crimes. Gang members not only held up banks but targeted and killed the police in shootouts. Booty gained from such ventures financed gang activities and was spread around as patronage in the Wareika and nearby communities.

But criminal activity in Wareika was also wedded to ideology and political agendas. Ideologically schooled leaders no doubt discussed with Hotstepper gang members the villainy of the capitalist-oriented JLP in contrast to the proud ideals and promise of the PNP's socialism. This outlook was also shared by the Christopher Henry gang, who combined left-wing political commitments with banditry against banks and vengeful killing of policemen as well.

Leaders Brown, Flash and Henry were clearly criminals who refused the option of their lawful anti-capitalist compeers who had either joined the PNP or created communist parties of their own. The Hotsteppers hewed instead to the belief among a minority and radical fringe that the only way to empower the poor was to overthrow the ruling class by force. Though this position was confined to the fringe Left, it was nonetheless an outlook informed by socialist political conviction.

In this sense, the Hotsteppers and their peers in the ghetto really belonged to that decades-long left-wing tradition that began in the 1930s. This heritage radiated throughout the country with powerful adhesion in Kingston's poorer precincts. It bound grassroots leaders and poor communities to a shared heritage of fighting for socialism, for which the Cuban Revolution was the inspiration after 1959. Flash, Brown and company had merely extended this long tradition into a new form by waging a guerrilla war against the state. In a real sense, then, the Hotsteppers represented that rare instance of genuine protest crime – banditry driven not so much by the quest for booty as by motivation to create an alternative political system. Indeed, the JLP was acutely aware of these political sympathies in its reminder to Parliament that "these criminal gunmen are unique in that they are ideologically motivated".[64]

No doubt this recognition reinforced the all-out war against the gangs. Anthony "Starkie" Tingle was the first left-wing gunman of note to die. He was deported to the island in July 1980 after serving time in Canada, was rearrested but then freed later that year. Gang members had seen to that by intimidating witnesses who subsequently failed to show up for his trial. After this tactic of jamming the wheels of justice Starkie returned to Arnett Gardens where he continued his predation with a hold-up that killed a lowly clerk at a betting shop.[65]

That murder reportedly incensed the Arnett Gardens community and led it to take punitive action against Starkie. It was one thing to rob unpopular banks, plunder other communities and even make war on a murderous police force. But it was unforgivable to carry this mayhem into one's own community and kill a hard-working shopkeeper. The urban poor may protect criminals from a legal system perceived to be unjust, but they will not countenance murderous acts that contravene community values.

After all, though the Kingston poor lived in communities where lawbreaking was taken for granted, moral culture in the ghetto also respected the value of hard work and entrepreneurial initiative. Residents looked to personal enterprise and property ownership as routes to mobility as much as they did crime. The poor expressed these traditional norms through informal, underground and illegal means precisely because they were denied opportunities to do so through legitimate institutions. Killing a community member who made a living through personal enterprise in a neighbourhood that also sheltered criminals invited outrage precisely because moral standards of the official society were not completely extinguished. In the terms of the community values outlined above, Arnett Garden residents were wholly consistent in retaliating against Starkie and expelling him from the community early in 1981. Thus a poor community that had otherwise been in collusion with gunmen had ousted one of its own. In the moral universe of these residents, there was moral culpability, a scale of values and norms of propriety which gunmen had to respect. Starkie had evidently violated this tacit code of honour and was summarily banned from the area.

In Kingston's political hot zones, the lifting of this community's protective veil was probably tantamount to a death sentence as Starkie was forced to retreat to the less secure environs of Jones Town. There, early on the morning of 1 June 1981, a detachment of policemen surprised him and several associates and mowed them down in a shootout. Starkie's death thus began a reign of terror that felled scores of left-wing gunmen including a surprising few who belonged to the communist Workers' Party of Jamaica (WPJ).[66]

The reader should not conclude from the foregoing discussion of left-wing criminal gangs that the policy of exterminism was directed solely at them. While armed left-wing groups were a threat, the major challenge for the state was not left-wing guns as much as autonomous guns in the hands of criminal gangs not domesticated by the parties. The 1970s had spawned a growing number of these gangs across Kingston. In their quest for booty, the majority of them cared little for political doctrines or for political patronage. Motivated by raw plunder and evolving forms of self-organization, this sector was a wholly disruptive force and a major source of criminal violence. Fighting crime therefore meant targeting violent criminals, isolating them from politically protected gangs and taking the war of attrition to them. The policy meant treating criminal gangs as an anomic force that had to be separated from the political parties and physically eliminated from the society.[67] Such a two-track policy of sheltering political crime from the reach of the law on the one hand, while striking at freelance gangs and gunmen on the other, ignored mutations within the cellular structures of the urban underground. The next chapter examines this development and related cultural phenomena.

10

Criminal Self-Organization and Cultural Extremism

THE PREVIOUS CHAPTER HIGHLIGHTED THE WAYS in which violent criminal enterprises were yielding their transforming effects on the island. Predation by criminal gangs had opened a troubling zone of illegal activities outside the immediate compulsion of state politics. Criminal enterprises in this period not only led to a rash of new crime, but they also produced "heroic" outlaws associated with it. In addition, gangs in this period had an arsenal of weapons that deterred all but the bravest of lawmen. In life and death, criminal gangs and notable gunmen enjoyed remarkable community support that confirmed their awesome social power.

While several gangs in this period engaged in predictable predation, they also displayed political inclinations. The Hotsteppers gang, the Christopher Henry gang, WPJ gunmen and Starkie's gang all showed clear political commitments and ideological sentiments. While not the only lawless force operating in Kingston's badlands, these left-leaning, pro-PNP gangs introduced a new twist in urban protest and insurgency. By including banditry among their activities they showed that groups inspired by left-wing values were not immune to the gangsterization of politics now pervasive in other realms.

Militarization of Left-Wing Politics: The Workers' Party of Jamaica

The resort to the power of the gun was a new development within the Left, for while it was not unusual for poor and working-class insurgents to take up arms against the state and to engage in outlawry, social banditry was highly unusual in left-wing organizations led by the middle class. Consequently, although ideologically driven insurrection involving guns and violence was not a novel development in post-war Jamaica, insurgency that wedded bank heists and radical politics was.[1]

That gun violence and bank hold-ups had become appealing not just to politically inspired outlaws but also to the WPJ – an organization that was led by middle-class intellectuals – was stunning testimony to the seduction of outlawry in this period.[2] Not only did top officials of that organization have armed bodyguards, but WPJ activists were involved in the political violence common at the time.[3]

Local politics did not change, however, the WPJ's allegiance to an imported model of radical politics. This workers' party hewed to the political style, organizational structure and ideological orientation typical of pro-Soviet communist parties. WPJ leaders spoke in the idiom of the world communist movement; they looked for ideological direction and support from the Communist Party of the Soviet Union and they adopted the organizational format of a communist vanguard party. In this sense, the WPJ exhibited a Eurocentric identity, albeit of a radical persuasion.

At the same time the WPJ displayed qualities typical of party formations in Jamaica. For instance, like the main political parties the WPJ also had its security apparatus and gunmen. While providing the usual protections for a vanguard party of this type, the WPJ security apparatus became militarized. As the party fought for position in a context of raging political violence and mounting crime, it invariably had to secure its own enclaves and shelter its cadres against hostile opponents in Kingston.[4] Under these circumstances, the WPJ's labourist politics adapted itself to Jamaica's warlord politics.

Moreover, while the WPJ held fast to the organizational rules and the severe ascetic style of a communist vanguard party, it was not immune to the compulsions of Jamaican popular culture and the boisterous etiquette of party politics on the island. At WPJ party conferences and mass rallies, top leaders won rank and file adulation and honorifics reserved for party bosses on the island. Here political hero-worship typical of the local political culture saturated the show of support for the organization's leaders and the party's cause.

This fawning over the communist elite was often reserved for General Secretary Trevor Munroe, who was celebrated for his role as brilliant strategist, champion of the downtrodden and inveterate critic of capitalism. The deafening accolades that greeted Munroe's approach and departure from the microphone at WPJ party conferences were not unlike the messianism encountered at public JLP and PNP rallies.[5] Thus, in a remarkable combination, the personalism in Jamaica's political culture was yoked to a bureaucratic leadership model – the communist vanguard party – imported from abroad.

A coupling of dissimilar cultures was also evident in the unseemly adaptation of the WPJ's communist politics to the island's warlord politics. Not only did state surveillance of the party find guns in the hands of WPJ activists, but this surveillance led to government allegations that several violent incidents in the country were linked to a WPJ-led guerrilla-style campaign of robbery and mayhem.[6] Because Jamaican governments in the past have often exaggerated the threat posed by political dissidents, these claims about the WPJ may well have been inaccurate or overblown.[7] Still, interviews with a former leading WPJ activist did confirm the party's complicity in both banditry and political violence.

In a curious process of Jamaicanization, the WPJ wedded imported norms of vanguard party politics to norms of vintage, local, gun-toting politics. As a consequence, rejection of criminal acts and the primacy that earlier Jamaican Marxists had given to reason over force and violence in politics was displaced by the politics of armed confrontation in the 1970s. As such, the traditional left-wing emphasis on achieving political victory by dint of labour's concerted political action against a capitalist system gave way in the 1970s to gun politics, tit-for-tat violence and the militarization of left-wing politics. In this respect, the militarization and gangsterization of Jamaican politics were no longer confined to the main political parties but had now seeped into the tactics of organizations and groups associated with the Left.

This corruption of left-wing politics in favour of the gun is compelling testimony to the enveloping violence and the militarization of relations that gripped the society in the 1970s and after. Political violence and calculated expediency informed the strategies of all political parties, and the WPJ was no different in this regard.

In the armed warfare that defined the 1970s, the militarization of the Left no doubt helped ensure the physical survival of its personnel. Counter-violence against gun-toting rivals no doubt enabled communists to remain a viable force in the killing field that urban Kingston became in the 1970s. Moreover, widespread belief among PNP partisans and the communist Left

that the country faced an externally instigated campaign of violent destabilization no doubt encouraged like-minded communists to take up arms
against this threat.

In this regard, finding weapons in communist hands would not have been
unusual for the time. After all, politics in Jamaica was never a genteel affair
and its violent factionalism offered no apprenticeship to the politically timid
and the martially unprepared. To survive in Jamaican politics contenders
invariably entered the political arena with steely nerves and martial dispositions. Regrettably, as this study has shown, violence and guns defined the
political game in urban Jamaica after the 1960s. To compete in this arena
entailed armed campaigns and the quest for victory through political violence. As such, WPJ cadres no doubt felt that the taking up of arms was necessary in order to have any chance of survival and gain any ability to outlast
militarized JLP and PNP opponents. Thus the militarization of political
contestation in the 1970s undoubtedly informed communists' resort to guns.

Hence, what is surprising about WPJ politics was not that the party had
a militia. Rather, what is unusual for a communist party of this type that
insisted on rank-and-file discipline and on moral incorruptibility as a hall-
mark of communist politics is that WPJ cadres exploited the breakdown in
law and order in Jamaica to engage in banditry.

While the extent of this activity is in dispute, party cadres were involved
in it, sometimes with the party's knowledge, and at other times not.[8] To be
fair, it should be said that party-sanctioned bank heists were rare; that banditry was certainly not the defining feature of WPJ politics in the 1970s; and
that when such acts did occur, personnel carrying them out were tightly
controlled.[9] Still, in a disordered society bereft of moral examples in the
political realm, a left-wing party's resort to armed robbery to secure funds
for the communist cause is more than troubling.

Such surrender to base criminality by an otherwise valiant champion of
the Jamaican people is awful testimony to the corrupting power that expediency had on advocates of social transformation, no matter their political
persuasions. Much like the PNP partisans who mistakenly waged war on the
hapless poor in the name of socialism in the 1970s, WPJ cadres robbed banks
to presumably fund what they regarded as an equally righteous cause.

The politics of expediency and a culture of gangsterism therefore
doomed what began in the 1970s as a high-minded quest for social change
by challengers to the status quo. Whatever else may be said of politics in the
1970s, the degeneration of left-wing activism into criminality sounded the

death knell for a long-standing tradition of radicalism in Jamaica that resisted thievery, had no truck with gunplay and offered itself as moral exemplar in opposition to the corruptions of a capitalist society in crisis.

Social Change and the Transformation of Crime

Apart from contributing to the degeneration of left-wing politics, gang-based criminal enterprise deepened the criminalization of the state. Theft, murder and the suborning of the courts and prisons accomplished this. Gang members intimidated witnesses, killed a civil servant investigating their activities, engineered prison breaks and freed outlaws. Gangsters jammed the wheels of justice and frustrated the hamstrung courts in the late 1970s. No authority seemed immune to the gangs' power as immigration, customs and municipal workers did their bidding. As a result, Copper, Starkie and their associates in the underground were able to travel abroad freely and sometimes return to the island without being jailed.

These problems became worse in the 1980s and they were not all due to criminality. Bureaucratic inefficiency abetted corruption. The director of public prosecutions would report, for example, that the courts faced a backlog of fifteen hundred criminal cases that were yet to have a hearing.[10] But poor police work that permitted the guilty to go free and excessive detention of suspects awaiting trials paled in significance compared with growing cases of bribed testimonies and juror misconduct, as panels delivered verdicts at odds with the evidence.[11]

Though these activities were clearly a feature of the growing criminalization of the Jamaican state, they cannot be subsumed under the parallel, often overlapping, but quite distinct corrupt practices directed from on high by party barons and state agents. Gang-based criminal enterprise belonged to a zone that was not subject to state dictation. Criminal enterprise had much in common with the party-based gangs and a state that straddled the boundaries between formal and informal politics; that crossed the divide between the official and underground economy. Nonetheless, criminal gangs were a distinct, corporate group with their own interests that were shaped by a history of independence outside the compulsion of partisan politics. Although these gangs had been drawn into the orbit of partisan politics, by the mid-1980s they had developed interests that were more and more independent of the state.

Still, it would be a mistake to think that a wall existed between party political gangs and gangs from the criminal underground. On the contrary, boundaries that existed were porous, and though a distinction can be made between groups that engaged in violent activities in the name of politics and others that did so in the name of crime, by the early 1980s changing circumstances blurred this distinction. As a result, some political top rankings moved away from purely partisan engagements and gravitated to criminal enterprise while others juggled both vocations. Because these developments occurred at the cusp of the new decade they represented an important social mutation and fateful transition in ghetto and national politics.

In a large measure, then, the changes that occurred here represented a parting of ways and a reordering of relations in the political and criminal underground. Because relations in both undergrounds were coextensive with developments in the wider society, transformations in the latter had ramifying effects on the former. The sum of all these changes would keep the level of violence below the threshold established in 1980 while increasing the intensity of criminal violence and expanding the number of recruits to it. These developments dealt a blow to the state's crime-fighting strategy. Indeed, structural and political changes had been undermining terror and exterminism as crime-fighting strategies and those changes made criminal violence more, not less, likely after 1980.

For one thing, the economic crisis encouraged resort to crime. The country's declining economy and "watchdog" IMF austerity measures since 1977 severely the reduced lavish patronage that was once heaped on political supporters. Cutbacks in state spending hurt favoured top rankings and directed potential gunmen and traditional supplicants to other pursuits. As patronage dried up, the pressure to move from politics to criminal employment increased. Hence, hardy souls who might have been drawn to politics in more flush times had to look elsewhere for a livelihood.

Other political factors hastened this parting of ways. Disillusionment with state predation, recrimination from the failed truce and the scorched-earth policies of the state turned all but the fanatically loyal against blind partisanship. Besides these defections, the defeat of democratic socialism in 1980 and the compromising of left-wing ideas by deadly gun politics deflated enthusiasm for the politics of radical change. After all, the very population that had twice elected the PNP turned it out of power in a landslide when it engaged in a blood-drenched rivalry with the JLP and failed to deliver the promise of a better life.

JLP Victory and Political Decline

By October 1983 the implosion of the Grenada revolution reinforced anti-communist attitudes in Jamaica and hastened disillusionment with the politics of the Left. Furthermore, rumours that the WPJ had backed the coup that killed Maurice Bishop, Grenada's popular leader, dashed whatever enthusiasm remained for socialist experiments among thoughtful members of the Jamaican Left, including the poor that had embraced that cause. Well before the 1989 collapse of communism in Eastern Europe, then, the militant poor as well as thoughtful progressives in Jamaica and throughout the Caribbean were beckoned toward a post-communist outlook marked by sharpened scrutiny of the ethics of Caribbean communists and disillusionment with left-wing causes.

Edward Seaga and the JLP seized on these sentiments and the unexpected turn of events in Grenada to call new elections in December 1983, fully two years before they were constitutionally required. Surprising erosion of political support prompted this pre-emptive action. Even though it had scored a resounding victory in 1980 the JLP faltered less than a year into its term. After the first flush of enthusiasm had worn off and the policy of satisfying pent-up consumer demand with high food and consumer imports had run its course, the JLP's honeymoon ended.

A confluence of factors trimmed the party's political support between 1980 and 1983.[12] First, an abundant supply of imported goods without a commensurate increase in purchasing power hurt sales and heightened frustration among merchants and agricultural producers. Second, high expectations of significant foreign investment were dashed, as a recession in the United States reduced investment flows to the island. Third, the JLP policy of encouraging foreign investment and ending protections for domestic manufacturers hurt local entrepreneurs and provoked their discontent. Fourth, unemployment remained high, hovering in the range of 30 to 35 per cent. This problem highlighted the JLP's inability to create enough new jobs to make a dent in the unemployment rate and that failure increased frustration among the jobless poor. Finally, the JLP's tendency to cater to foreign interests, accommodate itself to the luxury consumption of the rich, and tolerate skyrocketing prices for rentals and home sales all hurt its image with the public. By October 1982, the Stone Polls showed that support for the JLP had slipped to 47 per cent, from a high of 59 per cent two years earlier.[13]

Besides alienating a variety of classes including big importers and manufacturers, the JLP was increasingly perceived as a party that cared little for
the poor and working people. This was in sharp contrast to the party's 1980
election campaign that pledged to bring "deliverance" to the Jamaican
people and reward them with the "jingling" of money in their pockets.[14]
Disillusionment with the JLP reversed the public's negative opinions of the
PNP and its support rose steadily between 1981 and October 1983.

Indeed, support for the JLP tumbled even more when it announced a 77
per cent devaluation of the currency in November as a condition for securing a new standby agreement with the IMF.[15] This sharp devaluation delivered the *coup de grace* to Seaga's reputation as a prudent manager and financial
wizard. Prospects of a massive reduction in the standard of living of an
already overburdened population appeared to seal the JLP's fate and led the
PNP to call for Seaga's resignation.

It was this economic squeeze and crumbling support that drove the JLP
to link its call for new elections with the disastrous events in Grenada. The
JLP traded on revulsion of the Grenada coup and exploited Jamaicans' fears
of communism. Despite a PNP boycott of the election, the JLP rode to
power on the wave of public disgust with the murderous seizure of power
and widespread support for the American invasion that ended it.[16] But
whatever hopes the JLP had that this reprieve would give it time to fix the
economy and forestall public outbursts were dashed with the fuel price
protest of 15 and 16 January 1985.

Social Explosion: The 1985 Fuel Price Demonstrations

As with the 1979 upheaval, this protest revealed intense levels of impatience
among the poorer classes with governments that seemed only to destroy
their purchasing power. Four years of austerity policies, repeated price hikes
and two devaluations under the JLP dimmed public expectation of any
"deliverance" from what had now amounted to twelve years of unrelenting
economic pressure since the 1973 downturn. In a stark confirmation of the
structural character of the economic crisis, neither the PNP nor the JLP
seemed capable of relieving the country's distress. These parties' ideological
protestations were now largely irrelevant in the face of the country's structural dependence and the permanence of economic crisis. Thus when the

JLP announced a J$1.91 increase in the price of a gallon of premium gasoline, the frustrated urban poor took to the streets on Tuesday morning, 15 January.

Once again the Corporate Area of Kingston and St Andrew became a tinderbox. At major intersections and neighbourhoods across Kingston and St Andrew, the urban poor blocked roads, clashed with the police and demanded money from stranded drivers. Public transportation was interrupted and schools and business closed their doors. Security forces had their hands full throughout the city as militant demonstrators blocked roads that had been repeatedly cleared.[17]

The demonstration also showed its partisan face. JLP gunmen from the Southside enclave in Central Kingston assaulted Browns Town residents who were manning roadblocks there. Pro-PNP residents in East Kingston threw up barricades, fought with JLP invaders and registered their contempt by scrawling graffiti that declared "Away with Seaga. Elections Now".[18] Such was the fury of these partisans that four of the seven deaths from the disturbance occurred in the East Kingston area alone.

The protest also spread to the countryside. Major incidents occurred in the cities and larger towns of the central parishes. The parish of St Catherine, for example, became a secondary centre of opposition. Demonstrators there blockaded the city of Spanish Town, obstructed railway tracks and, more ominously, set fire to the Holland sugar estate.[19] Less ferocious demonstration also occurred in such far-flung locales as Port Antonio and Morant Bay. Although protests in the countryside were much less severe than in Kingston, rural protesters had nonetheless erected an estimated four hundred roadblocks in defiance of the authorities. On Wednesday, the protest led by the urban poor subsided without involvement by other classes. By day's end Michael Manley had joined the JLP in calling for an end to the demonstrations for the sake of the "national interest".[20]

Compared to events in 1979 this demonstration was more violent but less disruptive. That is, more lives were lost in 1985, but the protest was less intense and had fewer political consequences for the regime. The 1985 protest fizzled after only two days, while the 1979 demonstration was of longer duration. While the 1979 upheaval forced the state to back down and take a smaller price increase, the 1985 disturbance caused no rollback in prices. The JLP was therefore able to impose the entire J$1.91 increase that sent premium gasoline to J$10.90 per gallon, with related hikes for kerosene, another fuel used heavily by the poor.

Other differences set the two fuel price demonstrations apart. In 1979 the urban poor drew strategic industrial workers and other classes to their cause; in 1985 the militant unemployed were an isolated social force. Finally, where the 1979 strike found the political parties sharply at odds, in 1985 they set aside their partisanship and closed ranks as protesters moved beyond the orbit of partisan recrimination to burn the cane fields at the Holland Estate. Despite these handicaps the second fuel price protest in a decade did confirm the role of the unemployed as a "tripwire class", easily provoked and ever prepared, by dint of its hardships and martial tradition, to lead the outcry against hard times.

The Evolution of Criminal Self-Organization: The Rise of the Drug Don

The cooperation of political patrons in turning back the rioters and thwarting a rollback in prices may have produced another hiatus in the succession of public demonstrations. It did little, however, to reduce crime or halt the destruction of community life in the ghetto. Securing an unstable peace gave no advantage to those who hectored the alienated poor to turn away from crime. The imposition of the fuel price hike had closed off another route to relief, leaving the poor to face sharply reduced options. For the desperate minority among them, criminal employment remained an attractive option. As economic circumstances deteriorated in the ghetto and the society, defiant criminal gangs found recruits among this desperate minority.

In fact, political violence in the 1970s and its aftermath made criminal gang leaders' task that much easier. Violence and economic hardship winnowed the population, and in poor neighbourhoods across Kingston those who stayed behind in the gutted buildings and terminal squalor were primarily those who had no other options and were inured to partisanship, violence and crime. Political and criminal violence had driven countervailing forces such as charitable organizations, civic-minded leaders, citizens associations as well as public and private sector agencies from violence-ridden neighbourhoods. Teachers, clergy and community leaders now had little or no influence in them. In sum, political violence, pressing economic need, state terror and ideological deflation had cleared the ground of virtually all social forces whose interests were divergent from the political and criminal undergrounds. With the political gangs decimated by war and on the defensive, and their criminal counterparts looking for new vocations, both groups turned to the one activity that promised huge profits: drug trafficking.

As Laurie Gunst observed in her exposé of politics, drugs and guns in Jamaica, after 1980 the island became a transshipment point for cocaine with Jamaican gangs playing a vital role in the traffic. The drug was allegedly introduced by the JLP "when Seaga came to power, and several of his government ministers were said to be involved in protecting its movement into and out of Jamaica".[21] By 1984 the re-export of cocaine from the island and its use in the ghetto were sufficiently disturbing for the US Drug Enforcement Administration to sound an alarm in an intelligence report:

> Increasing evidence of cocaine traffic in Jamaica is of concern both because of the threat to the local population and because it involves foreign criminal elements. Some Jamaican traffickers are believed to have switched to cocaine because of the relative ease with which it can be shipped, in comparison to marijuana, and because of the large profits to be made.[22]

A lively international traffic in hard drugs now complemented the island's modest export trade in marijuana and this change in the illicit trade hastened the displacement of pure partisanship as vocation and source of livelihood in the ghetto.[23]

The transition to trafficking in hard drugs, with its potential for huge profits, was accomplished with extraordinary speed. As we have observed, 1980 was a watershed year. While the JLP's victory had forced several gangsters to flee the island for North America and Cuba, it had also prompted others on the island to look to criminal ventures abroad to sustain their enterprise. In the United States they not only established operations in the cocaine and marijuana trade in cities such as New York and Miami, but they also kept the gang names and partisan persuasions of Kingston's ghettos. Monies from the trade were then sent back to the drug dealers' old neighbourhoods in the form of patronage, along with sophisticated weapons that were smuggled to gang members on the island.

Gunst maintained that the advent of cocaine in Kingston's ghettos was no accident. It coincided, she argued, with a JLP electoral victory that opened up a protected transshipment trade that shielded drugs, the local pro-JLP gangs in the trade and the guns that were smuggled to them on the island. Moreover, the cocaine trade flourished even as the local marijuana trade was being stifled. As Gunst observed, "Jamaica's entry into the Caribbean transshipment trade dovetailed neatly and brutally with the island's American-funded ganja eradication program. As the ganja barons found it harder to get their product off the island, they began to piggyback their shipments on the cocaine trade."[24]

In the early 1980s, Lester Lloyd Coke, popularly known as "Jim Brown", was running a major portion of the trade out of the Tivoli Gardens enclave. Brown had emerged as Massop's successor in Tivoli, though it was said that Brown had neither the charisma nor the respect won by the slain top ranking.[25] As was the case with previous leaders in Kingston's ghettos, Brown was responsible for securing the Tivoli garrison and had men under his command to accomplish that. But unlike earlier top rankings, Brown and others like him became patrons in their own right as the cocaine trade brought new wealth that could not be matched by state sponsors. Befitting the new largesse that came with the cocaine trade, notables such as Jim Brown now became the "dons" of their neighbourhoods. They too possessed the key resources once monopolized by politicians: guns, money, violence and the social power of community support. As the new don in Tivoli Gardens, Brown therefore juggled the management of the drug trade and his political obligations to the West Kingston garrison. Politics and drug crime now fed each other in Tivoli Gardens.

By 1984 Brown had already established a major drug trafficking enterprise in the United States that required him to shuttle regularly between Jamaica, Miami and New York. Run by Jamaican loyalists abroad, Brown's organization, the Shower Posse, accumulated fabulous wealth. Some of it found its way back to Kingston's ghettos in the form of fancy cars, expensive jewellery worn by the don and his associates, powerful guns to protect the trade, as well as patronage in the form of handouts, street parties and festivities in poor neighbourhoods. A new wealth had come to the ghetto and it completely outstripped anything the politicians had hitherto delivered in their constituencies. Where politicians had been celebrated as saviours in poor communities, the new drug dons now threatened to displace their power and influence.

The new power in the ghetto was earned by dint of a savage indentureship. Decades of apprenticeship to the political parties had decimated the ranks of the supplicant poor. But that tutelage in factional politics also served the new gangsters well. The more ambitious among them put this forty-year heritage to effective use. They now leveraged their political connections, used the desperation in their neighbourhoods to seduce the young and the needy, and employed badness-honour, gunfire and brutality to overawe opponents and caution renegades within their ranks.

Politics had been a full-time occupation for party activists and enforcers. In the 1980s, they turned that apprenticeship to the business of the drug trade. After all, the gangs' political engagements required organizing communities for myriad political tasks. It entailed recruiting and training workers and gang members in the minutiae of activist politics ranging from delivering handouts to disrupting an election. Their apprenticeship included mastery of guns and other weapons of war, organizing "troops" for battle and outlasting political enemies in violent encounters. In Jamaica's slums, party militia leaders acquired skill more akin to guerrilla warfare than to electoral politics.

Top rankings were also responsible for disbursing funds to loyalists, providing transportation for violent forays against political opponents and coordinating tactics and strategy with political bosses. That required leadership, communication and organizational skills as well as political acumen. These were well-honed aptitudes and repertoires that showed a far more sophisticated sensibility than the stereotype of mere greedy desire for booty. Poverty and its interface with politics thus gave activists in the ghetto a peculiar apprenticeship in organized violence and in a species of "management training" and leadership which they put to other purposes.

But learning and sophistication also came from geo-cultural sources. Jamaica's political and criminal gunmen may have been poor and uneducated, but they were not political illiterates or cultural parochials. On the contrary, they were New World moderns of a particular stripe. Ghetto notables such as Copper, Starkie, Massop and Brown were more than hoodlums. They were worldly men because of foreign travel and exposure to world culture. More than that, these gunmen were avatars who had imbibed a unique curriculum. Its contents were as various as socialism, lessons in stubborn black self-help, factional democratic politics and organization, as well as criminal predation and the horizontal violence that claimed the lives of the black poor.

Moreover, the impact of global culture on Jamaica powerfully influenced these notables. Though they lived in a physical ghetto, gangsters shared that modernity of experience typical of the Caribbean diaspora as crucible of global culture. World historical ideologies such as liberalism, black nationalism, Marxism, and ideas of freedom and individual rights radiated in the ghetto with probably more intensity than in more privileged precincts in the country. Foreign travel and imported literature – as various as the mytho-religious books disseminated by the L.W. DeLaurence Publishing Company of Chicago as well as critiques of capitalism in Marxist texts – with its pro-crustean ideas, were means of social mobilization in Kingston's ghettos. Last, saturation by a global electronic media made sure Jamaicans of all classes imbibed their contradictory messages. Invariably, this cultural provocation led Jamaicans, including ghetto-dwellers such as Brown and Massop, to take their agonistic place in global culture.

Gangsters who set up criminal enterprises abroad took the risks and faced the dangers that came with their venturesome exploits. In this respect, they were merely the latest cohorts in Caribbean migrants' continuing quest for wealth, power and autonomy at home and abroad. Monies earned in foreign lands, whether from back-breaking work in factories or in the high-risk and murderous drug trade, were sent back to the island as remittances. These funds supported families, rewarded natal communities, established criminal enterprises or secured a coming retirement.

In appreciating the connection between world culture and the advent of the new dons, it may not be an exaggeration to argue the following. If contemporary Caribbean history is one epicentre of upheaval in world experience, then the turbulence in Kingston's urban ghettos and the pro-tean consciousness exhibited there represent fault lines in the unity of that global experience. In other words, gang culture in Jamaica was less a pecu-liarity of Jamaican experience than it was a disruptive, radiating force in global culture.

This summary of the instructive impact of history and experience on contemporary leadership in Kingston's ghettos is no moral paean to the criminal gangs. It is, however, an account of the vast forces that shaped them and buttressed their claim to a new social power.

Mystique of the Gun: Source of Mobility and Measure of Social Power

Several incidents involving Jim Brown between 1984 and 1988 made that power painfully obvious to Jamaicans. In May 1984 Brown and a large con-tingent of Tivoli gunmen laid siege to the Rema enclave and killed twelve residents there. The assault was retaliation for Rema's attempt to break with its status as Tivoli's vassal and stepchild to the JLP. While Rema languished from neglect, Tivoli remained the citadel of JLP power in Kingston and it got the lion's share of state largesse. This subordination offended Rema-ites to the point where they not only flirted with the PNP but also contemplated launching their own assault on Tivoli Gardens.[26] Brown and his men brutally put down this incipient revolt with the resulting loss of life.

On 16 May and again on 4 October, islanders were shocked when shipments of high-powered weapons were discovered in containers on the Kingston docks. While the May discovery revealed four semi-automatic rifles and seven automatic pistols, the October shipment was a stunning confirmation of the growing traffic in illegal guns. It included a "twenty-two-gun arsenal that included an M16, and an M1 Enforcer, five assault rifles, two .44 magnums, and more than six thousand rounds of ammunition".[27] Jim Brown's Shower Posse in the United States, it was revealed, had sent both shipments to the island.

If the interdiction of these weapons stripped JLP gangs of their coveted weapons, the seizures had no immediate effect on Brown's criminal activities in Jamaica. They did, however, erode the political protection he enjoyed there. A warrant for his arrest was issued after the murders in Rema, but Brown was able to flee the island for the United States in October. In March 1987 he eluded US authorities and returned to Jamaica where he was charged with the crimes in Rema. However, like Starkie and others before him, Brown was freed when an intimidated witness changed her testimony, presumably to save her life. With this acquittal jubilant supporters from Tivoli Gardens gave the don a rousing welcome as he left the courthouse. In another display of contempt for the legal system, supporters fired their weapons in a cacophonous "gun salute" outside the Supreme Court and lifted the don aloft in a frenzy of popular enthusiasm.[28] The chatter of celebratory gunfire outside the nation's highest court did more than confirm the extent of criminals' disrespect for the legal system. The gunfire affirmed the consolidation of a rival and new power in the ghetto with its unalloyed challenge to the political bosses and the society at large.[29]

Indeed, widespread access to guns permitted unmediated exercise of power and enjoyment of exalted status in the ghetto. Guns were no longer just a weapon in political wars or merely means to a criminal end. In prior years, armed criminals wreaked havoc and engaged in a derring-do that, on the whole, did not invest the gun with the kind of social potency and cultural meaning it assumed in later years.

In the 1970s and after, guns were celebrated as sources of personal power and measures of social authority. Criminals and non-criminals alike regarded the gun as a social equalizer. Guns and their use therefore enabled hitherto demeaned persons from the ghetto to exercise unprecedented personal authority and social power. Guns in criminal hands wrested coveted goods from frightened citizens and claimed the lives of public officials.[30] In criminal hands, guns were means to predation, instruments of political assassination and not least a tool of compensatory social respect. Gun violence and badness-honour were forms of social power. Together they opened avenues of upward mobility and permitted armed members of the lumpenproletariat an elevated status in a highly status-conscious society.

To be sure, both gunmen of all political stripes as well as criminal gangs committed horrible crimes. Yet crime bore a highly personal charge that expressed both personal inclinations and larger social divisions. This social energy was expressed in the settling of scores with insolent rivals and in the rough justice meted out to victims. Personal will informed dyadic power relations that became evident in the readiness of gunmen to be remembered for exhibiting a fearsome and stylized form of power. This repertoire included the infamous "dog-hearted" readiness to hurt, humiliate or degrade victims with no concern for their humanity. Victims of criminal violence therefore experienced that tyranny not as chance, impersonal objects, but as socially implicated and often vulnerable persons. Often they were targets that appeared to be easily vanquished. Usually they were persons against whom vengeance was exercised in the name of a raw, atomized show of personal power. Whether it was the rape of defenceless women in the ghetto, the murder of public officials or the settling of personal scores with other gunmen, such instances of horizontal violence had nothing to do with social protest and everything to do with crime. Yet even here, power intruded as gunmen using a stylized violence sought to exercise their unchecked will over others or tried to alter by force social arrangements that got in their way. In these cases, marginality led not to "protest crime" but only to crime.

The use of the gun was therefore much more than a means to predation. It was also a means to a newer kind of social power, one that thrived on the asymmetries of power between a sophisticated, socially mobilized, armed cohort from the ghetto and an unarmed population. Guns were no longer the exclusive possession of the security forces. Both criminal and political gangs, who were all from the ghetto, possessed a competing and sometimes far more powerful arsenal. The gun therefore gave huge authority and status to hitherto marginal groups. This reversal of status and the means that achieved it encouraged a swaggering bravado in the ghetto. Guns and gun use had become gradually but inexorably linked to power struggles within and beyond party politics. Part of that contestation entailed a battle for individual honour and personal respect among gunmen. It is not surprising, then, that in their predation gunmen were sensitive to matters of respect and deference. For armed criminals in the 1980s, wresting deference from reluctant others was almost as important as grabbing coveted booty.

Commenting on this interface between power-seeking gunmen and the weapons of their trade, Stone observed that

> it gives them power stature and status. Women dare not refuse them. Men shudder in fear of the mention of their names. Their top ranking status was earned by killing and maiming and they can only keep that reputation by continuing to perform daring deeds of violence with the gun. To give up the gun involves loss of status and power and makes the gunman a vulnerable target to challengers, enemies and rival gang members.[31]

Guns and their nexus with crime and power therefore went beyond satisfying the quest for personal enrichment. Guns increasingly became a source of personal pride, an object of individual finesse and expertise, and a source of compensatory personal power. In this regard, fighting crime became doubly difficult precisely because criminal acts were simultaneously acts of personal and social power. Criminal gangs had become both agents of social power and brokers of personal power. Hence, drugs, the guns that protected the drug trade and the social power of the don now threatened, as never before, the politicians' hold on power.

Like Michael Manley before him, Edward Seaga in the 1980s encountered the shock of insurgency by boisterous supplicants and power-seeking gunmen. With the gunfire outside the courthouse, these groups had once again breached the boundaries of good etiquette and violated the tacit understanding between party bosses and supporters that their actions not embarrass the patron or reveal too starkly the vulgarity of party politics. Edward Seaga was therefore compelled to denounce the gun salute as "illegal behaviour" and to register his disapproval by boycotting a Tivoli function to honour the freed drug lord.[32]

Despite this retreat from the violent excesses of the urban poor, Seaga's predicament in the 1980s was very different from Manley's in the 1970s. On the one hand, the PNP leader encountered challenges that conceded the party's authority, even as supplicants demanded a share of power and pressured municipal bodies to disgorge state funds to them. PNP insurgents clashed with powerful patrons, but these supplicants still looked to the state's bounties to satisfy their needs.

Seaga, on the other hand, faced a new situation in which Jim Brown had resources all his own and did not rely exclusively on the politician for disbursing benefits to the poor. A nested structure of power linking the political world and the criminal underground had emerged in Tivoli Gardens. But evolving relations in this citadel and beyond were putting Jim Brown less and less in Seaga's debt while raising the don's stakes among the JLP's rank and file. Brown's independent wealth and far-flung criminal enterprise were more serious challenges to this party boss's power than the opposition Manley encountered a decade earlier.

Though these reordered relations between patrons and the new dons would persist, politicians were not without resources in a corrupted political system. Those resources included terror, assassination and the levers of law and public opinion. Notwithstanding growing public knowledge of the ties between gunmen and politicians, for the most part elite groups accommodated the unflattering sight of cooperative relations between politicians and gangsters. Privileged groups in the society held fast to a greater contempt for the black-skinned, ghetto-confined poor than for their elite sponsors.

Social Domination and Compensatory Honour in the Slums

This contempt for the violent, unlettered blacks in the ghetto was a formidable cultural barrier to their advance. Acquisition of wealth and display of the trappings of success in the ghetto only intensified the society's visceral contempt for ghetto residents. It is worth recalling that this scorn had little to do with repulsion for conspicuous consumption and gaudy display. On the contrary, in a society where middle- and upper-class status relied on consumption values and vulgar displays of success, the handicap for ghetto residents was not gaudy exhibitionism but dislike of unlettered blacks that refused to know their place.[33]

Crime and social protest in the slums fed unyielding perceptions of ghetto blacks as "de ole dutty criminal dem".[34] This prejudice had been the key cultural resource that politicians relied on to wreak atrocities on the unruly poor since the days of Alexander Bustamante and Wills Isaacs. This strange complicity between law-breaking, corrupt politicians and a fearful society inured to racist images of the black, stifled concern for the ongoing, violent annihilation of the ghetto poor.

These sentiments and the cultivated indifference that attended them worked to Seaga's advantage as he responded to the social power that threatened his rule. Two developments eased the politician's dilemma. On the one hand, Brown killed again in Jamaica and the political protection the don once enjoyed was removed. The trigger was an offence to Brown's personal honour. He was arrested in June 1988 for murdering a minibus driver who made the fatal mistake of challenging the don after "bad driving" him and nearly forcing his car off the road.

On the other hand, the amassing of federal charges against Brown in the United States and a request for his extradition put the Jamaican government in an unenviable position. It had to either accede to the US demands with the risk that Brown might divulge incriminating information, or refuse the extradition request and antagonize a powerful ally. Brown, who had beaten the June murder charge when witnesses refused to come forward, was held for extradition in 1990.[35] But in a surprising turn of events the don, who no doubt knew much about the traffic in drugs, the flow of guns and their nexus with Jamaican politics, was killed in a mysterious fire while awaiting extradition in his maximum-security cell.[36] Not surprisingly, Brown's death fed rumours that he was killed to assure his silence. For those who held this view, Brown's death merely confirmed the continuing brutality of state power in Jamaica.[37]

Such views helped inspire a Jamaican brand of outlawry marked by orgiastic violence. State predation fed on the society's racist contempt for the urban poor, using it to both mobilize and throttle ghetto supplicants. This experience spawned a peculiar agonism that combined badness-honour and martial identities with the disillusionment of the downtrodden who believed they were socially dead. While communal clashes provoked proud partisan identities, and though criminal gangs built solidarities based on derring-do and heroic outlawry, both groups did succumb to the dark side of identity formation in the ghetto, namely the impulse to self-immolation. Orgiastic political and criminal violence overwhelmingly consumed the poorer classes, not the well-heeled or complicit politicians.

Yet this stark reality of life in the ghetto should be qualified. Cultural contempt, class marginality and ceaseless parasitism undoubtedly drove the poor to despair, rage and social cannibalism. These dispositions won favour with politicians and "badness" in search of honour was harnessed by them and canalized into political rivalries.

At the same time, deprivation also fed a species of redemptive immolation. It was premised not so much on the quest for transcendent collective ideals as on rejection of the psychic effect of political domination: that effect produced a mobilized but throttled persona. It was a condition in which social and political mobilization offered prospects of freedom and autonomy even as the quest for it was denied rebellious blacks. For the militant poor, social inequality and the state predation that backed it up merely confirmed perceptions of themselves as persons who were socially dead. Reggae music culture, popular culture and everyday talk in Kingston's congested ghettos constantly strummed this theme of social death in which the enjoyment of moral belonging to the national community was constantly denied.[38]

However, rather than lead only to despair, massive social and political mobilization in Jamaica also fed notions of compensatory honour. In the 1980s the "ready fi' dead" attitude among the alienated poor clearly expressed this sensibility in which hopelessness and hopeful honour were joined. In these terms, the self-immolation of the mobilized poor carried both nihilism and redemptive impulse as cultural freight.

On the one hand, hopelessness and blocked aspirations produced "born fi' dead" and "done dead a'ready" attitudes among the enraged poor. On the other, the agonism of the poor betrayed not just nihilism, lack of hope or obsession with death. Rather, ghetto contention also disclosed a determination that violent extremism and physical death were better, even redemptive options, more preferable to the far worse fates of social death and crucifying violence that the society deemed as a normal, if unfortunate, part of life in Jamaica. By the late 1980s, this was undeniably the common sense among the most alienated groups in Kingston's ghettos.

Crime and Social Honour: The Case of Wayne Smith

Gang leader Wayne "Sandokhan" Smith, holed up in the Waterhouse community in the West Central St Andrew constituency, typified this outlook among criminal gangsters beyond the confines of West Kingston and South

St Andrew. Smith's tortured career as a drug don and community patron offers another vantage point for examining the conjunction of state politics, social inequality, crime, moral culture and notions of community in the ghetto.

Wayne Smith was born on 2 May 1962. By the time he was seventeen years old, he had already dropped out of school for three years and was facing imprisonment for larceny.[39] After his release he returned to the Waterhouse–Olympic Gardens community which had become a battle-scarred zone in the 1979–80 political upheaval. But where political war had torn apart Trench Town and Tivoli Gardens and made those regions emblematic of political strife, the communities of Riverton City, Waterhouse and Olympic Gardens in West Central St Andrew shared in that upheaval and more.

On the one hand, political divisions mimicked conflicts elsewhere. In Olympic Gardens, PNP political gangs operating from areas they dubbed "Moscow" and "Havana" clashed with hostile JLP gangs in the Tower Hill area. Firebombing and gunfire destroyed lives and decimated the homes and businesses of poorer residents. According to a noted journalist, of the more than eight hundred persons killed in 1979–80 over three hundred came from the Tower Hill and Waterhouse areas.[40] The result of this was a collapse of community life and descent into anarchy and political murder. Against the backdrop of this hollowing of souls and neighbourhood buildings, at-gunpoint political evictions in West Central St Andrew secured the expulsion of all but the most stalwart of residents.

On the other hand, even as political violence in the constituency mimicked factionalism elsewhere, residents in West Central St Andrew suffered even greater hardships than some Trench Town communities. Besides being one of the most densely populated areas in the country, the constituency had the dubious distinction of being the site of the city dump. It was located in Riverton City and the stench of rotting garbage suffused the air there.

As populations fled other war-torn areas over the years, they had decamped in parts of West Central St Andrew. Over the years this constituency became the new Back-o-Wall with its shacks and scenes of humans foraging for food at the dumpsite. Hence, where thousands in West Kingston and South St Andrew tenanted modern dwellings with their infrastructure of party-delivered community services, residents in Riverton City, Tower Hill and Waterhouse enjoyed no such bounties. In the worst areas, shacks rather than modern housing were the typical dwellings. In a city where unemployment was rampant and deprivation high, Waterhouse and its environs were communities *in extremis.*

Ten years of structural adjustment policies combined with currency devaluation had driven down national living standards and invariably poor neighbourhoods such as Waterhouse and Riverton City were hit hard. Between 1980 and 1988, for example, the cost of living in the country increased a whopping 48 per cent with an annual average increase of 14 per cent. The years 1983 to 1985 were especially difficult, as the cost of living ballooned to 86 per cent with an annual average increase of 87 per cent. Even as the national unemployment rate between 1983 and 1985 dropped from 26.4 per cent to 25.4 per cent, the rate went from 28.3 per cent to 31 per cent in Kingston and St Andrew Parish alone.[41]

The consequences for the Waterhouse poor were uniformly negative. While political gangs laid waste to the area, criminal gangs flourished in the political mayhem and its aftermath. They robbed the poor and preyed on defenceless women, raping many of them. Anti-crime sweeps and indiscriminate assaults by the security forces compounded these difficulties. Poorly trained, often outgunned and lacking community support, the security forces resorted to counterproductive crime-fighting measures. Assault, intimidation and indifference to the distinction between the law-abiding but uncooperative majority and the armed gangs only hardened community attitudes against lawmen.

Facing brutality from the security forces on one side, and plunder from criminals on the other, desperate Waterhouse residents looked to whatever source could deliver relief from the pincers of economic want and violent predation, whether criminal or lawfully sanctioned. In the absence of political favours and public welfare, only the "charity" of criminal gangs and that of a few missionaries in the neighbourhood remained.[42] In the bombed-out, war-ravaged environment and demoralized communities of Waterhouse, Olympic Gardens and Riverton City, Sandokhan emerged as the don and avenging outlaw.

Like other gang leaders across Kingston who saw an opportunity in the enervation of the state and in the crippling of society, Sandokhan rose to prominence as a don freed of constraining ties to political parties. In a lawless environment, he and other gunmen laid down the law. For populations neglected by the state, he became the new patron. For women and others who feared rape and the terror of marauding criminals, he was both protector and avenging lawman.

The decay of civil society and the criminalization of the state were pre-conditions for Sandokhan's power. The debilities of state power in the 1980s permitted Sandokhan's ready access to guns and ties to the network of the international drug trade. By 1988 Sandokhan's links to the drug trade reached from Olympic Gardens to the far-flung environs of New York and Kansas City, where drug rings carrying his name had established operations. Sandokhan's power in the Waterhouse area was based, therefore, on the connections among drugs, money and guns in the international economy. Drug trafficking created the means to buy guns abroad, to recruit gang members at home and distribute patronage to the poor. The guns, in turn, overawed opponents and protected the drug trade. All three factors fed Sandokhan's accumulation of social power in the poorer communities of West Central St Andrew. Between 1986 and the summer of 1988, the gunman's exploits confirmed this awesome power and highlighted the conjunction of power, crime and alternative notions of law and community.

Notwithstanding the fact that he was a wanted man, Sandokhan evidently moved about freely, seemingly without fear of interdiction. However, this bold disregard for the law was interrupted on 19 November 1986 when a patrol attempted to interdict him as he rode with his wife on a motorbike. In a remarkable show of force, Sandokhan single-handedly fought his way out of the ambush and fled to safety, leaving his wife in the hands of the police.[43]

Yet rather than instil caution in the gunman, Sandokhan's brush with the police emboldened him, and he and several associates mounted what the local press called a "guerrilla-type assault" on the Olympic Gardens police station that very night. Three policemen inside the station were killed, and Sandokhan and his associates fled with several weapons including an M16 machine gun.

Less than a week later, this stunning display of power was followed by a bold attempt to leave the island. On 26 November, Sandokhan passed through the customs checkpoint, and was already aboard a departing flight when the police at the Sangster International Airport seized him. Yet even this arrest failed to deter the gunman and he engineered several other escapes, both before and after he was sentenced to hang for the murders of the policemen.

Sandokhan's latest escape on 15 June 1988 from the St Catherine District Prison showed how thoroughly criminalized the security and judicial apparatus had become and how immune to restraint a powerful gangster such as

Sandokhan was. Repeated escapes by the "most wanted" man in the country exposed continuing official corruption in the prisons, despite the incredulity of press reports of an escape that allegedly "baffled laymen and criminologists alike".[44] But more than the prison staffers were compromised. The gunman evidently recruited members of the security force. As the minister of national security and justice discovered during the manhunt, several policemen who had volunteered for that duty were actually seeking to be informants for the gunman.[45]

Notwithstanding this penetration of the security forces, Sandokhan's enmity for the police expressed more than the defensive response of a wanted man and revealed something far more troubling in the law enforcement ranks. According to informants, the gunman's fury and hostility for the police was partly explained by the seizure and operation of his drug trade by policemen who had moved into the shadow economy. Their intervention, according to one press report, "was not part of a moral crusade to rid the community of drug pushers. They concurred with Sandokhan's enterprise."[46] The import of this development was not lost on a resident who remarked during the manhunt that the police "dem change him life the very day dem mash up him business and teck it over fe demself".[47] That policemen also beat Sandokhan's wife while she was in detention only encouraged the gunman's unforgiving attitude toward the law.

As the clash between the avenging gunman and the state unfolded, terror backed by law was matched by criminal terror in the West Central St Andrew communities. In the hunt for Sandokhan, lawmen persisted in reckless assaults on residents, arresting and beating citizens who committed no crime. Grandmothers, children and women were hauled into the dragnet and threatened. Women and youths who refused to cooperate became, according to the *Sunday Gleaner*, "prime targets" of the police and were roughed up by lawmen.[48] The hunt for Sandokhan spared no one as marauding soldiers and police squeezed the community to deliver the gunman. As one frightened woman confided to a reporter, "Them say them na stop terrorise we unless we turn over Sandokhan."[49]

For his part, Sandokhan was even more violent in dealing with perceived enemies. He not only targeted policemen for murder but was equally vicious with those in the community who threatened his enterprise. He summarily executed a likely witness to his deeds; he brutally murdered a youth he merely suspected of being an informer; he expelled rival gunmen by means of superior arms; and he and his small gang terrorized all who might have stood up to him. According to the police's count, Sandokhan, by the first week of August 1988, had killed nine people.[50]

This predation together with state terror and Sandokhan's expulsion of other criminals gave the gunman the community protection he needed. Indeed, residents expressed relief at the gunman's return after his latest prison break. According to one, "Since him come back me sleep wid me windows opened very night without fear because him always fight against the robberies and the rapes and me know say that the thief them nu like that."[51] Those who knew him best, his mother and wife, spoke only of a gentle, kind and friendly person who bore no resemblance to the savage "Public Enemy No. 1" villain depicted in police notices and lurid newspaper accounts.[52] At the height of the punishing manhunt even old women that crossed paths with Sandokhan thought him kind. One recommended the gunman to the neighbourhood priest who later recalled her telling him, "Father, help him, he is a good boy for when he is here the police and bad men can't trouble us."[53]

Father Richard Albert, neighbourhood priest and American-born rector of St Patrick's and St Jude's Roman Catholic churches, joined in the community's paeans to Sandokhan. In a speech to the Kiwanis Club, Father Albert spoke as priest and sociologist to the elite gathering, observing that Sandokhan was akin to a Robin Hood who

> watched politicians use young boys for violent, political reasons and he knows the daily struggles of old people who look for food and shelter. I make no excuses for Sandokhan or for the crimes he might have committed: I in no way want to say to you that poverty gives any man the excuse to commit crimes. . . . But, I do beg of you to try to understand that when the social conditions around you are so bad, when the health services do not come anywhere near fulfilling even the basis [sic] needs of the community, and unemployment, [and] political rivalries cause young men to search for other alternatives to support themselves, I want you to understand how a man like Sandokhan could emerge.[54]

This challenge to the society, and the priest's disclosure that he had met several times in public with the gunman to persuade him to surrender, produced a political firestorm. The security minister denounced the speech and expressed amazement that "a man in Fr. Albert's position could meet with and know of the whereabouts of Sandokhan and not pass on this information to the Police".[55]

The press, with rare exception, concurred in this opinion. One prominent columnist averred that the priest "ought to be given a taste of the
lockup". Another opined that the clergyman's real crime was glorifying
Sandokhan and concluded that Father Albert was "too busy playing politics,
advancing worldly causes and striking poses for the gallery to have retained
a sense of moral direction".[56]

As the debate raged, Sandokhan penned a letter to the clergyman the day
after his speech. In the two-page letter written on the leaves of a school-
book, the gangster acknowledged the priest's effort to arrange his surrender:

> The last time I speak with you it was great. Father you're influencing me to give
> in myself, but father you're a great friend of mine, and I've heard your speech
> on the radio yesterday and it was good. I know you don't want to see me die
> on the dungle, I know you care about me and my family.

The letter then turned to a complaint and issued a threat:

> Father Tuesday the Police curfew water house and held my wife and that same
> Police D.C Colt boxed up my wife and beat her up, and I want some action
> to take against the Policeman soon. If no action don't take against that police-
> man he's going to go on doing the same. And father I promise you I will never
> molest the Police, but if the Police continue doing things to my wife they will
> get me doing things to them. Father I want this cassette to play over the air. I
> know the police are not going to stop looking for me.... action must be taken
> now on that policeman. If no action is taken against that Policeman, he's going
> to make things worse on other Policeman.[57]

A Fateful Collision: Crime, Politics and the Law

The letter leaves no doubt about Sandokhan's hostility to the police.
However, this missive to the clergyman is equally revealing of the gunman's
other values and moral orientation. First, the outlaw revealed the importance
of his family and particularly of his wife, Jenice Smith, whom he married in
1985 when she was fifteen years old.[58] He took the hardships she endured
at the hands of policemen personally. However, the rough justice she
received in detention backfired on the lawmen. Rather than cause his capitulation, the abuse intensified his contempt for the law.

Second, Sandokhan may have been semi-literate, but like many from his social class who depended on face-to-face communication, the radio was almost certainly his primary access to news and public affairs. All the achievement of global society and its horrors were transmitted to ordinary Jamaicans through this medium, thereby informing and socially mobilizing men like Sandokhan. Television news broadcasts from home and abroad, and, more recently, the hugely popular local call-in radio programmes, alerted the rebelling poor to both public sympathy and ridicule of their actions. Hence, local media exposed the poor and working people not just to the "news ideology" reinforcing the status quo but also to the counter-ideologies such as those expressed by Father Albert in the speech that Sandokhan heard on the radio. Precisely because he knew that listeners and callers from his social class dominated the call-in programmes it is little wonder that Sandokhan urged the clergyman to get the gunman's audio-cassette tape aired on the radio.

Finally, though Sandokhan's case became a *cause célèbre* that riveted the nation and depicted a struggle between good and evil, the gunman's letter revealed a far different narrative. It expressed that distinct and recurrent feature of social conflict and power in Jamaica: its intimate and highly person-alized character. Sandokhan, the letter shows, sought redress for his impugned honour. He wanted to settle scores with a particular policeman for showing disrespect to the gunman's family. In his fury at being disre-spected, Sandokhan took note of the offending policeman by name and rank. It was not lawmen at this or that police station that angered him, but "D[etective] C[orporal] Colt" who earned his enmity. Because of this policeman's personal slight, Sandokhan sought to settle scores with him.

In the morality of the ghetto, hunting for a gunman and trying to kill him was one thing; those were the terms of the war in Kingston's badlands. But impugning Sandokhan's family honour was another. It had to be corrected by means of a personal vendetta against a single policeman and, by implica-tion, the entire police force. For Sandokhan, the Jamaican state was a distant entity; he knew it not as the "committee of the bourgeoisie" but only in the person of an arrogant lawman who had cut to the quick of Sandokhan's honour by slapping his wife. Fighting the state meant a vendetta against one policeman.

A reciprocal relationship of personal hostility held for the security forces. In this dramaturgy of mutual personal revenge, securing honour and repu-tation seemed more important than upholding the law. Policemen sought out Sandokhan not merely as a lawbreaker, but as a rude, facetious "bwoy" who challenged their swaggering power. He had fired on them with impunity, killed three from their ranks, kept them at bay for months and embarrassed them in the public's eye. This was not only criminality, but also an offence that mocked their competence as armed men. Sandokhan had to be taught a lesson, not just to pay for his crime against society, but also to recover the integrity and manhood of other powerful men whom he had violated by his defiance and prolonged escape. The manhunt for Sandokhan therefore became highly personal as state agents in their role as dishonoured men sought their elusive quarry.

These cultural preoccupations informed the motivations of Jamaica's vigilante policemen and reduced gunfights to duels of offended honour between armed men. In these kinds of conflicts, it is arguable that law enforcement on the streets in urban Jamaica was less a matter of uphold-ing public law than of defending the manhood of armed men whose integrity and respect had been tested and violated by armed and impudent criminals.

It is little wonder, then, that policemen in West Central St Andrew dealt harshly with communities that threw up a wall of silence against them. In this battle for honour and struggle of personal wills, the Riverton City and Waterhouse communities stubbornly held out against the security forces. They did so not because they were irredeemably lawless, but because the state's power radiated to them in the form of known-by-name corrupted policemen who exacted punishments as if settling personal scores with each victim. Indeed, one policeman alerted Sandokhan's wife to the personal vengeance he would take when her twenty-two-month-old son became a man. She reported him as saying, "When the boy grow up, me goin' shoot him. Me goin' waste him and drop him off the causeway."[59]

In this zone where crime, law and politics collided, traditional notions of community, justice and propriety collapsed. At the ground zero of mutual terror, ghetto moral culture and law enforcement culture became flexible and expedient as both lawmen and rebels jettisoned proprieties. Lawmen killed with impunity and victimized residents had no compunction in defi-antly embracing the criminal who protected them from predators. Men like Sandokhan became one of "us" against "them", the predatory outsiders, rep-resented by policemen who were known by name.

For many in South Central St Andrew, the Waterhouse retort to law-givers in the society could be interpreted as follows:

Sandokhan is our protector; he is a loving son, and a devoted father. Compared to the terrorism of the security forces and the criminality of policemen, Sandokhan's crimes do not detain us. We are socially dead, and Sandokhan is our Robin Hood. In a debased society with its savagery against the poor, we, the black poor of Waterhouse, are "done dead a'ready". We therefore feel no remorse in embracing and hiding our kin, Sandokhan.[60]

This "done dead a'ready" moral culture and the exilic community it spawned in Waterhouse and Riverton City protected Sandokhan for an astonishing eighty-six days.

But even as he sheltered under its protective cover, the breakdown of the judicial and law enforcement apparatus threatened Sandokhan's enterprise and endangered his life. Where law and justice are lacking, or where their functions are seriously eroded, "self-help justice" tends to prevail. On the one side, the turn to rough justice benefited outlaws such as Sandokhan, who exploited the fear of crime to become a community protector. On the other, the breakdown of law threatened such outlaws as fear of increased violence from within and without made rough justice commonplace.

As a result, the security force's determination to root out Sandokhan at any cost, the hiking of the reward money to J$50,000 and the enabling state discourse depicting him as a quarry to be destroyed on sight encouraged vigilantism. Already mob killings had increased in the late 1980s as citizens threatened by crime took the law into their own hands. Vigilantes killed some seventeen persons in 1987, up from five in the previous year. In this context where the black poor were being violently squeezed to deliver the gunman, and collective punishment was being meted out to the whole community, vigilantism became attractive. This was true despite "the police's own violent violation of the poor as a social class in the country".[61]

In the end, vigilante gunmen, not the police, felled Sandokhan on 8 September 1988. As a result, yet another outlaw and self-appointed champion of the downtrodden was brought to heel in Kingston. With this success, police pressure on West Central St Andrew lifted and the state conducted its gory ritual of displaying the gunman's body as object lesson for the unruly poor. Yet even in death Sandokhan remained an avatar of a deep social crisis. The combustible forces in state and society that had produced him only persisted, and they exploded with stunning force around issues of popular culture and morality.

Morals, Manners and Social Power: Slackness versus Civility

If lawgivers and politicians had hoped to regain their authority by killing the Jim Browns, Starkeys and Sandokhans of the ghetto, overlapping and disruptive processes in the society thoroughly undermined that hope. Raging political violence which had diminished since 1980 continued in episodic but muted forms. In fact, the disillusionment with party politics that alienated many in the ghetto hardly affected that 10 per cent minority of voters who made up the hard-core activists. They remained tied to the structure of communal violence and their factional violence persisted.

Thus, after a period of relative quiet, violence erupted in the balloting for the July 1986 local government elections. Reporting on the incendiary nature of political loyalties during the balloting, a commission of inquiry reported that "roving bands of hooligans purporting to be supporters or activists of the two major political parties and armed with guns, knives, sticks and other weapons, moved freely about in parts of Kingston and St Andrew, and parts of St Catherine".[62] In this resurfacing of Jamaican-style balloting in violently contested communities, political gangs entered polling stations "where they terrified the election officers and in some case assaulted them and inflicted injuries".[63] These partisans, the commission reported, "forcibly seized ballots and marked them for their chosen candidates, forcing the presiding officer to sign the counterfoils when their names did not appear on the official list of electors".[64] As this episode shows, though the intensity and frequency of violent political incidents had diminished, the fanaticism and violence of the previous decade were alive and well in 1986.

Just the same, no matter how serious political violence remained, criminal violence was far worse. Indeed, the marked increase in criminal, as opposed to political, violence barred any search for a quick end to social disorder and to the pre-eminence of the new dons. As the drug trade spread, violence linked to crime outstripped violence linked to politics. This remained true even as "actual crime *rates* for all major or serious non-drug-related crimes declined in the period 1980–1989".[65] Criminologist Bernard Headley identified this irony of rising criminal violence and falling crime rates for non-drug related crimes, and attributed it to a statistical artefact: Jamaican crime statistics do not list drug-related crimes under "serious" crimes. This procedure obscured another reason for the undocumented increase in criminal violence: street criminals' transition from petty crimes to the more lucrative drug trade. "The consequence", as Headley points out, "was one less reported housebreaking and one less burglar, but one more pusher or drug 'Don' ."[66]

Their acquisition of weapons and formation of gangs ensured the eclipse of politically inspired violence by criminal mayhem. A minority of outlaws who were becoming more sophisticated drove this gang-led violence. According to one estimate, by the close of 1987 there were "over 30 highly mobile and well-armed gangs" operating across the country.[67] Their feuds and skirmishes over the drug and contraband trade contributed massively to the growth in criminal violence and murder in the 1980s and after.[68] As one commentator noted of these independent gangs, they are a

> highly organized and motivated minority armed with superior firepower . . . those who reach the top, are professionals who approach their chosen vocation in much the same way as the successful doctor, engineer or architect. They enjoy recognition and seniority within their fraternity for constantly demonstrating high standards of excellence as they execute murder, mayhem, robbery and rape.[69]

The power of these gangs was such that their illicit activities jeopardized the country's flagship airline and threatened its access to US ports. The gangs' bid to smuggle large quantities of drugs into the United States aboard Air Jamaica resulted in the repeated impounding of its planes. These incidents and the huge fines required to release the carrier delivered a blow to the country's pride, even as the smuggling revealed the growing criminalization of public and private institutions. In sum, killing individual gangsters was having hardly any effect either on reducing crime or in halting the formation of criminal gangs. Moreover, summary executions proved useless in deterring the black lower class from the norms and values politicians and the dominant classes increasingly blamed for the country's woes.

The true fear of the social power of the urban poor, therefore, came not from the damage criminal gangs caused the island's reputation and the tourist trade. Rather, the stubborn expansion of the new dons, a relatively autonomous group of ghetto influentials who had harnessed guns, drugs, dollars and ghetto moral culture into new forms of social power, was the real threat to the status quo and to power holders.[70] In the late 1980s, this threat united a diverse coalition. Politicians, the middle and upper classes, entrepreneurs, and wide swaths of the peasantry, workers and the urban poor bemoaned this development.

Of all these, the consternation of complicit politicians was noteworthy. By 1988 politicians from both parties that previously had thrown in their lot with rebels from the black lower class moved to break ties with them. Politicians, who had harnessed badness-honour to political power, lashed out at armed gangs from the criminal underworld. It was equally significant that they now decried the influence of the black lumpenproletariat that flaunted the new moral culture in the ghetto. Former prime minister Michael Manley took pains in a 1987 interview to make a distinction between "political crime" and "drug crime" and to dissociate himself from both.[71] A year later, Manley continued this defection by calling for a return to earlier ideals of tolerance and persuasion as a path to national development.

But where Manley dithered in confronting the issue on everyone's mind, one of the strongest statements marking the political retreat from all gunmen came in mid-1988. Pearnel Charles, then minister of public utilities and transportation in the JLP's administration, and defeated candidate for the murderously contested South West St Andrew seat in the 1970s, left no doubt about where he stood. Gripped by the force of the predicament and evidently fearing the eclipse of politicians by the two armed branches of the black lumpenproletariat – the criminal and political gunmen – Charles publicly broke with them with the following statement:

> I wish to declare that in the upcoming general elections and any subsequent election that I may participate in, I do not want the backing, nor support of any drug man or gunman. I do not need their political support or their financial support, or their backing. I do not wish to represent them at all.[72]

The capstone for this hasty retreat from "gun politics" came in the form of yet another peace truce, this time brokered not by the black poor, but by frightened politicians of both parties.[73] Organized gun violence, linked to drug trafficking, whose profits formed a new source of ghetto community patronage and drug don social power, was the main impetus for this agreement.[74] In another instance in Jamaica's postcolonial political history, the inexorable claims of political self-preservation – not the primacy of law, democracy or probity – governed these leaders' reaction to rising crime.

Recognizing the inadequacy of the politicians' pact on crime, the left-wing PNP politician Arnold Bertram aptly noted that "any agreement to isolate criminals from the political parties does not necessarily diminish crime, it only redirects it".[75] This assessment was confirmed as criminal and political violence returned with a vengeance in subsequent years.[76] In the long run, the truce was therefore a flawed achievement enabling the parties to enjoy only a pyrrhic victory.

The hiatus in political violence was interrupted on 12 September 1988 by a massive hurricane that hit the island with destructive force. But rather than inspiring comity and a joining of hands, the hurricane disaster was greeted by political opportunism, corrupt practices by commercial importers, and wanton looting and theft of emergency supplies by the urban poor and others. Bertram took the occasion to excoriate commercial entrepreneurs for their greed and plunder in a time of crisis. "This group", he lamented, "has with singleness of purpose callously exploited the misery of the destitute by over-charging not only for food, but for every item crucial to the recovery of shelter."[77] *Jamaica Record* editorialists joined him in decrying not just the looting and theft of relief supplies, but also the profiteering of merchants who sold zinc, nails and other supplies at exorbitant prices.[78]

Criticism of profiteers was joined by rebuke of the lumpenproletariat. Here the Left and the Right were unanimous in their censure. Bertram, like Michael Manley and Pearnel Charles, broke morally and politically with the unruly lumpenproletariat. He indicted the group for "engaging in every form of anti-social behaviour known to man".[79] In perhaps the strongest language yet coming from the Left, Bertram also denounced the group for a social dominance that not only threatened the national community, but also barred the way to national reconstruction.

In a remarkable convergence, intellectual gadfly Wilmot Perkins matched Bertram's critique with a raking assessment:

> Their concern is only with their urges and appetites. When they are hungry they must eat. When they are angry they must destroy. When their bowels move they defecate [in public places], and when opportunity offers they loot. And politics by giving them the vote, has given them the best of all opportunities. Economic recovery or reconstruction is of no concern to them; for that is work; and what they want is freeness. It is they who provide the driving force for entropy.[80]

Where Bertram was even-handed in his reproof of a "lumpen bourgeoisie with their 'fistful of dollars' and a lumpenproletariat whose 'guns don't argue' ",[81] Perkins, not unlike most Jamaicans, blamed only the unruly poor.

Regardless of Perkins's one-sidedness, a broad consensus had emerged against the defiant poor. It seemed to be saying that poverty was no excuse for depravity.

As the battle against guns and gunmen stalled, this moral outcry intensified. Most groups outside the ranks of the rebellious poor spoke out against what they perceived as a fundamental challenge to the national identity and the society's basic values. The latest moral danger was identified as the black lumpenproletariat's descent into "slackness" – a condition narrowly associated with uninhibited sexuality and moral depravity, but more broadly identified with the norms and behaviours of the black urban poor.[82]

For Jamaicans of all classes who embraced traditional religious values and norms of moral propriety, "slackness" was any breach of moral conservatism by the black lumpenproletariat. For dominant groups and subordinate strata that shared their perspective, "slackness" was the transgression of Jamaica's traditional norm-identity. Jamaicanness was premised on traditions rooted in the island's protean cultural inheritances. In the late twentieth century, these were a Christianizing European colonialism, Afrocentric Ethiopianism and a secular, North American materialism. The intersection of all three had produced a norm-identity of Jamaicanness that privileged the dominance of white over black, "haves over have-nots" and the scribal classes over the orally and kinetically profuse masses. These markers complemented obeisance to status consciousness and possessions over merit and achievement. Fealty to notions of the Christian-modern, over fears of the profane and the savage-primordial, completed these polarizing beliefs.

Although all Jamaicans breached these binary opposites and lived their everyday lives according to a jamboree of values, these binary linkages formed part of the normative chain-link fence that barred the black urban poor from full moral membership in Jamaican society. For dominant groups, "slackness" was the distillate of all the cultural deficits preventing the black poor from being accepted fully into the Jamaican community.

Slackness as moral indictment regarded the "careless sexuality" of the black poor as a moral crime. Slackness meant indecency, public sexual licence, moral degeneracy and erotic lawlessness among the rebellious black poor. In the realm of popular culture, "dancehall culture" with its sexually explicit lyrics, revealing costumes worn by women, and frenzy of its music and erotic dancers confirmed this degradation arising from ghetto culture.[83] Hence, slackness, and the moral weaknesses associated with it, were not conditions that afflicted the guardians of moral propriety. Slackness was not associated with theft from the public purse. Nor was it related to rampant private greed and the widening graft of merchants, entrepreneurs and state bureaucrats. On the contrary, slackness was a debased moral status from which the ghetto poor had to be rescued.

For the "uptown" and privileged classes, the slackness of the "downtown" lumpenproletariat was more than a menace; it was a civilization threat. For the uptown elite, the black rabble and "dutty criminals" from the slums, with whom the term "culture" could not be associated, were threatening to substitute their debased norms for the civil "values and attitudes" of their social betters. The values evident in popular music, ghetto lifestyles, dance forms and "roots plays" were regarded as a cultural blight, appealing only to the lowest common denominator and to the basest of instincts.

To the better-off classes, to the moral purists among workers, peasants and the urban poor, slackness was to moral culture what street violence was to politics. In this view, the violence of the black poor had invaded and corrupted national politics causing the better-off classes to flee from it. Now, the critics argued, slackness endangered the national culture in the same manner. For the defenders of moral orthodoxy, slackness threatened to replace social etiquette, civility and moral propriety with debauchery.

The intensity of the outcry that greeted the turn to sexually explicit lyrics in reggae music and the denunciations of the morality of the related dancehall phenomenon highlighted, as perhaps no other issue, fundamental social divisions in Jamaican society. These polarizations threw into sharp relief conflicts between power holders and the black lumpenproletariat. They also provoked clashes between black lower-class champions of the new, radical otherness and their more respectable working-class and urban poor kin. This intra-class conflict arrayed defenders of earlier, anti-systemic cultural and political orthodoxies against exponents of the turn to sexual extremism.[84]

The intensity of these differences over "slackness" was so acute that it rent the society, tearing apart traditional alliances, exposing sharp class divisions and triggering moral panics. Most interesting of all, "slackness" unleashed an inchoate mix of discourses. On one side, it valorized cultural exterminism directed at expunging the black lower-class moral influence on the society. On the other, it offered prospects of democratization, acceptance of cultural difference and even the recession of social oppression.

Why rival claims to sexual propriety in the form of an outrage against "slackness" should simultaneously have destructive and recuperative potentials, requires closer examination. My own view is that "slackness" is a form of sexual transgression and as such was merely another repertoire employed by the black lumpenproletariat in its ongoing clash with dominant groups. Just as racial identity and class allegiance disrupted social relations in earlier periods, slackness now provoked huge social divisions. Slackness had this effect in the 1980s because the social crisis had ignited a stubborn issue underlying historic conflicts among the Jamaican people-nation: the moral status of disadvantaged, but combative blacks. Dominant groups in the late twentieth century echoed the fears and concerns of powerful groups a century earlier. In the 1980s, they affirmed the "savage" identity of rebelling blacks and wondered whether they could be rescued for civilization.

What made slackness so incendiary in the 1980s was partly the conflictual social relations that gave moral culture predominance as symbol and crystallization of the social crisis. Criminalization of the state, breakdown of law and order, and predation within and beyond the slums all provoked debates over moral and political culture. That moral injunctions were being handed down by political and economic elites who were weakened politically and who were seen as morally compromised only worsened matters. Yet this double handicap did not deter powerful elites in their claim to moral relevance and propriety. Political debility and perceptions of elite moral weakness therefore led to clashes between these elites and an uncaptured lumpenproletariat equally determined to assert its own moral claims. That many of these claims revolved around disputed sexual norms only sharpened the conflicts.

Racially embedded sexuality had, in effect, converged with disputes over unequal social relations. This wedding set off major social tremors. This was the case because many Jamaicans agreed that together with crime, undisciplined black sexuality in the ghetto was the final rupture of the civilization-identity of the people-nation. Raw sexuality in the ghetto further strained ideas of a "common culture" that some sections of the dominant classes had invoked to hail the ghetto poor in the postcolonial period. Contested notions of "race" in the 1960s and after had already undercut dominant notions of a common culture. Now a disputed black sexuality posed new challenges to dominant notions.

But while "race" remained a potent cultural marker and incendiary cultural force in Jamaica, sexuality and gender identities also generated conflict and change. Sexuality and gender, like race and class in this postcolonial society, were bases of social stratification and determinants of social inclusion and exclusion. Sexual identity and the uses of the erotic helped determine cultural membership in Jamaica's postcolonial society. In this racially divided and class-stratified society, the more the black poor policed their sexuality and kept their erotic displays out of public view, the better were their chances of social approval and the more likely their inclusion in the community of the respectable people-nation.

However, the dominant society's emphasis on disciplining a fugitive sexuality among the rebellious black poor made that membership increasingly unlikely in the postcolonial period. Errant sexuality in the ghetto in the late 1980s came to be regarded as much a threat to stable cultural relations as riotous acts of defiance were to peaceful political relations. Full cultural membership for the black poor in Jamaica was therefore premised, in part, on acceptance of a dominant class, norm-identity that privileged black submissiveness and black docility. Uncritical deference to power, not the norm of moral infrangibility, became the measure of black lower-class civility and criterion for moral inclusion. Sexual docility in the slums was therefore as important to dominant class power as political submissiveness there.

The black poor undoubtedly recognized these compulsions and challenged them. "Slackness" and the celebration of it by ghetto youth and popular performers in the 1980s seemed to announce to the society the end of its moral sway over the black lower class. In song, dance and theatre, orthodox sexual morality gave way to uninhibited celebration of all things libidinal. Sexual extremism for its own sake and as a repertoire for challenging social conventions now became the dominant form of expression within an otherwise variegated ghetto culture.

The erotics of power were therefore wrested from moral guardians in a manner not too dissimilar from the violence seized from the control of politicians. By their sexual extremism, the black lumpenproletariat appropriated, stylized and inverted a form of power that defined the boundaries between the morally legitimate and the morally depraved. Undisciplined black sexuality on public display was now used not merely for libidinal release, but also to intimidate and to threaten. Flaunting sexuality was now a means of social struggle, and an expression of badness-honour. The racial, sexual and social class tensions that were latent in the postcolonial period were now awakened by the "slackness-civility" conflict.

In Jamaica's tormented history as a former slave society and colonial territory, sex and power were inextricably linked, and race and class relations suffused both sex and power. Dominant classes that were white or brown feared black lower-class sexuality, deeming it a source of anarchy and agent of cultural disruption. It is arguable that throughout Jamaica's modern history middle- and upper-class fear of unbridled lower-class sexuality was as intense as fear of unchecked, lower-class political violence. Both imperilled the public weal if not the identity of the people-nation. The policing of black lower-class sexuality was thus as central to the management of social and political power as the policing of black lower-class violence.

Sexual extremism in the ghetto was therefore not an accident. It was instead a conscious, wilful political choice in reaction to dominant class power. Inversion of the dominant sexual norms in the 1980s was merely the latest tactic of a black lumpenproletariat engaged in a protracted class war. In the 1980s, this war was fought on the terrain of moral culture and the ideological lines were sharply drawn between the depraved and the civilized.

Unflattering as it might appear, sexual extremism in the slums did not occur because the ghetto poor did not know better. Even the most alienated of them knew right from wrong. Many gangsters deferred to Christian values and a few even read their Bibles. More than that, the rebelling poor strove constantly to juggle dominant norms of propriety with contingent resort to moral licence. Furthermore, the same criminal that a poor mother in the Waterhouse area could refer to as a "good boy" and the same bandit that could seek out and share repeated confidences with a Roman Catholic priest belonged to the same moral universe as the rest of the society. Hence, the eroticism of dancehall queens and the licence of gun-praising DJs were unvarnished expressions of shared cultural practices.

This did not make extremist behaviours morally right. Black sexual extremism in the ghetto primarily offered the negative emancipation of instincts and not the solutions to the poor's most urgent needs. Moral depravity was as disabling for the ghetto poor as it was for better-off groups, even if the latter were spared withering public criticism. Contrary to apologists for the self-satisfied, "uptown" classes and defenders of the rebelling "downtown" poor, there were not two cultures on the island: one depraved and the other civilized. Rather, there was only a single culture in which excess and licence, and their condemnation, were widely shared.

Having said that, it is worth noting that black nationality and its nexus with class inequality had trumped sexuality as source of conflict and fulcrum of change in the early postcolonial period. Black nationalism and lower-class insurgencies based on it forged new identities and secured significant social change in the period from 1962 to 1972. By the late 1980s, however, sexuality and its nexus with race, class and power had redefined social conflicts, complementing already incendiary markers.

In the 1980s, expressions of black sexuality in the ghetto were akin to the celebration of black nationality in the 1960s. Exhibitionist erotic displays in the dancehall and explicit sexual lyrics in song and in the theatre mocked the sexual etiquette of the middle and upper classes. Dancehall culture, with its celebration of the erotic, the sexually vulgar and the gangster lifestyle, had therefore opened another front in the war on a tottering and defensive society. Sexual indiscipline by ghetto youth, by male and female dancehall DJs, and by middle-class defenders of the dancehall, was another and later means by which the black lumpenproletariat raised the ante in an ongoing social struggle. "Slackness" had become the terrain of conflict and a highly charged cultural force in the 1980s.

In this respect, the sexual extremism of slackness made it a potent "weapon of the weak". Much like terrorism in politics, the hurling of "slackness" into an inflamed society was a disruptive, even seditious act. The inversion of the core value of civility endangered the whole society and imperilled its norms. Slackness compelled social actors to choose sides. And that often produced unorthodox alliances and contorted ideological positions.

In doing all this, "slackness" as the sexual extremism of the black poor called attention to historic grievances, highlighted the hypocrisy of dominant groups and rallied respectable defenders to its cause. By provoking acute social divisions over the uses of sexuality, the transgressive slackness of the lumpenproletariat raised anew old and delicate civilization issues. It opened up questions of racial domination, gender inequalities and human rights in Jamaica.

Social conflict over sexuality therefore resonated with issues of economic justice, the need for democratization and the prospects for social reform. But it also raised troubling issues of governance and its relationship to moral culture. One nagging problem was whether the cultural orientations expressed in ghetto extremism contained an alternative, emancipatory culture for a new society. If bourgeois middle-class civic morality and its defence of a cultural standard were repressive and class-ridden, as some critics maintained, what were the criteria for determining a new cultural standard? Should civic values be jettisoned because strategic elites violated them? Is an anomic and dissident sensibility sufficient to set an alternative standard?

The dispute over slackness also raised the vital issue of the relationship between "culture" – the beliefs, values and underlying assumptions of a society – and the quality of governance and the prospects for economic development in Jamaica. Was there a relationship between political culture in Jamaica and the form of its government? Clashes over slackness raised concern about the relationship between the culture of the society and the quality of its government. In sum, conflict over slackness disclosed the nexus between culture and power. It also raised questions about the fit between norms in Jamaica's shared and dissident culture and the civic norms required for a democratic order. In a surprising turn of events in the 1980s, clashes over sexuality starkly posed the issue of whether moral culture as an independent force was having negative consequences for Jamaican governance and economic development.

Sexual extremism did not liberate the ghetto exponent, but it did create ruptures that freed the society to address fundamental issues. This opening, not the freeing of black libidinal energy, was the real transforming effect of lower-class sexual extremism and responses to it. Of course, for the defenders of the status quo, fear of slackness and its resonance with fear of the black poor limited opportunities for change. The effect of that reluctance was panic and fear of an entire group of Jamaicans.

As the 1990s dawned, Jamaicans faced a stark reality. On the one hand, naked use of state power and rampant criminalization of state and society complemented dominant class moral panic. On the other, spiralling crime, social indiscipline among the rebellious poor and widespread acceptance of vigilantism revealed acute lower-class discontent. These reciprocal processes yielded forms of social cannibalism in what was now a brutish, Gorgonian society.

But these epic developments did more than snare an agonized society in the web of its own doing. The twin processes powerfully beckoned social actors to a fateful choice – whether to persist in making the rebellious black poor the moral pawns of a profound social crisis, or to engage the crisis in ways that would make the alienated poor beneficiaries of a recuperated and reformed democratic society.

11

The Cultural Contradictions of Power

Badness-Honour and Liberal Democracy

IN CONTRAST WITH PERIPHERAL SOCIETIES ELSEWHERE, the form of power in Jamaica reflects a special type of rule. I have referred to it as predatory not so much because of theft and pillage of public funds, but because of a parasitic impulse that draws willy-nilly on antagonistic socio-political tendencies to maintain dominance. The Jamaican state has pursued a variety of engagements marked by dissonant political forms and contradictory repertoires. Surprisingly, integration of these clashing elements led not to political collapse but to viable political unities. State dilation across antinomies – political, economic and cultural – showed not just versatility but also a seemingly limitless capacity to use clashing political norms to reproduce political domination. This achievement shows the state's dynamic flexibility, dilating reach, and capacity for forging unities from incompatible political forms and social interests.

The harnessing of such sharply conflicting attributes produced unique alliances within the country's democratic political structure. Political leaders established enduring ties with the mobilized urban poor and reserved a progressively influential role for armed loyalists among them. Despite this corrupt association, both political parties maintained ties to labour, entrepreneurs and the middle class.

Moreover, cohabitation of political gangsters, party bosses and the main social classes did not lead to equilibrium of political influence. On the contrary, defenders of democratic values were marginalized and even routed as champions of street-based norms became ascendant. Political gangsters' communal loyalties, their savage violence and predatory instincts altered the country's moral and ideological direction. Middle-class party leaders and political activists matched this subversive incursion in the name of power and honour. Invariably, this savage power and honour-driven politics increasingly subverted democratic politics.

These developments transformed the character of the Jamaican state. On the one hand, it retained a political identity at odds with typical forms in the developing world. Where several states in Africa and the Middle East remained wholly anti-democratic, politicians in Jamaica deferred to democratic norms and practices. Where regimes in poor countries collapsed under the weight of official corruption, succumbed to military rule or descended into violent anarchy, Jamaican governments that faced similar impulses avoided these pitfalls but did not totally escape their allure. In this regard, state politics and Jamaican politicians were not exemplars of a wholly corrupted order marked by tyrannical rule or state-destroying anarchic violence.

But neither have they been champions of an invigorated democracy. Rather, Jamaican politicians have been bold interventionists who have harnessed incompatible socio-political tendencies and made them instruments of political domination. These politicians moved confidently into normatively hostile social spaces not to destroy them but to use them as political resources. This predation on anti-systemic social spaces, mostly occupied by alienated groups, as well as the harnessing of their disruptive political norms and activities is revealing. It shows that Jamaican politicians are not so much political tyrants or exemplary democrats as they are creative agents of a parasitic apparatus whose power they determinedly reproduced.

Neither model democrats nor tyrants, these politicians are like moral and political ridge-riders drawing on contrary norms and repertoires to sow social divisions and forge complex political unities. The result is a dominating structure of shaky coherence whose incompatible social interests produced not political collapse, but a race for survival among competing interests. Political domination in democratic form persists in Jamaica as social groups alternate between battles for ascendancy on the one hand and grudging accommodation of each other's disputed access to power and resources on the other.

Befitting their role as arbiters of these clashing interests, state agents quelled lower-class insurgencies with patronage and solicitousness and repelled others with terror and brutality. State politics deployed shifting repertoires simultaneously embracing democratic practice, warlord tactics, as well as criminality and terror. This form of state exhibited novel combinations of power and employed a variety of structures. In them, a traditional democratic apparatus gave power to a criminal underground, to "big men", political militias and emboldened partisans who violently enforced group patronage rights.

In its turn, a multi-vocal state ideology unified and invigorated these contradictory obligations using elliptical but culturally appealing idioms. This multi-vocality and dilation across incompatible political forms evidence of political novelty and protean power in the Caribbean. Such patterns also dramatically illustrate state parasitic tendencies that draw on seemingly incompatible and nominally antagonistic interests to wield a durable power. Both democratic practice and illiberal, even lawless, measures helped renew this predatory power.

State power increasingly used crime and nimble resort to informality in bold displays of ubiquity. Amid enormous challenges political actors ineluctably moved the state into illegal practices and toward a variety of informal spaces. Processes and norms in all of such spaces – the informal economy, the urban ghetto, the criminal and political underworlds – were at odds with the tenets of democratic rule. Despite this incompatibility, politicians saw opportunities for political leverage in these spaces.

In moving into them, hardy politicians boldly relocated power, sharing it with others there, but without surrendering their authority or wholly subverting the state's democratic identity. Indeed, the novel uses of power led to a change in the political order whose identity was not reducible to known and familiar forms in most developing countries. Social conflict in Jamaica and the state's responses to it led neither to a vigorous democracy nor to a brutal oligarchy. Rather, a parasitic power avoided them both, preferring instead to execute brilliant, inventive options that contained traces of these political forms without embracing their fullness.

In daring moves marked by resourceful permutations, politicians across the decades straddled the chasm between dictatorship and democracy. Rather than moving the state toward one or other of these exclusive forms, state agents in Jamaica instead forged a new type of power. Its identity shows a capacity to mold contradictory political and ideological tendencies in ways that had powerful appeal for constituencies whose interests were often at odds. These contrary state tendencies included badness-honour and the violence of political militias. Conversely other tendencies exhibited the etiquette and substance of democratic rule, solicitousness for disadvantaged groups, attention to the needs of "big men", as well as exterminist terror against armed "badmen".

Creative permutation of these tendencies solidified the power of politicians. However, lower-class gunmen helped consolidate this power as much as patronage-seeking big entrepreneurs. Both were joint, if uneasy, supplicants who were wedded to this power. This state power that neither strengthened democracy nor affirmed brazen autocracy retained marked cultural and political appeal and exercised compulsion over all social classes. Both morally and politically, this dilating power had a seductive attraction for alienated slum-dwellers inured to violence and patronage.

It had the same compulsion on entrepreneurs, the civic-minded but fearful middle class and most law-abiding citizens that saw themselves as beneficiaries and guardians of the island's democratic tradition. This consensus prevailed despite the state's incapacity in the face of increasing social disorder that provoked demands for a return to civil politics in which the rule of law applied to all.

Power in Jamaica was therefore distinctive in the following sense: its authority was based on summoning often-incompatible social interests to recognize their own legitimate claims in the fusion of warlordism, political gangsterism and democratic politics. The wedding of all three elements in Jamaican statecraft tapped powerful cultural sentiments in the society and the marriage had broad appeal for important sectional interests.

Each could find, in this ensemble, points of leverage and culturally familiar idioms. Thus rather than narrowing its political reach and muting its ideological appeal, Jamaican statecraft embraced repertoires that ensnared clashing groups. This straddling to achieve political preponderance and the broadest range of social support persisted in the face of harsh criticism, continuing group discontent, and dissatisfaction with what some saw as the state's moral and political indirection.

The state's retention of an inherited constitutional democratic order is one example of the continuing appeal of civic politics. This order prevailed despite the fact that politicians increasingly hived off important activities to parallel structures and gave informal actors from both the political and criminal underworlds significant power. Political rule in Jamaica was therefore remarkable for maintaining substantive democratic liberties amidst the informalization, creeping corruption and gangsterization of national politics.

A durable, centuries-long democratic culture had helped institutionalize fundamental rights of speech, association and voting, as well as the right to establish countervailing organizations independent of state control. Though this was first accomplished under a racially exclusivist democracy, that tradition was gradually reformed and progressively extended to incorporate native groups. The process culminated in the 1944 constitution that extended suffrage to the majority population.

During the passage of the post-war and postcolonial years, competing political parties and alternating native regimes acknowledged and appealed to these rights, employing them to establish their political identities and affirm their legitimacy. Except for massive violations in select urban and rural constituencies, ruling parties generally abided by democratic rules. The most important of these pertained to the free exercise of the franchise, deference to the constitutionally mandated rotation of political office-holders, and acceptance of bargaining and negotiation to resolve disputes. Despite serious erosion of this democratic culture and notwithstanding politicians' subversion of its tenets over the years, support for the democratic rules-of-the-game remained strong among the political class.

The mass public also endorsed the democratic order and vigorously insisted on its retention particularly in times of stress and instability. Even when state agents and a growing number of partisans massively violated democratic principles, the democratic order remained intact in large part because of substantial support for it among all classes. In sum, despite serious violations and marked abuse, democratic norms were widely endorsed and remain a defining feature of Jamaica's political culture. Jamaica's predatory state thus drew part of its strength and legitimacy from widespread obeisance to this powerful political tradition.

At the same time, however, politicians of both parties prevented the population in the poorer precincts of urban Jamaica from enjoying basic rights. In these communities, the parasitic state forged an unusual alliance with the rebellious urban poor. The state established parallel underground structures and devolved vital political functions to informal entities there.

Nonetheless, violence against the rebellious poor was typical of state intervention in the ghetto. Hence, even as the constitutional form of the state remained democratic, the "everyday" form of power was unabashedly repressive. For a minority of alienated citizens in the slums, democratic rights were brutally denied, highly circumscribed or hedged about with other impediments. In the most grievous cases, terror, forced relocations, violent cleansings of neighbourhoods and harsh brutality against rebellious sectors of the population characterized political rule in Jamaica. Yet unlike dictatorships and military rule in parts of Asia, Africa and Latin America, political power in Jamaica could not be classified, then or now, as either a dictatorship or as a form of oligarchic rule.

Political repression in Jamaica is real and often horrific. But it is not the kind of repression that was exclusively directed at expunging mainstream political movements and parties that were opposed to incumbents. Nor was violence directed primarily at populations whom the state arrested, jailed or even killed because of their ethnicity, religious beliefs or revolutionary commitments. Although they were often subject to political interference and hampered in their functions, dissenting political parties, elite activists and most protesters were not subject to arrests or "disappearances". In fact, political dissenters beyond the slums seem relatively immune from state violence as state security forces – the police and the army – did not routinely murder these citizens because of their political opinions.

The same agents acting on behalf of the parties did routinely commit political murder in the ghetto. Duelling party militias committed most of the political murders across the decades. These murders, forced expulsions and intimidation of ghetto populations were imposed to maintain state dominance, suppress independent politics, curb dissent and eliminate political choice in urban constituencies. The state therefore waged a savage war against the expression of democratic opinion and political choice in the slums and used rival political militias to enforce it.

Armed-to-the-teeth political militias were allowed to kill and maim with impunity to bar political competition in the slums. State terror came mostly in the form of violence by these militias that wreaked havoc in a few urban communities. Then as now, formal state security forces were rarely used to harass these politically protected militias and this status insulated them from the reach of the law and the judgement of the courts.

Unlike ghetto-dwellers, however, most citizens beyond the slums enjoyed the protections of a democratic society. In particular, middle- and upper-class dissenters and political opponents as well as countervailing civic institutions in the society functioned without harassment or intimidation. Dissenting leaders of all stripes, crusading journalists, outspoken priests and other proponents of contrary opinions were free to express their views and to mobilize their constituencies against unpopular regimes and their policies. Notwithstanding the fact that the society was becoming progressively more violent and increasingly brutal, the overwhelming majority of Jamaicans did not experience this worsening condition as the effect of tyrannical state power directed against them.

Rather, death was exacted and terror regularly exercised against a small but politically significant sector of the population, namely the mobilized, rebellious black urban poor. The Jamaican state used two strategies to terrorize and exterminate this group. On the one hand, the state through the parallel structure of the party militias violently assaulted the poor by means of the proto-national communal war. On the other hand, politicians used the official security forces to hunt and execute criminal gunmen by means of a widely endorsed war on crime.

State security forces, acting much like vigilantes, summarily killed "most-wanted" gunmen and marauding criminals that lacked party political protection. In its abusive and punitive reach, state terror was thus tightly focused and aimed at dismembering a distinct and troublesome lower class. State terror – whether by means of political militias or by the official security forces – targeted only the black urban poor. The politically driven among them were therefore mowed down in the communal war organized and instigated by the political parties. Other lower-class militants who took up arms to engage in criminal predation or protest crime succumbed not to the violence of political militias but to the terror of state security forces.

A key objective of Jamaica's democratic order, then, was an everyday form of rule that terrorized the ghettos. The fight against crime, the bid to stifle opinion and the parties' blood-drenched struggle for power winnowed the ranks of the armed and mobilized poor. This parasitic power that drew on democratic values, yet expunged the lives of the black poor for the political choices they made, produced its politically noxious and predictable results: extreme bloodletting, exterminism and dismemberment, and the social disorganization of the defiant poor.

In terms of the massive toll in death and physical injury to this group, it hardly mattered whether its members accepted or refused the political protection of the state in exchange for their supplication. Fanatic loyalists, party militia members, captive residents in political garrisons and marauding criminal gunmen all met a similar fate in violent encounters with this power that policed opinion in the ghetto and harshly restricted choice there. By targeting for punishment only the supplicant black poor on opposite sides of the political divide and by hunting their kin in the criminal underground for extermination, political power throttled and dismembered the rebel cultures of the urban poor.

In accomplishing this feat, parasitic power slyly established ties with society's loathing of an unruly black population that refused to accept its place in the structures of class domination and cultural contempt. Racist language wedded to an exterminist doctrine fed public prejudice against unlettered, outlaw blacks. This terrorism against the black lower class drew powerful social support from significant sectors of the population, especially among the middle and upper classes who turned a blind eye to this sustained abuse.

Yet for all its viciousness, predatory state power was no mere autocracy that only expelled disadvantaged groups from the arena of power or denied them cultural and political consideration. On the contrary, power in Jamaica evinced protean, solicitous attributes that mobilized the defiant poor, summoning them to participate in the dynamics of the state's parasitic authority. Indeed, politicians developed inventive repertoires that established a seductive political terrain that drew in the supplicant poor.

Resourceful politicians turned to the state's treasury to fund a variety of politically conditioned benefits. These ranged from the distribution of housing and state contracts to the issuing of tickets to the faithful for farm work abroad. In the handout of political patronage, state policy also made it clear that important "big men" were not the only ones to share in this bounty. Supplicants and "small men" from the unemployed and working class, as well as the peasantry and urban poor, enjoyed significant benefits across the decades.

Notwithstanding the sneering and humiliation the poor had to put up with, there is no denying that the state gave disadvantaged groups significant benefits and that these handouts for which they fought meant much to them. Moreover, where the middle and upper classes were repulsed by the squalor of the urban ghettos and were aghast at lower-class illiteracy and rowdiness, resourceful party bosses and other activists stayed in the slums to accumulate and distribute power there.

Duelling politicians therefore linked their parties' fortunes to a most unlikely social force: the socially mobilized lumpenproletariat. This group was decisive for the ascent of party bosses to national power and their creation of notable reputations. Where leaders in other poor countries might have shied away from this motley group in the ghetto, Jamaican politicians embraced its members. They were variously incorporated as political contractors, personal bodyguards and "comrades", electoral observers, odd job-bers, and praetorian guards of captive communities. Still others participated in formulating party strategy and tactics and these non–middle-class types contributed to partisan ideological debates at the constituency and national levels. This social power of the poor was thus invigorated as politicians decentralized state violence, transferring its use to a political underground dominated by the partisan lumpenproletariat.

Similarly, where the wider society held the black poor in cultural con-tempt, competing urban politicians accorded them *cultural* recognition. In a further display of flexibility and capacity for political straddling, jousting politicians deferred to the cultural claims of the black poor and affirmed their right to cultural distinction. Thus, early leaders of both political par-ties incorporated adepts of traditional religions into party campaigns and established personal ties with them. Other leaders backed champions of black nationality in their quest for equal identity, and most politicians gave creative artists and cultural leaders from the lower class an iconic space in public life and party affairs. Of course, top-ranking ghetto leaders and polit-ical dons also enjoyed party-sponsored positions that brought them respect and social honour in their communities.

This legitimization of the culture of the black poor breached structures of cultural apartheid in the country and reoriented the cultural balance of power in ways that were politically meaningful and irreversible. Thus where the urban poor lacked authority to impose their cultural claims on a reluc-tant society, astute urban politicians buttressed these claims by according disadvantaged groups a major role in the country's cultural and political life. In sum, a political power that was punitive toward non-compliant rebels and destroyed their ability to exercise democratic rights also held open, for their more pragmatic and compliant kin, authoritative institutions and cul-turally familiar social spaces from which to influence politics and society.

Forms of engagement by the mobilized poor also revealed distinctive responses to power and domination. Unlike disadvantaged groups in poor countries who remained quiescent, rose up in revolutionary violence or overthrew oppressive states by insurgent "people power", discontent among the militant poor in Jamaica disclosed neither of these polarizing traits. Instead, popular response to harsh disadvantage took a novel form. It expressed itself as an agonism that had more to do with unrequited affairs of honour than with establishing coalitions of the oppressed or with seek-ing the overthrow and seizure of state power.

The contrast between the intensity of group mobilization and high levels of social consciousness in the ghetto on the one hand and the throttled expression of the social power produced, on the other, is a remarkable feature of alienation in urban Jamaica. On the one side, lower-class social and political alienation produced high levels of activism and compelling varieties of culturally informed engagements. Lower-class social discontent triggered massive violence, unleashed disruptive social dynamics and fed clashing, destabilizing relations of power.

Still, these mighty exertions seemed more attuned to securing lower-class social honour and escaping atomized personal and group power than to toppling state actors or even embracing an alternative elite. There was no shortage of lower-class defiance and no protest that escaped the influence of cultural grievance. Rioters objected to repeated price hikes, non-party gunmen turned to criminal plunder and some like Sandokhan affirmed that concern by defying lawmen's claim to deference. The outlook of party militia leaders was also redolent of this alienated sensibility and for a time they broke with their political bosses. In their turn, urban traders mimicked these sentiments as they engaged in disruptive tactics in a bid to move up within the commercial sector.

Yet even as economic deprivation fed all such engagements, their political expression showed acute concerns that went beyond the satisfaction of economic need. Emotionally laden and deeply felt identities and racially charged concerns animated lower-class activism. Across ghetto communities, heightened awareness of stigmas and their cultural injuries fed individual and group belligerence. While the urban poor could hardly ignore political matters, political considerations did not dim alertness to urgent group cultural needs.

Indeed, group cultural claims seemed overwhelming in their influence. The lower-class quest for wealth, power and cultural standing depended less on the official political discourses of the day than on affirming the poor's own doctrinal commitment and belief in an inviolate black personhood. In the slums, a near-sacred defence of imperilled black humanity fed racially saturated claims to honour, power and economic need. Self-ownership, social ambition and competitive individualism in the cause of personal and racial-group achievement became core values. As a result, volitional rights and cultural respect for subordinated *black persons* became the common sense in poor communities. These twin considerations, and an arch response to their violation, fed and maintained defiance of law, political authority and social conventions.

Such premium values pertained, therefore, to unrequited affairs of honour. They provided positive impulses for the rebel cultures of the urban poor. Indeed, they drove trusted political loyalists such as George "Feathermop" Spence, Claude Massop and even Jim Brown to defy their political sponsors. These defections were thus powerfully influenced by a self-owning race pride and by the search for equal social standing and equivalence of volition. This honorific fundamentalism permeated all forms of dissidence.

Notwithstanding their variety, the multiple involvements of the urban poor had one thing in common: anxieties of black personhood and acute sensitivity concerning reputation, social honour and respect. The urban poor made them priorities and the social power of the group used these cultural claims to defend a variety of interests well beyond cultural matters. This preoccupation was so powerful that the mobilized poor seemed less concerned with unseating predatory power than with assuring that both state and society respected the volitional identity and the status claims of a racially proud but throttled black population.

In reaching for this elusive goal, disadvantaged groups and over-loyal fanatics fought less for freedom of political opinion and independent political choice than for the indivisibility of cultural respect and lower-class volitional rights. In brief, regardless of their agendas, the socially mobilized urban poor were not so much champions of free political choice in the ghetto as they were exponents of that durable and unyielding brand of cultural fundamentalism we call freedom.

Poor people's fundamentalism for themselves insisted, above all else, on volition, self-management and black dignity. This lower-class cultural essentialism made personal honour and racial-group respect the *sine qua non* of social existence and insisted that both state and society defer to these core values. As a consequence, the fundamentalism of racial respect, and the badness-honour that accompanied it, became all consuming. These honorific values reached into far-flung domains and affected myriad issues well beyond the cultural sphere.

As a consumatory norm, the cultural absolutism of the militant urban poor formed the basis of sharp social divisions that had ramifying effects beyond questions of political power. It impinged on interpersonal relations in poor neighbourhoods; it reached into the drama of sports and entertainment; it affected relations at the workplace and the home; and it inflected motivation to crime and abetted the lure of gangsterism. The insinuation of this overriding impulse for self-ownership into every relation – from the seemingly innocuous to the most politically charged – made social encounters antagonistic and potentially lethal.

This agonism of the mobilized Jamaican poor was overdetermined for it joined deeply held concerns of personal worth to large public issues. Anxieties about the loss of moral citizenship – a major issue for those in the public realm – resonated with private fears of impugned honour. This association was recurrent and insistent, and its incendiary contents infiltrated other relations and provoked huge contentions. Insistence on *equal identity* and the battle for *equivalent volition* revealed a peculiarity of lower-class alienation. This was its production of a newer martial tradition organized not so much around economic class relations as around claims of personal dignity and cultural respect. Matters of self-regard and anxieties for a throttled identity thus motivated this combativity.

Such a fighting spirit had as its fundamentalism the claim of black social competence. The fundamentalism of black competence therefore made lower-class personal and racial-group respect the main standard against which all engagements and all social relations were judged. The encounters of criminal gunmen with disrespectful policemen, disputes between top-ranking notables and party bosses, and armed clashes between political militias and rival communities all confirmed the priority of this doctrine and its broad, national impact. Black competence – and the tortured quest for it – became the political religion of the poor.

Like state parasitism, insistent lower-class claims of volitional rights and cultural respect produced novel repertoires of power. Supplicancy and dependence on a patronizing state alternated with bold bids for autonomy. Dependence gave notables and the loyalist rank and file some of what they wanted though many had to pay a huge price for such gains.

This search for racially inflected volitional rights yielded a test of wills that was fought on several fronts. In the clash between state power and the want of black competence, party militia leaders chafed at their political reins and broke away to exercise group- and self-owning ventures. Other gladiators used their complicity with power to wrest advantages from the state and political patrons. Hence political hirelings plundered the state's largesse, often to the chagrin of party patrons.

These were clearly acts of lower-class predation, yet they also registered an insistent, albeit negative, claim to black competence. Needless to say, other rebels breached traditional intercultural ramparts. Notably, they transgressed the boundaries of proper etiquette and class deference to flaunt norms of badness-honour that proved embarrassing to their sponsors.

In the realm beyond partisan politics, alienated groups employed badness-honour as a political resource, and all linked it to their disparate projects in the quest for competence and for its recognition. In the name of volitional rights, cultural regard and political liberation, alienated groups resorted to this testy agonism. Ne'er-do-wells, mercenary criminals – including communist and left-leaning gunmen – made ultra-violence and badness-honour their stock-in-trade.

Spurred by the parasitic state's divisive patronage and dismembering violence, gunplay and outlawry became the order of the day for these groups. Hence, where party-linked supplicants had used badness-honour, intrigue and guile to leaven their complicity with power, a motley collection of politically inspired gangsters, heroic bandits and left-wing gunmen made armed confrontation and derring-do their deadly vocation. In an ostensible war against capitalism, they robbed banks, challenged the security forces with hit-and-run tactics, and mocked the rule of the two parties. Yet for all their disruptiveness, such groups were a minority among the poor and their armed extremism and ultra-violence lacked broad social support.

In some respects, the urban poor's errant engagements – sly complicity with power and Gorgonian violence against it – set Jamaica apart from poor countries with disadvantaged but rebellious urban populations. For where the urban poor elsewhere were inclined to completely disengage from the state, take up arms against it or plunder its resources in violent civil wars, the alienated urban poor in Jamaica were only marginally involved in these activities.

For the most part, the complex engagements of the Jamaican poor inclined influential contingents to seek and retain ties to powerful incumbents. Such avid connections produced a debilitating internecine war. But the prize for which these groups fought was not the seizure of state power per se; it was the amount of patronage warring contenders received. Shares of the state's largesse, and not capture or displacement of the powerful, animated these partisans. For most of these rebels, the state seemed less a cruel nemesis than a means of minimizing hardships.

Predatory state politics assured this sensibility. Indeed, power in Jamaica sought out the majority of the poor not so much to expel them as to co-opt them. In a bizarre twist, political violence in Jamaica came not so much from the exclusion of the poor from political power as from their integration and complicity with it. Therefore, deep filiation and identification with power and not distance from power triggered political violence in Jamaica.

The political engagements of the urban poor were different in other respects. Whatever might be said of alienation and its links to political violence in Jamaica, it was not driven by religious zeal. Nor was mobilized ethnic nationalism a source of contention. Moreover, though political differences increased tensions in the country, for the most part such differences did not pit political authorities against a majority of insurgents making secessionist claims.

It is also worthy of note that the rebellious poor did not respond to the denial of political options by forging alternative organizations with appeal beyond the ghetto. While gangs, militias and peace councils led by political gunmen found legitimacy in the slums, these units and their leaders only elicited hostility and incomprehension from the wider society. By dint of their normative and anti-systemic character such units earned the derision of official society if not the security force's determination to expunge them.

This repression probably drove a minority of alienated slum-dwellers from party politics into crime even as continued blandishments and terror encouraged the vast majority of their kin to accept continued dependence. Consciousness of impugned status honour in the ghetto did not therefore result in far-reaching demands for social and political change that excluded existing political parties. In short, lower-class claims for equal competence fell victim to the politics of partisanship: such claims neither insisted on the right to choose between political parties nor sought to empower their alternatives by seeking support beyond the slums. In these ways, factional violence, blandishments and limited forms of dissent throttled the search for emancipation.

Still, the salience of cultural competence in the ghetto created a new political situation in the country. The accumulation of social power in the ghetto – in complicity with and antagonistic to state power – imposed on politicians and a reluctant society the troubling fact of dual power. On the one hand, politicians – standing astride incompatible organizational structures and divisive normative orientations – exercised state power in parasitic form. On the other hand, this very fact helped confirm the social power of the poor. Dependent on the state initially, groups that exercised this social power became increasingly autonomous and by 1989 they exerted a near unchecked moral sway over both politics and society. Distinctive forms of lower-class social power had checkmated state power.

The emergence and interaction of these two forms of power in Jamaica leave no doubt about the vital impact of cultural obligations on national politics. Power relations showed a marked susceptibility to cultural inflection. Protagonists not only took cultural imperatives for granted in their encounters, they cherished and boldly affirmed them. Conflicts in which personal honour, reputation or group racial claims were repeatedly invoked exposed the cultural roots of power. Social rank and knowing one's place in a pecking order both smoothed and disrupted relations within and beyond the political arena. Aspirants to power within and beyond the ghetto increasingly made their authority claims on the basis of group competence as well as on the basis of abridged or achieved status rights.

To be sure, protagonists in Jamaica undoubtedly fought huge battles in which unabashed use of raw power for advantage and booty was on display. However, encounters as various as the struggles over political turf, claim of leaders to class deference, and war between the security forces and criminal gunmen were shot through with powerful cultural impulses. Matters of impugned manhood, anxieties concerning violations of class and ethnic identities and agonism over transgression of rank in a social hierarchy aggravated encounters and raised the political stakes for all involved.

Not surprisingly, protagonists fought over competing claims to competence and respect. Fear of losing face – with its attendant humiliation – became a common feature in these power struggles. Party bosses, top-ranking notables, criminal gangsters, performance artists, avenging lawmen and ordinary citizens all recognized and acted on these powerful cultural impulses. In these ways, "culture" became more than just a cohesive and disruptive force in Jamaican political life. It was also a normatively familiar lever of political and social power and a legitimate basis of authority claims. For both state and society, cultural inflection gave power its authority and transmitted deep personal meanings to protagonists. Indeed, cultural resonance became a major source of power renewal. More specifically, decades-long habituation to the communication politics of badness-honour in Jamaica guaranteed this outcome.

Based on this sketch of the power-culture nexus, it is clear that the dilemma for Jamaica is the apparent and growing disjunction between this cultural expression of power – with its communication politics of "badness", "slackness" and exterminism – and the norms of a democratic politics. The power and legitimacy of the latter are to be found in the practice of civil politics and in the resolution of political differences through law and peaceful negotiation.

The contrast between democratic politics and the communication politics of predatory power and resistance to it could not be more extreme. Party activists, state actors, fanatical voters, criminal bandits, army and police forces, and ordinary citizens in Jamaica had turned massively to violence and self-help indiscipline to affirm their claims. Aggression became a lever of power, a means of self-defence and a source of invigorated identity. In a society increasingly regarded as Gorgonian and socially cannibalistic, the struggle for self-protection displaced any interest in or support for the state's historic function as defender of the public interest and guarantor of public safety.

The post–1972 crisis years in Jamaica had therefore spawned a violent, disruptive political culture that had become universal in scope and multi-class in character. Violence, incivility and indiscipline defined the emergent and broadly shared political culture. Needless to say, this uncivil political culture imperilled persons and was profoundly threatening to democratic institutions and to citizens' respect for them.

Ironically, however, this threat to well-being and hostility to democratic values was no bar to the accumulation of social power across all sectors of society. Social disorganization produced disruptive but compelling forms of political and social power. Invasive state strategies, ubiquitous party politics, the penetration of a subversive global culture and the island's structural economic dependence shattered stable social relations, encouraged social oppression and provoked uncivil political responses. Yet these very destabilizing forces spawned awesome forms of power shot through with deeply felt cultural motivations.

Weakened democratic institutions were no match for such disruptive forces. Raging violence coarsened social relations, and self-help indiscipline progressively displaced respect for law and public institutions. In this context, liberal-democratic ideals pertaining to the civic uses of power and the priority of the public interest collapsed. Factional political violence, the progressive criminalization of the state, and the turn to a generalized outlawry at the level of both state and society drove such ideals and their defenders to the political margins. In sum, during the post–1972 crisis period democratic forces and public institutions lost their vigour. Having become instruments of social oppression, public corruption and lawlessness for decades, democratic institutions lost legitimacy and public support.

A major contradiction thus lay at the heart of power and its exercise in Jamaica. The conditions for gaining political support, for securing an honourable identity and for maintaining power were all at odds with the conditions for creating a civil and democratic society. The one thrived on vicious factionalism and martial displays of honour, while the other required accommodation, trust and negotiation of difference as well as respect for law. Predation politics was manifestly inconsistent with democratic politics. This incompatibility weakened the appeal of democratic norms, it eroded respect for democratic institutions and it trimmed public trust in their capacities.

It is clear, then, that the political culture that generated powerful personal meanings and buttressed state politics was not the political culture that invigorated democratic politics. Widely shared agonism and highly charged honorific impulses fed the contention and factionalism that gave vigour to proud martial identities. These vital identities were being formed, however, by resort to aesthetics and a dramaturgy that were completely alien to democratic politics. Because predation politics summoned Jamaicans' status anxieties and fed their testy agonism, violent factionalism undercut democratic methods. Oddly enough, the very cultural impulses that undermined democratic norms were the same ones that gave power its authority and social groups their potent identities and measure of social honour.

Consequently, despite their dysfunctional effects, summonings that invoked honour through combativity had great appeal for leaders and supplicants alike. State agents found in them a powerful repertoire of power, and rebel cultures of the urban poor used them to build an equally potent means of power and identity. Badness-honour in this context was the crystallization of a brand of cultural fundamentalism that was thoroughly opposed to civil politics. Badness-honour was more than merely disruptive; clearly, it was also socially productive. Badness-honour enhanced the authority of the politically powerful; it summoned ordinary citizens to its siren call; and it won massive allegiance from the criminal class and the mobilized poor.

Those seeking personal and social respect therefore no longer looked to democratic institutions or its civic norms to validate their identity claims. Rather, persons in search of a social identity in a context of threat and uncertainty drew on a historic agonism and widely held authoritarian values and set them to new purposes. In the changed circumstances of the time, authoritarianism and agonism in the guise of badness-honour were transformed into decisive influences. As they became ubiquitous, myriad relations succumbed to their influence. In the twenty-year span between

1972 and 1992, the norm of badness-honour went from being a local tradition among alienated subcultures in the urban ghetto, and for a minority
of politicians and party activists, to being a near-universal political culture
that roiled the society.

In light of these cultural conditions of power and their close nexus with
social identities, it should be evident that Jamaica's social crisis will not be
susceptible to quick solutions. There will be no easy road to the reinvigoration of Jamaica's fractured democracy. Indeed, the restabilization of society and the cessation of social aggression and incivility are probably not
amenable to orthodox, short-term forms of political management, to easy
cultural fixes or to simple economic remedies.

This is apparent for a several reasons. First, the tottering Westphalian inter-
state system will make recovery difficult. The structure that formed the political edifice of world society since 1648 is now breaking up. National states
outside the industrialized democracies have either collapsed or are experiencing major crises. A notable feature of this unravelling is the onset of civil
strife ranging from nationalism and ethnicity, to religious fundamentalism
across the world. Collapsed civic norms, the dispersal of violence to non-
state actors, and the rise of criminal gangsters and Mafiosi as major social and
political actors all testify to the erosion of state authority in a weakened
inter-state system. Jamaica's turmoil is partly due to its membership in this
crisis-ridden inter-state system. Its convulsions are inexorably linked to the
local "Jamaican" forms of upheaval and conflict described in this book. Any
effort at recovery will necessarily have to acknowledge the continuing
impact of this destabilizing connection.

Second, efforts to invigorate democracy in Jamaica will come to naught
where structures of democratic factionalism that feed predation politics and
reproduce racist images of Afro-Jamaicans are left untouched. An unfortunate aspect of Jamaica's membership in the inter-state system was
the embrace, on behalf of its leaders, of a culturally compromised nation-
statehood. That is, local thralldom to Westphalian structures based on cultural
"modernity" and "progress", and on their engendered and ethnicized hierarchies, abetted political strategies and social ontologies that fed both
gender subordination and racial domination.

In truth, Jamaica's reproduction of liberalism's ideology of modernity and
progress produced a savage and destructive effect on poor Afro-Jamaicans.
Political reform will require an end to state and party politics that
impose forms of domination that insist on limiting political choice in the

slums and purging the majority population of Africanist forms of civilization identity.

Finally, any political renewal must address the crisis of widening allegiance to honorific fundamentalism. This brand of cultural fundamentalism among poor Afro-Jamaicans is historical in character though variant in its manifestations. In the post-war years, the lumpenproletariat and the urban unemployed poor have been honorific fundamentalism's outspoken champions and its irrepressible vanguard. Their insistent claim to moral infrangibility based on equivalent identity and volition, and their demand for both a better life and an end to the racism embedded in Jamaica's factional democracy identify them not as a rogue culture, but as the avatars of liberation in Jamaica.

Honorific fundamentalism is not a claim to an exclusionary racialism or a demand for racial supremacy. Least of all is it a threat to a freer, more humane and fully democratic Jamaica. At its best, honorific fundamentalism is a powerful expression of Afro-Jamaican civilization identity under duress. Its claim to the moral infrangibility of Afro-Jamaicans represents a sweeping, radical thrust for the full democratization of Jamaican society. Short-term reform measures now under review or currently being implemented can certainly make a difference in the lives of the poor, but they are not sufficient. Such measures as dismantling garrison constituencies, ending the benefits politics associated with it, reforming the police and passing anti-corruption laws are all to the good.

However, while honorific fundamentalism is certainly about the desire for free expression of political choice and opinion, and though it has always insisted on "full employment" and an end to police brutality, its claims are more far-reaching and hence more threatening. Honorific fundamentalism among poor Afro-Jamaicans is premised on a radical reordering of domestic class and institutional relations. Its demands have always carried an explicit challenge to all forms of social domination dealt with in this book.

There can be little doubt that decades of dissent during the post-war years have drastically reordered these domestic relations. The urban poor have undoubtedly become more socially empowered, even as the group remained politically throttled and more culturally demeaned. The huge contradiction between forms of social empowerment for the poor on the one hand, and marked political throttling and cultural scorn for the group on the other, weakened democracy and spawned the phenomenon of "badness-honour".

As Jamaica makes its inevitable transition from predation politics and democratic factionalism in the era of globalization, badness-honour may well be eclipsed. Barring a major upheaval in the interim, however, it is probable that the transition could well usher in newer and possibly more subversive forms of the fundamentalism of black competence.

Epilogue

The Ordeal of Social Reconstruction in Jamaica

POLITICAL STUDIES AND COMMENTARIES ON JAMAICAN politics offer ample accounts of the social crisis in that country.[1] Indeed, the political dimensions of the Jamaican ordeal are so well known and their effects so horrific, that these disabilities provoked a desperate search for answers and spurred a frantic quest for alternative forms of governance.

As the 1990s drew to a close, two remarkable developments connected to the ongoing crisis appeared on the political scene. First, politicians and public officials began to articulate a language of political reform. In fact, commitment to reform went beyond mere talk and resulted in a raft of legislation and other measures to restore confidence in government.[2] In the context of this book's indictment and critique of Jamaica's brutal and predatory state politics, the initiation of reform measures from above, and politicians' public disavowal of anti-democratic practices are remarkable developments that raise questions about the survival of predatory rule.[3] Jamaican politicians' rhetorical statements and legislative initiatives to reform the rapine and predatory political system they helped to create – and did much to maintain – represent a sufficiently notable shift that warrants close examination for its theoretical and political significance.

Second, the ongoing social crisis was so acute that it stirred sections of the alienated middle class into political activism and drove disadvantaged

groups to violent protest in the streets. There the disaffected urban poor –
decades-long victims of a crucifying state violence and an indifferent society – became even more emboldened in expressing their disgust with social
and political authority.

Lacking leadership and organization, and having no intention to seize
state power, spontaneous protesters in the street nonetheless frontally challenged the state's legitimacy and its right to rule. When not spontaneously
mounting roadblocks to air their grievances or burning tires to express their
frustration, the urban unemployed went beyond plaintive protest to invade
and even attack the very citadels of state power.

In September 1998, for instance, the militant urban poor from the
Matthews Lane area in West Kingston blocked roads in downtown Kingston
and marched *en masse* to the Central Police Station after they learned that
the police had detained their ghetto community leader. At the police station,
the incensed crowd demanded and won the right to see their leader, the better to satisfy themselves that he had remained unharmed while in police
custody.

The appearance of Donald "Zeeks" Phipps – the so-called don from the
Matthews Lane community – on the balcony of the Central Kingston Police
Station sent shock waves throughout the island. With arms raised to calm his
supporters, Zeeks assured the demonstrators that all was well, and that they
should return peacefully to their community. The capitulation of the police
to popular demand and the daring confrontation on behalf of a local patron
and lawgiver from the ghetto laid bare in the starkest terms the gradual
transfer of legitimacy and social power in Jamaica from the state and its
agents to community enforcers and the new patrons in the ghetto.

As if this insult to state authority was not enough, Gordon House, the
parliament and seat of national government, was bombed a month later.
This unravelling of public authority and affirmation of popular challenge
continued as the urban poor struck again six months later. This time they
rose up in April 1999 in violent protest against a hike in fuel prices. The
scope and ferocity of this upheaval stunned PNP political leaders enough to
cause them to trim the price hike, thereby handing another decisive victory
to the seething urban poor.[4]

The corrosive effects of these attacks on the authority of the state left no
doubt about the ongoing reconfiguration of power in the society. Indeed,
the mixture of incredulity and outrage that greeted these events only confirmed the society's recognition of this uncomfortable fact. Given the inten-

sity of popular social mobilization and the militant poor's confrontational stance, it is clear that any proposal for reform and social renewal, from whatever source, must necessarily address the powerful grievances that led to these outbursts and challenges.

More worrisome, however, from the standpoint of social renewal is the mobilized urban poor's rejection of the norm of civility and their repudiation of the state itself. This socially powerful group's withdrawal from society in favour of self-enclosure inside a nihilistically oriented counter-society opposed to public law and conventions of social morality raises serious questions for all reformers. Both the group's rejectionist stance and allegiance to an anti-system cultural otherness are not amenable to easy prescriptions. Indeed, simplistic suggestions that employment is all that would be needed to reverse the dissenters' hostility to state and society completely underestimated the cultural factor and its importance to any resolution of the crisis.

Beyond that, the militant rebels' near-absolute and long-standing rejection of institutional forms of political power (because of the historical and current role in their oppression) also suggests that proposals for social renewal that call for sacrifice, discipline and social restraint on the part of the alienated poor are likely to fail. Building social consensus and rallying the alienated but socially powerful urban poor to a new project that can win their allegiance will be a major challenge for reformers.

That challenge, it appears, has been taken up by an awakened civil society. Critical broadcast and print media, new political parties and movements, and myriad civic organizations, lobby groups and influential personalities hostile to predation politics added their voices of dissent and proposals for change. In doing so, they made important contributions to the debate on social renewal, although the effectiveness and durability of these groups remain in doubt.

This epilogue describes the anguished search for social and political renewal in Jamaica. It examines the unfolding politics of reform for assumptions about social progress, democratic rule, cultural identity and the deeper meaning of Jamaicans' engagement with global society and modernity.

These issues that are central to the process of social renewal and national development have been typically ignored in favour of solving immediate and pressing problems.[5] But reformers' assumptions about the foregoing issues matter because reformers' prescriptions, while appealing on their face, may harbour restrictive notions of freedom and democracy where such prescriptions do not herald a confining politics in new garb.

In discussing the ordeal of social reconstruction, then, this epilogue assesses the politics and ideologies of change-makers for clues as to whether their new politics represents a break with the status quo in ways that suggest alternative methods of engaging modernity and harnessing power to achieve democratization and social liberation.

Crisis in the Parties

As is the case with major social crises, the disintegration of the old order in Jamaica has been accompanied by unsettling and contradictory realities. This is apparent both inside the state and within society itself. For example, the deepening crisis has had a destructive effect on the two major political parties. Both political parties faced massive disillusionment not only among the voting public, but also within the ranks of their leadership.[6] Growing conflicts among party notables was one reflection of the pressures being felt inside the parties in response to the mounting demands for change on behalf of alienated groups. In addition, party dissidents' own frustration with a corrupt system and the lack of internal party democracy was another contradiction occasioned by the crisis.

This dissension at the top was especially acute inside the JLP. For example, the "Gang of Five" episode in 1990, in which party leader Edward Seaga accused five senior members of plotting to remove him from power, mirrored the ongoing democracy deficit in the country. Thus instead of addressing dissenters' concerns about the quality of his leadership through democratic debate within the JLP, Seaga merely issued a diktat to his critics to submit to his leadership or leave the party.[7] Since this episode that forced out several JLP dissenters, other top party figures, including Deputy Leader Bruce Golding, subsequently resigned in frustration from that organization.[8]

In contrast with the JLP's autocratic rule and the public squabbling it provoked, disagreement inside the PNP expressed itself somewhat differently. There, rather than trying to displace the leader for his shortcomings, party notables typically used the more open PNP political culture to air disagreements in hopes of bringing about reform. However, as the social crisis deepened and as PNP predation, corruption and debasement of political life persisted, PNP notables such as Maxine Henry-Wilson, the party general secretary, publicly expressed concern for PNP shortcomings.[9]

Others went further, however. In November 2000 Danny Melville, a respected business leader and PNP member of Parliament for North East St Ann, quit the party in disgust. Remarking on the nexus among corruption, crime and politics, Melville drew the unflattering lesson about his tenure in politics: "My role as a parliamentarian seems to be defined as an attender of funerals, co-ordinator of patronage and a symbol of tribalism."[10]

Evidently expressing the widely shared sentiment among the professional classes that party politics – despite PNP leaders' protestations to the contrary – was not a place for their talents, the businessman-turned-politician lamented his entry into politics:

> I find I can no longer be a part of a system that glorifies mediocrity and denigrates any vision of excellence. Now that I have been part of our present system, whereby politics reigns supreme over all other considerations, it is clear to me that it is a system that cannot deliver success. I began in 1997 with hope. And sadly I have ended with disillusionment.[11]

Melville's departure was followed by still another defection from the PNP as Francis Tulloch – the representative for North West St James – quit his post for similar reasons in August 2001.

Defections such as these had no impact, however, on the politics of predation. Both parties continued in their old ways, though mounting pressures for change inside the country and a changing international conjuncture would impel only the PNP to modify facets of its political rule.

The Politics of Reform

The movement for political reform in Jamaica took several forms. Besides defections and internal conflicts over the lack of inner party democracy, a few politicians began publicly divorcing themselves from an aspect of the political order that had triggered the greatest public outcry: the parties' recruitment, financial backing and protection of gunmen as co-governors in strategic urban constituencies.

By the late 1970s, these gunmen threatened the very system that had created them. The gunmen's growing independence from their political sponsors, as well as their mayhem and ultra-violence that provoked murder and chaos in the streets, encouraged the parties and their notables to close ranks against this threatening force. Spiralling crime, ever-increasing murder rates and general lawlessness not only damaged politicians' credibility, but also threatened the country's economic well-being. Mayhem hurt the tourist trade and damaged prospects for foreign investment. These concerns and worry for their hold on power no doubt drove politicians into a tactical retreat from political gunmen.[12]

Still, it is worth remembering that politicians' repudiation of the nexus of guns and politics was not wholly driven by tactical considerations. Sorrow and guilt moved the disenchanted among them – especially former PNP and JLP activists – to decry the predatory system they once served and acknowledge their complicity in its murderous ways.

Time and sober reflection on decades of bloodletting and the massive social division it caused spurred this confessional group to take up the cause of social reform and to make public their belated misgivings about predation politics. Moreover, assaults under questionable conditions by the security forces in Tivoli Gardens that killed four persons in May 1997 and another twenty-five in July 2001 stirred outrage in these communities and elsewhere.

A similar savage attack by the security forces in Braeton, St Catherine, in March 2001 that took the lives of seven young men suspected of criminal acts, added to the revulsion as human rights groups gathered evidence suggesting that the seven were murdered by the police.[13]

Unremitting state terror in the fight against crime in poor communities therefore pricked consciences and rallied opposition. The discarding of elementary procedures for enforcing the law and the trampling of basic rights of the accused in these episodes, alarmed the now-penitent former public officials, themselves hardened veterans of Jamaica's martial politics. They therefore sounded an alarm against that country's devouring state and decried its merciless violence against the black poor.

Beginning in the late 1990s, former PNP and JLP politicians uttered their *mea culpas* before an equally grateful and exasperated public.[14] For example, in 1999 Dudley Thompson, former PNP law-and-order hardliner and ex–minister of national security, apologized for having said in 1978 that the security forces that lured, ambushed and shot dead five unsuspecting inner-city men at the Green Bay firing range in St Catherine killed "no angels".[15]

Bruce Golding, JLP defector and the then leader of the National Democratic Movement (NDM), joined the refrain in the same year by offering his regret for having consorted with gunmen when he was the member of Parliament for the garrison community of Central St Catherine.

Acknowledgement of the link between crime and politics also came in the same year from Anthony Abrahams, a former JLP minister of tourism. In his case, Abrahams promised to tell all he knew, but only on condition that he be granted immunity from prosecution.

Of all the *mea culpas* coming from these former public officials, perhaps none roiled the waters as much as the speech of the former PNP general secretary D.K. Duncan at a fundraising banquet before a JLP audience on 28 September 2001. In an unprecedented act, Duncan criticized the party he once served for its complicity with terror and murder in the 1970s and after. And he did so not at a PNP gathering, but before an upset JLP audience still seething from the murderous police assault on the Tivoli Gardens community in July.

In a rejection of Jamaican politicians' conspiracy of silence concerning the political parties' organization of political violence and murder, Duncan broke from the ranks, spoke up for justice and disclosed the sordid facts about Jamaican politics "to let you know that these things were not done accidentally".

To wit, Duncan exposed how both the Gun Court Act and the Suppression of Crime Act of 1974 – to which he and others in the PNP assented despite knowing that both were unconstitutional – were used to violate the basic rights of the black poor in the ghetto. This, Duncan implied, was done largely to satisfy middle-class and public concern that something be done about crime and violence.[16]

As Duncan observed, the result of applying what then party leader Michael Manley called "shock therapy [in inner-city communities] in the hope that this would buy time for the society" was not the suppression of crime or violence, but the institutionalization of repression and terrorism by the state.[17]

Speaking in the context of both the Braeton killings and the recent deaths at the hands of the police in Tivoli Gardens, Duncan backed JLP criticism of PNP high-handedness and indifference to accusations of police misconduct. Duncan also dismissed attempts to discredit him by asserting that accusations of political disloyalty for decrying JLP deaths and endorsing Edward Seaga's warning about the abuse of Jamaicans' civil rights were irrelevant in the face of unchecked state terror.[18] PNP terror had to be stopped now for the sake of justice and the rule of law, Duncan warned. For "whereas in a particular point in time the Suppression of Crime Act allowed them to just kick off the door, come in, and gun-butt you and take you to jail, now, them come in and gunbutt you, and shoot you in your head!"[19]

Coming from a former PNP stalwart, strongman and political warrior of the 1970s, this *mea culpa* and biting critique of power had the predictable effect. His former party dissociated itself from his statement and rejected "any notion that the PNP administration had ever planned or executed any form of terror on the Jamaican people".[20] For their part, media commentators seemed confounded by Duncan's disclosures, with some praising his forthrightness while others condemned him and his ilk for having "blood on their hands".[21]

Whatever the disagreements about Duncan's complicity, there can be no doubt that a former member of the inner circle and a one-time perpetrator of political violence who knew the intimate details had spoken out and had shattered a taboo. Duncan's bombshell was therefore significant not so much for what it revealed about how short-term thinking and cynicism led to political murder and injustice for Afro-Jamaicans – though that was important – but for its breach of the wall of silence maintained by Jamaica's politicians.[22]

Thus no matter the outcry against social disorder in the country, what is clear is that both civil and uncivil forms of protest against injustice and terror had struck a blow against the governing class by heightening contradictions within the group. Their fabled unity was crumbling and the resulting splits and divisions were now pitting former allies against each other, while uniting historic enemies.

Narratives of Reform

One effect of this deepening crisis was its impact on narratives of reform. At the level of the state, its attempt to come to grips with the crisis produced an unseemly and wholly unconvincing ideological discourse. As the defensive responses to Duncan's disclosures revealed, the PNP's commitment to democratic reform seemed insincere if not cynical. Not only did the PNP's National Executive Council wholly reject Duncan's claim, but Prime Minister P.J. Patterson in his address to the National Executive Council asserted that neither he nor the party had anything to confess. Evidently stretching the bounds of credulity, the party leader and long-time senior

PNP executive declared himself personally innocent of Duncan's charges, since he neither "participated [nor] subscribed to any decision by the party or the government in the 1970s, that was intended to bring terror to the people of Jamaica".[23]

This claim of political innocence probably rang hollow with long-time observers of the Jamaican political scene as well as with those familiar with the inner workings of Jamaican politics. Indeed, Patterson's protestations seemed wholly insensitive to the dire nature of the ongoing crisis and heedless of the urgent constitutional issues posed by the security forces' continued killing of Jamaicans on a mass scale.

Indeed, state agents' efforts to discredit human rights activists who spoke out against police killings only reinforced perceptions that the government was more concerned with holding onto power at all costs than with fulfilling its stated commitment to building democracy. As the local human rights group Jamaicans for Justice reported, police harassment of its members and the state's repeated attempts to discredit its work on behalf of victims threatened the organization's survival and put the lives of its activists in jeopardy.

As the organization noted in a recent report, despite Jamaica's treaty obligations under the UN's Declaration on Human Rights,

> Statements made to the media by the Minister of National Security and Justice, the Police Commissioner, various chairmen of the Police Federation and a civilian support group, have been, at times, anti human rights defenders, and seem calculated to foment public rejection of human rights defenders. Some statements have tended to portray HR defenders as supporters of criminals, uncaring about the rights of victims, [and] contributors to the upsurge in criminal activity.[24]

This attack on human rights groups and the authoritarian ideological assault that accompanied it obviously clashed with the democratic accent in the state's narrative. How, then, to reconcile the language of reform in the prime minister's April 1999 budget speech in which he declared that "our institutions, political systems and bureaucracy must either change quickly, or disintegrate and be swept away" with subsequent actions and talk which repudiated that claim?

The answer lies, I think, in the desperate attempt of the governors of the Jamaican State to preserve their power while searching for a new basis for political legitimacy. What we are witnessing is the predatory state's untidy and contradictory search for a way out of the impasse created by its rule. The tangle of contradictions and the seeming incoherence in the state's narrative of reform is an aspect of this unfolding drama.

A Turn to Political Neo-liberalism and Managerialism

I have characterized this pattern of response to crisis as a species of political dilation in which the state absorbs the contradictory movement of ideas and sentiments in society, the better to deploy them as part of its hegemony. In doing so, the predatory state today articulates a reform narrative, accompanies it with relevant legislation, but drains the shift to reform of its substantive content. This it does by means of foot-dragging, weak implementation and outright opposition to meaningful change on key issues that threaten its power. To this list should be added the absence of any effort at mass mobilization on the scale of the 1970s to enshrine principles of democratic honour, ethnic competence in power-sharing and moral infrangibility as inalienable rights of Afro-Jamaicans.

What is remarkable about Jamaica's ostensible shift to democratic renewal is the technocratic and managerial enunciation that has accompanied it. The seeming readiness with which representatives of the Jamaican state embraced the Organization of American States' call for transparency and good governance, and the Jamaican government's imitative adoption of the Washington Consensus on political neo-liberalism for peripheral societies, offers a clue to local state agents' motivations and agendas.

It will be recalled that in bringing Jamaican law into conformity with the country's treaty obligations under the Organization of American States Convention against Corruption, the PNP willingly agreed to put in place the legal framework and legislative policies for assuring clean government and political transparency.[25] However, in countries such as Jamaica, where a free vote and substantive rights already exist, transparency of decisions, the elimination of corruption and the effective delivery of services to so-called political consumers are seen within the neo-liberal mindset as representing the deepening of democracy. It is this understanding of democracy that the Jamaican state and even its harshest critics have so powerfully embraced.

For all its compelling appeal, however, the seductive vogue of good government and political openness in peripheral societies such as Jamaica is deeply flawed. That is because political neo-liberalism with its siren calls for the professionalization of Third World politics favours an elitist agenda that conflicts with popular demands. These demands include the democratization of political institutions in ways that include mass involvement; the democratization of elite political culture to curb its historic conceit as bearer of progress, champion of modernity and exemplar of "civilization" for all Jamaica. Most important, however, is the awakening of political power in a majority black country to its unfulfilled ontological obligations. That is, the exercise of political power in a former slave society and in an ex-colonial territory such as Jamaica is unlikely to succeed where it fails to connect institutional change to the diverse positive cultural sensibilities of the Afro-Jamaican majority. So far the admirable calls for the professionalization of Jamaican politics remain deaf to this neglected civilization project.

The framework of political neo-liberalism is equally problematic in another respect because it depends on political technique and political management as its "organizational rationality".[26] That is, consistent with its notion of good governance and political efficiency, political neo-liberalism sees governance as the application of technical expertise to political problems. In these terms, Jamaica's piratic politics is attempting to make the transition from a system of domination based on the odious patronage-driven structure to a cleaner, less contentious method that I shall call political managerialism.

This form of organizational rationality, in which governance becomes a form of techno-political management, rests on three pillars. First, economic decisions would be insulated from social pressures and demands – the better to give economic planners and decision-makers autonomy from the political.[27]

Second, governance would become a type of political steering of the ship of state. Redefining political relations in ways that demobilize popular protest and that channel political action into bureaucratic modes involving only pragmatic choices "for the good of the country" appears to be the new state ideology in Jamaica. Politics would therefore become less and less about the contestation between conflicting ideologies over unequal distribution of social goods and shares of social honour, and more about achieving efficiencies in attracting foreign investment, fighting crime and growing the economy.

Third, political managerialism would affirm its legitimacy through a seductive results-oriented discourse. Practical results – not the means by which they were achieved or the moral consequences of political decisions – would be the measure for determining political success.

To resonate with loyalists and other symbol-sensitive constituencies this narrative of ends over means would be joined to a reinvigorated political nationalism. In the new period of the late 1990s, however, political nationalism would now hail rebellious Jamaicans not as criminals and moral bankrupts, but as empowered patriotic citizens and cultural moderns called to partnership with the state in the civic renewal of democratic Jamaica.[28]

In sum, political managerialism in Jamaica would employ an updated form of political nationalism to transform Jamaica's acute social divisions into a usable resource for the recomposition of political power. This state agents tried to accomplish by the sleight-of-hand of empowering technocrats and politicians over the people as the difficult process of political transition unfolded, by the technique of dressing power in new garb, and by assigning the practitioners of predatory politics new roles as champions of a people-oriented democracy.

Correlatively, under this new dispensation the stubbornly insolent and non-conformist black poor would be offered an ostensibly democratic option: partnership in the search for social renewal and reconstruction on condition of docility and obeisance to the agendas of technocrats and political managers.

By offering a significant advance over recent and more brutal forms of power, this sly tactic of political rule had the desired effect. It divided its already weak opponents, drew middle-class champions of reform into its ideological orbit, and seduced them with its limited definition of democracy as improvement and reform from above.[29] Hence, in announcing a new crime initiative late in 2002, PNP politicians under duress resorted to the tried-and-true tactic of co-opting the political opposition. As one commentator noted approvingly in late 2002,

> The Government has, effectively, disarmed the human rights lobby by including its three most vocal and media-friendly spokespersons on the two critical bodies it has set up to monitor the Jamaica Defence Force (JDF) and to advise the Ministry of National Security on crucial crime-fighting issues.
>
> The Executive Director of Jamaicans for Justice (JFJ), Dr Carolyn Gomes, ubiquitous talk show guest; JFJ chairperson Susan Goffe, a regular voice on the electronic media, Breakfast Club member and sometime co-host; Dr Lloyd Barnett, the highly respected constitutional lawyer and chairman of the

Independent Jamaica Council for Human Rights (JCHR), now have an official platform in the corridors of power to champion their human rights causes.[30]

This endorsement of the affirmative uses of power in dealing with opponents is clear-eyed and unromantic and is wholly consistent with my own dark view of power. Yet in Jamaica's political culture that knows nothing but quick fixes and short-term remedies for social problems, my critical "theory" of domination as not simply harsh repression or dissembling, but rather as the rendering of positive initiatives in ways that opponents find appealing, is likely to be derided as fanciful, if not naïve. What is so wrong, ever-pragmatic Jamaican critics might ask, with an approach that gives opponents a voice in the corridors of power? Is that not, after all, a measure of the unfolding process of democratization?

The answer to this query might insist that from the standpoint of the opponents of the system, inclusion may not result in empowerment but rather the opposite. This is especially so in highly volatile transitional contexts where defenders of the old order are most inclined to hew to the principle of making short-term reforms in order to preserve their long-term hegemony.

Despite this problem with short-term measures, their appeal for opponent and hegemons alike is undeniable. As noted journalist and political commentator Ian Boyne is fond of reminding critics of state terror and of "hard policing", the short term is all that matters in a society fighting for its life in the face of an orgy of criminal violence.

Evidently deaf to the assessments by D.K. Duncan and other critics, that hard policing has already cost too many innocents their lives, abridged liberties and has never worked in curbing either crime or violence, Boyne and others sympathetic to his view continue to argue for the simultaneous adoption of brutal short-term measures and enlightened pursuit of political reform.[31]

Whether any government could long survive in the face of violent protest and public criticism of the moral and political consequences of pursuing such a policy is not a moot question, however; Jamaica's state agents are relying on precisely this approach as they feel their way through the crisis. Judging from the mounting social discontent and upheaval between 1999 and 2002, however, the prospects are not good that this deployment of contradictory repertoires of power can be extended indefinitely.

Equally worrisome for the future is whether middle-class challengers to the status quo can survive long enough to impose their agendas on a reluctant state while also winning the hearts and minds of an equally reluctant and jaded society. Here again, if the record of the many reform organizations that appeared on the political scene after 1992 is any indication, their limited achievement does not bode well for the future.

Civil Society and Social Change: Reform Movements

It is something of a paradox that Jamaica has a diverse civil society and myriad civic organizations but a dulled capacity for vigorous civic involvement in the social and political realm. While it is partly true that in the past predation politics either swallowed politically available organs of civil society such as sports clubs, community groups and even religious organizations – or drained them of their vigour by making political involvement unattractive – state politics is not entirely responsible for Jamaica's shrunken associational life and the limited involvement of civic groups in the social and political arena.

The burden of this deficit must be shared with an embedded moral economy in which involvement in public affairs is seen as relevant only insofar as it advances the private and personal interests of groups and individuals. This privatistic view of the significance of public affairs has largely determined the scope and intensity of social and political involvement in Jamaica in recent decades. It is this privatism and not so much the mighty reach of an allegedly totalitarian state that is responsible for stunted civic life in Jamaica.

The country's wrenching social crisis has only intensified this privatism as groups and individuals withdraw from public affairs and socio-political engagement in favour of a retreat to enclosures that suit them. Thus while it is true that Jamaica has experienced a revival of civic engagement in limited areas and has seen the emergence of new civic groups, the countertrend to privatism, self-enclosure and indifference to public affairs across the country is extremely powerful.

The New Beginning Movement

Reforming movements that appeared in the 1990s and after had to overcome this hurdle and none of them has so far succeeded. The New

Beginning Movement (NBM) that began with such promise and high expectations in 1992 could not surmount this obstacle.

That leading NBM members were former PNP, JLP and WPJ stalwarts was both a blessing and a curse. On the one hand, the group, which included such notable figures as D.K. Duncan from the PNP, Douglas Vaz of the JLP and Trevor Munroe of the WPJ, had instant name recognition and enjoyed the favour of being the first elite formation to emerge with a sharp critique of predation politics and a counter-narrative of democratic reform in the 1990s.[32] On the other hand, because these notables were familiar to the public and were known for holding highly partisan views, this ideological provenance probably earned them as much condemnation as praise.

Moreover, these notables' sudden shift from using the harsh language of communist politics and the uncompromising discourse of JLP–PNP "tribal" politics probably took their audience some time to adjust to the new liberal-democratic accent. No doubt for some the sight of Trevor Munroe, the former hard-line communist leader, speaking up for the political virtues of the capitalist system he had only recently denounced in the harshest terms, was perhaps too much of a shift in belief to be accepted readily by his detractors.

The same would be true for D.K. Duncan, an equally polarizing figure from the 1970s, who had found his conscience in the 1990s and was now challenging the murderous politics he had helped to perpetuate.

That the NBM had powerful notables who were seasoned in Jamaican politics became an obstacle in another respect. The different and conflicting ideological provenance of NBM members probably made unity difficult. For while all could agree on the indictment of the status quo and concurred on the need for the democratization of a corrupted system, it was less clear what else NBM members stood for and how they planned to implement their agenda.

The weakness of the NBM was its failure to stir public enthusiasm after the first flush of excitement that greeted its founding. And the movement's unity was not enhanced by constant PNP and JLP inducements to individuals in the group to return to those organizations to implement their ideas.

Against a background of public indifference and internal disagreements, the NBM passed from the scene. As one of its founders observed a decade later, the NBM "fell apart after the main leaders simply absented themselves". These would-be champions of a political alternative to the established system later found a new political vocation as "former NBM convenors today are members of parliament and senators on both sides of the house, and [are] prominent in public life. The NBM was a wonderful opportunity missed."[33]

The National Democratic Movement

More recent political formations did not fare much better. Bruce Golding's creation of the NDM foundered on similar shoals. Founded in October 1995, the NDM offered itself as an alternative to the two main political parties and their politics of predation and violence. However, the NDM's message of national unity, constitutional reform and the creation of a new political culture failed to win broad public support.

The new party's failure became apparent in the 1997 general national elections in which NDM candidates failed to win a single seat. This setback was all the more worrisome given that in recent years polls were reporting that over 40 per cent of likely voters had declared themselves uncommitted and independent.

By the end of 1998, the writing was on the wall for the NDM, as speculation about Golding's return to the JLP increased. In March 2001 Golding resigned from a near-moribund NDM that garnered only 740 of the more than 15,000 votes cast in the St Ann North East by-election.[34]

How in the midst of a massive defection of voters from the two main political parties and widespread public disillusionment with their tenure did another promising third party movement fade into obscurity?[35] Much of the answer has to do with political allegiances in Jamaica.[36] For all their weakness and enfeebled condition, the two major parties still control the giant share of votes cast. And although the winning party has been garnering an ever-declining share of the total vote and although fewer and fewer voters are turning out at the polls, the PNP–JLP monopoly at the polls remains unchallenged.[37]

Aside from this two-party hegemony that has historically doomed third parties, NDM politics also hurt its chances. For instance, it appears that Golding did not convince potential voters that he had indeed made a clean break with the old system. Besides being damned for being a JLP defector, Golding could never quite shake the perception that he was merely biding his time before returning to the JLP. Moreover, potential voters were put off by the perception that the NDM – as one wag put it – was "nothing more than a 'baby JLP' " because of its composition of defecting JLP politicians.[38] This problem of credibility and of the leader's larger ambition dogged Golding and the NDM during its existence. In fact, Golding's last-minute return to the JLP as a candidate in the 2002 general elections proved that the doubters were right all along.

The collapse of the NDM, and Golding's return to the JLP, are ominous developments for other fledgling third parties. Neither the Jamaica Alliance for National Unity nor the United Progressive Party has any significant support among the voting population. In a poll in 2002 of public preference for political parties, only the United Progressive Party among the two new parties got poll results of any significance, and then the percentage of respondents who thought the United Progressive Party was "best suited to run the country right now" was a mere 3.3 per cent.[39] In sum, whatever messages of reform the new parties hoped to convey were ignored because of public indifference, two-party dominance and lack of credibility.[40]

The collapse of third parties like the NDM is an awful indictment not only of these parties and their leaders, but also of the unforgiving and still hobbled character of Jamaican political culture. That is, for all the talk about the need for a new politics, potential supporters of these third parties and others punished or rewarded them based on criteria from the old politics.

For example, expectations associated with the culture of political patronage hurt the NDM because it had little to give partisans hungry for handouts. Similarly, intense personalism and identification of the party with the leader was alive and well in the NDM's relationship with its rank and file as the latter projected their hopes and fears onto NDM leader Golding. The same concern for personalities over organizational issues was evident in the unrelenting media commentary and sniping at NDM leader Bruce Golding.

The NDM's fortunes fared no better in a conjuncture where cynicism born of disillusionment led to pre-emptive public assessments of reform movements and parties as quixotic, if not an occasion for ridicule. These new parties learned the hard way that public disenchantment with the traditional parties can cut both ways. Disillusionment can favour reformers with new opportunity and it can cast them down if popular yearnings outrace reformers' achievements.

It is equally true that third parties such as the NDM hurt themselves by creating the illusion that power could simply be picked up like a fallen fruit under a dying tree. This illusion was in woeful neglect of the fact that it was not so much the fruit of power that was to be seized but rather the dying society that had to be resuscitated. How to both renew a jaded and cynical society and still keep an eye on the attainment of power over the long haul was a challenge third parties seemed not to have mastered.

Civic Reform Movements

Against the background of this failure and collapse of reforming third parties and their ilk, it is remarkable that non-partisan civic organs that entered the political arena fared better. The relative effectiveness and subversive achievements of civic-oriented groups such as Citizens Action for Free and Fair Elections, and Jamaicans for Justice are well known.[41] These organizations were more effective in large part because they were not political parties. Thus Citizens Action for Free and Fair Elections earned public respect despite the parties' attempts to sabotage its effort and it helped clean up the more odious aspects of voting and electioneering in Jamaica. In their turn, Jamaicans for Justice championed the cause of victims of police violence and spoke out against the flagrant disregard for the basic rights of the accused.

This is not to say that human rights organizations such as Jamaicans for Justice had an easy time of it. For although the wider society sympathized with Jamaicans for Justice's challenge to what it called the state's "culture of impunity", public sentiment seemed to overwhelmingly favour the rights of the victims of criminal violence over the rights of the accused and the prerogatives of the security forces over the rights of their victims. Despite attempts to discredit their efforts, organizations such as Jamaicans for Justice are educating and alerting an insensitive government and society about their panicked embrace of a culture of vigilantism and summary police justice in the streets.

Universalism and Imperial Encroachment

This step forward for social justice cannot be denied. However, it should be remembered that this advance occurs within a global framework in which universalist ideas of human rights, social justice and reform are being articulated with imperial projects that seek continued domination of peripheral societies. Consequently, even as local groups struggle to achieve small victories against the now defensive Jamaican state, it is also true that external actors such as the United States, the World Bank, and the Organization of American States are interested in this project of democratization for their own ends. These pertain to restructuring socio-political relations in peripheral societies to facilitate the penetration of capital and promotion of the sway of political neo-liberalism as humanity's destiny.

Transferred to the periphery and embraced by states there, this political neo-liberalism may be regarded as a new form of imperial encroachment. Much like its kin, neo-liberal economics, political neo-liberalism exploits the contradictions of peripheralization that previous forms of global hegemony had produced in state-society relations abroad. Those contradictions produced predation politics in Jamaica. The complications it produced now threaten not just the accumulation of capital but also the very idea of a "society" – not to mention the erosion of state power and authority.

The encroachment of the diktat of political neo-liberalism, then, is the attempt to inaugurate a new hegemonic phase at both the world-level and at the level of local societies. This imperial project hopes to harness to its reform agenda the current movement of ideas for change in Jamaica and the vigour of popular resistance to predatory politics there. Consequently, clientelism, political violence, extra-judicial killings and the like are to be done away with in favour of "democracy". Such a hegemonic scheme hopes to arrest the movement of ideas and the mounting protests against liberalism's rule in Jamaica by expanding its range and enhancing the "rule of law", governmental accountability and so on.

We are witnessing the transition to this renovated order with all its promises and risks. Insofar as these adjustments bring about meaningful changes that hamper state terror and eliminate flagrant abuse of power, they are an improvement. However, because political neo-liberalism's organizational rationality is informed by a technocratic impulse and has a politically arresting logic that throttles transformative change, reformers should be alert to these limitations and should push beyond them.

Modernity, Power and Social Ontology

The conundrum facing Black Atlantic societies such as the Caribbean has been how to understand their relationship to capitalist civilization, to modernity and also how to address these issues in order to achieve an emancipated existence. In the Caribbean, and in Jamaica in particular, several projects since 1938 offered answers to this puzzle by way of a succession of reforms. One of these – political independence – according to recent polls was judged by a majority of Jamaicans to be worse than living under colonial rule.[42]

No matter the bruised sensibility that led to this indictment and the quarrels it unleashed, the truth is that the creole nationalist project of 1938 has exhausted itself. This project evolved through three phases.

The first and critical phase from 1938 to 1969 saw a reform agenda of liquidating colonial rule, achieving sovereignty and inaugurating national development. Despite important improvements, this phase collapsed. It broke up because it was embedded in Euro-American racist notions of cultural difference, it was grounded in liberalism's arrested understanding of democratic rule and it was wedded to catch-up models of developmental economics.

Enlightenment ideas of "progress" and "civilization" buttressed these weaknesses. The moral summoning of the Jamaican people in this first phase depended on articulating a relationship to modernity that made Afro-Jamaicans into backward peoples who were to be led to "civilization" by its bearers, the brown middle class. The ontological expression of power in this first phase was experienced by Afro-Jamaicans mostly as a devouring system of class and racial oppression.

The second phase began in 1970 and lasted through 1989. This was a turbulent juncture with huge upheavals, great gains and sharp reversals. By any standard this was a period of the greatest social upheaval and transformation in modern Jamaica. The reforms that unfolded in this period swung between empowerment for the Afro-Jamaican majority under the rubric of democratic socialism between 1974 and 1980, and attempts by the JLP and the PNP between 1980 and 1989 to demobilize the popular classes by means of state terror, neo-liberalism and ideological pragmatism. Reform in the 1980s meant restoration of capitalist market relations to pre-eminence and withdrawal of the state from its traditional welfarist functions and ideological connections with society.

In the years 1980 to 1989 the increasingly rebellious population was hailed as criminal and barbaric and in need of harsh discipline. At the same time, the not-yet-defecting middle and working classes were summoned as New World Moderns and urged to draw on their cultural capital and positive cultural sensibilities to help lift the society out of its crisis. In these years, progress meant satisfying externally imposed neo-liberal economic expectations and bringing a violent society back to normal through law and order and the restoration of civility as a lost cultural ideal. However, the alienated Afro-Jamaican poor experienced this period as brutally exterminist, while the better-off classes saw the period as a thoroughgoing decay of politics and culture.

Neither the democratic socialist agenda nor a revivification of capitalist market relations after 1980 could surmount the growing crisis. Indeed, between 1980 and 1989 the social crisis worsened as traditional authorities and already weakened institutions were unable to cope with an orgy of violence and the shock of sustained challenge from the rebellious poor.

The third phase – from 1989 to the present – is the one described in this epilogue. Its reform agenda echoes concerns of earlier phases but with accents on certain themes. Thus civility, law and order, and economic neoliberalism are emphasized along with ideas of democratization.

This phase is experienced as an all-compelling crisis of transition. Here state agents see modernity and capitalist civilization less as panaceas than as interlocutors of the Jamaican population's commitment to progress and development. If the state's discourse is to be believed, hitching to the neoliberal economic bandwagon and returning to civility and civism are the only means to realize these purposes.

It should be clear from the foregoing that manners and morals are recurring themes in Jamaican politics and they continue to inform reform agendas. Public lamentations concerning the population's moral failings combine with bracing accounts of Jamaicans' moral potential – raging from their tradition of civism to the benefits of their cosmopolitanism. But underlying this concern for morals and their relationship to political futures is the idea that social progress has become impossible because of a lack of civility on the part of the rebelling Afro-Jamaicans. In the discourse of the state and in the language of reformers, incivility has largely arrested the march of progress in Jamaica.

Unfortunately, casting the issues in this way has created confusion, not the least because notions of progress and civility are themselves contested. Moreover, these twin concepts are too much bound up with the still appealing European enlightenment project and the systems of thought and structures of power it has wrought. It is arguable that "civility" and the "civilized" are concepts so integral to the cultural logic of capitalist modernity, with its stress on hierarchical racial difference, that they should be jettisoned.

Uncivil otherness and the flight from civility in Jamaica today are perfectly fitting in a context where discourses on civility have been used much like truncheons to beat defiant Afro-Jamaicans into cultural submission. Again, it is arguable that civility's political rule has been experienced by Afro-Jamaicans not as a means to their full moral incorporation into the people-nation, but rather as an instance of devouring violence and cultural dismemberment.

In sum, the notions of "civility" and the "civilized" have been too much linked to anti-black racism and to ideas of African primitivism, African primordialism and African cultural atavism. Briefly, the problematic of civility is ontologically biased and its application in Jamaican state politics has barred Afro-Jamaican unity, fragmented the group's identity and brutalized its members.

The creole nationalist project of 1938–69, the democratic socialist agenda of 1974–80, the hard-line 1974–90 Workers' Liberation League/WPJ bid for power and the current episode of political neo-liberalism have all expressed stronger or weaker versions of this notion of what it means to be modern and civilized. In all of them we find a politically noxious claim and an organizational rationality that deny Caribbean Africanism its gainful expressive life in the organization of political power.

Implicitly or explicitly, every one of these social projects has taken up this issue of how to relate Caribbean Africanisms to the exercise of power. Where such projects have not suppressed this life-world in favour of Europeanist ontology, they have pandered to Caribbean Africanisms in the most vulgar ways. The effect has not been the positive incorporation of Afro-Jamaican expressive life to lift the spirit of the people and to give power its liberating ethno-national reference point. Instead, predatory power in Jamaica has pandered to cheapened versions of this sensibility and has engaged in a corrupted incorporation of aspects of this expressive life.

The Caribbean has experienced the ontology of European colonial power. Here as elsewhere, a noxious variant of white European ethnic consciousness was given expressive life in supremacist state policies and in racist social relations. Under colonial rule, power unabashedly displayed its ethnonational ontological life based on notions of cultural differences between Africans and Europeans. Because anti-colonial nationalists in the Caribbean recognized the white supremacist basis of colonial state power and challenged it by promising to displace that power's expressive life, the nationalist movement won broad mass support. Yet in the eyes of alienated

Afro-Jamaicans today, that nationalist reform in the name of political sovereignty is regarded as a continuation of the diktat of colonial rule.

Given this perception of cultural and political betrayal, it should be clear that the Jamaican crisis is not really about the lack of civility or disrespect for the rule of law. Rather, it is about abuse of political power and the absence in it of a culturally resonant Afro-Jamaican expressive life that has not been shamelessly manipulated and corrupted. Alienated Afro-Jamaicans' flouting of law is therefore not disrespect for law as such. Rather, it is defiance of liberalism's rule in Jamaica – predation politics – in a class and racially divided peripheral society.

If this is the case, then currently fashionable proposals for a hygienic suspension of the rights of criminal suspects and for harsh policing of criminals in poor communities are likely to fail. That is because such proposals assume that a clinical separation can be made in practice between applying punitive law to criminal suspects in poor communities, while also respecting the rights of innocent but hostile populations with powerful memories of racial abuse in these same communities. In the highly inflamed conditions in the inner cities today and in the wider society more generally, applying harsh policing to the hostile and criminally involved perpetrator, while sparing his neighbour, the hostile but innocent poor, seems most unlikely.

Conclusion

A rebellious counter-society in Jamaica has dramatically raised questions about the expressive life of liberalism's rule there. As I have argued above, the ontology of that power is manifest in Jamaica's predation politics. Challengers to this power have made it clear, however, that they reject the state, its institutions and its laws.

In particular, protesters have rejected claims on their moral conduct by resorting to cultural inversions. These resistances to conventional manners and morals subvert political power and mock the state's ability to define the proper conduct of its subjects. By challenging predatory power in uncivil ways, members of this counter-society have, in effect, attacked liberalism's weak link in Jamaica: its insistence on Afro-Jamaican cultural and political subordination on pain of social dishonour and punitive violence.

Will social theory and those searching for new knowledge recognize the significance of the popular refusal of modernity's progress and liberalism's rule by means of predation politics? Thus far it appears that social theory and critical intellectuals in the Caribbean are still offering renovated versions of liberalism's political rule and reformed versions of its expressive life.

In the difficult passage to social renewal and reconstruction, reformers should not be repeating the old, nationalist, middle-class discourse of extractive and sacrificial nation-building based on outworn narratives of modernity. That story of humanity's grand march to a universal, ethnically co-equal, democratic destiny under capitalist rule is no longer credible or compelling for most Afro-Jamaicans.

The current crisis therefore indicates a need for theoretical renewal as much as for social renewal. That renewal of social theory will depend on contributions from intellectuals, but only in a dialogical relationship with the contributions of contemporary social movements.

In the politics of these movements, there are critiques of modernity and criticisms of liberalism's idea of progress. The same is true for this anti-systemic movement's capacity for suggesting alternative ways of living. The popular movement possesses immanent and positive ideas about power, forms of social organization and moral values. These alternatives derive from the lived experience of Afro-Jamaicans that reflects their values and their solutions to the challenges of everyday life.

Suggestions for renewal drawn from this lived experience are too many to list here, but they include the Rastafarian notion of "social living" and that group's communitarian, democratic idea of "reasoning" and "grounding" as means of solving problems.[43] What this implies is not modernity's fearful notion of a mystical and atavistic return to barbarism involving the smoking of marijuana around a backwoods fire, but rather the organization of democratic problem-solving at the community level.

Embedded in the notion of "grounding", therefore, is the wholly unremarkable idea of community self-organization and democratic discussion. In practice, this might mean nothing more threatening than the creation of community-based councils that act as deliberative bodies and forums for resolving problems.

Likewise, the "partner" system of lending among the Jamaican poor that has been regarded as a stubborn throwback to the past ought to be seen for what it is – a creative expression of Afro-Jamaican community economics. As with the previous example, the Afro-Jamaican "traditional" partner system is nothing more ominous than today's modern micro-credit system that is now all the rage in development programmes for peripheral societies.

Finally, as Brian Meeks, the Jamaican political scientist, has suggested, the insistence in Afro-Jamaican popular culture that "each one [should] teach one" ought not be regarded as a chant merely for initiates of a religious cult. On the contrary, this dictum should also be recognized for what it is – the affirmation of that elusive civism and volunteerism whose alleged absence a heedless middle class now bemoans.

These sketches of Caribbean Africanisms as they relate to politics and society highlight the current disconnection between the identity of power in Jamaica and the expressive life of Afro-Jamaicans. In thralldom to limiting notions of modernity and progress, political power in Jamaica has thus far resisted the incorporation of Caribbean Africanisms in ways that are not vulgar and corrupted.

Critical intellectuals would do well to repair this breach by learning from popular movements and by displacing narratives of modernity with new concepts and problematics that are informed by the contributions of Caribbean Africanisms. In doing so, critical intellectuals will air liberalism's ontological silences and maybe discover how to incorporate now fugitive Caribbean Africanisms into relations of power in positive ways that reinvent power's expressive life in Caribbean societies.

Notes

Chapter 1

1. See, for example, Göran Hydén, *Beyond Ujamaa in Tanzania: Underdevelopment and an Uncaptured Peasantry* (London: Heinemann, 1980); James Scott, *Weapons of the Weak* (New Haven: Yale University Press, 1985); and Victor Azarya and Naomi Chazan, "Disengagement from the State in Africa", *Comparative Studies in Society and History* 29, no. 1 (1987): 1.
2. These symbolic forms of protest are emphasized in James C. Scott, *Domination and the Arts of Resistance* (New Haven: Yale University Press, 1990).
3. For a commentary on these matters pertaining to the Caribbean and Africa respectively, see Carolyn Cooper, *Noises in the Blood: Orality, Gender, and the "Vulgar" Body of Jamaican Popular Culture* (New York: Heinemann, 1994); and Jean-Francois Bayart, *The State in Africa: The Politics of the Belly* (New York: Longman, 1993).
4. See Eric Hobsbawm, *Bandits* (New York: Pantheon Books, 1981).
5. See, for example, Donald Crummey, ed., *Banditry, Rebellion and Social Protest in Africa* (London: Heinemann, 1986).
6. For a sharp critique of outlawry as a form of social protest, see Samir Amin, "Social Movements at the Periphery", in Ponna Wignaraja, ed., *New Social Movements in the South: Empowering the People* (Atlantic Highlands, N.J.: Zed Books, 1993).
7. See, for example, Robin D.G. Kelly, *Race Rebels: Culture, Politics, and the Black Working Class* (New York: The Free Press, 1994); and Achille Mbembe, *On the Post-Colony* (Berkeley: University of California Press, 2001).
8. For an excellent study of African politics that makes this point, see Robert Fatton Jr., *Predatory Rule* (Boulder: Lynne Rienner, 1992).
9. Carl Stone, *Class, State, and Democracy in Jamaica* (New York: Praeger, 1986).
10. Ibid., 189.
11. Ibid., 194.

12. Stone's political journalism in the *Daily Gleaner* – the island's largest news-paper – typically called attention to the violent and undemocratic character of the Jamaican state.

13. For a list of the emoluments and multi-million dollar salaries paid to some of these executives, see the *Jamaica Observer,* 13 October 1999, http://www.jamaicaobserver.com/.

14. Widespread public outcry against allegations of official corruption resulted in the passage of anti-corruption legislation in October 1999.

15. In the 1990s, for example, JLP leader Edward Seaga – long known for his defence of political gunmen as community leaders in his constituency – found it necessary to give the commissioner of police the names of eight men from the Tivoli Gardens enclave in West Kingston who had challenged his leadership. Evidently recognizing the irony in this situation, and citing a lack of evidence of criminal acts, the police commissioner declined to arrest the men.

16. In trying to enforce the norm of reciprocity on the state, the militant poor have often forced it to disgorge its benefits to them. Detractors of the poor have often used the epithet "freeness" to describe these handouts to the poor.

17. For a compelling account of this unravelling of political authority, see Brian Meeks, *Radical Caribbean: From Black Power to Abu Bakr* (Kingston: University of the West Indies Press, 1996), especially chapter 8.

18. The growing authority of ghetto-based patrons who also act as lawgivers in the slums – the so-called inner-city dons – is a stunning realization of this power.

19. Political supporters in the inner cities are so zealous in defending their party, and affirming their partisan identities above all else, that they do resemble communally minded groups. Hence the shibboleth "political tribalism" to describe party rivalry in Jamaica.

20. Carl Stone, "Community Councils", *Daily Gleaner,* 6 December 1978, 10.

21. For a recent study on the political significance of the Rastafarians, see Barry Chevannes, *Rastafari Roots and Ideology* (Syracuse: Syracuse University Press, 1994).

22. For example, as late as June 2001, the president of the Jamaica Exporters' Association was decrying the growing importance of outlaw patrons in the inner city: "The vast majority of people who live in our decaying urban areas couldn't care less about private sector leadership and our struggles to build a productive sector and develop an export led economy." As the president of the Jamaica Exporters' Association aptly confirmed, "They do care, however, whether the 'don' lives or dies, and they do care whether he is able to fulfil his obligations to lead and protect them." Cited in the *Jamaica Gleaner,* 19 June 2001, http://www.jamaica-gleaner.com/.

Chapter 2

1. For a review of the 1938 revolt and its political consequences, see Ken Post, *Arise Ye Starvelings: The Jamaica Labour Rebellion of 1938 and Its Aftermath* (The Hague: Martinus Nijoff, 1978).
2. Ibid., chap. 11.
3. These judgements concerning Bustamante's personality are based on Ken Post's meticulous research on the labour leader's role in Jamaican politics. See Post's *Arise Ye Starvelings*.
4. For an assessment of the ideological temperament of both leaders, see George Eaton, *Alexander Bustamante and Modern Jamaica* (Kingston: Kingston Publishers, 1975), 131–33.
5. Ibid., 90.
6. This description of changes in Kingston relies on Ken Post's valuable work on the period. See Post, *Arise Ye Starvelings*, 131–34.
7. Eaton, *Alexander Bustamante and Modern Jamaica*, 123.
8. Public works projects such as repairs to the often flooded Sandy Gully were among the earliest programmes converted to unabashed political patronage by Bustamante and the JLP.
9. Eaton, *Alexander Bustamante and Modern Jamaica*, 115.
10. Ibid.
11. Ibid., chap. 5.
12. Ibid., 118.
13. Accompanying Bustamante in the assault on the hospital was a determined enforcer, known for his fearsome and violent partisanship. Nicknamed "Black Saturday" for his violent partisanship at the hospital, this political fighter would be remembered in the legend of partisan enforcers as one of the earliest political badmen spawned by this violent partisanship. Interview with Arnold Bertram, interview by author, Kingston, Jamaica, August 1996.
14. Eaton, *Alexander Bustamante and Modern Jamaica*, 118–20.
15. Ibid., 139–40.
16. Bertram, interview.
17. Eaton, *Alexander Bustamante and Modern Jamaica*, 125, 129–30.
18. It is noteworthy that PNP historian Arnold Bertram and JLP historian George Eaton both agree on the significance of the PNP's counter-violence with regard to the outcome.
19. For a former resident's account of life in West Kingston in the 1940s and 1950s, see the *Sunday Gleaner, Outlook Magazine*, 19 November 1978, 2.
20. Recalling the condition of port workers of the day, one aging Kingston resident noted that although the port workers were the best paid of the Negro

residents in the area, their miserable clothing testified to their woeful circumstances: "We used to call them 'Joseph Coat of Many Colours', because
they walked barefoot [*sic*] and wore patched clothing with many colours."
Ibid.

21. Ibid.
22. For a discussion of Bustamante's attitude toward the Rastafarians, see
   Chevannes, *Rastafari Roots and Ideology*, 148–51.
23. Eaton, *Alexander Bustamante and Modern Jamaica*, 122.
24. Ibid., 120. Bustamante was eventually tried and acquitted of the charges in
   June 1946.
25. This Bustamante bravado and seeming recklessness in brandishing guns is
   documented by Eaton, *Alexander Bustamante and Modern Jamaica*, 54, 121,
   137. For yet another Bustamante gun-toting incident, see Chevannes,
   Rastafari Roots and Ideology, 150–51.
26. Eaton, *Alexander Bustamante and Modern Jamaica*, 263n17.
27. The crusading journalist and PNP partisan John Maxwell would recall that
   this JLP victimization of PNP supplicants provoked the latter to sing the following ditty about the JLP, in protest against its abuses in the early 1950s:
   "Gully govament, ah wha me do yu? Workhouse govament, ah wha me do
   yu? Old clothes govament, ah wha me do you?" This latter reference to clothing derided the JLP for its meagre aid to the poor, a system that depended on
   charity in the form of second-hand clothing sent from the United States. John
   Maxwell, interview by author, Kingston, Jamaica, August 1996.
28. Both political parties had to respond to the growth of urban Rastafarianism.
   Chevannes reveals the complicated and divergent responses this exilic movement elicited from labour leaders in the PNP and JLP. See Chevannes,
   Rastafari Roots and Ideology, 145–52.
29. One noteworthy instance of banditry involved the case of the heroic and
   feared criminal of the late 1940s, Vincent "Ivanhoe" Martin, alias Rhygin.
   His story of defiance and heroic banditry is compellingly depicted in both
   the book and the film *The Harder They Come*.
30. A religious revivalist from that period recalled Seaga as "a very courteous
   man, well mannered and kind, I accepted him. The following Sunday we
   were having a 'duty' . . . and I invited him. He came with a camera, climbed
   a housetop, took pictures and taped the whole meeting. From then he used
   to visit the tables regularly." *Sunday Gleaner, Outlook Magazine,* 19
   November 1978, 2.
31. Cited in the *Daily Gleaner, Festival Supplement,* 3 August 1988, 5.
32. Chevannes, *Rastafari Roots and Ideology*, 11–33.
33. One revivalist of the day recalled years later that, "when I first met him, I
   really didn't like white men. But I had to accept him as a practical man,

especially after he became a member of parliament." *Sunday Gleaner, Outlook Magazine,* 19 November 1978, 2.

34. The less fortunate among these revellers, who were called "ragga ragga people" and "Jagabats", typically went barefooted to these dance halls. See Tony Laing, *Daily Observer,* 20 March 1996, 9.

35. For a good discussion of the development of this music culture and industry, see Timothy White, *Catch a Fire: The Life of Bob Marley* (New York: Holt, Rinehart and Winston, 1984).

36. Ibid., 150.

37. For a review of these developments in the 1960s, see Obika Gray, *Radicalism and Social Change in Jamaica, 1960–1972* (Knoxville: University of Tennessee Press, 1991).

38. Surprisingly, much of this criticism came from disillusioned younger PNP members and their radical sympathizers outside the party.

39. For a discussion of the disputed Federation, see Eaton, *Alexander Bustamante and Modern Jamaica,* 169–95.

40. Ibid., 188–89.

41. Maxwell, interview; and Eaton, *Alexander Bustamante and Modern Jamaica,* 188–92.

42. For Thompson's account of his years in East Africa, see his *From Kingston to Kenya: The Making of a Pan-Africanist Lawyer* (Dover, Mass.: Majority Press, 1993).

43. As late as the 1961 Referendum, a nattily dressed Thompson could still be seen at political rallies in the blazing heat wearing Oxford loafers, sporting a stylish imported long-sleeved shirt and dressed in warm, pleated trousers. For comments on Thompson's African-inspired dress in 1962, see Carl Stone, *Daily Gleaner,* 2 September 1987, 8.

44. *Daily Gleaner, Festival Supplement,* 3 August 1988, 5.

45. Obeah, a feared folk practice, employs sorcery and cultic rites designed to bring harm to others.

46. Other candidates in this election who emphasized racial issues included the Rastafarian Sam Brown and Millard Johnson of the neo-Garveyite People's Political Party. Despite their appeal to cultural sensibilities of the poor, these working-class contenders were no match for the PNP and the JLP with their patronage and hegemonic grip on the electorate.

47. For observations on Tavares's pioneering role in using gunmen to protect his constituency, see Carl Stone, *Daily Gleaner,* 14 March 1990, 6.

48. Bertram, interview.

49. For a review of voting patterns in West Kingston, Seaga's tactics in the elections and the role of race in this contest, see Carl Stone, *Daily Gleaner,* 2 September 1987, 8.

Chapter 3

1. For details on these outbursts in the slums, see Gray, *Radicalism and Social Change,* chaps. 3–4.
2. For an account of the founding of these organizations, see Easton, *Alexander Bustamante and Modern Jamaica.*
3. For a discussion of the early post-war social experiences of rural migrants to the city of Kingston, see Chevannes, *Rastafari Roots and Ideology,* 57–77.
4. Although the parties and trade unions did cast a wide net, others opposed to these organizations also organized slum-dwellers. Poor residents did find a militant advocate in the Unemployed Workers Council, an organization that was led by one of their own. For a discussion of the politics of the Unemployed Workers Council, see Gray, *Radicalism and Social Change,* 67–69.
5. For a discussion of the Jamaican elites' struggle to establish their moral leadership and of the opposition to it among the urban poor, see Rex Nettleford, *Mirror Mirror* (Kingston: Collins and Sangster, 1970).
6. See Post, *Arise Ye Starvelings.*
7. For Post's elaboration on this claim, see his *Strike the Iron,* vol. 1 (Atlantic Highlands, N.J.: Humanities Press, 1981).
8. Post, *Strike the Iron,* 1: 190.
9. Cited in Post, *Arise Ye Starvelings,* 95–96. Emphasis in the original.
10. For a discussion of this prejudice in the North American context, and of efforts to correct it within the US Left, see Anthony Bogues, *Caliban's Freedom: The Early Political Thought of C.L.R. James* (London: Pluto Press, 1997), chap. 5.
11. Commenting on the Jamaican Left's difficulties with the black struggle, Post would observe: "The Communists never were able to find a suitable theoretical formula by which they could link the racial and class struggles." *Arise Ye Starvelings,* 96.
12. With respect to the nexus of race and political nationalism in the consciousness of the middle strata, it is worth remembering that the group did exhibit a racial sensibility. However, it expressed itself not in terms of a self-conscious cultural nationalism based on awareness of civilizational differences between the colonizers and the colonized. Rather, the brown-skinned and coloured middle strata came to race consciousness by way of their resentment of whites and ethnic minorities who held coveted positions in the polity and the economy. For a discussion of these matters, see Ken Post, *Strike the Iron,* vol. 2 (Atlantic Highlands, N.J.: Humanities Press, 1981), 430.
13. Millard Johnson, a black lawyer and champion of Marcus Garvey's ideas of racial uplift, founded the People's Political Party in 1961.

14. The People's Political Party's racial appeal was sufficiently threatening to this elite that it caused Vernon Arnett, the PNP minister of finance, to warn his party: "It is clear that it would be unsafe to treat the Millard Johnson movement lightly. He is succeeding in holding interest and he is known to be a determined and persistent person." Cited in Gray, *Radicalism and Social Change*, 60.

15. Cited in the *Daily Gleaner*, 25 October 1960.

16. From a July 1959 pamphlet distributed by Claudius Henry. Cited in the *Daily Gleaner's* account of Henry's trial for treason. 11 October 1960, 5.

17. Cited in Gray, *Radicalism and Social Change*, 50.

18. Frustrated by having to turn away hundreds of supporters he had summoned to Kingston for an exodus to Africa, Henry blamed Prime Minister Norman Manley for not providing monies he allegedly had promised for the repatriation of blacks to Africa. This thwarting reportedly caused Henry to fulminate that if his supporters did "not get to leave Jamaica back to Africa, they should take off his [Manley's] head and kick it up Rosalie Avenue like [a] football". Cited in Gray, *Radicalism and Social Change*, 50–51.

19. *Daily Gleaner*, 7 April 1960.

20. Cited in Gray, *Radicalism and Social Change*, 56.

21. *Daily Gleaner*, 19 October 1960.

22. Foremost among them were lower-middle-class blacks who aspired to jobs as bank tellers, salespersons, secretaries and clerks. They were embittered by what they perceived as exclusion from banking, tourism and sales jobs on the basis of colour. This racially informed grievance targeted Chinese nationals. They were seen as a racially favoured group that held coveted positions desired by upwardly mobile lower-class blacks.

23. For example, speaking for Chinese retailers who had become targets of xenophobic racial anger among the black lower middle class, one letter writer averred, "all I can now say is, be careful all of you who are teaching race-hatred, lest the present situation in Alabama does not develop here in years to come but with the Chinese and white Jamaicans being victimized. . . . This whole concept now held by many Afro-Jamaicans that Jamaica is a Black Man's Country and Black Man Must Rule no matter what, even if the country is probably ruined in the process, is all wrong and makes a complete mockery of our motto." Cited in Gray, *Radicalism and Social Change*, 84.

24. In national elections between 1944 and 1962, West Kingston voters gave the winning margin in this constituency to each of the parties in the following manner: 1944, JLP; 1949, PNP; 1955, JLP; 1959 PNP; 1962, JLP.

25. They included the Jamaica Federation of Trade Unions and the Unemployed Workers Council, founded in 1953 and 1962 respectively.

According to Richard Hart, one of the founders of the Jamaica Federation of Trade Unions, that organization was "nothing more than a committee. It only got one union off the ground – the Sugar and Agricultural Workers' Union which was, for a while, quite successful at [the] Appleton [Sugar Estate] and in West Hanover." Cited in Trevor Munroe, *Jamaican Politics: A Marxist Perspective in Transition* (Kingston: Heinemann Caribbean, 1990), 141.

26. People's Freedom Movement candidates contested the 1955 general elections and the 1956 parish council elections in the parishes of Clarendon and Kingston. Except for a victory in the Clarendon sugar belt in the Parish Council vote, the few candidates put forward by the People's Freedom Movement in these elections were soundly defeated at the polls. See Munroe, *Jamaican Politics,* 150–51.

27. In August 1965, unemployed West Kingston residents stoned and set ablaze Chinese-owned establishments in a fury over allegations that an employer had beaten a female sales clerk in a job-related dispute.

28. Hal Draper, *Karl Marx's Theory of Revolution,* volume 2, *The Politics of Social Classes* (New York: Monthly Review Press, 1978), 478.

29. Scott, *Domination and the Arts of Resistance.*

30. Frantz Fanon, *The Wretched of the Earth* (New York: Grove Press, 1966).

31. Ibid., 103.

32. Here Fanon concurred with Marx by noting that "colonialism will also find in the lumpen-proletariat a considerable space for maneuvering. For this reason any movement for freedom ought to give its fullest attention to this lumpen-proletariat." Ibid., 109.

33. Scott, *Arts of Resistance,* 136.

34. Among these were self-helping predators primarily concerned with the satisfaction of their own needs, but at the expense of the state's largesse and without deference to political elites; social bandits laying waste to life and property, but also meeting social patronage obligations to their communities; and paid political enforcers that killed their kin in partisan wars, while retaining the anti-system cultural armoury of the poor.

35. It is precisely this heightened awareness of the costs of this engagement that caused the urban poor in Jamaica to describe their circumstances as subjection to "politricks".

36. Widespread rowdyism in Kingston among unemployed urban youth typified this lawlessness in 1964, provoking a call from civic leaders to stamp out this "hooliganism". Still, as Percival Gibson, the Anglican bishop, reminded the leaders, misbehaviour among the young suggested something far more ominous. "The real problem in Jamaica so far as hooliganism is concerned, is not just a question of a few hundreds of youngsters here and there who disturb the public weal and are a nuisance to the community, but it is that people of

all ages, particularly between the ages of 15 and 22 . . . come under no influence whatever either of Church or state." Cited in Gray, *Radicalism and Social Change,* 117.

37. For a discussion of the role of the Youth Development Agency – a department within Seaga's portfolio in 1963 – in distributing benefits to the youths of West Kingston in exchange for JLP political affiliation, see Barry Chevannes, "The Rastafari and the Urban Youth", in *Perspectives on Jamaica in the 1970s,* ed. Carl Stone and Aggrey Brown (Kingston: Jamaica Publishing House, 1981), 392–422.

38. William Strong, a leading columnist for the *Daily Gleaner,* disclosed the anxieties of civic leaders and the political elite. Responding to growing race consciousness and assertions of black nationalism among the urban poor, Strong gave this blunt retort to lower-class claims on the nation's identity: "Jamaicanism is not a colour . . . or a fiercely aggressive attitude towards people who are not black. Jamaicanism is a state of mind, based on a sense of civic responsibility, on good manners, on respect for all others who inhabit our island . . . Jamaicanism is not 'black man time'. Jamaicanism is raceless . . . Jamaicanism is realization and acceptance of the fact that Jamaica is neither a black nor a white nor a pink country, but a country in which all men may dwell together in unity and good fellowship." *Daily Gleaner,* 10 October 1963, 8.

39. Cited in Gray, *Radicalism and Social Change,* 61.

40. *Daily Gleaner,* 19 April 1961.

41. As Barry Chevannes notes, by 1963 the incumbent JLP was using its largesse to create "programmes aimed especially at organizing the youths" of West Kingston. See Chevannes, "The Rastafari and the Urban Youth".

42. *Daily Gleaner, Festival Supplement,* 3 August 1988, 6.

43. Aside from Seaga's cultural reforms at the state level, both parties competed at the constituency level to show their support for working-class leisure pursuits such as soccer, cricket and music.

44. Maxwell, interview.

45. For an authoritative account of this phenomenon in the Jamaica bauxite industry and the violence it provoked, see Michael Manley, *A Voice at the Workplace* (London: André Deutsch, 1975) 143–50.

46. The irrepressible Unemployed Workers Council led the grassroots opposition to the eviction of these slum-dwellers.

47. Unemployed Workers Council pamphlet, "The Right to Work", 28 November 1963. Ben Monroe's personal files, Kingston, Jamaica.

48. Maxwell, interview.

49. See Gray, *Radicalism and Social Change,* 254n16.

50. For a discussion of the formation of these early gangs, see Chevannes, "The Rastafari and the Urban Youth", 392–96.
51. Ibid.
52. Ibid.
53. Ibid., 394.
54. As the electoral competition for West Kingston between 1944 and 1962 shows, no political party was able to score consecutive electoral victories in the constituency. This failing would end once and for all with the JLP's 1967 electoral triumph from which it never looked back.
55. "Churchill", interview by author, May 1994. "Churchill" was a former JLP loyalist of the 1960s.
56. This much is suggested by Chevannes's previously cited research on the early political gangs in Kingston.
57. For the JLP's use of political largesse in the early 1960s, see Chevannes, "The Rastafari and the Urban Youth", 394.
58. Seaga, it will be recalled, had a close familiarity with the Salt Lane community from his years as an ethnographer and politician.
59. For a revealing journalistic account of the early political gangs, see Laurie Gunst, *Born Fi' Dead: A Journey through the Jamaican Posse Underworld* (New York: Henry Holt, 1995).
60. See Chevannes, "The Rastafari and the Urban Youth", 395.
61. Thus fleeing Kingston Pen squatters typically ran to the nearby Riverton City slums in West Kingston.
62. In the volatile and underdeveloped economies of Third World countries such as Jamaica, where employment for the unskilled is uncertain and irregular, those agents in the very low-wage ranks of the urban working class are often part of the lumpenproletariat. This is precisely because of their meagre wages and unpredictable employment. Moreover, including the lowest earners from the ranks of the urban working class as part of the lumpenproletariat captures the potential for political overlap between both groups. In addition to capturing the flexible, often-shifting economic status of both groups, this demarcation is also sensitive to the ideological affinities between them. That is, because of their economic status and problematic social relations with better-off groups, both low-wage urban workers and the lumpenproletariat have evinced a marked antagonism and hostility toward the dominant classes in Jamaica.
63. Upheavals in the turbulent 1960s occurred overwhelmingly in urban centres and especially in the capital city.
64. This creative transmutation of cricket into personal and sociologically significant acts by West Indian sportsmen is marvellously reviewed by C.L.R.

James. See his *Beyond a Boundary* (London: Hutchinson Publishers, 1963), especially chap. 4.

65. This was certainly the case for disaffected intellectuals at the University of the West Indies in Kingston, who grew increasingly sympathetic to the claims of the urban poor.

66. See M.G. Smith et al., *The Rastafari Movement in Kingston, Jamaica* (Kingston: Institute of Social and Economic Research, University of the West Indies, 1960).

67. The cultural upheaval in the 1960s provoked undergraduates at the university to march in support of Walter Rodney, a Guyanese historian at the university, who was declared persona non grata by the Jamaican government in October 1968 because of his views on Black Power and his open association with the Rastafarians.

68. The ideological impact of this social power was noticeable among minority sections of the middle class whose offspring now turned against their parents' values and began to adopt the Afro hairstyle and other trappings of the unfolding black consciousness movement in Jamaica.

69. Disaffected groups, and especially the young, increasingly took up these locutions of Rastafarian origin.

70. The rude boy phenomenon was also notable for its sexist verbal harassment of young women in their communities. For a discussion of this development, see Maureen Rowe, "Gender and Family Relations in Rastafari: A Personal Perspective", in *Chanting Down Babylon: A Rastafari Reader,* ed. Nathaniel Samuel Murrell et al. (Kingston: Ian Randle Publishers, 1998), 72–88.

71. This was most notable, for example, in the *Abeng* newspaper movement led by academics and other dissidents in the late 1960s.

72. For a detailed discussion of these matters, see Gray, *Radicalism and Social Change,* chap. 10.

Chapter 4

1. The Rastafarians, for example, emerged and evolved as a group largely outside the orbit of party politics. For a recent account of the group's development in Jamaica, see Chevannes, *Rastafari Roots and Ideology.*

2. Ibid., chap. 1.

3. For a discussion of Marcus Garvey's role in intensifying this sensibility, see Rupert Lewis and Patrick Bryan, eds., *Garvey: His Work and Impact* (Kingston: Institute of Social and Economic Research, University of the West Indies, 1988).

4. For the classic statement of this idea, see Edward Kamau Brathwaite, *History of the Voice: The Development of Nation Language in Anglophone Caribbean Poetry* (London and Port of Spain: New Beacon, 1984). For a restatement of this thesis in the context of Jamaican popular culture in the 1980s, see also Cooper, *Noises in the Blood.*

5. For the application of this idea to the game of cricket, see C.L.R. James, *Beyond a Boundary.*

6. Afro-Jamaicans' awareness of this immanent freedom is best represented by the popular expression "man free". Don Robotham makes exactly this point in his "Freedom Ossified or Economic Crisis? A Comment on Holger Henke", *Identities: Global Studies in Culture and Power* 8, no. 3 (September 2001): 451–66.

7. For a discussion of the social and cultural aspects of this condition in this period, see Erna Brodber, "Socio-cultural Change in Jamaica", in *Jamaica in Independence: Essays on the Early Years,* ed. Rex Nettleford (Kingston: Heinemann Caribbean, 1989), 55–74.

8. For an extended discussion of exilic space and its function under conditions of domination, see Scott, *Domination and the Art of Resistance,* especially chap. 5. For a brief review of the same phenomenon in Caribbean life, see Rex Nettleford, *Inward Stretch, Outward Reach* (London: Macmillan, 1993), 80–90.

9. Lower-income groups saw significant upgrading of their shelter as successive governments built modern dwellings for the poor. For a discussion of these and other post-war social improvements, see Carl Stone, "Power, Policy and Politics in Independent Jamaica", in *Jamaica in Independence: Essays on the Early Years,* ed. Rex Nettleford (Kingston: Heinemann Caribbean, 1989). 19–53.

10. Middle-class dissenters also encountered repressive legislation in the early postcolonial years. However, unlike the poor who were sentenced to long prison terms and even whippings in jail for their infractions, the middle class and political dissenters among them were treated less harshly. For instance, in the early 1960s, middle-class radicals encountered only travel bans and the censorship of socialist and black nationalist literature. For a discussion of repressive legislation to curb black nationalist and communist activity in this period, see Gray, *Radicalism and Social Change,* chap. 3.

11. For a discussion of Jamaican law-making, see Lloyd Barnett, *The Constitutional Law of Jamaica* (London: Oxford University Press, 1977).

12. As middlemen, these political hirelings disbursed jobs, favours and benefits to the supplicant poor.

13. The striving, iconic popular reggae singer best captures this contradictory sensibility of affirming an overweening individualism in the quest for recognition as well as a caustic rejection of dominant moral values.

14. For a brief review of this phenomenon and its gender implications, see Rowe, "Gender and Family Relations in Rastafari", 72–88.

15. For a review of the political impact of this cultural shift, see Colin A. Palmer, "Identity, Race, and Black Power in Independent Jamaica", in *The Modern Caribbean,* ed. Franklin W. Knight and Colin A. Palmer (Chapel Hill: University of North Carolina Press, 1989), 111–28.

16. The West Kingston area has been a repeated target for the imposition of states of emergency.

17. Carl Stone, "Decolonization and the Caribbean State System – the Case of Jamaica", in *Perspectives on Jamaica in the 1970s,* ed. Carl Stone and Aggrey Brown (Kingston: Jamaica Publishing House, 1981), 16.

18. Ibid., 17.

19. Ibid.

20. I am indebted to Orlando Patterson for making this point with respect to the denial of moral citizenship to African Americans. See Patterson, *The Ordeal of Integration* (Washington, D.C.: Civitas, 1997), 137–42.

21. The concept of time-spaces is borrowed from Jean-Francois Bayart. See his *State in Africa.*

22. I am indebted to Erna Brodber for her insistence on the importance of "Ethiopianism" among Afro-Jamaicans. See her "Re-engineering Blackspace", *Caribbean Quarterly* 43, nos. 1 and 2 (March–June 1997): 70–81

23. Rex Nettleford, the Jamaican sociologist, has emphasized this point in all his work. For a recent reiteration of this theme, see his *Inward Stretch, Outward Reach.*

24. For a recent discussion of these conjugal patterns, see Christine Barrow, "Caribbean Masculinity and Family: Revisiting 'Marginality' and 'Reputation' ", in *Caribbean Portraits,* ed. Christine Barrow (Kingston: Ian Randle Publishers, 1998), 339–58.

25. For the relationship between sports and nation-building in Jamaica, see Jimmy Carnegie, "Sport in National Development in Jamaica", in *Jamaica in Independence: Essays on the Early Years,* ed. Rex Nettleford (Kingston: Heinemann Caribbean, 1989), 257–90.

26. For a review of Jamaica's economic development after 1962, see Omar Davies and Michael Witter, "The Development of the Jamaican Economy since Independence", in *Jamaica in Independence: Essays on the Early Years,* ed. Rex Nettleford (Kingston: Heinemann Caribbean, 1989), 75–101.

27. For an extended discussion of the tourist sector, see Owen Jefferson, *War Economic Development of Jamaica* (Kingston: Institute of Social and Economic Research, University of the West Indies, 1977), especially chap. 7.

28. For the American influence on Jamaican reggae music, see White, *Catch a Fire,* chap. 9.

29. For the authoritative statements on this phenomenon in the global cultural economy, see Arjun Appadurai, *Modernity at Large* (Minneapolis: University of Minnesota Press, 1996).

30. The Rastafarian-influenced rude boys were among this group.

31. Both terms are of local vintage and refer to the *savoir-faire* of the ladies' man. For a recent discussion of the aesthetics of black manhood in the United States, see Richard Majors and Janet Mancini Billson, *Cool Pose: The Dilemma of Black Manhood in America* (New York: Simon and Schuster, 1992).

32. The term refers to the menacing pose adopted by local would-be gangsters. The cult classic Jamaican film *The Harder They Come* accurately captured this adaptation of Hollywood gangster images to the realities of urban life in Jamaica.

33. Remarking on these colonially derived stigmas, Rex Nettleford writes, "A maid insists that she would never work 'for black people'. . . . A watchman in a private compound coldly informs a black-skinned student that he cannot proceed on the compound for the authorities have instructed him (the watchman) not to let 'any black people pass there after six o'clock'. . . and an older black woman insists that she is giving her vote to a white candidate 'for no black man can help me in this yah country these days'." Cited in Nettleford, *Mirror Mirror,* 34.

34. Besides this result, the integration of race consciousness with gangsterism caused many in this group to justify their crime and outlawry as the political acts of a racially victimized group.

35. For a discussion of the ska beat, see White, *Catch a Fire,* 18–19.

36. For a review of these musical styles and their relations with identity and culture in the Caribbean, see Dick Hebdige, *Cut 'n' Mix: Culture, Identity, and Caribbean Music* (New York: Routledge, 1990).

37. See Carnegie, "Sport in National Development in Jamaica", for an apt discussion of this achievement.

38. I am indebted to C.L.R. James for this socio-political and aesthetic approach to the meaning of sports in the Caribbean. See his *Beyond a Boundary.*

39. Champion athletes such as Arthur Wint and Herb McKenley, and fabled cricketers such as George Headley, established this trend long before the achievement of political independence.

40. Thus the celebrated footballer Allan "Skill" Cole accepted public recognition for his talent by playing for Jamaica in international competition. However, this recognition from politicians and from Jamaica's official society never dimmed Cole's enthusiasm for his working-class roots nor weakened his allegiance to Rastafarianism.

41. As reggae icon Bob Marley would demonstrate in his own life, belated official recognition was unimportant. What mattered more was the unity of poor Afro-Jamaicans in the quest for full empowerment.

42. For a quantitative assessment of class attitudes and awareness in Jamaica, see Carl Stone, *Democracy and Clientelism in Jamaica* (New Brunswick, N.J.: Transaction Books, 1980), chap. 2.

43. Jamaica's ethnic minority groups include South Asian, Chinese and Jewish populations.

44. Reggae music and its lyrics became a major vehicle for this critique of power. Bob Marley's song "Small Axe" nicely captures this trend with the following refrain: "If you are the big tree, we are the small axe ready to cut you down." Bob Marley and the Wailers, *Burnin'* (Tuff Gong/Island, ILPS 9256, 1973).

45. It became a commonplace for defecting middle-class youths to greet each other and the poor with the popular Rastafarian salutation: "Selassie I!"

46. Junior Byles's reggae hit "Beat Down Babylon" is but one example of this torrent of invective against an oppressive society. See Junior Byles, *Beat Down Babylon* (CD: Trojan CDTRL 253; produced by Lee Perry).

47. I am indebted to Edward Kamau Brathwaite for his early understanding of Caribbean kinetic morality. For his classic statement on this subject, see his *History of the Voice.*

48. Gray, *Radicalism and Social Change,* chap. 4.

49. Hence, in speaking of the unruly poor in 1962, editorialists in the *Daily Gleaner* suggested that no means should be spared in interdicting them: "Every citizen has a responsibility to keep an eye on them, to keep a finger on them and if necessary to use violence against them in order that they may be made subordinate to good order." Ibid., 244n.

Chapter 5

1. Remarking on the impact of these political gangs, Carl Stone noted that "in the 1970s most of our street gangs were political although many of the gang members used their guns to rob citizens and business enterprises. In that period they visited a reign of terror on this society. Tens of thousands of Jamaicans in the inner city had to flee from their homes under fear of the political guns and many hundreds were slaughtered by these terrorists." Cited in Carl Stone, "Logic Versus Hysteria", *Daily Gleaner,* 13 May 1991, 6.

2. For a useful comment on this dimension of Jamaican political culture, see David Scott, "The 'Culture of Violence' Fallacy", *Small Axe,* no. 2 (September 1997): 140–47.

3. In several neighbourhoods and enclaves throughout Western and Central Kingston, law-abiding citizens of both working- and lower-middle-class origins held onto the old ways. This group was the self-conscious, if numerically declining, custodian of the stock of cultural capital in these communities.

4. Nowhere was this cultural turn more evident than in popular music. In it, scores of male reggae singers proclaimed the message and authority of anti-social behaviour in the slums. One typical response came from Bob Marley, whose popular song – "I Shot the Sheriff" – offered the proud refrain from the urban rebel culture: "I shot the sheriff, but I didn't shoot the deputy." Bob Marley and the Wailers, *Burnin'*.

5. This development was hastened by the PNP's populist victory at the polls in 1972 and by its declaration of democratic socialism two years later.

6. For a discussion of these contrary ideological tendencies within the Jamaican class structure, see Stone, *Democracy and Clientelism in Jamaica*, chap. 2.

7. Hence the typical salutation – "Hail mi bredrin" (Hello my brother) – used by working- and lower-class males on the streets of Kingston.

8. By 1974 the PNP's pro-socialist declaration and its radical foreign and domestic policies polarized Jamaican politics and provoked an equally intense pro-capitalist and pro-Western orientation by the JLP. For a discussion of these developments, see Evelyne Huber Stephens and John D. Stephens, *Democratic Socialism in Jamaica* (Princeton: Princeton University Press, 1986).

9. Stone, *Class, State, and Democracy in Jamaica*, 49.

10. Ibid., 51.

11. Stone, *Democracy and Clientelism in Jamaica*, 99–100.

12. With the PNP's declaration of democratic socialism in 1974, commitment to these identities grew more intense as ideological divisions – between supporters of the socialist and anti-imperialist PNP, and backers of the pro-capitalist and pro-Western JLP – fed old enmities.

13. I am grateful to Anthony Bogues, the Jamaican political scientist, for explaining to me the honorific and disciplinary uses of badness-honour by top party figures in Jamaica.

14. In the late 1960s, Walter Rodney, the Guyanese scholar and Black Power activist, gave a boost to this challenge to state power in Jamaica by identifying with the cause and moral culture of the urban poor. He was expelled for his activism in the slums and elsewhere. See his *The Groundings with My Brothers* (London: Bogle L'Ouverture Publications, 1969).

15. Stone, *Democracy and Clientelism in Jamaica*, 108.

16. One need only consult the current editorial and op-ed pages of Jamaica's major newspaper, the *Daily Gleaner*, to read the typically mistaken view that social outlawry is a uniquely Jamaican phenomenon.

17. Scott, *Domination and the Arts of Resistance*, chaps. 1–3.

18. Michael Manley succeeded his father, Norman Manley, as party leader upon the latter's retirement from politics in 1969.

19. For a definitive statement of the moral and political concerns underlying the PNP's turn to the left after 1972, see Michael Manley, *The Politics of Change* (London: André Deutsch, 1974).

20. In this election, the PNP won 56.1 per cent of the popular vote and 36 seats in the legislature, to the JLP's 43.2 per cent and 17 seats. For a discussion of the PNP's 1972 electoral campaign, see Stephens and Stephens, *Democratic Socialism in Jamaica,* chap. 3.

21. For a discussion of the tactic of establishing politically homogeneous, garrisoned political communities through violence and intimidation, see Stone, *Class, State, and Democracy in Jamaica,* chap. 4.

22. It is worth remembering, however, that where outlawry from below threatened the predominance of the two-party system and its grip on power, party-backed endorsement of political violence could be repudiated even when the parties themselves instigated this violence.

23. For a review of PNP campaign themes and appeal to popular culture in the 1972 electoral campaign, see Anita M. Waters, *Race, Class and Political Symbols: Rastafari and Reggae in Jamaican Politics* (New Brunswick, N.J.: Transaction Books, 1989).

24. For the chorus of denunciations of this outlawry from respectable quarters in the late 1960s, see Gray, *Radicalism and Social Change,* chap. 3.

25. In the 1972 election and after, both political parties won extensive backing from this group. In 1972, 52 per cent supported the PNP compared to 48 per cent for the JLP. By 1980, when the PNP lost the national elections in a political landslide, support for the PNP among the unemployed and unskilled had slipped to 40 per cent compared to 60 per cent for the JLP. For a discussion of these fluctuations, see Stone, "Power, Policy and Politics", 31–32.

26. PNP politicians, for example, switched from Western-style suits to African kareba outfits as a gesture to cultural decolonization. Similarly, in a fit of enthusiasm for things local, PNP politicians began mouthing the utterances and locutions of the now widely popular Rastafarian movement.

27. These benefits were the usual ones involving myriad favours ranging from contracts for public works and jobs for the boys to the distribution of shiny new S-90 Honda motorbikes for political enforcers.

28. The corollary was also true of the JLP. In defence of the free market and in opposition to communism, the JLP accommodated its supporters' display of badness-honour.

29. It will be recalled that the PNP had declared itself for socialism on the model of the British Labour Party. For a discussion of the PNP's political history, see Munroe, *Jamaican Politics,* chap. 2.

30. For a nuanced account of US opposition to the PNP left-turn after 1974, see Stephens and Stephens, *Democratic Socialism,* chap. 4.

31. Ibid., 139.

32. For a first-hand recounting of this viewpoint, see Michael Manley, *Jamaica: Struggle in the Periphery* (London: Writers and Readers Publishing Cooperatives Society, 1982).

33. Address at the thirty-eighth annual conference of the PNP, Kingston, Jamaica, 19 September 1976.

34. As the 1980 general elections approached, JLP leader Edward Seaga warned his supporters of the PNP threat: "They talk with Communists. They plan with Communists. They march with Communists. They hold meetings together with Communists. They do everything that they can possibly do with Communists. I say that if you look like duck, and if you walk like a duck; if you swim like a duck, and if you quack like a duck, you can't be anything else but a duck!" "Get Up, Stand Up", *Americas,* episode 8 (video-tape, Annenberg/CPB Collection, 1993).

35. States of emergency were declared in Jamaica in the 1940s, 1960s and 1970s.

36. In a bid to reduce crime, the PNP in 1974 passed the draconian Suppression of Crime Act that seriously infringed on political liberties.

37. It is well known that with respect to party factionalism the JLP had a different problem. Its inner party factionalism and challenge to the leadership occurred at the top, among competing party notables, rather than between leaders and the rank and file.

38. For a review of these relations, see Munroe, *Jamaican Politics,* chaps. 3–4.

39. For an extended and highly informed discussion of populism, see Ernesto Laclau, *Politics and Ideology in Marxist Theory* (London: Verso, 1977), chap. 4.

40. This interpretation of the role of reason in ideology, in opposition to perspectives that regard political ideology as mind-inflaming and irrational, is borrowed from Alvin Gouldner. See his *The Dialectic of Ideology and Technology* (New York: Seabury Press, 1976), chap. 2.

41. For a discussion of the nature of these closed communities, see Stone, *Class, State, and Democracy in Jamaica,* chap. 4.

42. Barry Chevannes, "The Formation of Garrison Communities" (paper presented at the symposium Grassroots Development and the State of the Nation, in honour of Professor Carl Stone, University of the West Indies, Mona, Jamaica, 16–17 November 1992), 3.

43. See David D'Costa, "Green Bay: Dangerous – and Deadly Lessons", *Sunday Gleaner,* 4 June 1978, 13.

44. Cited in the *Daily Gleaner,* 28 January 1976, 6.

45. JLP Member of Parliament Edwin Allen, evidently enjoying the coup scored by possession of the tape recording, triumphantly peppered Manley with embarrassing questions in the House of Representatives.

46. Confronted with the secret recording, Michael Manley issued a tortured and unconvincing denial. For an account of Manley's exchanges with his hostile interlocutor in Parliament, see the *Daily Gleaner,* 28 January 1976, 6. See also David D'Costa's report in the *Sunday Gleaner,* 4 June 1978, 13.

Chapter 6

1. For two notable studies on the politics of democratic socialism in Jamaica, see Michael Kaufman, *Jamaica under Manley: Dilemmas of Socialism and Democracy* (Westport, Conn.: Lawrence Hill, 1985), and Stephens and Stephens, *Democratic Socialism in Jamaica.*

2. In these years, the PNP announced several programmes to benefit the poor. They included a jobs programme for the urban unemployed, a literacy programme, free secondary and university education, and equal pay for women. For a year-by-year list of programmes initiated by the PNP between 1972 and 1979, see Stephens and Stephens, *Democratic Socialism in Jamaica,* 70–71.

3. Jamaica's foreign policy moved sharply to the left during the PNP's tenure between 1972 and 1980. For a discussion of this shift, see Don Mills, "Jamaica's International Relations in Independence", in *Jamaica in Independence: Essays on the Early Years,* ed. Rex Nettleford (Kingston: Heinemann Caribbean, 1989), 131–71.

4. Stone, "Power, Policy and Politics", 45–46.

5. Michael Manley, address to the thirty-eighth annual conference of the PNP, Kingston, Jamaica, 19 September 1976.

6. Stone, "Power, Policy and Politics", 45.

7. For polling data on Jamaicans' positive perception of the United States, see Stone, "Power, Policy and Politics", 50–51.

8. For an account of these clashes, see Stephens and Stephens, *Democratic Socialism in Jamaica,* chaps. 4–6.

9. For a discussion of Jamaica's patron-client politics, see Stone's classic study, *Democracy and Clientelism in Jamaica.*

10. In this episode, Allan Isaacs, PNP minister of mining and a critic of socialism, was forced from his post.

11. Eight hundred is the most widely cited figure for the deaths caused by political violence in 1980 alone.

12. For a review of *Gleaner* criticisms of the PNP, see Stephens and Stephens, *Democratic Socialism in Jamaica,* 205–10.

13. For a discussion of the gathering opposition to the PNP after 1974, see Stephens and Stephens, *Democratic Socialism in Jamaica,* 116–47.

14. Stone, *Class, State, and Democracy in Jamaica,* 85.

15. This was certainly the case for West Kingston, but the South St Andrew constituency had also moved in this direction.

16. In this period, for example, PNP epithets for JLP loyalists included not only the older "dutty [dirty] Labourite" label, but also the new and now highly charged "capitalist" denunciation.

17. Stone, the political sociologist, was the pioneer in calling attention to this aspect of Jamaican political culture. See in particular his *Class, State, and Democracy,* chap. 4.

18. This fact has been at the core of clientelist politics in Jamaica.

19. Because of their political connections, top political enforcers from both parties were treated for the most part as untouchables, subject neither to arrest nor to prosecution.

20. Politics in contemporary Africa, for example, confirms this overlap between class politics and ethnic politics. For a discussion of the relation between class and ethnicity in Africa, see Naomi Chazan et al., eds., *Politics and Society in Contemporary Africa* (Boulder: Lynne Rienner, 1992).

21. This repression of the poor as a social class was most notable when states of emergency were declared in 1966 by the JLP and in 1976 by the PNP.

22. The most dramatic example of this break with political patrons came with the 1978 peace movement in the ghetto that was led by rival party gunmen.

23. Interview with former associate of Massop, "Churchill", interview by author, Kingston, Jamaica. Summer, 1994.

24. See Chevannes, "The Rastafari and the Urban Youth".

25. For a discussion of the relationship between powerful interest groups and the Jamaican state, see Stone, *Democracy and Clientelism in Jamaica,* chap. 10.

26. Stone, *Class, State, and Democracy in Jamaica,* 65.

27. Paul Burke, interview by author, Kingston, Jamaica, Summer 1994.

28. "Churchill", interview.

29. "Churchill", interview.

30. Gunst, *Born Fi' Dead,* 81.

31. Stone, *Class, State, and Democracy in Jamaica,* 57.

32. According to one of Massop's close associates, the gunman respectfully addressed the constituency leader as "Mr Seaga". Informant, interview by author, Kingston, Jamaica, Summer 1994.

33. See for example, George Beckford and Michael Witter, *Small Garden . . . Bitter Weed: Struggle and Change in Jamaica* (London: Zed Books, 1980), and Fitzroy Ambursley, "Jamaica: from Michael Manley to Edward Seaga", in

Crisis in the Caribbean, ed. Fitzroy Ambursley and Robin Cohen (New York: Monthly Review, 1983), 72–104.

34. This apartment block was located in the so-called Rema enclave that housed JLP loyalists.
35. Maxwell, interview.
36. For official documentation of this link between politicians and gunmen in South St Andrew, see excerpts from the Rema eviction inquiry report, *Daily Gleaner,* 26 July 1978, 1, 17.
37. For an authoritative pro-PNP interpretation of these developments, see Manley, *Struggle in the Periphery.*
38. By late 1975, the communist WPJ had given its "critical support" to the PNP while denouncing the JLP as a political stooge of the United States.
39. For opposing party programmatic statements, see "The 1976 Election Manifestoes (PNP and JLP)", in Stone and Brown, *Perspectives on Jamaica in the Seventies,* 275–98.
40. In local parlance, this cunning and guile in matters personal and political is referred to as "Anancyism".
41. In 1975 these developments included a sharp downturn in bauxite production; increased criminal activity involving murder, rape and armed robbery; and deepening fears that the PNP's ties to Cuba and to Fidel Castro would lead to the establishment of a communist state in Jamaica. For a discussion of Jamaica's foreign relations in the 1970s and the polarization it caused, see Kaufman, *Jamaica under Manley,* 85–91.
42. It was estimated that imposition of this levy would increase bauxite revenues sevenfold for a yield of J$170–$200 million between January 1974 and March 1975. See Stephens and Stephens, *Democratic Socialism in Jamaica,* 78–80.
43. *Daily Gleaner,* 21 January 1975, 1.
44. JLP leader Edward Seaga, who called for a halt to the gang's mayhem, gave this litany of misdeeds to the press. See *Daily Gleaner,* 22 January 1975, 2.
45. *Daily Gleaner,* 7 December 1974, 1, 33.
46. *Daily Gleaner,* 22 January 1975, 2. See also *Daily Gleaner,* 28 January 1976, 6, 13.
47. *Daily Gleaner,* 27 January 1975, 12.
48. *Daily Gleaner,* 22 January 1975, 1.
49. *Daily Gleaner,* 15 March 1975, 1.
50. *Daily Gleaner,* 24 March 1975, 1.
51. Arnold Bertram, interview by author, Kingston, Jamaica, August 1996.
52. *Daily Gleaner,* 4 July 1975, 1 and 6 July 1975, 1.
53. See David D'Costa's account in the *Sunday Gleaner,* 4 June 1978, 13.

Chapter 7

1. Between 1972 and 1977 in just the Rema enclave alone, more than 300 people were shot dead, 306 were wounded and some 252 gunmen were arrested. See testimony by the police before the commission investigating the violence in Rema, *Daily Gleaner,* 22 March 1977, 1.

2. In 1974 the tough Suppression of Crime Act was passed. As the violence increased, the PNP declared a state of emergency in 1976.

3. Carl Stone, "The Crime Problem", *Daily Gleaner,* 22 April 1991, 6.

4. Carl Stone, "Managing Crime", *Daily Gleaner,* 9 December 1987, 6.

5. Cited in Bernard D. Headley, "Jamaican Crime and Violence at Home and Abroad: An Ideological Perspective" (manuscript, West Indies Collection, University of the West Indies, Mona, Jamaica, 1994), 13.

6. Anthony Harriott, *Police and Crime Control in Jamaica* (Kingston: University of the West Indies Press, 2000), 9.

7. Ibid., 11.

8. Ibid.

9. Carl Stone reported, for example, that while political gunmen carried high-powered rifles, the police were largely confined to .38 revolvers and "old fashioned .202 rifles". See Stone, "Managing Crime", 6.

10. For example, on 19 May 1976, gunmen set fire to a tenement on Orange Lane in Kingston, killing some ten persons, including children. Despite initial and widely believed PNP allegations that JLP thugs had committed the murders, recent disclosures from more credible sources point to PNP thugs as the perpetrators. For the shocking disclosure of PNP collusion in suppressing this finding, see Laura Tanner, "The Orange Lane Fire Enquiry", *Jamaica Gleaner,* 7 March 2000, http://www.jamaica-gleaner.com/.

11. As political scientist Carl Stone noted: "Our crime problem mirrors a deadly combination of easy access to guns to immature tough and street wise teenagers; cocaine habits among the ghetto and uptown youth, political gangs, and a frightening level of illegal importation of high-powered weapons." See Stone, "The Threat of Violence", *Daily Gleaner,* 14 September 1987, 8.

12. A notable exception in the late 1970s was the "Wild Bunch" gang whose leader, Anthony Tingle, threw his support to the PNP's Arnett Gardens gang in Trench Town. Burke, interview.

13. Headley, "Jamaican Crime and Violence", 22.

14. Statistics for reported violent crimes do not distinguish between domestic, criminal and politically motivated violence. Hence, aside from problems of reliability and definition, it is impossible to tell from aggregate crime data whether criminals or the politically motivated committed these crimes.

15. For a valuable discussion of the political and cultural impact of reggae music on the poor, see Kwame Dawes's *Natural Mysticism: Toward a Reggae Aesthetic* (Leeds: Peepal Tree Press, 1999); and Cooper, *Noises in the Blood,* especially chap. 7.

16. Observers of the Jamaican poor rightly dismiss a revolutionary vocation for the lumpenproletariat. Yet in focusing narrowly on the group's capacity for revolution, these critics typically ignore the vast social power of the lumpen-proletariat and its capacity to checkmate the predatory state. See Alan Eyre's comments in "Political Violence and Urban Geography in Kingston, Jamaica", *Geographical Review* 74, no. 1 (1984): 24–37. For other critical comments, see Headley, "Jamaican Crime and Violence", 27.

17. In the early 1960s, several reggae artists, including Bob Marley and the Wailers, warned the rebellious poor against engaging in reckless violence.

18. This is where I part company with scholars, including Bernard Headley, who, in order to dismiss the claim that the lumpenproletariat has a revolu-tionary sensibility, throw out the proverbial baby with the bathwater by completely rejecting any social content in criminal acts.

19. *Daily Gleaner,* 1 May 1978, 13.

20. *Daily Gleaner,* 1 May 1978, 1. See also White, *Catch a Fire,* 102–3.

21. *Daily Gleaner,* 29 September 1978, 1.

22. Burke, interview.

23. For a discussion of the relationship between bandits and politics, see Hobsbawm, *Bandits.*

24. Burke, interview.

25. Ibid.

26. *Daily Gleaner,* 1 May 1978, 13.

27. Cited in the *Daily Gleaner,* 1 May 1978, 13.

28. Ibid. Reportage by the *Gleaner* indicates that the name of the ring refers to the L.W. DeLaurence Company of Chicago, publishers of metaphysical and occult literature. Though its publications were on the colonial government's watch list, various titles from the company were in the hands of the poorer classes and were popular with them. This acceptance of literature elaborating on the occult was no doubt due to its resonance with indigenous religious practices. For a recent discussion of the latter, see Chevannes, *Rastafari Roots and Ideology,* chap. 1.

29. Burke, interview.

30. The state's frustration at being thwarted by residents who protected Barth is aptly registered in the comments of Dudley Thompson, the minister of national security. According to Thompson, "It is certain that 'Copper' and his gang could not have remained at large for so long if there were not people who helped him to hide." Cited in the *Daily Gleaner,* 2 May 1978, 11.

31. Burke, interview.
32. This was certainly the stereotype drawn by the minister of national security who, after Barth was shot dead in a bungled robbery, advised the poor in the ghetto that Barth "was no sufferer looking for employment. . . . He chose a life of crime, and as I said, crime does not pay . . . . He has now come to the end of the trail shot down in his youth like a wild animal. Yes, like a mad dog should be, like all mad dogs will be." Cited in the *Daily Gleaner,* 2 May 1978, 11.
33. Of course, no such justification could be offered for predation and violence against the poor. Hence, the plaintive strain in popular music for peace and the cessation of violence against "your brother".
34. Carl Stone, *Daily Gleaner,* 9 December 1987, 6.
35. This was particularly so in election years, which saw incidents of violent crimes soar from 15,893 in 1976 to 24,201 in 1980. Cited in Harriott, *Police and Crime Control,* 10–11.
36. For a good discussion of the creation of political garrisons, see Chevannes, "The Formation of Garrison Communities", 1–11.
37. Burke, interview.
38. *Daily Gleaner,* 6 January 1976, 1.
39. *Daily Gleaner,* 9 January 1976, 16.
40. *Daily Gleaner,* 8 January 1976, 15.
41. See Michael Manley's address to the nation, *Daily Gleaner,* 10 January 1976, 20.
42. For PNP allegations of this destabilization campaign, see Manley, *Struggle in the Periphery,* chap. 9.
43. Ibid., 20. For a day-by-day account that documents PNP claims of subversion, see in particular, the "Destabilization Diary" in the appendix of Manley, *Struggle in the Periphery.*
44. *Daily Gleaner,* 5 February 1988, 3. See also Kaufman, *Jamaica under Manley,* 112–20.
45. Political violence soared after the PNP's return to office. As both sides clashed over the country's political direction between 1977 and 1980, the contestation brought a major run-up in crime and a shocking display of destructive violence on both sides. That violence destroyed already meagre housing stocks in working-class neighbourhoods while claiming the lives of hundreds of poor Jamaicans.
46. PNP leader Michael Manley argued as much when he insisted that "clearly, the multinational corporation, the conservative elements of the Western press, the champions of the capitalist system, the US establishment and those who defended the *status quo* generally, were lined up solidly behind the JLP". Manley, *Struggle in the Periphery,* 199.

47. For one view that avoids conspiratorial explanations while distributing blame to all parties, see Stephens and Stephens, *Democratic Socialism in Jamaica,* 128–37.

48. See the "Commission of Enquiry into the 1976 State of Emergency" (Government of Jamaica).

49. Years of PNP violence and blandishments had apparently borne fruit as a few Rema-ites began to warm to the PNP and its benefits. For the tension between these defectors and Tivoli Gardens' hard-liners, see *Daily Gleaner,* 20 August 1978, 7.

50. *Daily Gleaner,* 10 August 1978, 11.

51. See the 1978 report on the Rema eviction issued by Commissioner Justice Ronald H. Small. Cited in the *Daily Gleaner,* 26 July 1978, 1. Hereafter referred to as Report of the Small Commission.

52. In rejecting Spaulding's rationale, Justice Small noted: "The totality of the evidence indicates quite clearly that . . . there was a positive political confrontation of the two political parties and not a dispassionate administrative exercise as the ministry officials would have this commission to find." Report of the Small Commission, cited in the *Daily Gleaner,* 30 July 1978, 13.

53. *Daily Gleaner,* 10 August 1978, 11.

54. JLP activists and residents bitterly complained that even as they fled their homes and sought shelter at the Denham Town police station in 1976, officers there ignored their plight and turned them away. *Daily Gleaner,* 8 January 1976, 15.

55. This epithet for the police was not peculiar to Rema residents. In fact, by the late 1970s the politicization of the police had become so widespread that ghetto residents regarded them, according to one commentator, as "merely another gang on the scene". See David D'Costa, "Green Bay: What Made Them Do It". *Sunday Gleaner,* 28 May 1978, 12, and also his "Green Bay: Dangerous – and Deadly Lessons", *Sunday Gleaner,* 4 June 1978, 22. This derision of policemen as bloodsuckers on the collective body of the poor continued into the 1990s.

56. *Daily Gleaner,* 10 August 1978, 11.

57. Cited in the *Daily Gleaner,* 16 March 1977, 1.

58. *Daily Gleaner,* 11 March 1977, 16.

59. Testimony by Anthony Spaulding before the Small Commission. Cited in the *Daily Gleaner,* 20 August 1978, 7.

60. For a sharp critique of the corruptions of democratic socialism, see Wilmot Perkins's "The Feeding Tree of Corruption", in the *Sunday Gleaner,* 2 July 1978, 13.

61. Report of the Small Commission, cited in the *Daily Gleaner,* 10 August 1978, 11.

62. Report of the Small Commission, cited in the *Daily Gleaner,* 30 July 1978, 13.

63. Report of the Small Commission, cited in the *Daily Gleaner,* 10 August 1978, 11.

64. Ibid.

65. *Daily Gleaner,* 30 July 1978, 13.

66. Police testimony before the Small Commission. Cited in the *Daily Gleaner,* 10 August 1978, 11.

67. Report of the Small Commission, cited in the *Daily Gleaner,* 26 July 1978, 1.

68. Report of the Small Commission, cited in the *Daily Gleaner,* 30 July 1978, 13.

69. Report of the Small Commission, cited in the *Daily Gleaner,* 26 July 1978, 17.

Chapter 8

1. Obika Gray, "Power and Identity among the Urban Poor of Jamaica", in *Globalization and Survival in the Black Diaspora,* ed. Charles Green (Albany: SUNY Press, 1997), 199–226.

2. The one social space – popular culture and especially reggae music – into which the poor had retreated and in which they exercised a predominant influence – had also been penetrated by the state and seemingly colonized at strategic moments. This invasion is apparent from Edward Seaga's, Dudley Thompson's and Michael Manley's thorough appropriation of popular culture including its symbols and idioms.

3. See, for example, Stone, *Class, State, and Democracy in Jamaica,* chap. 4.

4. For a discussion of intra-party PNP conflicts in the 1960s, see Gray, *Radicalism and Social Change,* chap. 5.

5. A sevenfold increase in bauxite revenues yielded J$170–$200 million between January 1974 and March 1975. For a discussion of the bauxite levy, see Stephens and Stephens, *Democratic Socialism in Jamaica,* 76–81.

6. Carl Stone, "Of Self-Reliance and Dependency", *Daily Gleaner,* 24 October 1988, 6. For a discussion of this employment programme, see Stephens and Stephens, *Democratic Socialism in Jamaica,* 72–73.

7. Not all those among the young were attracted to the PNP because of patronage. A significant and influential minority in the PNPYO (People's

National Party Youth Organization), the party's radical youth wing, was drawn there because of ideological commitments.

8. See *Daily Gleaner,* 13 June 1977. The Sandy Gully has been a prominent site of patronage and political conflict in post-war Jamaica. Since the 1940s both parties have alternated in directing their loyalists to this site to earn a living by doing repairs. At the same time, both parties recruited workers from the site to mount assaults on the political opposition.

9. Burke, interview.

10. See *Daily Gleaner,* 8 July 1975, 1.

11. *Daily Gleaner,* 6 July 1975, 1.

12. Burke, interview.

13. The assassinated official was Edward Ogilvie, permanent secretary in the Ministry of Public Works.

14. By 1977 the public outcry against this theft was sufficiently deafening that the PNP had to accept the formation of a commission of inquiry into the theft of the public funds. In addition, critical journalists such as Wilmot Perkins of the *Daily Gleaner* minced no words in excoriating the PNP for maintaining a "feeding tree of corruption" for the PNP's "socialist birds". *Daily Gleaner,* 2 July 1978, 13. See also Carl Stone, "The Politician as 'Boops'", *Daily Gleaner,* 4 March 1991, 6.

15. Wilmot Perkins, "No Certificate of Poverty, Please", *Daily Gleaner,* 8 March 1977, 8.

16. Carl Stone, "The Long Road from 1938", *Sunday Gleaner,* 21 May 1978, 13.

17. For a list of some fifty policies and initiatives, the majority of which benefited the poorer classes, see Stephens and Stephens, *Democratic Socialism in Jamaica,* 70–71.

18. The otherwise discerning journalist Wilmot Perkins was particularly culpable here, preferring to emphasize history's creation of the lumpenproletariat as nothing but "a monster without conscience, bereft of fine feelings, remorselessly vicious, coarse, grasping and improvident". *Daily Gleaner,* 8 March 1977, 8.

19. The term "freeness" antedates the 1970s. It had been used approvingly by the poor and was positively associated with political patronage. However, as the distribution of patronage became more contentious, the word became a term of derision and contempt for the supplicant poor. For an early use of the term in this sense, see Colin Gregory, "Of This and That", *Daily Gleaner,* 28 January 1975, 10.

20. Burke, interview.

21. Edward Seaga of the JLP was well known for his insistence that supplicants not look to him for patronage that would be used purely for conspicuous consumption.

22. Michael Manley, "Aspects of a Caribbean Development Strategy", in "Proceedings of a Regional Seminar on Caribbean Sovereignty", 112. Cited in *Sovereignty: Mobilization for Development and Self-Reliance; The Tasks of Political Education* (Kingston: PNP, 1984).

23. For additional critical commentaries, see Kaufman, *Jamaica under Manley;* Beckford and Witter, *Small Garden . . . Bitter Weed*; and Ambursley, "Jamaica: From Michael Manley to Edward Seaga".

24. Manley, "Aspects", 114.

25. Wilmot Perkins, "Opportunities in the Ghetto", *Daily Gleaner,* 13 January 1978, 6.

26. The truth of this observation is bitingly expressed in Bob Marley's wonderful lyric: "Never make a politician grant you a favour / They will always want to control you forever." From the song "Revolution", Bob Marley and the Wailers, *Natty Dread* (Island Records, ILPS 9281, 1974).

27. The songs of the Wailers, separately and together, repeatedly invoke this image of the bloodsucking beast.

28. Gray, "Power and Identity", 205.

29. Only a shrinking, marginal group of activists continued to hold the view that the lumpenproletariat was a revolutionary vanguard and avatar of liberation. For a discussion of the latter issue, see Obika Gray, "The Jamaican Lumpenproletariat: Rogue Culture or Avatar of Liberation?" (paper presented at the twenty-third annual conference of the Caribbean Studies Association, Antigua, 26–30 May 1998), 1–30.

30. In 1982 this area of 75 square kilometres had approximately 750,000 persons or about 36 per cent of the country's population. At the same time, it was responsible for the largest percentage of violent crimes in the country. See Eyre, "Political Violence and Urban Geography", 26. See also his "The Effects of Political Terrorism on the Residential Location of the Poor in the Kingston Urban Region, Jamaica, West Indies", *Urban Geography* 7, no. 3 (1986): 227–42.

31. For a discussion of the development of the drug trade in the 1990s, see Ivelaw L. Griffith and Trevor Munroe, "Drugs and Democratic Governance in the Caribbean" in *Democracy and Human Rights in the Caribbean,* ed. Ivelaw Griffith and Betty N. Sedoc-Dahlberg (Boulder: Westview Press, 1997), 74–94.

32. In a dramatic example of the security forces' link to the trafficking of guns, four Sterling submachine guns were stolen from the military in December 1976. These weapons were allegedly being sold to criminals in the McGregor Gully and Angola precincts of South St Andrew. See *Daily Gleaner,* 9 September 1978, 1.

33. Most turfites betting on the horses at the Caymanas Park racetrack were
     probably unaware of the underworld's extensive penetration of the sport.
     There horses, jockeys and grooms had long been fair game for a variety of
     mobsters from the precincts of West Kingston. They worked tirelessly in the
     1970s to fix the races there. Anthony Bogues, interview by author, Kingston,
     Jamaica, Summer 1996.
34. Carl Stone, "The Crime Problem", *Daily Gleaner,* 22 April 1991, 6.
35. In the ghetto, as in the wider society, the rites of manhood entailed proving
     one's manliness to other men. In many precincts of the ghetto, manliness
     was defined by skill in sports and games and the use of weapons. In other
     precincts, manliness might be associated with a capacity for smoking "quan-
     tities" of the marijuana weed, consuming liquor, enjoying the fineries of life
     and most importantly being able to control women or have sexual access to
     as many of them as possible.
36. Gray, "Power and Identity", 219.
37. Carl Stone was the first to recognize this trait. In describing routes to
     upward mobility and power in Jamaica in the 1970s, he wrote the following:
     "Just as money and status create social rank in middle class suburban com-
     munities, the capacity to exercise violence and to be the 'baddest of the bad'
     create their own pecking order of power in ghetto communities." See his
     "Guns and Politics", *Daily Gleaner,* 2 October 1978, 6.
38. Carl Stone, "Garrison Politics", *Daily Gleaner,* 26 February 1992, 6.
39. An advertisement bearing Barth's picture and offering a J$3,000 reward for
     the twenty-six-year-old was published in the island's largest daily newspaper.
     See *Daily Gleaner,* 11 November 1977, 2.
40. Burke, interview.
41. *Daily Gleaner,* 3 November 1977, 2.
42. I am indebted to David D'Costa for this and other penetrating insights into
     the political meaning of the Green Bay deaths. See his "Green Bay: What
     Made Them Do It", *Sunday Gleaner,* 28 May 1978, 12, 23.
43   For a summary of the testimony before the commission of inquiry into the
     incident, see *Daily Gleaner,* 16 April 1978, 23.
44. For an account of the plot and a description of the incident by the victims
     themselves, see Gunst, *Born Fi' Dead,* 87–110. See also D'Costa's two articles
     on the subject: "Green Bay: What Made Them Do It", 12, and "Green Bay:
     Dangerous – and Deadly Lessons", *Sunday Gleaner,* 4 June 1978, 13, 23.
45. *Daily Gleaner,* 6 January 1978, 1.
46. This account, as described by D'Costa, remains the most plausible explana-
     tion for the ambush. See D'Costa, "Green Bay: Dangerous – and Deadly
     Lessons", 22.
47. Gunst, *Born Fi' Dead,* 103–4.

48. John Hearne's interview with an unemployed youth in the aftermath of the executions. See Hearne, "Green Bay to Beeston Street", *Daily Gleaner,* 13 January 1978, 6.

49. Gunst dates the manifestation of the truce on the very night of the killings, when "the men from Tivoli and Rema, Concrete Jungle and Tel Aviv began crossing the no-man's-land that divided them, smoking chalices full of ganja and talking peace". *Born Fi' Dead,* 104. The first of several rallies celebrating the truce occurred, however, on 9 and 10 January.

50. Gunst, *Born Fi' Dead,* 95 and 104.

51. Ibid., 94.

52. Cited in the *Daily Gleaner,* 11 January 1978, 1.

53. *Daily Gleaner,* 16 January 1978, 1.

54. *Daily Gleaner,* 13 January 1978, 11.

55. Cited in the *Daily Gleaner,* 11 January 1978, 1.

56. *Daily Gleaner,* 12 January 1978, 1.

57. *Daily Gleaner,* 13 January 1978, 6.

58. Gray, "Power and Identity", 217.

59. *Daily Gleaner,* 16 January 1978, 1.

60. Ibid.

61. See John Hearne, "The Peace and Truce: A Second Look", *Daily Gleaner,* 22 January 1978, 6.

62. *Daily Gleaner,* 10 March 1978, 1. The policy of exterminism of the violent poor did not, it must be said, begin with the PNP or with Dudley Thompson. State terror and extra-judicial murder in the ghetto became state policy in the late 1960s. It was captured in then prime minister Hugh Shearer's infamous directive to the security forces to "read no beatitudes" to gunmen before killing them. See my *Radicalism and Social Change,* chap. 7.

63. *Daily Gleaner,* 19 March 1978, 1. Not all journalists looked askance at the dirty war against the gunmen. Carl Stone, the respected scholar and *Gleaner* columnist, supported the terror and denounced as "bleeding heart liberals" those who decried the policy of assassination and summary execution. See his "No Tears over Green Bay", *Daily Gleaner,* 31 May 1978, 8.

64. Ibid., 1. Thompson also denounced as "traitors" those soldiers who chose to break with the army's cover story and testify truthfully before a commission of inquiry into the incident. See the investigative reports of David D'Costa in the *Gleaner* and especially his report "Senator Thompson and Green Bay", *Daily Gleaner,* 17 June 1978, 8.

65. It is important to note here that despite the mailed fist that Dudley Thompson showed to the poor, other influentials inside the PNP were either in open sympathy with the gunmen or implicitly critical of their own party's policy toward them. Paul Burke of the PNPYO was in the former

category and Hugh Small, minister of youth and sports, belonged to the latter. See Small's critical and prescient comments about the cunning of political power in Jamaica in *Daily Gleaner,* 12 January 1978, 1.

66. In response to the crisis, the state approved some J$500,000 to be disbursed
through the Kingston and St Andrew Corporation for infrastructural
improvements and employment generation. However, four months into the
truce, none of the money had been disbursed. See the urgent plea for action
by journalist Evon Blake, *Daily Gleaner,* 5 May 1978, 8.

67. The advisory body headed by churchmen was known as the Central
Advisory Peace Council.

68. In October, the United States Agency for International Development
donated to the poor some 1,404 tons of food worth J$1.2 million. See the
Sunday Gleaner, Outlook Magazine, 3 December 1978, 1–2.

69. In addition to earning an estimated J$40,000, the concert was notable for
Marley's valiant and ultimately successful effort to get the reluctant Edward
Seaga and Michael Manley to clasp hands on the concert stage in a gesture
of peace. For a discussion of Marley's long-standing ties to the truce leaders,
see White, *Catch a Fire,* chaps. 15–16.

70. *Daily Gleaner,* 5 May 1978, 13.

71. *Daily Gleaner,* 1 May 1978, 1.

72. The total funds from all sources, other than the government, was approximately J$94,000 – with the lion's share coming from receipts from Bob
Marley's peace concert.

73. For Reverend Reid's reflections on the truce, see *Daily Gleaner,* 24 February
1994, 6.

74. Upon closing its peace fund, the *Gleaner* reported that the largest corporate
contribution was a mere J$500. *Daily Gleaner,* 1 May 1978, 1.

75. *Sunday Gleaner,* 19 March 1978, 13. For references to the dangers of "Trench
Town Ideology", see *Daily Gleaner,* 19 March 1978, 13. In his frenzied rejection of protest from the ghetto, Dudley Thompson continued the state's
response to social crisis by seeking the cultural expulsion of the poor as well
as their physical extermination. This was usually accomplished by using the
pretext of crime control. For Thompson's comments, see *Daily Gleaner,* 10
March 1978, 1.

76. Wilmot Perkins, "No Certificate of Poverty, Please", *Daily Gleaner,* 8 March
1977, 8.

77. Ibid., 8.

78. D'Costa has described the policy in the following manner: "Contrary to the
argument that we have been 'wishy washy' in dealing with crime in the past
and have failed to apply adequate doses of terror, the irrefutable fact is that
this society (God help us) has always relied upon terror to 'control' its

under-classes." See "Green Bay: Dangerous – and Deadly Lessons", 13.
Others, such as Carl Stone, spoke on the side of law and order. Yet even
Stone was compelled to admit, "political terrorism by the state against the
people is being used under the guise of fighting crime". See Stone,
"Violence by the State", *Daily Gleaner,* 7 March 1979, 6.

79. *Daily Gleaner,* 9 December 1978, 23.
80. *Daily Gleaner,* 1 May 1978, 1. What went wrong at the track is unclear.
    Gunst writes that Tivoli gunman, Lester "Jim Brown" Coke, "set Copper up
    to rob the racetrack office and then tipped off the police". Gunst, *Born Fi'
    Dead,* 107. Paul Burke averred that the gunman died in a firefight when the
    clip of ammunition fell from his machine gun. Burke, interview.
81. *Daily Gleaner,* 2 May 1978, 11.
82. *Daily Gleaner,* 1 December 1978, 1.
83. D'Costa, "Green Bay: Dangerous – and Deadly Lessons", 22.
84. For a discussion of this reciprocal terror, see Carl Stone, "The Balance of
    Terror", *Daily Gleaner,* 14 June 1978, 8.
85. D'Costa, "Green Bay: Dangerous – and Deadly Lessons", 22.
86. The Reverend C.S. Reid recalled an occasion when "Bucky" Thompson
    "let loose some awful language about the PNP Mayor of the KSAC who
    seemed to be dragging his feet about certain promised improvement in part
    of his Thompson's community". *Daily Gleaner,* 22 February 1994, 6.
87. Ibid., 6.
88. *Daily Gleaner,* 21 April 1978, 8.
89. In mid-June, for example, self-appointed defenders of the truce in Arnett
    Gardens summarily executed two accused rapists for violating the peace.
    Daily Gleaner, 14 June 1978, 1. It is worth noting that the social power that
    initiated this system of rough justice also suborned the legal system by
    intimidating witnesses who then refused to testify against lawbreakers for
    fear of their lives. For the public outcry that greeted this development, see
    the editorial, "Justice in Jeopardy", *Daily Gleaner,* 17 June 1978, 8.
90. *Daily Gleaner,* 9 December 1978, 1. Before the evening was over, pro-PNP
    warmongers had slashed the tires of Claude Massop's car and threatened JLP
    supporters.
91. JLP residents responded to this new threat in December by vigorously
    defending the peace and seeking state protection from the predation of
    Starkey and his men. See *Daily Gleaner,* 13 December 1978, 1.
92. *Daily Gleaner,* 1 November 1978, 1. The three persons whose signatures
    were needed to approve withdrawals were Trevor Phillips, chairman of the
    Central Peace Council; Diane Jobson, Bob Marley's assistant; and
    Archimandrite Abba Laike Mandefro, administrator of the Ethiopian
    Orthodox Church.

Chapter 9

1. Carl Stone, "The Long Road from 1938", *Sunday Gleaner*, 21 May 1978, 12.
2. Ibid.
3. For a discussion of the economic crisis that led to the adoption of these measures between 1973 and 1978, see Stephens and Stephens, *Democratic Socialism in Jamaica,* chaps. 5–6.
4. For a list of increases in the price of gasoline between November 1973 and May 1978, see the *Daily Gleaner,* 9 January 1979, 1.
5. *Daily Gleaner,* 3 January 1979, 1. Prior to January 1973 a gallon of premium gasoline was sold for 44.2 cents.
6. Wilmot Perkins, "Gas Price Politics", *Daily Gleaner,* 14 January 1979, 11.
7. See Dennis Forsythe, "The People's Revolt", *Daily Gleaner,* 14 January 1979, 11.
8. According to one estimate, demonstrators erected some five hundred roadblocks in Kingston alone. *Daily Gleaner,* 12 January 1979,1.
9. One wit's placard urged the regime to "Sell Ganja: Left the Poor" (Sell Marijuana. Stop Interfering with the Poor), *Daily Gleaner,* 9 January 1979, 1.
10. *Daily Gleaner,* 11 January 1979, 6 and 11.
11. Columnist Carl Stone observed that the intensity of the demonstrations in Kingston was such that the PNP on Monday had its "goons, bully boys and badmen on the street with instructions to clear the streets and beat back the forces blocking the streets". *Daily Gleaner,* 15 January 1979, 6.
12. *Daily Gleaner,* 9 January 1979, 1.
13. *Daily Gleaner,* 10 January 1979, 13.
14. Ibid.
15. The act, which had been in place in ten parishes, was lifted in December 1978. It was now extended to the parishes of Hanover, Westmoreland, St Elizabeth, Manchester, Clarendon, St Thomas, Portland, St Mary and St Ann. *Daily Gleaner,* 10 January 1979, 1.
16. *Daily Gleaner,* 10 January 1979, 1.
17. Ibid., 13.
18. As the PNP turned to austerity measures in the 1970s, ties between unionized workers and political parties began to fray. The result, as the 1979 demonstration showed, was an increasing divergence between the economic interest of unionized workers and the state's agenda of tight economic management.
19. It is worth noting that the striking mineworkers belonged to the National Workers Union, and not the BITU. Guided by their leader, Hugh Shearer, BITU workers affirmed unionized labour's independence by remaining aloof from JLP partisanship.

20. Hence premium gasoline went to J$3.20 and regular to J$3.10. The PNP also announced that further increases would be coming in April, July and October to meet upcoming OPEC price hikes.

21. Wilmot Perkins, "Gas Price Politics", *Daily Gleaner,* 14 January 1979, 11.

22. Ibid., 11.

23. Manley's broadcast to the nation on Wednesday, 10 January 1979. Cited in the *Daily Gleaner,* 12 January 1979, 1.

24. *Daily Gleaner,* 11 January 1979, 11.

25. Ibid., 1.

26. Ibid.

27. See John Hearne's commentary, "The Shroud of Disgrace", *Daily Gleaner,* 13 January 1979, 16.

28. See Edward Seaga's complaints against the police in Kingston in the *Daily Gleaner,* 11 January 1979, 11.

29. For Carl Stone's estimation of the importance of the protest, see the *Daily Gleaner,* 15 January 1979, 6. For reports on the politics of the bauxite workers, see *Daily Gleaner,* 12 January 1979, 2.

30. In a startling turn of events, an alliance of left-wing organizations including the WPJ, the Communist Party of Jamaica, and the Revolutionary Marxist League threw their "critical support" to the PNP and joined it in denouncing the demonstrations. For critiques of these left-wing organizations, see Dennis Forsythe, "The People's Revolt", *Daily Gleaner,* 14 January 1979, 11.

31. Political scientist Carl Stone developed this point in his *Politics versus Economics* (Kingston: Heinemann Caribbean, 1989).

32. Arnett Gardens was the first of several communities to leave the Central Peace Council, yet Massop kept West Kingston in the council long past its effectiveness.

33. Cited in the *Daily Gleaner,* 1 November 1978, 17.

34. For a detailed discussion of the JLP's political offensive between 1977 and 1979, and its impact on economic aid, see Stephens and Stephens, *Democratic Socialism in Jamaica,* chaps. 5–7.

35. In a challenge to the explanation that the police had their own motive for killing Massop, gossip and rumours placed the blame instead on power brokers in West Kingston and elsewhere in the western belt. It was alleged that they wanted Massop dead because the gunman's defection had made him a force for grassroots unity and a rival to party barons. Indeed, a stubborn claim was that the gunman and his allies harboured ambitions for his candidacy for political office in West Kingston. That he was killed within the confines of his own domain only lent credence to this allegation.

36. Starkie would be arrested within two days of his arrival in Canada. He was imprisoned there before being deported to Jamaica in July 1980. *Daily*

Gleaner, 2 June 1981, 1. See also Lloyd Williams, "The Posses and Their Roots", *Sunday Gleaner,* 7 February 1988, 8A.

37. The ease with which these gunmen left the country points to the criminalization of state functions in this period. Indeed, this state collusion with the political and criminal undergrounds would be repeated in the 1980s as successive "most wanted" gunmen left the island with impunity as politicians and even the police escorted them to the aircraft. For a discussion of this development, see Headley, "Jamaican Crime and Violence", 51.

38. On 30 October, Roy McGann, junior minister of national security and member of Parliament, was killed in a political fracas in Gordon Town. For the PNP's account of its travails in 1980, see Manley, *Struggle in the Periphery,* chap. 15.

39. In the so-called Gold Street Massacre, several persons were murdered when PNP gunmen fired on JLP revellers in East Central Kingston. This incident was the most horrific case of violence directed at non-violent JLP supporters. Gunst, *Born Fi' Dead,* 58; and Manley, *Struggle in the Periphery,* 195.

40. Stone, *Politics versus Economics,* 14.

41. The Eventide Home for the Aged, for example, was consumed in a horrific case of arson that claimed 153 lives.

42. Commenting on this development, Manley noted that "Up to 1976, the .357 Magnum was the deadliest weapon in common use in the political battle. . . . The 1980 campaign was to be dominated by the M16 rifle, smuggled into the country in large but unspecified numbers at that time. Their rapid-fire chatter became like a theme song of the campaign." *Struggle in the Periphery,* 194.

43. Carl Stone, "The Peace in Trench Town", *Daily Gleaner,* 12 September 1988, 8.

44. These figures are cited in Kaufman, *Jamaica under Manley,* 188.

45. Eyre, "Political Violence and Urban Geography", 32. Carl Stone, also citing Eyre, reports him as estimating that a grand total of forty thousand persons were forcibly expelled from their homes during political warfare in the 1970s. See Stone, "A Country Playing with Fire", *Daily Gleaner,* 14 March 1990, 6.

46. Stephens and Stephens, *Democratic Socialism in Jamaica,* 244.

47. Ibid., 246.

48. Kaufman, *Jamaica under Manley,* 192.

49. Stone, *Politics versus Economics,* 6.

50. Ibid., 7.

51. For discussion on the shift in the PNP's class support between 1976 and 1980, see Kaufman, *Jamaica under Manley,* 192–93; and Stephens and Stephens, *Democratic Socialism in Jamaica,* 244–46.

52. Gray, "Power and Identity", 207.

53. The highly publicized case of Dexter Rose, head of the State Trading Corporation during the PNP second term, captured the scale of state agents' corruption at the highest levels.

54. Michael Witter, "The Role of Higglers/Sidewalk Vendors/Informal Commercial Traders in the Development of the Jamaican Economy" (paper presented to a symposium on higglers and informal commercial importers, University of the West Indies, Mona, Jamaica, 21 May 1988), 4.

55. Ibid.

56. Robert Fatton Jr. has emphasized this point with respect to African states. See his *Predatory Rule*.

57. Gray, "Power and Identity", 209.

58. For a discussion of patrimonialism in Africa, see Thomas Callaghy, "The State as Lame Leviathan: The Patrimonial Administrative State in Africa, in *The African State in Transition,* ed. Zaki Ergas (New York: St Martin's Press, 1987), 87–116.

59. Gray, "Power and Identity", 210. See also Donna McFarlane-Gregory et al., "The Informal Commercial Importers of Jamaica" (research project on Jamaican micro-enterprises, University of the West Indies, Mona, Jamaica, June 1993), 4.

60. Gray, "Power and Identity", 210.

61. McFarlane-Gregory et al., "The Informal Commercial Importers", 4.

62. *Jamaica Record,* 26 July 1988, 3A. No doubt reflecting dramatically changed circumstances in the urban complex, the venerable Kingston and St Andrew Corporation – the KSAC – was renamed and given the new acronym "MPM" – Metropolitan Parks and Markets.

63. The extent of the JLP's favour with the Americans was revealed with Seaga's visit to the Reagan White House in 1981. Seaga, representing the tiny island of Jamaica that had allegedly fought off a communist takeover, was the first head of state to be received by the new president.

64. "Brief for Debate on the Suppression of Crime Act" (Government of Jamaica mimeo, n.d.), 42.

65. *Daily Gleaner,* 2 June 1981, 1.

66. For a roster of dead or wanted left-wing gunmen, see "Brief for Debate on the Suppression of Crime Act", 5–42

67. Arnold Bertram, PNP activist and occasional minister, makes exactly this point in discussing the futility of the 1988 peace accord. See his "Certain War – Uncertain Peace", *Jamaica Record,* 29 July 1988, 7.

Chapter 10

1. Whatever may be said of the 1959–60 insurrection of Claudius Henry and his son, Ronald, bank hold-ups were not part of their modus operandi.

2. For a list of robberies attributed to WPJ cadres by the Jamaican State, see "Brief for Debate on the Suppression of Crime Act", 1–56. While a former leading member of the WPJ dismissed the state's allegations in this document as fabrications, this informant did concede in interviews that some robberies may have had party approval.

3. Former WPJ activist, interview by author, Kingston, Jamaica, Summer 1996.

4. For example, the WPJ had a political beachhead in Greenwich Town, and party militants defended its presence there against hostile opponents.

5. This assessment is based on the author's attendance at the public session of WPJ party conferences and at public rallies held by the JLP and PNP.

6. See "Brief for Debate on the Suppression of Crime Act", 15, 34.

7. Given that the allegations against the WPJ were included in a public document that was the basis of a parliamentary debate on the Suppression of Crime Act, it seems unlikely that the state's evidence pointing to WPJ complicity in outlawry contained only fabrications.

8. Former WPJ activist, interview.

9. Former WPJ activist, interview.

10. *Daily Gleaner,* 1 December 1987, 20.

11. Ibid.

12. The explanations for the JLP's loss of support are borrowed from Carl Stone's review of the 1980–83 period. See his *Politics versus Economics,* chaps. 2–3.

13. Ibid., 27.

14. See Stephens and Stephens, *Democratic Socialism in Jamaica,* 263.

15. Since March of 1981, the JLP signed several agreements with the IMF. In September 1983, the JLP failed the Fund's performance test, and thus a new agreement had imposed the massive devaluation.

16. Because of the boycott, the JLP won all sixty seats in Parliament, including six seats which were won in constituencies that were contested by independent candidates. It should be noted that this victory by default earned public disapproval. As the Stone Polls showed, 59 per cent of the electorate disagreed with the JLP's decision to call the election without first drawing up a new voters' list. See Stone, *Politics versus Economics,* 46–52.

17. *Daily Gleaner,* 16 January 1985, 3.

18. Ibid.

19. Ibid., 13.

20. *Daily Gleaner,* 17 January 1985, 1.

21. Gunst, *Born Fi' Dead,* 117.

22. Ibid., 118.

23. On at least six occasions between 1984 and 1987, US customs impounded Air Jamaica, the national airline, for having large quantities of marijuana on board.

24. Gunst, *Born Fi' Dead,* 118.

25. Opinions of Brown's personality are uniform in their depiction of him as a new type of leader. He has variously been described as lacking the common touch, devoid of grassroots ideological convictions and wholly preoccupied with money.

26. Burke, interview. See also "The 'Jim Brown' Story", *Daily Gleaner,* 26 February 1992, 1 and 13.

27. See Gunst, *Born Fi' Dead,* 42. See also Lloyd Williams, "The Posses and Their Roots", *Sunday Gleaner,* 7 February 1988, 8A.

28. *Daily Gleaner,* 7 July 1987, 1. Hugh Small, a lawyer and former minister in the PNP's administration, wrote the following of the trial: "The crowd was so disorderly on one occasion that they jostled the Chief Justice as he made his way into the building and on another they prevented a judge from having access to the building." *Daily Gleaner,* 9 July 1987, 1.

29. By the late 1980s, gun salutes were a commonplace in popular songs, at the dance halls, at soccer matches and at New Year's Eve festivities across the island. See Carl Stone, "Subverting the Rule of Law", *Daily Gleaner,* 20 July 1987, 8.

30. In September 1988, a commentator lamented the death by assassination of the Registrar of the Supreme Court. See Wilmot Perkins, "Of Murder and Murderers", *Jamaica Record,* 25 September 1988, 9A.

31. Carl Stone, "The Parole System", *Daily Gleaner,* 21 December 1987, A8.

32. *Daily Gleaner,* 9 July 1987, 1.

33. David D'Costa captured aspects of this fear of the black ghetto poor by likening it to the nineteenth century planters' fear of blacks during the 1865 Morant Bay Rebellion. See his "Green Bay: What Made Them Do It", 23.

34. The reference is from Lloyd D'Aguilar. See his "Police Control", *Sunday Herald,* 3 March 1996, 6A.

35. Despite the JLP's close ties to Washington, the latter rankled the Jamaican government by refusing to accept the principle of reciprocity in its extradition treaty with Jamaica. Errol Anderson, former minister of national security in the JLP administration, interview by author, Kingston, Jamaica, Summer, 1996.

36. Acrid smoke from a fire in his cell asphyxiated Brown on 23 February 1992. Earlier that month PNP gunmen had killed his son, Mark Coke, after the latter had succeeded his father as Tivoli's don.

37. Brown's death triggered no commission of inquiry nor did it deter the prime minister and other JLP officials from attending Brown's funeral.
38. I am indebted to Orlando Patterson for his discussion of the principle of moral infrangibility. See his *Ordeal of Integration,* 139–42.
39. *Daily Gleaner,* 10 September 1988, 2, 9.
40. Byron Buckley, "No Tears for 'The Forgotten Ones' ", *Sunday Gleaner,* 10 April 1988, 8A.
41. These statistics are taken from Omar Davies and Pat Anderson, "The Impact of the Recession and Structural Adjustment Policies on Poor Women in Jamaica" (paper presented at the fourteenth meeting of the Caribbean Studies Association, Barbados, 23–27 May 1989), 1–44.
42. The most notable of these were St Jude and St Patrick's Roman Catholic churches, run by the rector and expatriate Father Richard Albert.
43. Press reports listed the woman on the motorbike as "his girlfriend", but later reports confirmed that she was, in fact, Sandokhan's wife. See the *Daily Gleaner,* 8 August 1988, 1 and 32.
44. *Jamaica Record,* 24 July 1988, 1.
45. Anderson, interview.
46. *Jamaica Record,* 24 July 1988, 4A.
47. Ibid., 1 and 4A.
48. *Sunday Gleaner,* 11 September 1988, 8A.
49. *Jamaica Record,* 25 August 1988, 2.
50. *Daily Gleaner,* 8 August 1988, 1.
51. Cited in the *Jamaica Record,* 11 September 1988, 4A.
52. *Sunday Gleaner,* 9 October 1988, 9A. In a retort to the negative media coverage of the gunman, Sandokhan's mother-in-law offered this lament to reporters: "Sometimes what oonu write, is like oonu working for the police" (What you have written gives the impression that you are working for the police).
53. Cited in the *Daily Gleaner,* 26 August 1988, 3.
54. Ibid.
55. Statement issued to the press. *Jamaica Record,* 28 August 1988, 3A.
56. Wilmot Perkins, "A Kind of Corruption", *Money Index,* 6 September 1988, 33.
57. Wayne Smith's letter to Father Richard Albert, dated 26 August 1988.
58. *Sunday Gleaner,* 11 September 1988, 2. The couple also had a twenty-two-month-old son.
59. Ibid.
60. This jaundiced view of a renegade security force began finding support from several respectable quarters. In its 1986 report, the human rights group America's Watch cited the island for its high rate of police killings. In addi-

tion, the *Daily Gleaner,* whose editorialists were generally supportive of the police, vigorously protested the resort to "summary police justice" in a series of editorials in late 1987. Finally, Arnold Bertram, a leading PNP politician and contributor to the *Jamaica Record,* disclosed what was common knowledge in the criminal underground: that huge numbers of policemen were on the take. According to Bertram, some 285 of them were convicted of a variety of criminal offences between 1984 and mid-1988. See his "Certain War – Uncertain Peace", *Jamaica Record,* 29 July 1988, 7.

61. Carl Stone, "Law and Society", *Daily Gleaner,* 30 December 1987, 8. In this controversial and inflammatory article, Stone correctly notes the high cost of crime to the poorer classes. Unfortunately, he drew the wrong lessons from this fact to demand that human rights concerns be set aside, in favour of a policy of exterminism.

62. For verbatim excerpts of the Duffus Report, see the *Daily Gleaner,* 9 September 1987, 1.

63. Ibid.

64. Ibid.

65. Headley, "Jamaican Crime and Violence", 16. Author's emphasis.

66. Ibid., 17.

67. Carl Stone, "The Parole System", *Daily Gleaner,* 21 December 1987, A8.

68. Between 1985 and 1989, there were, on average, 435.6 murders per year. Between 1990 and 1995, that number had increased to 642.5. See James Walsh, "Crime Statistics", *Daily Gleaner,* 28 June 1996, A4.

69. Arnold Bertram, "Certain War – Uncertain Peace", 7.

70. Carl Stone acknowledged the role of guns and the "money power" of the drug dons as a source of social power. "The gun", he argued, "is the new power base in this country and the ultimate objective of those who control it is to impose their will on the society". See "More Thoughts on Crime in Jamaica", *Daily Gleaner,* 7 October 1987, 8.

71. *Sunday Gleaner,* 27 September 1987, 9A. Prior to the collapse of this rationale in the late 1990s, denial of the direct relationship between political gunmen and politicians was the stock response of political office holders.

72. Cited in the *Daily Gleaner,* 4 July 1988, 1.

73. JLP and PNP leaders signed the peace accord on 26 August 1988.

74. War-weariness and public yearning as well as pressure for the peace, within and beyond the ghetto, also pushed politicians to make what turned out to be a hollow gesture.

75. Bertram, "Certain War – Uncertain Peace", 7.

76. The truce did not disarm either criminal or political gunmen and it did not attend to the fundamental social and economic problems that fed crime.

77. Arnold Bertram, "Man, Politics and Reconstruction", *Jamaica Record,* 4 October 1988, 9.
78. See the editorial "Where Is Our Community Spirit?" *Jamaica Record,* 28 September 1988, 8A.
79. Bertram, "Man, Politics and Reconstruction", 9.
80. Perkins, "Of Murder and Murderers", 9A.
81. Bertram, "Man, Politics and Reconstruction", 9.
82. For a useful literary discussion of the phenomenon of slackness, see Cooper, *Noises in the Blood,* chap. 8.
83. For a book-length discussion of Jamaican dancehall culture, see Norman C. Stolzoff, *Wake the Town and Tell the People: Dancehall Culture in Jamaica* (Durham: Duke University Press, 2000).
84. For the varying political positions on dancehall culture, see Stolzoff, *Wake the Town,* chap. 8.

Epilogue

1. For a recent assessment of the Jamaican crisis, see Trevor Munroe, "Voice, Participation and Governance in a Changing Environment: The Case of Jamaica" (discussion draft, Caribbean Group for Cooperation in Economic Development, June 2000), 1–42; and Selwyn Ryan, "Democratic Governance in the Anglophone Caribbean: Threats to Sustainability", in *New Caribbean Thought: A Reader,* ed. Brian Meeks and Folke Lindahl (Kingston: University of the West Indies Press, 2001), 73–103.
2. These included the Bail Act, the Justice Reform Act and the repeal of the Suppression of Crime Act. Equally important, a new Corruption Prevention Act was finally approved in 2000 to replace the 1931 act. This breakthrough was accomplished only after years of debate in the 1990s and after much pressure from advocates of clean government at home and abroad that eventually overrode government efforts to weaken the bill. Indeed, motivation for this legislation, and for the Prevention of Corruption Commission it would establish, came not so much because of massive domestic pressure on the government but rather from external factors. Primary among these was the need to bring Jamaican law into conformity with the country's treaty obligations under the Organization of American States Convention against Corruption to which Jamaica is a signatory. For information on Jamaica's anti-corruption act, see *Combating Corruption in Jamaica: A Citizens Guide* (Atlanta: The Carter Center, 1999).
3. In the aftermath of the April 1999 riots, Jamaica's chastened prime minister, P.J. Patterson, averred that political rule using old dictatorial methods was no

longer possible. Patterson therefore warned members of the political class to avoid becoming "part of the problem to be swept aside by the emerging new social order". Befitting the turn to a new discourse and strategy of power, Patterson acknowledged the necessity of adopting a more democratic approach to governance. Cited in Trevor Munroe, "Transforming Jamaican Democracy through Transparency: A Framework for Action", in *Fostering Transparency and Preventing Corruption in Jamaica,* ed. Laura Nelson (Atlanta: The Carter Center, Emory University, 2002), 13.

4. Faced with three days of angry demonstrations, Finance Minister Omar Davies accepted the recommendation of the Moses Committee to roll back petroleum taxes by 50 per cent. See the *Jamaica Gleaner,* 28 April 1999, http://www.jamaica-gleaner.com/.

5. In emphasizing the need for immediate implementation of myriad new legislation, leading reformers such as PNP senator and University of the West Indies academic Trevor Munroe tend to gloss over the deeper problems of the society that have little to do with successful implementation of laws.

6. Munroe notes, for example, the massive decline in voter turnout and cites the increasing number of voters – some 45 to 55 per cent of the electorate in the 1990s – who have declared themselves as either "uncommitted" or as "independent". See Munroe, "Transforming Jamaican Democracy", 15–16.

7. For a compelling account of dictatorial rule inside the JLP, see Pearnel Charles, *A Cry from the Grassroots* (Kingston: PC Publishers, 1999).

8. Golding left the JLP in 1995 to form the ill-fated third party, the National Democratic Movement. In late 2002, Golding, after much dithering, returned to the fold under Seaga's ever-weakening leadership, as the latter led the JLP to its fourth consecutive electoral defeat since its loss in the 1989 election.

9. This much was apparent from Henry-Wilson's criticism of PNP mistakes that led to the April 1999 riot and her opposition to the partisan distribution of contracts. Consistent with the mood of self-criticism inside the PNP, PNP leader Patterson also vowed to re-establish the party's formerly close contact with its supporters.

10. *Jamaica Gleaner,* 11 November 2000, http://www.jamaica-gleaner.com/.

11. Cited in Peter Espeut, "Danny Melville: A Conscious White Boy", *Jamaica Gleaner,* 15 November 2000, http://www.jamaica-gleaner.com/.

12. No matter politicians' protestations that they were done with dependence on political gunmen and the captive communities they help secure, to this day (May 2003) not one of these garrison communities has been dismantled.

13. See Jamaicans for Justice, "Jamaica's Human Rights Situation".

14. The public was understandably grateful for any public admission of guilt from politicians who were more famous for closing ranks behind a wall of silence than for making public disclosures about the dark side of Jamaican politics. Yet the public was also exasperated by the disclosures, for they invariably came only after the politicians had long left office. Even then the disclosures stopped short of naming names and giving a full account of the inner workings of crime and party politics.

15. Thompson's comment in 1978 stirred public outrage amidst charges that the men had been executed. His 1999 apology occurred not so much as a considered declaration, but rather as a comment on "talk radio" concerning the society's continued tolerance for extra-judicial killings by the security forces. See the *Jamaica Gleaner*, 27 August 1999, http://www.jamaica-gleaner.com/.

16. To be fair to Duncan, he did complain to Michael Manley, the party leader, about the consequences of pushing through the Suppression of Crime Act. Faced, however, with middle-class pressure to curb crime, Manley averred in effect that the risks of violating the rights of poor Jamaicans were worth it because "the people will say we are soft on crime". Cited in Michael Burke, "Pontius Pilate Politics in 1974", *Jamaica Observer*, 4 October 2001, http://www.jamaicaobserver.com/.

17. The quoted statement is by Michael Manley and is taken from the text of Duncan's address. See the *Jamaica Gleaner*, 7 October 2001, http://www.jamaica-gleaner.com/.

18. As Duncan noted, "It must not happen to anybody! People say, 'if yuh sey dat people going misunderstand and sey you are a labourite'. If my support for and concern for what happened in Tivoli is shared by Edward Seaga and that makes me a labourite, then make me a labourite. But it's not for my own personal self, it's because I know where we are coming from because I was a part of it and for that I am sorry. Because I could have left the People's National Party in 1974 when that thing was introduced." Ibid.

19. Cited in the *Jamaica Gleaner*, 30 September 2001, http://www.jamaica-gleaner.com/.

20. Statement by the National Executive Council of the PNP. Cited in the *Jamaica Observer*, 2 October 2001, http://www.jamaicaobserver.com/.

21. For a typical condemnation of politicians' atrocities, see Peter Espeut, "Blood on their Hands", *Jamaica Gleaner*, 3 October 2001, http://www.jamaica-gleaner.com/.

22. That silence, it should be remembered, was not only about misdeeds and abuse of power. It pertained as well to a fundamental distrust of the Jamaican people and to a lack of party democracy, since insistence on party unity fed self-censorship which in turn hurt democratic debate. Thus while

the Suppression of Crime Act generated much debate inside the PNP's inner circle, nobody spoke out publicly. By tacit but compelling agreement, that debate was kept inside the party and not carried to the rank and file. In this respect, the PNP's democratic socialism of the 1970s was neither socialist nor democratic.

23. Patterson's statement to the National Executive Council. Cited in the *Jamaica Observer,* 2 October 2001, http://www.jamaicaobserver.com/.

24. Jamaicans for Justice, "Jamaica's Human Rights Situation" (presentation to the Inter-American Commission on Human Rights, 14 November 2001).

25. See note 2.

26. The term is borrowed from Caribbean sociologist Percy C. Hintzen. See his "Rethinking Democracy in the Postnationalist State", in *New Caribbean Thought,* ed. Brian Meeks and Folke Lindahl (Kingston: University of the West Indies Press, 2001), 104–27.

27. It is arguable that Omar Davies, the incumbent minister of finance, is playing precisely this role although the April 1999 riot imposed its own correction of this technique.

28. The PNP's current outlook and victory in the 2002 elections fits this assessment best.

29. I am indebted to David Scott for this insight on the limitations of democracy as improvement. See his "Government of Freedom", in *New Caribbean Thought,* ed. Brian Meeks and Folke Lindahl (Kingston: University of the West Indies Press, 2001), 428–50.

30. Ian Boyne, "Government Scores with Crime Initiative", *Sunday Gleaner,* 8 December 2002, http://www.jamaica-gleaner.com/.

31. In a remarkable convergence of views, Don Robotham, former WPJ activist and former pro vice chancellor of the University of the West Indies, also called for tough measures in dealing with criminals, including the suspension of *habeas corpus* and rule by decree. See his "Crime Has Put Jamaica in a State of Emergency", *Sunday Gleaner,* 17 November 2002, http://www. jamaica-gleaner.com/. For Boyne's defence of his own position late in 2002, see his "Country Not United Against Crime", *Sunday Gleaner,* 10 November 2002, http://www.jamaica-gleaner.com/.

32. For a sustained articulation of the liberal democratic reformist views of a leading member of the New Beginning Movement, see Trevor Munroe, *For a New Beginning* (Kingston: CARICOM Publishers, 1994).

33. Peter Espeut, "Blood on their Hands", *Jamaica Gleaner,* 3 October 2001, http://www.jamaica-gleaner.com/.

34. *Jamaica Gleaner,* 19 March 2001, http://www.jamaica-gleaner.com/.

35. The NDM still limps along under new and ineffectual leadership in 2003 but does so in name only.

36. As pollster Mark Wignall reported in 2001, "If sheer poll percentages were the final arbiters of a political party's success, then the NDM would have to be considered a failure to date. From a high of 18 percent in 1995 to two percent in the June 2001 Stone polls, the NDM has moved from a party neck-and-neck with the PNP/JLP to an entity now struggling to find a foothold among an increasingly angry and apathethic [*sic*] electorate." *Jamaica Observer*, 23 August 2001, http://www.jamaicaobserver.com/.

37. According to one report, only 56.3 per cent of eligible voters turned out for the October 2002 general elections and the PNP received only 53 per cent of the popular vote. See the *Jamaica Observer*, 17 October 2002, http://www.jamaicaobserver.com/.

38. See Lloyd B. Smith, "Should the NDM be Allowed to Die?" *Jamaica Observer*, 24 November 1998, http://www.jamaicaobserver.com/.

39. *Jamaica Observer*, 13 September 2002, http://www.jamaicaobserver.com/.

40. There is not much to distinguish the Jamaica Alliance for National Unity from the United Progressive Party, as both formations stood for similar values including national unity. If a distinction were to be made, it would be that while the Jamaica Alliance for National Unity emphasizes Christian values the United Progressive Party stresses cultural authenticity and the recovery of indigenous values. See Robert Buddan, "New Parties and What They Stand For", *Sunday Gleaner*, 1 September 2002, http://www.jamaica-gleaner.com/.

41. Citizens Action for Free and Fair Elections has been widely hailed for helping to restore integrity to the electoral process. See, for example, "The CAFFE Verdict" for one editorial appreciation of the organization's work. *Jamaica Gleaner*, 23 March 1998, http://www.jamaica-gleaner.com/.

42. According to the Stone Poll conducted in 2002, 53 per cent of Jamaicans reported that the island would have been better off under colonialism. For a discussion of the significance of the poll, see Dennis Morrison, "We Can Succeed Alone", *Jamaica Observer*, 31 July 2002, http://www.jamaicaobserver.com/.

43. I am grateful to Brian Meeks for reminding the audience of these contributions during his presentation at the 2003 meeting of the Caribbean Studies Association.

Selected Bibliography

Ambursley, Fitzroy, and Robin Cohen, eds. *Crisis in the Caribbean*. New York: Monthly Review, 1983.

Appadurai, Arjun. *Modernity at Large*. Minneapolis: University of Minnesota Press, 1996.

Azarya, Victor, and Naomi Chazan. "Disengagement from the State in Africa: Reflections on the Experiences of Ghana and Guinea". *Comparative Studies in Society and History* 29, no. 1 (1987): 106–31.

Barnett, Lloyd. *The Constitutional Law of Jamaica*. London: Oxford University Press, 1977.

Barrow, Christine. "Caribbean Masculinity and Family: Revisiting 'Marginality' and 'Reputation' ". In *Caribbean Portraits,* edited by Christine Barrow, 339–58. Kingston: Ian Randle Publishers, 1998.

———, ed. *Caribbean Portraits*. Kingston: Ian Randle Publishers, 1998.

Bayart, Jean-Francois. *The State in Africa: The Politics of the Belly*. New York: Longman, 1993.

Beckford, George, and Michael Witter. *Small Garden . . . Bitter Weed: Struggle and Change in Jamaica*. London: Zed Books, 1980.

Bogues, Anthony. *Caliban's Freedom: The Early Political Thought of C.L.R. James*. London: Pluto Press, 1997.

Brathwaite, Edward Kamau. *History of the Voice: The Development of Nation Language in Anglophone Caribbean Poetry*. London and Port of Spain: New Beacon, 1984.

Brodber, Erna. "Re-engineering Blackspace". *Caribbean Quarterly* 43, nos. 1 and 2 (March–June 1997): 70–81.

———. "Socio-cultural Change in Jamaica". In *Jamaica in Independence: Essays on the Early Years,* edited by Rex Nettleford, 55–74. Kingston: Heinemann Caribbean, 1989.

Callaghy, Thomas. "The State as Lame Leviathan: The Patrimonial Administrative State in Africa". In *The African State in Transition,* edited by Zaki Ergas, 87–116. New York: St Martin's Press, 1987.

Carnegie, Jimmy. "Sport in National Development in Jamaica". In *Jamaica in Independence: Essays on the Early Years,* edited by Rex Nettleford, 257–90. Kingston: Heinemann Caribbean, 1989.

Carter Center. *Combating Corruption in Jamaica: A Citizens Guide.* Atlanta: The
    Carter Center, 1999.

Charles, Pearnel. *A Cry from the Grassroots.* Kingston: PC Publishers, 1999.

Chazan, Naomi, Robert Mortimer, Donald Rothchild and John Ravenhill, eds.
    Politics and Society in Contemporary Africa. Boulder: Lynne Rienner, 1992.

Chevannes, Barry. "The Rastafari and the Urban Youth". In *Perspectives on Jamaica
    in the 1970s,* edited by Carl Stone and Aggrey Brown, 392–422. Kingston:
    Jamaica Publishing House, 1981.

———. "The Formation of Garrison Communities". Paper presented at the
    symposium Grassroots Development and the State of the Nation, in honour
    of Professor Carl Stone, University of the West Indies, Mona, Jamaica, 16–17
    November 1992.

———. *Rastafari Roots and Ideology.* Syracuse: Syracuse University Press, 1994.

Cooper, Carolyn. *Noises in the Blood: Orality, Gender, and the "Vulgar" Body of
    Jamaican Popular Culture.* New York: Heinemann, 1994.

Crummey, Donald, ed. *Banditry, Rebellion and Social Protest in Africa.* London:
    Heinemann, 1986.

Dawes, Kwame. *Natural Mysticism: Toward a Reggae Aesthetic.* Leeds: Peepal Tree
    Press, 1999.

Draper, Hal. *Karl Marx's Theory of Revolution.* Vol. 2, *The Politics of Social Classes.*
    New York: Monthly Review Press, 1978.

Eaton, George. *Alexander Bustamante and Modern Jamaica.* Kingston: Kingston
    Publishers, 1975.

Eyre, Alan L. "Political Violence and Urban Geography in Kingston, Jamaica".
    Geographical Review 74, no. 1 (1984): 24–37.

———. "The Effects of Political Terrorism on the Residential Location of the
    Poor in the Kingston Urban Region, Jamaica, West Indies". *Urban Geography*
    7, no. 3 (1986): 227–42.

Fanon, Frantz. *The Wretched of the Earth.* New York: Grove Press, 1966.

Fatton Jr., Robert. *Predatory Rule.* Boulder: Lynne Rienner, 1992.

Gouldner, Alvin. *The Dialectic of Ideology and Technology.* New York: Seabury Press,
    1976.

Gray, Obika. *Radicalism and Social Change in Jamaica, 1960–1972.* Knoxville:
    University of Tennessee Press, 1991.

———. "Power and Identity among the Urban Poor of Jamaica". In *Globalization
    and Survival in the Black Diaspora,* edited by Charles Green, 199–226. Albany:
    SUNY Press, 1997.

———. "The Jamaican Lumpenproletariat: Rogue Culture or Avatar of
    Liberation?" Paper presented at the twenty-third annual conference of the
    Caribbean Studies Association, Antigua, 26–30 May 1998.

Green, Charles, ed. *Globalization and Survival in the Black Diaspora*. Albany: SUNY Press, 1997.

Griffith, Ivelaw, and Betty N. Sedoc-Dahlberg. *Democracy and Human Rights in the Caribbean*. Boulder: Westview Press, 1997.

Gunst, Laurie. *Born Fi' Dead: A Journey through the Jamaican Posse Underworld*. New York: Henry Holt, 1995.

Harriott, Anthony. *Police and Crime Control in Jamaica*. Kingston: University of the West Indies Press, 2000.

Headley, Bernard D. "Jamaican Crime and Violence at Home and Abroad: An Ideological Perspective". Manuscript. West Indies Collection, University of the West Indies, Mona, Jamaica, 1994.

Hebdige, Dick. *Cut 'n' Mix: Culture, Identity, and Caribbean Music*. New York: Routledge, 1990.

Hobsbawm, Eric. *Bandits*. New York: Pantheon Books, 1981.

Hydén, Göran. *Beyond Ujamaa in Tanzania: Underdevelopment and an Uncaptured Peasantry*. London: Heinemann, 1980.

James, C.L.R. *Beyond a Boundary*. London: Hutchinson, 1963.

Jefferson, Owen. *The Post-War Economic Development of Jamaica*. Kingston: Institute of Social and Economic Research, University of the West Indies, 1977.

Kaufman, Michael. *Jamaica under Manley: Dilemmas of Socialism and Democracy*. Westport, Conn.: Lawrence Hill, 1985.

Kelly, Robin D.G. *Race Rebels: Culture, Politics, and the Black Working Class*. New York: Free Press, 1994.

Knight, Franklin W., and Colin A. Palmer, eds. *The Modern Caribbean*. Chapel Hill: University of North Carolina Press, 1989.

Laclau, Ernesto. *Politics and Ideology in Marxist Theory*. London: Verso, 1977.

Lewis, Rupert, and Patrick Bryan, eds. *Garvey: His Work and Impact*. Kingston: Institute of Social and Economic Research, University of the West Indies, 1988.

Majors, Richard, and Janet Mancini Billson. *Cool Pose: The Dilemma of Black Manhood in America*. New York: Simon and Schuster, 1992.

Manley, Michael. *The Politics of Change*. London: André Deutsch, 1974.

————. *A Voice at the Workplace*. London: André Deutsch, 1975.

————. *Jamaica: Struggle in the Periphery*. London: Writers and Readers Publishing Cooperatives Society, 1982.

Mbembe, Achille. *On the Post-Colony*. Berkeley: University of California Press, 2001.

McFarlane-Gregory, Donna, et al. "The Informal Commercial Importers of Jamaica", 1–73. Research project on Jamaican micro-enterprises. University of the West Indies, Mona, Jamaica, June 1993.

Meeks, Brian. *Radical Caribbean: From Black Power to Abu Bakr.* Kingston: University of the West Indies Press, 1996.

Meeks, Brian, and Folke Lindahl, eds. *New Caribbean Thought: A Reader.* Kingston: University of the West Indies Press, 2001.

Munroe, Trevor. *Jamaican Politics: A Marxist Perspective in Transition.* Kingston: Heinemann Caribbean, 1990.

————. *For a New Beginning.* Kingston: CARICOM Publishers, 1994.

————. "Voice, Participation and Governance in a Changing Environment: The Case of Jamaica". Discussion draft, Caribbean Group for Cooperation in Economic Development, June 2000.

Murrell, Nathaniel Samuel, William David Spencer, and Adrian Anthony McFarlane, eds. *Chanting Down Babylon: The Rastafari Reader.* Kingston: Ian Randle Publishers, 1998.

Nelson, Laura, ed. *Fostering Transparency and Preventing Corruption in Jamaica.* Atlanta: The Carter Center, Emory University, 2002.

Nettleford, Rex. *Mirror Mirror.* Kingston: Collins and Sangster, 1970.

————. *Inward Stretch, Outward Reach.* London: Macmillan, 1993.

————, ed. *Jamaica in Independence: Essays on the Early Years.* Kingston: Heinemann Caribbean, 1989.

Patterson, Orlando. *The Ordeal of Integration.* Washington, D.C.: Civitas, 1997.

People's National Party (PNP). *Sovereignty: Mobilization for Development and Self-Reliance; The Tasks of Political Education.* Kingston: PNP, 1984.

Post, Ken. *Arise Ye Starvelings: The Jamaica Labour Rebellion of 1938 and Its Aftermath.* The Hague: Martinus Nijoff, 1978.

————. *Strike the Iron.* Vols. 1 and 2. Atlantic Highlands, N.J.: Humanities Press, 1981.

Robotham, Don. "Freedom Ossified or Economic Crisis? A Comment on Holger Henke". *Identities: Global Studies in Culture and Power* 8, no. 3 (September 2001): 451–66.

Rodney, Walter. *The Groundings with My Brothers.* London: Bogle L'Ouverture Publications, 1969.

Rowe, Maureen. "Gender and Family Relations in Rastafari: A Personal Perspective". In *Chanting Down Babylon: A Rastafari Reader,* edited by Nathaniel Samuel Murrell et al., 72–88. Kingston: Ian Randle Publishers, 1998.

Scott, David. "The 'Culture of Violence' Fallacy". *Small Axe,* no. 2 (September 1997): 140–47.

Scott, James. *Weapons of the Weak.* New Haven: Yale University Press, 1985.

————. *Domination and the Arts of Resistance.* New Haven: Yale University Press, 1990.

Smith, M.G., et al., *The Rastafari Movement in Kingston, Jamaica*. Kingston: Institute of Social and Economic Research, University of the West Indies, 1960.

Stephens, Evelyne Huber, and John D. Stephens. *Democratic Socialism in Jamaica*. Princeton: Princeton University Press, 1986.

Stone, Carl. *Democracy and Clientelism in Jamaica*. New Brunswick, N.J.: Transaction Books, 1980.

————. *Class, State, and Democracy in Jamaica*. New York: Praeger, 1986.

————. *Politics versus Economics*. Kingston: Heinemann Caribbean, 1989.

————. "Power, Policy and Politics in Independent Jamaica". In *Jamaica in Independence: Essays on the Early Years,* ed. Rex Nettleford, 20–52. Kingston: Heinemann Caribbean, 1989.

Stone, Carl, and Aggrey Brown, eds. *Perspectives on Jamaica in the Seventies*. Kingston: Jamaica Publishing House, 1981.

Stolzoff, Norman C. *Wake the Town and Tell the People: Dancehall Culture in Jamaica*. Durham: Duke University Press, 2000.

Thompson, Dudley. *From Kingston to Kenya: The Making of a Pan-Africanist Lawyer*. Dover, Mass.: Majority Press, 1993.

Waters, Anita M. *Race, Class and Political Symbols: Rastafari and Reggae in Jamaican Politics*. New Brunswick, N.J.: Transaction Books, 1989.

White, Timothy. *Catch a Fire: The Life of Bob Marley*. New York: Holt, Rinehart and Winston, 1984.

Wignaraja, Ponna, ed. *New Social Movements in the South: Empowering the People*. Atlantic Highlands, N.J.: Zed Books, 1993.

Witter, Michael. "The Role of Higglers/Sidewalk Vendors/Informal Commercial Traders in the Development of the Jamaican Economy". Paper presented to a symposium on higglers and informal commercial importers, University of the West Indies, Mona, Jamaica, 21 May 1988.

Index